Realism –
"the cult of the
immediately
ascertainable fact."
(means of rapid &
easy consumer
satisfaction)

The Coffee House

The Coffee House

A CULTURAL HISTORY

Markman Ellis

Weidenfeld & Nicolson
LONDON

First published in Great Britain in 2004
by Weidenfeld & Nicolson

A CIP catalogue record for this book
is available from the British Library.

ISBN 0 297 84319 2

Typeset, printed and bound in Great Britain
by Butler and Tanner Ltd, Frome and London

Weidenfeld & Nicolson

The Orion Publishing Group Ltd
Orion House
5 Upper Saint Martin's Lane
London, WC2H 9EA

www.orionbooks.co.uk

For Becky

CONTENTS

ILLUSTRATIONS

The Art Archive: 1
Corbis: 2, 10, 14
Getty Images: 3, 5, 12, 13
Guildhall Library, Corporation of London: 6, 8
The Bridgeman Art Library: 9
The Lewis Walpole Library, Yale University, 738.0.3 (1738 etching and engraving, 26.5 × 20.8 cm., plate): 7

PREFACE

The Conversible World

Caffeine is the most widely used drug in the world, exceeding all other common drugs including nicotine and alcohol. The value of the coffee traded on international commodity markets is surpassed only by oil. Yet for most of human history, coffee was unknown outside a small region of the Ethiopian highlands. Coffee itself has been consumed in Europe only in the last four centuries. There is no coffee in the Torah, or the Bible, or the Koran. There is no coffee in Shakespeare, Dante or Cervantes. After initially being recognised, in the late sixteenth century, by a few sharp-eyed travellers in the Ottoman Empire, coffee gained its first foothold in Europe among curious scientists and merchants. The first coffee-house in Christendom finally opened in London in the early 1650s, a city gripped by revolutionary fervour. In this sense, coffee's eruption into daily life seems to coincide with the modern historical period.

A coffee-house exists to sell coffee, but the coffee-house cannot simply be reduced to this retail function. In his *Dictionary*, Samuel Johnson defined a coffee-house as 'A house of entertainment where coffee is sold, and the guests are supplied with newspapers'.[1] More than a place that sells coffee, Johnson suggests, a coffee-house is also an idea, a way of life, a mode of socialising, a philosophy. This book seeks to explain how the coffee-house came to have these connotations, how a simple commodity rewrote the experience of metropolitan life. Yet the coffee-house does have a vital relationship with coffee, which remains its governing symbol, lending it connotations of alertness, sobriety and volubility. These convivial and conversational associations grant the coffee-house a unique place in urban life and manners, in sharp contrast to its alcoholic competitors.

The story of the coffee-house is a historical narrative, in which the seventeenth and eighteenth centuries take central stage. In the hundred years after the first coffee-houses opened in London, they came to be ubiquitous features of the modern urban landscape, indispensable centres for socialising, for news and gossip, and for discussion and debate. In the coffee-house, men learnt new ways of combinational friendship, turning their discussions there into commercial ventures, critical tribunals, scientific seminars and political clubs. As the following chapters explain, the legacy of the early coffee-house is not simply to be found in Starbucks and other modern retailers of coffee, but also in the stock market, in insurance companies, in political parties, in the modern regard for public opinion, in the institutions of literary criticism, in the research cultures of modern science and in the Internet. As many commentators have noted, the coffee-house has provided many websites with a powerful metaphor for all kinds of collaborative intellectual enterprise. From the cyber-cafés of the 1990s, to the wi-fi enabled coffee-house of the new century, the overlap between the coffee-house and the information age has never seemed so exact.

The history of the coffee-house is not business history. The early coffee-house has left very few commercial records. But historians have made much use of the other kinds of evidence that do exist. In the archives of government, a rich seam of evidence details the reports of state spies and ministers on conversations heard and alleged in coffee-houses. Further evidence is found in early newspapers, both in their advertisements and news reports. Legal records, such as probate inventories, parish registers and property records, also contribute to this story. The eminent diarists of the seventeenth and eighteenth centuries, including Samuel Pepys, Robert Hooke and James Boswell, testify to the centrality of the coffee-house in the social life of the period. This book makes use of all these kinds of evidence.

In depicting the life-world of coffee-houses, however, much of the most compelling testimony is literary. The variety and nature of the coffee-house experience have made it the subject of a huge body of satirical raillery, jesting humour and deliberately partisan misrepresentation.[2] Considered as literature, this body of writing is linguistically rich and exciting, enlivened by currents of enthusiasm and vituperation, freighted with the arcana of particular and local disputes. In representing the coffee-house, these literary materials, more than anything else, established and confirmed the place of coffee in modern urban life. Using this literary evidence, however, is not straightforward and has long troubled historians. When the distinguished nineteenth-century historian Thomas Babington Macaulay mined these satires in his *History of England* for evidence of the lived experience of coffee-houses, using them to add colour, flavour and nuance to his account, he wagered that these satires offered a transparent view into the social life of Restoration England.[3] Yet satire rarely offers such a simple picture. It is in the nature of satire to exaggerate what it depicts, to amplify folly and vice, and to cast its material in the most brightly hued language. In this book the coffee-house satires are considered as works of literature as well as historical evidence: these low and vulgar satires are not a simple indictment of coffee-house life, but part of their conversation, one voice in the ongoing discussion of the social life of the city.

A note on dates

Until the reform of the English calendar in 1753, the civil year (used in official and legal documents, for example) began on 25 March, so that, for example, 31 December 1675 was followed by 1 January 1675. Many people wrote dates between January and 25 March so as to indicate both dates, thus the date which is 14 February 1676 in modern notation was written 14 February 1675/76. This book has silently followed modern practice, by writing dates between 1 January and 25 March according to modern notation.

ACKNOWLEDGEMENTS

I am very grateful to the following people for their invaluable advice on the project at various stages: Becky Beasley, Richard Hamblyn and Anne Janowitz, as well as John Barrell, Ben Buchan, Marilyn Butler, Georgina Capel, Vincent Caretta, Emma Clery, David Colclough, Richard Coulton, Elizabeth Eger, Charlotte Grant, Gavin Jones, John Mitchinson, Miles Ogborn, Chris Reid, Morag Shiach and Sue Wiseman.

I would also like to thank the many people who generously suggested leads for research: Ava Arndt, Jennie Batchelor, Paul Bayaertz, Giles Bergel, Martha Campbell, Brycchan Carey, Ezri Carlebach, Adriana Craciun, Greg Dart, Rebecca Garwood, Naftali Goldberg, Pat Hamilton, Paul Hamilton, Megan Hiatt, Lisa Jardine, Lawrence Klein, Leya Landau, Katherine Marino, Joseph Monteyne, Paul Montgomery, Michael Moriarty, Graham Rees, John Reynolds, Patrick Reynolds, Mike Rossington, Sandra Sherman, Charlotte Sussmann, Stephen Twining, Maria Wakeley and David Worrall.

I have benefited, too, from the advice of numerous seminars in London, Cambridge, Warwick and Sydney, most especially the London Eighteenth-Century Reading Group at Queen Mary. I would also like to thank Sharon Ellis, Briony Ellis and Roger Woods, Stead and Marianne Ellis, and Brian and Mary Beasley for their kindness and support while writing the book. Key research for this book was undertaken in Peets, Berkeley; Café de Flore, Paris; Caffè degli Specchi, Trieste; John's Diner, Auckland; and Bar Italia and the Algerian Coffee Stores in London.

I am especially grateful to the staff at the Rare Books Reading Room of the British Library, but also to the Corporation of London Record Office; Guildhall Library, London; University of London Library; Queen Mary University of London Library; Cambridge University Library; the National Archives, London; the Lewis Walpole Library, Farmington, Connecticut; the Beinecke Rare Books Library, Yale University; the archives of R. Twining & Co., Andover; and the Harry Ransom Research Center at the University of Texas at Austin. I am also grateful for the research leave awarded by Queen Mary and the Arts and Humanities Research Board.

CHAPTER ONE

First Encounters

George Sandys and the Coffa-Houses of Constantinople

Anchoring below the customs house steps at Constantinople on the evening of 28 September 1610, the *Armado*, out of Simo, a Greek sponge divers' bark not much larger than a Gravesend wherry, must have made a singularly unimposing impression on the officers of the Sublime Porte. Along with a cargo of sponges, the bark carried a thirty-two-year-old English gentleman, George Sandys. Having left London over four months earlier, from Venice Sandys had island hopped on English merchant ships, until at Chios he abandoned the comforts of the *Great Exchange* of London for the fishermen's tiny vessel. For two weeks he sailed with them, sleeping among their sacks of sponges and sharing their meagre rations. In his journal he noted that their meals were composed of 'Biskot, Olives, Garlicke and Onions', occasionally augmented with the samphire they picked from the rocks, or a small fish that he knew in Italian as *riceio* (burre), washed down with a daily draught of wine. Sandys was delighted by the uncomplicated life of the sponge divers: they were, he said, 'a happy people that live according to nature; and want not much, in that they covet but little'. But now he had arrived in Constantinople. The contrast between the simple world of the sponge divers and the splendours of the Ottoman Empire could not be greater. In 1610, Constantinople was the richest and most populous city in the world. The capital of the most powerful empire in Europe, it was a repository of treasures and unequalled luxury, yet also of despotism and cruelty.

Once known as Byzantium, then renamed Nova Roma by the Christian emperor Constantine when he took it as the capital of the Roman Empire, the city had been the centre of the civilised world for centuries. Conquered by the Turks in 1453, it was rebuilt as the capital of the empire of the Ottomans, who came to know it as Istanbul or, more poetically, the Abode of Sovereignty, or the Threshold of Bliss. In 1610, under the rule of Sultan Achmet, the city was home to more than a million people: not only Islamic Turks, but also to large populations of Jews, and of Christians from Armenia, Greece and Italy, both free and enslaved. Sandys was struck by the weight of this extraordinary historical legacy. 'This Citie by destinie appointed, and nature seated for Soveraigntie, was first the seate of the *Romane* Emperours, then of the *Greeke,* as now it is of the *Turkish*: built by *Constantine* the sonne of *Helena*, and lost by *Constantine* the sonne of another *Helena* ... to *Mahomet* the second, in the year 1453, with the slaughter of her people and destruction of her magnificent structures'[1] For a historian and classicist like Sandys, the city was a relic of exalted richness, like a vast indecipherable book demanding translation and interpretation. A journey to Constantinople was a journey to the centre of the world, the Lord of the horizons.

> Than this [city] there is hardly in nature a more delicate object, if beheld from the sea or adjoyning mountains: the loftie and beautifull Cypresse trees so intermixed with the buildings, that it seemeth to present a citie in a wood to the pleased beholders. Whose seven aspiring heads [hills] ... are most of them crowned with magnificent Mosques, all of white marble, round in forme, and coupled above; being finished on the top with gilded spires, that reflect the beames they receive with a marvellous splendour.[2]

In Constantinople, there was much that was foreign to the eye of the traveller, and even some which was entirely new and undescribed.

From his little sponge divers' boat, Sandys came ashore and took leave of his Greek companions. He then crossed the harbour of the Golden Horn to the suburb of Pera, where he presented himself at the imposing residence of Sir Thomas Glover, the English ambassador, 'a man full of spirit, able to defend and offend, if our neighbours should go about in any way to wrong us'.[3] Pera had long been the suburb where foreigners were tolerated and where the embassies of the Christians were located. As a guest of the ambassador, Sandys found hospitality as well as protection. The hospitality was lavish: in his four-month stay, Sandys reported that he barely had cause to pay for anything. Located among the vineyards, the ambassador's residence provided food and lodging for all English nationals and, if some travellers are to be believed, nightly entertainment of wine drinking and whoring, both activities that could be punishable by death outside the embassy. The protection the ambassador offered was a necessity, not a luxury: as infidels, the Christian foreigners, or Franks as they were generally known, were frequently attacked by the populace and even by the forces of the law. From the ambassador's house in Pera, Sandys went on daily excursions to see the sights of the city, safe for as long as he was accompanied by a heavily armed bodyguard, drawn from the famed military caste of the janissary. The protection was often needed. During his visit to the great mosque of Santa Sophia in 1597, the English gentleman Fynes Morison was surprised by the sudden appearance of the Sultan in the crowd, and his janissary had to protect him from the attack of an old man wielding a mace, angered that a Christian should have got to within two or three paces of the Great Turk.[4] A few weeks later an old woman, seeing Morison and his servant being conducted by the janissary, concluded that they were his captives and slaves, and asked their price. Seeing the comedy of the situation, the janissary entertained the offer, upon which she suggested 100 aspers (about 5 shillings) for the 'slender and weake' Morison, and 400 for his vigorous servant.[5] As Sandys discovered, the janissary was guide and protector, but he was also warder and prison keeper.

To many travellers, scholars and traders, Turkey was a paradox: a 'daintie fruit growing out of a dunghill', as a later commentator described it.[6] In his study of Islamic Constantinople Sandys had to admit that the city was better organised, cleaner, more pious and more charitable than London. Politically, Ottoman society was more egalitarian, as there was no aristocracy and the meanest born might through merit end up in positions of great power. Furthermore, its justice was both less arbitrary and quicker. Ottoman commerce was more advanced, its merchants richer and the markets for luxuries more prosperous. It was truly the wonder of the world. Yet, paradoxically, Constantinople also demonstrated the corrupting influence of wealth and power. In the spectacle of the city Sandys saw not only abundance, but also 'the pride of a sterne and barbarous Tyrant possessing the thrones of ancient and just dominion'.[7] Like many Northern European visitors, Sandys was perplexed by how these riches had fallen upon a people who were not Christian. Of all the countries he visited on his travels, he concluded, Turkey represented the most clearly fallen state of the world.[8]

Describing the everyday life of the Ottomans, Sandys was caught again and again between opposing signs of magnificence and poverty. In their opulent palaces he was perplexed by the lack of furniture. Although they have splendid '*Turkie* carpets' on the floor, and ceilings of 'inlaid wood, adorned with gold and azure of excessive costliness', there are nothing 'but bare white walls', with 'neither tables nor stools'. Their food, too, was plain and austere 'so that they live for little or nothing, considering their fare, and the plenty of things'.

> Their most ordinary foode is pillaw, that is, rice which hath been sod [boiled] with the fat of mutton. Potage [thick soup] they use of sundry kinds, egges fried in hony, tansies (or something like them), pasties of sundrie ingredients: the little flesh which they eat is cut into gobits, & either sod, or tosted in a furnace. But I thinke there is more in *London* spent in one day then is in this Citie in twenty.[9]

In Turkish food, then, Sandys finds another version of his paradox: despite the plenty of provisions, the Turks choose to eat these incomprehensible nothings. That they exercise their taste in this way must be explained, but it cannot be comprehended by recourse to the system of values he used at home. As an aberration, Turkey might be dismissed as a kind of barbarism, were it not also powerful, rich and strong. Seizing upon Turkey's radically foreign qualities, Sandys hoped to reveal its essence. And of all the unfamiliar fruits of this oriental paradox, coffee was by far the strangest.

As one of the most visible signs of the discipline required by Islam, the food and manners of the Turks were of great interest to Christian travellers. Diet was one of the key ways in which Muslims set themselves apart from 'unbelievers', as they were forbidden by the Koran to consume wine and pork. Although Islamic Constantinople furnished many examples of unfathomable differences, the prohibition on drinking wine (and other spiritous liquors) seemed the most perverse. 'Wine is prohibited by their Alcoran: they plant none, they buy none.' Nonetheless, he observed the Turks' taste for wine when they could get it, for in the protected environment of an ambassador's residence they drank it so liberally, he noted, that there were 'few go away unled' from the table. William Biddulph, 'Preacher to the Company of English Merchants at Aleppo' in the period 1601–6, thought that these dietary regulations were the epitome of the Koran's teaching and an example of their heathen hypocrisy. 'The two chiefest points forbidden in the Alcoran, are, the eating of swines flesh, and the drinking of wine. Yet many of them drinke wine until they be drunken: but I never heard of any Turkes would eat swines flesh.'[10] Punishments for possessing wine were severe. So scared were they of being caught in possession of wine by the Ottoman officers, that the Greek sponge divers with whom Sandys had travelled to Turkey had consumed all their stocks in a single session the day before they arrived in Constantinople. But instead of wine the Turks had a mysterious drink, which they held in great regard.

'Their most common drinke is *Coffa*,' Biddulph wrote, 'which is a blacke kind of drinke made of a kind of Pulse like Pease, called *Coava*; which being grownd in the mill, and boiled in water, they drinke it as hot as they can suffer it; which they find to agree very well with them against their crudities and feeding on hearbs and rawe meates.'[11] Coffee drinking, Biddulph proposes, is a necessary antidote to the diet of the Turks. While 'coffa' agrees very well with the constitution of the Turk, he implies it will not suit that of the Englishman. Again, coffee was the sign of Turkish difference and, in a sense, the perfect symbol of Islam. William Lithgow, the eccentric Scottish traveller who made a 'pedestriall pilgrimage' from Paris to Jerusalem between the years 1609–14, examined the laws of Mahomet and the Prophet's life in order to expose the hypocrisy of a religion he repeatedly declared idolatrous:

> *Mahomet*, chiefly prohibiteth in his *Alcoran*, the eating of Swines flesh, and drinking of Wine, which indeed the best sort doe, but the baser kind are dayly drunkards: Their common drinke is *Sherpet*, composed of Water, Honey and Sugar, which is exceeding delectable in the taste: And the usual courtesie, they bestow on their friends, who visite them, is a Cup of *Coffa*, made of a kind of seed called *Coava*, and of a blackish colour; which they drinke so hote as possible they can, and is good to expell the crudity of raw meates, and hearbes, so much by them frequented. And those that cannot attaine to this liquor, must be contented with the cool streams of water.[12]

Sandys, following Biddulph and Lithgow, was of the opinion that the Turks drank coffee simply because they were forbidden to drink wine. Not knowing what else to call it, Sandys called this drink 'Coffa', a word he derived from the Arabic word for the berries from which it was made. He knew, from his own experience, that it was served as hot as the tongue would permit, in dainty little porcelain cups, and that it was as black as soot. Sandys concluded that the taste was not much better than soot either: burnt, bitter and gritty.

Coffee was an oddity not only in taste and appearance, but also in the effects it had on the body. These effects or 'vertues' occasioned much debate among physicians and natural philosophers. In 1601 George Manwaring, a gentlemen engaged with the embassy of Sir Anthony Sherley to Persia, noted, 'They have a certain kind of drink which they call koffwey, it is made of an Indian seed; they drinke it extreme hot; it is nothing toothsome, nor hath any good smell, but it is very wholesome.'[13] Such estimates of coffee's taste and effects do not suggest a lengthy interaction, although Manwaring's estimate of its toothsome qualities at least suggests he tried it himself. Another of Sherley's party, William Parry, further observed, 'They sit at their meat (which is served to them upon the ground) as Tailers sit upon their stalls, crosse-legd: for the most part, passing the day in banqueting and carowsing, untill they surfet, drinking a certaine liquor which they do call *Coffe*, which is made of a seede much like mustard seede, which will soone intoxicate the braine, like our Metheglin.'[14] A spiced variety of Welsh mead, metheglin was flavoured with therapeutic herbs like rosemary, hyssop, thyme and sage, with a distinctly medicinal taste.

To a drinker not habituated to it, Parry suggests, coffee tasted like medicine. That people might actually be fond of this brew was an idea beyond his comprehension. The Portuguese Jewish merchant Pedro Teixeira, who encountered coffee in the Ottoman provincial capital of Baghdad in October 1604, found it a rather insipid drink. 'Coffee is a vegetable of the size and appearance of little dry beans, brought from Arabia [. . .] It is black and rather tasteless; and, although some good qualities are ascribed to it, none are proven.'[15] Coffee drinking, William Biddulph noted in 1609, was primarily social. 'It is accounted a great curtesie amongst them to give unto their friends when they come to visit them, a Fin-ion or Scudela of *Coffa*, which is more holesome than toothsome, for it causeth good concoction, and driveth away drowsinesse. Some of them also drink Bersh or *Opium*, which maketh them forget themselves, and talke idly of Castles in the ayre, as though they saw Visions, and heard Revelations.'[16]

Biddulph and Sandys were curious, too, about the effects coffee had on the mind. They thought it acted like opium, another exotic comestible they first encountered in Turkey. Inasmuch as coffee 'driveth away drowsinesse', Biddulph thought it was conducive to conversation. The visionary reveries engendered by opium similarly made conversation flow, although with rather different results. While the narcotic poppy made men fanciful, talking of castles in the air, coffee kept them awake. Straight after his description of coffee, Sandys noted that

> The *Turkes* are also incredible takers of *Opium*, whereof the lesser *Asia* affordeth them plenty: carrying it about them both in peace and in warre; which they say expelleth all feare, and makes them couragious: but I rather thinke giddy headed, and turbulent dreamers; by them, as should seeme by what hath been said, religiously affected. And perhaps for the same cause they delight in Tobacco; they take it through reeds that have joined unto them great heads of wood to containe it: I doubt not but lately taught them, as brought them by the English: and were it not sometimes lookt into [. . .] no question but it would prove a principal commodity. Neverthelesse they will take it in corners, and are so ignorant therein, that that which in England is not saleable, doth passe here amongst them for most excellent.[17]

By linking together the three commodities of coffee, opium and tobacco, Sandys identifies their common property. He observed that these little-known products affect the way people think and act: coffee gives men 'alacrity' or speedy readiness, just as opium makes them giddy and turbulent dreamers. Both opium and tobacco were well-known in Northern Europe. Indeed, tobacco had been introduced to Constantinople in the year 1600 by English merchants of the Levant Company, who imported it from North America by way of London. The Turkish historian Ibrahim-I Pechevi, writing in about 1635, declared that it was brought by the 'English infidels' in the year 1009 in the Islamic calendar (that is, 1600–1), who 'sold it as a remedy for certain diseases of humidity'. Pechevi admitted that 'Sensualists and pleasure seekers' took it up, but in truth he argued its harmful and offensive effects offered 'no possibility of spiritual pleasure'. Furthermore, he added, 'its abominable smell taints a man's beard and turban, the garment on his back and the room where it is used'.[18]

In Constantinople, George Sandys was repeatedly struck by the magnificence of this great city. He was constantly reminded of its antiquity, reading Roman inscriptions on columns and obelisks, and making comparisons between the ruins of antiquity and the modern splendours of Ottoman architecture.[19] In seeking to describe the city, he sought to find its secret. Freighted with scholarship and erudition, however, his account gives very little sense of his own subjective response to his experience. Like many travellers of the time, he was fascinated by the fate of his body in these strange climes, scrupulously noting the effects of food, drink and weather on his health. Coffee was clearly a curiosity worth attention, as one of those special signs of Ottoman exceptionalism. But in detailing his account of his body, and his scholarship, Sandys left little room for his encounters with other people.

As a resident of London for nearly a decade, Sandys had enjoyed the friendship of the public houses near the Inns of Court, where he made the acquaintance of other young men interested in the law, in poetry and witty debate. Later in his life he revelled in the erudite society attracted to London by the royal court and in the 1630s he was a good friend of Lucius Cary, second Viscount Falkland. In the refreshing rural atmosphere of Falkland's country house at Great Tew in Oxfordshire, Sandys was included among the famous gathering of scholars, poets, wits, theologians, statesmen and courtiers, including Edmund Waller, Ben Jonson and Sidney Godolphin.[20] But in Constantinople, one senses Sandys's struggle to find connection among the merchants and courtiers of the ambassador's residence, or among the Turks. He was unable to discover men of learning or philosophy, and as the city was without taverns he was unable to establish his own network of friends. As he noted in his pocketbook,

> Although they are destitute of Taverns, yet have they Coffa-houses, which something resemble them. There sit they chatting most of the day; and sippe of a drinke called Coffa (of the berry that it is made of) in little *China* dishes, as hot as they can suffer it: blacke as soote, and tasting not much unlike it.

In the 'coffa-house', as he called it, he recognised the kind of convivial social encounters that he enjoyed in the taverns of his London: like-minded men meeting for conversation, for pleasantries and debate, over a sociable drink.[21] The difference was that in it the Turks consumed coffee.

A few years earlier, Biddulph had stated, 'Their *Coffa* houses are more common than Ale-houses in England; but they use not so much to sit in the house as on benches on both sides the streets neere unto a *Coffa* house, every man with his Fin-ion ful; which being smoking hot, they use to put it to their noses & eares, and then sup it off by leasure, being full of idle and Ale-house talke whiles they are amongst themselves drinking of it: if there be any news, it is talked of there.'[22] Other English travellers had observed these places of public coffee drinking too, even though they didn't coin a name for them. George Manwaring, who travelled with Sir Anthony Sherley's embassy to Persia in 1601, made note of the 'koffwey' house in Aleppo, which he too thought resembled a tavern. Manwaring noted in his travel diary, 'As in England we used to go to the tavern, to pass away the time in friendly meeting, so they have very fair houses, where this koffwey is sold.' Well-appointed and well-attended, the 'koffwey house' was availed upon by all Turks who wished to pass away the time in friendly meeting. What attracted men to the coffa-house was socialising. Sandys observed that men found it an ideal place to while away the time, 'chatting most of the day'. Coffee, Pedro Teixeira observed, is 'prepared and sold in public houses built to that end; wherein all men who desire it meet to drink it, be they great or mean. They sit in order, and it is brought to them very hot, in porcelain cups holding four or five ounces each. Every man takes his own in his hand, cooling and sipping it.' The ritualised habits of coffee drinking introduced an important principle to the coffee-house. Not only did the great men of the city, such as officers of the basha's court, merchants and janissaries, meet with the mean populace, but they did so in a condition of equality. The rituals of coffee drinking reinforced this egalitarian idea, because all were served in turn, no man served another and, furthermore, each was seated according to the order in which he arrived, rather than that of precedence usually encountered in the hierarchical Ottoman state.

Yet it seemed to some travellers unlikely that coffee itself drew men to the coffee-house. Teixeira, although he noted the Turks' and Persians' belief in the beverage's medicinal properties, refused to see this as the reason for the popularity of the coffee-house. 'Only their custom induces them to meet here for conversation, and use this for entertainment; and in order to attract custom there are here pretty boys, richly dressed, who serve coffee and take the money; with music and other diversions.'[23] Sandys, too, found it unlikely that the drink motivated the men's attendance at the coffee-house. He suggests there was an ulterior, sexual motive, observing that many of the coffa-men kept 'beautiful boyes, who serve as stales to procure them customers'.

Sandys's hunting metaphor is revealing: a 'stale' was a decoy bird, used to entice other birds into a snare or net. These 'beautiful boyes', then, entrapped their customers in the coffa-house. As Sandys knew, the term 'stale' was often used to describe the lowest classes of prostitute common on certain streets of London, who lured their customers into situations where they were preyed upon by thieves. Other travellers to the Ottoman Empire were less coy in describing the waiter boys as male prostitutes. George Manwaring in Aleppo in 1601, observed that 'gentlemen and gallants resort daily' to the 'koffwey' house. In addition to the pleasures of coffee and conversation, Manwaring suggested more diverse pleasures were on offer:

> The owners of these houses do keep young boys: in some houses they have a dozen, some more, some less; they keep them very gallant in apparel; these boys are called Bardashes, which they do use in their beastly manner, instead of women, for all the summer time they keep their women very close in the houses, and have use of boys.[24]

The term he uses for the young waiters, 'Bardash', is perhaps derived from the Arab word for slave (*bardaj*), but was better known in English as a transliteration of an Italian term, '*bardascia*', meaning catamite, a boy or youth with whom a man has sexual intercourse. Manwaring states unequivocally that the coffee-boys are used in 'their beastly manner, instead of women'. It would be hazardous to doubt such a candid observer, although it is worth noting that Protestant attacks on Islam often made accusations of this kind. William Parry, for example, wrote in 1601 that he considered the Ottomans 'damned Infidells, and Zodomiticall Mahomets'.[25]

On his return to England, Sandys was to find fame as a poet and politician, cultivating a reputation as a sober and erudite man devoted to learning. An account of his travels, published in a prestigious edition, served as his calling card to men in high office and to his fellow scholars. Illustrated with copperplate engravings derived from Italian books collected in Venice, Sandys's *Relation of a Journey* was first published in 1615 and was dedicated to the young Prince Charles (the future Charles I). He rewrote his daily journal, in which he had recorded observations of folk customs and manners, his excusions among the ruins and his visits to the great sights. In the manner of Italian travel writers, he leavened his factual account with quotations and references to ancient geographers, church historians, biblical commentary and, especially, the great poets of the classical era. Such a combination was almost unknown in English and the book sold well, with nine editions that century and a substantial extract (including his remarks on coffee) in *Purchas his Pilgrimes* in 1625. His verse translations of Ovid's *Metamorphosis* in 1621 and 1626 sealed his reputation as a writer and ensured his place in court circles. A stockholder in the Virginia Company and the Bermuda Company since 1607, he was propelled into colonial politics by his brother, who had him appointed a colonial administrator to the fledgling colony. As the Virginia colony at Jamestown lurched from one crisis to another, the Sandys brothers were loud among those who pressed for reform. In 1621, having been given the job of promoting industry in the colony, Sandys was sent to Virginia, where he remained until 1625 in the position of Treasurer, promoting an unsuccessful scheme for a glass factory.[26]

Sandys's career forms the first connection between America and coffee, although it is most unlikely that he took coffee with him, as some have alleged. On his return, he capitalised on his relations with the newly crowned Charles I, and as a Gentleman of the Privy Chamber pursued the prestige, influence and wealth that comes with preferment. He died in March 1644 at Boxley Abbey in Kent, before the execution of his beloved king, less than a decade before the first coffee-house opened in London.

CHAPTER TWO

The Wine of Islam Discovered

When he visited Constantinople in 1610, George Sandys had found the coffee-houses well established. But in fact they were a comparatively recent phenomenon, no more than six or seven decades old. According to the Turkish historian Ibrahim-I Pechevi, who wrote in about 1635, they were unknown in Constantinople until the year 962 in the Islamic calendar (1554), when they made their appearance during the reign of Suleiman the Magnificent (1520–66). As translated by the eighteenth-century English historian James Douglas, Pechevi (or Bichivili as he is known to Douglas) states that in the year 1554, 'two Men, nam'd *Schems* and *Hekim*, the one from *Damascus*, the other from *Aleppo*, set up each of them a Coffee-House in that Quarter of *Constantinople* call'd *Takhtacalah*'. Situated near the bustling *kapan* or market near the port and the shops around the Rustem Pasa mosque, the coffee-house of these enterprising Syrians was 'furnish'd with very neat Couches and Carpets, on which they receiv'd their Company'. Schems and Hekim offered their coffee at 'an easy Charge': Pechevi reports that 'a Dish of Coffee cost but an *Aspre*, which is not an Halfpenny of *English* Money'. The first coffee-house customers of Constantinople, related Pechevi, 'consisted most of studious Persons, Lovers of Chess, Trictrac [an early form of backgammon], and other sedentary Diversions; and as the generality of the Turks came soon to relish this sort of Meeting-Places, call'd in their Language *Cahveh Kaneh*, the number of them multiplied insensibly'. From the first, then, the Kahveh Kaneh were places in which customers found as much society as coffee:

> They look'd upon them as very proper to make acquaintances in, as well as to refresh and entertain themselves [. . .]. Young people near the end of their publick Studies; such as were ready to enter upon publick

> Posts; *Cadhis* out of Place, who were at *Constantinople* making Interest to be restor'd, or asking for new employments; the *Muderis*, or Professors of Law, and other Sciences; and, in fine, Persons of all Ranks flocked to them. At length even the Officers of the *Seraglio*, the *Pathas*, and others of the first Quality, were seen to go openly to the Coffee House; and as this serv'd to increase the Reputation, so it multiplied the number of them to too great an Excess.[1]

As they became more popular, the typical clientele of the coffee-house became increasingly associated with indolence: students, professors and out of work *kadis* (judges). As the coffee-houses grew more numerous, different kinds of establishment emerged. Some of these businesses, as the Turkish traveller Evliya Çelebi notes in Cairo, were little more than coffee shops. Such small and local concerns served coffee to a small neighbourhood or quarter, often delivering a pot of coffee or a tray of cups to nearby businesses, or accommodating a few men on benches outside their door.[2] In Aleppo in 1609, William Biddulph observed that customers of the '*Coffa* house' spilled out into the surrounding streets, noting that it was their practice 'not so much to sit in the house as on benches on both sides the streets neere unto a *Coffa* house'.[3] Building a grand coffee-house became one of the first things Ottoman rulers did in newly conquered cities, to demonstrate the civility of their rule. Not long after Baghdad was conquered the basha began building defensive ditches, a market place, a merchant lodge or *Khan* and a coffee-house. Pedro Teixeira, who travelled overland from the Persian Gulf to the Mediterranean in the winter of 1604–5 on his way home from India, noted that Baghdad possessed a 'Casa de Kaoáh' among its magnificent public buildings, built by 'Açen Baxá Wazir' (Hasan Pasha Wazir) in 1601: 'These places are chiefly frequented at night in summer, and by day in winter. The house is near the river, over which it has many windows, and two galleries, making it a very pleasant resort. There are others like it in the city, and many more throughout Turkey and Persia.'[4] The coffee-house in Aleppo, he discovered, was similarly grand and impressive. 'The coffee-houses are well built and furnished, adorned with numerous lamps, for that their chief custom is at night, though they have enough by day also.'[5] In search of cooler and fresher air, these coffee-houses were frequently sited next to rivers, or with terraces overlooking the city walls.

When Schems and Hekim opened for business in Constantinople in

1554, coffee itself was also considered something of an innovation. Coffee drinking emerged as a practice in southern regions of the Arabian peninsular in the early fourteenth century, although knowledge of the coffee bean and the coffee shrub among physicians and herbalists can be dated some centuries before that. Nonetheless the Ottoman and, before that, the Arab, history of coffee is a difficult story to tell, as there is little firm evidence and the story is confused, and enlivened, by some fairly tall stories. What hard evidence there is suggests that as a beverage, coffee was first consumed by Sufis living in Yemen, in the southern reaches of the Arabian peninsula (Arabia Fœlix). The Sufis used coffee in the performance of their religious ceremonies, for they found that its wakeful properties incited them to mystical raptures during the performance of their lengthy and repetitive recitations. It is not clear when this practice first developed, but it is unlikely to be before the fourteenth century and its use remained relatively uncommon for the rest of that century. In tracing the history of coffee, the principal sources used by Ottoman historians are edicts and opinions given by jurists and judges on the legality of its consumption. The earliest such opinion is recorded in 1438 in Aden, while another implies that coffee was consumed in Mecca by the end of the fifteenth century. As with the Sufis, coffee was taken at first as a medicinal delicacy to enable the pious and the studious to stay awake during their devotions. Coffee-houses were soon established, where men met together to consume coffee, listen to music and play chess or backgammon. Such sociable encounters piqued the curiosity of the authorities, for these activities looked remarkably like those that went on in the proscribed wine taverns. Even the manner in which the little finions or cups of coffee were passed around reminded jurists of wine drinking.[6]

One evening in 1511, as Khair Beg (Kha'ir Bey), the chief of police of the holy city of Mecca, was returning from prayers at the mosque, he was scandalised to notice that in one corner of the mosque there was 'a company of Coffee-Drinkers, who were thus fortifying themselves in order to pass the whole Night in Devotion'. The sight filled him with rage, for he 'imagined they were drinking Wine', an impression that was only confirmed when he heard of the properties of the mysterious drink. His enquiries led him to the coffee-houses, too, where the numerous 'Merry-makings' decided for him that coffee 'must make People drunk, or at least dispos'd them to commit Disorders forbidden by the Law'. Chastising the coffee drinkers in the mosque, he called an assembly of jurists of the different schools of Arabic law, together with physicians and officers of the police, to debate the status of coffee the next day. Evidence suggesting that its effects were intoxicating and dangerous were eventually persuasive, and the *kadis* signed a protocol describing the properties of coffee and declaring it unlawful for Muslims. However, when the protocol was presented to the Mufti of Mecca, Kansuh al-Ghawiri, an aficionado of the drink himself, he refused to co-operate with its declaration, even though it left him open to some damaging criticisms by zealots. Despite the Mufti's opposition, Kha'ir Bey used his powers as governor of the city to 'visit all the Quarters of the Town, shut up all the Coffee-houses, and burn all the Coffee they could lay their hands on'.[7] Knowing they had the support of the Mufti, however, the coffee drinkers continued to drink it in their houses. Their confidence grew in the next year, when Kha'ir Bey was replaced as Chief of Police.[8]

Other Arabic documents confirm the spread of coffee drinking beyond the Arabian peninsula in the sixteenth century. Coffee is known to have been consumed in Cairo in the first decade of the sixteenth century by Sufis inhabiting the Azhar quarter of the city. Religious zealots again raised the complaint that it was intoxicating and should be forbidden. In 1532, incited by an incendiary *fakih*, a mob rioted against the coffee-houses, destroying their contents and attacking the clients. Investigating the cause of the riots, the *kadi* sought the opinion of prominent scholars on the intoxicating effect of coffee. His enquiries suggested that coffee should be permitted, and although in the following years it was from time to time forbidden, devotees were in general allowed to drink it unmolested.[9] Essays, dissertations and even poems considering the effects of coffee were issued over the following decades. One such text by Abdalcader Alanzari entitled 'What ought to be sincerely and distinctly believ'd concerning Coffee that is, if it be lawful for a Mussulman to drink it', written in the year 996 Hegira, or 1587 AD, discussed the etymology of the word *Cahouah* (coffee), its properties and history, then surveyed the religious disputes at Mecca and finished with a collection of verses in praise of coffee.[10] As well as a polemical defence of coffee drinking, situated within controversy on its legality in Islamic law, this document was a beautiful example of Arabic calligraphy. When the Marquis de Nointel – appointed the French ambassador to the Sublime Porte in 1672 – returned from

Constantinople in 1679, he brought back to Paris a copy among his collection of oriental treasures intended for the Bibliotheque du Roy of Louis XIV. There, the manuscript was translated by Antoine Galland, an Arabic scholar and traveller who later wrote the famous twelve-volume *contes arabes, The Thousand and One Nights*. Galland's translation formed the basis of his treatise *De L'Origine et du Progrez du Café*, published in a small edition in Caen in 1699, which became central evidence in subsequent treatises on coffee by the French travel writer Jean de La Roque in 1716 and the Scottish physician James Douglas in 1727.[11] By this method, then, Arabic coffee lore was brought to the Europe of the Enlightenment.

It was in Aleppo in 1573 that coffee was first certifiably noticed by a Christian European, a natural philosopher from Augsburg called Leonhard Rauwolf, who is sometimes credited with the 'discovery' of coffee. Leaving home in Augsburg in 1573, he travelled overland to Marseilles and from there by ship to the Ottoman port of Tripoli on the Syrian coast, then to Baghdad and Jerusalem before returning home.[12] Rauwolf's first real contact with the Levant was in Aleppo, the commercial hub of Ottoman Syria, located on a fertile plain at the crossing point of important caravan routes between the Mediterranean and Persia. It was there, in the coffee-house overlooking the river Quwayq, that he observed the Turks drinking something they called '*Chaube*', a drink 'as black as Ink'. Alerted by the medicinal qualities attributed to the drink, he realised that the plant from which it was made was unknown to him (it was, in the botanical expression, a *non-descript*). Acquiring some of the coffee berries (evidently raw and unroasted), Rauwolf made the first botanical description of the species later called *Coffea arabica*: 'they take a fruit called *Bunru*, which in its Bigness, Shape, and Colour, is almost like unto a Bay-berry, with two thin shells surrounded, which as they informed me are brought from the *Indies*; but as these in themselves are, and have within them two yellowish Grains in two distinct Cells.'

Without a European name for this plant, Rauwolf transliterated the Arabic terms: the drink is *chaube*, or coffee as we now know it, and the berry he calls *bunru*, an approximation of the Arabic word *bun*. As his description suggests, there was no coffee plant for him to examine in Aleppo and he is misinformed that the berries come from the Indies.[13] Of its preparation, or even roasting, he is silent. 'This Liquor is very common among them, wherefore there are a great many of them that sell it, and others that sell the Berries, everywhere in their *Batzars*.' Although their common drink was water, Rauwolf noted that coffee was consumed in a notably sociable manner, in 'an open Shop', where 'you sit down upon the Ground or Carpets and drink together [...] without any fear or regard out of *China* Cups, as hot as they can, they put it often to their Lips but drink but little at a time, and let it go round as they sit'.[14] Although it is as a botanist that Rauwolf takes an interest in this medicinal plant, it is as an observer of human nature that he is directed to coffee, drawn by the spectacle of 'company' using it as an excuse for socialising.

By the time Rauwolf returned from his travels he was in his late thirties. In the following decades he directed his energies towards cataloguing his discoveries, and disseminating his new knowledge among his fellow botanists through his publications and the assembly of his herbarium. Among the 'the rare Oriental plants' he encountered, coffee was one of the thirty-four that Rauwolf was the first to identify in Western science.[15] In developing a herbarium, a collection of dried plants systematically classified and labelled, Rauwolf was building one of the most powerful scientific instruments of his day. Through his correspondence with other botanists of the period, such as Gesner and Clusius, he exchanged seeds and samples, and extended his knowledge of exotic plants. A herbarium was, to use a Renaissance commonplace, a 'hortus siccus' or dried garden. He carefully mounted dried and pressed samples of the plants on to paper leaves. While it was often a struggle to nurture rare and exotic plants in the botanical gardens of Northern Europe, the botanist could study his herbarium in all weathers. Rauwolf's travels to the Levant, then, were motivated by a desire to extend the coverage of 'exotics' both in his collection and in the botanical community at large. This was not mere classificatory zeal, but also reflected his interest in discovering 'simples', that is, herbs which have medicinal properties, sometimes known as officinal herbs, indicating that they were to be kept in stock in a pharmacopoeia. Such herbariums were important tools for medical research and very valuable. After his death, Rauwolf's collection was acquired by the Kunsthammer in Munich, from where it was subsequently looted by Swedish troops during the Thirty Years War and taken to Stockholm. In Sweden, it was acquired by Isaac Vossius in about 1650, a Dutch scholar, who took it to Holland in 1655 and on to London in 1670, where it was consulted by eminent English botanists, including Robert Morison and John Ray. After Vossius's death, Rauwolf's herbarium was acquired by the University of Leiden, where it remains a treasure of the Nationaal Herbarium Nederland.

In 1582 Rauwolf's account of his travels, developed from his pocket journal, was published in his native Swabian-German dialect.[16] In writing his book, he correlated the plants he had encountered with those described by classical and Arabic authorities. In difficult cases he sought guidance from a network of fellow botanists, the most prominent among whom was his old student friend Charles de l'Ecluse (known in the scientific world as Carolus Clusius), who had risen to be the director of the imperial botanical gardens in Vienna. While students together at the University of Montpellier in the 1550s, they had studied Latin translations of medieval Arabic natural histories by Avicenna and Rhases.[17] Rauwolf invoked these works in his description of the coffee beans. 'Being as they agree in their Virtue, Figure, Looks, and Name, with the *Buncho* of *Avicen*, and *Bancha* of *Rasis ad Almans* exactly, therefore I take them to be the same, until I am better informed by the Learned.' Although an inspired guess, his identification was to prove controversial and misleading, suggesting, for example, that Arabic use of coffee extended back to the tenth century.[18]

In addition to Rauwolf's claim, there are more fanciful stories of the origin of coffee. One of the most widely repeated, both in the seventeenth century and to this day, is that first related in 1671 by an Italian historian of coffee, Faustus Naironi:

> A certain Person that look'd after Camels, or, as others report it, Goats, (this is the common Tradition amongst the *Eastern* People) complain'd to the Religious of a certain Monastery in the Kingdom of *Ayaman* [Yemen], that is *Arabia Felix*, that his Herds twice or thrice a Week, not only kept awake all Night long, but spent it in frisking and dancing in an unusual Manner. The Prior of the Monastery, led by his Curiosity, and weighing the Matter, believ'd this must happen from the Food of the Creatures: Marking, therefore, diligently, that every Night, in Company with one of the Monks, the very place where the Goats or Camels pastur'd, when they danc'd, found there certain Shrubs or Bushes, on the Fruit or rather Berries of which they fed. He resolv'd to try the Vertues of these Berries himself; thereupon, boiling them in Water, and drinking thereof, he found by Experience, it kept him awake

> in the Night. Hence it happen'd, that he enjoin'd his Monastery the daily use of it, for this procuring Watchfulness made them more readily and surely attend their Devotions which they were obliged to perform in the Night. When, by this frequent Use of it, they daily experienced its Wholsomness, and how effectually it conduc'd to the preserving them in perfect Health, the Drink grew in Request throughout the whole Kingdom, and in Progress of time, other Nations and Provinces of the *East* fell into the Use of it. Thus by a meer Accident, and the great and wonderful Providence of the Almighty, the Fame of its Wholsomness spread itself more and more, even to the *Western* Parts, more especially those of *Europe*.[19]

In Naironi's fable the power of coffee was discovered by accident. As he remarked, many of the great medical advances in physic, in which 'occult Vertues and properties of natural Beings' have been discovered, happened by accident. He made no claim as to the historical period in which this story took place and, indeed, the timelessness of the story makes it sound like a fairy tale or myth. It is thus both specific – a story of a particular event – and imprecise, in that it features 'goats or camels' and is without date or place or names. As such it can be endlessly repeated, with minor variations. According to Stewart Lee Allen in *The Devil's Cup* (2000), he was told this tale repeatedly in Yemen and Ethiopia in the 1990s, including one pornographic version.[20] The story of the dancing goats, then, mythologises the origins of coffee in a providential account grounded in natural processes. Ironically, the story is also an object lesson in practical 'simpling', botanising for medical herbs: the monk observes the practice of the animals, experiments with methods of consumption and records the physiological effects upon his body. The myth that this story relates, then, is not only the origin of coffee, but also the empirical art of the new science of the seventeenth century.

After the brief mention of coffee in Rauwolf's *Itinerary* (1582), other botanists working in the field began looking out for these 'seeds' or beans, including them in their herbals. Rauwolf's friend, Charles de l'Ecluse, included a brief description of the beans, together with an illustration, in his flora of exotic plants published in Antwerp in 1605.[21] In 1592 the Italian botanist Prosper Alpin published a description of the coffee shrub, which he had found in Cairo in the 1580s, growing in the garden of 'a certain Turk, called Aly Bey', a captain of the janissaries, 'there planted as a rarity, never seene growing in those places before'. After his travels in Egypt, Alpin returned to Padua as Professor of Botany, where he created a renowned Botanical Garden. In his *Book of Egyptian Plants* (1592), he presented the first illustration of the coffee 'tree' to a European audience:[22]

> The tree ... is somewhat like unto the *Euonymus* Pricketimber tree, whose leaves were thicker, harder, and greener, and alwayes abiding greene on the tree; the fruite is called Buna, and is somewhat bigger then a Hazell Nut and longer, round also, and pointed at the one end, furrowed also on both sides, yet on one side more conspicuous then the other, that it might be parted into two, in each side whereof lyeth a small long white kernell, flat on that side they joyne together, covered with a yellowish skinne, of an acide taste, and somewhat bitter withal, and contained in a thinne shell, of a darkish ash-colour: with these berries generally in *Arabia* and *Egipt*, and in other places of the *Turkes* Dominions, they make a decoction or drinke, which is in the stead of Wine to them, and generally sold in all their tappe houses.[23]

In this translation by the English apothecary John Parkinson from 1640, the coffee tree is likened to the family *Euonymus*, a deciduous shrub variously known in English as pricketimber or spindlewood, from the use to which its wood was applied. Like the coffee tree, *Coffea arabica*, euonymus, now a widely grown ornamental shrub, has opposite leaves, white flowers and bunches of bright-red fruits. The two plants are, however, not of the same genus. As Alpin observes, the tree's berries are used throughout the Ottoman dominions to make a decoction or drink, generally sold in their 'tappe houses' or taverns – the first explicit reference in a European language to the coffee-house. Nonetheless, Alpin is not aware how the decoction is made, nor that the beans must be roasted before use.

Knowledge of this exotic plant, and its medicinal uses, were widespread among European botanists by the end of the sixteenth century. Rauwolf's discovery was noted in 1596 by a Dutch physician, Bernard ten Broeke, known to science by the latinised name Paludanus. In the village of Enkhuizen, on the shores of the Zuider Zee, ten Broeke had assembled a well-known cabinet of curiosities, based on the 'chests filled with the wonders of nature' that he had collected in his own journey to Syria, augmented by the gifts of many other travellers.[24] In

1594 he co-operated in the compilation of a book describing the travels of a local merchant, Jan Huyghen van Linschoten, who had returned from a long voyage to the Portuguese colony of Goa in India between 1583 and 1592. Linschoten's *Itinerario* took the form of a description of his travels but was also an advertisement for the commercial potential of the Far East. While Linschoten described what he saw and learnt in Goa, Paludanus adumbrated the scientific details. In a section describing the food of Japan there is a description of the Japanese tea ceremony, collected second-hand from Dutch sailors. Here Paludanus inserted a section describing coffee, noting the curious analogy between the Turkish 'Chaona' or coffee and the Japanese 'warme water', made with 'the powder of a certaine herbe called Chaa [green tea]'. Paludanus remarked here:

> The Turks holde almost the same manner of drinking of their Chaona, which they make of certaine fruit, which is like unto the Bakelaer, and by the Egyptians called Bon or Ban: they take of this fruite one pound and a half, and roast them a little in the fire, and then sieth them in twentie poundes of water, till the half be consumed away: this drinke they take every morning fasting in their chambers, out of an earthen pot, being verie hote, as we doe here drink aquacomposita in the morning: and they say it strengtheneth and maketh them warme, breaketh wind, and openeth any stopping.

Paludanus, probably from his own experiences in the Levant, is the first to describe the preparation of coffee, noting that the beans are roasted before being seethed or boiled. The beans he likens to the bitter-tasting 'Bakelaer' or laurel berries used in some apothecaries' preparations. As the drink is taken very hot and in the morning, Paludanus relates it to the *Aquacomposita* or *Brandewijn* (brandy or gin spirits) that the Dutch took in the morning, for its salutary physical effects. After Linschoten's book was published in 1596 an English translation was quickly prepared by William Phillip in 1598, alongside others in German, Latin and French. By showing how weak Portuguese control of the India trade was, and the extent of its potential, the *Itinerario* was a gold mine of commercial information and gained a wide readership. The book was a powerful influence on the merchant traders of both Amsterdam and London, opening their eyes to the prospect of direct trade with the East Indies.

The enthusiastic commentaries on the powers of coffee by travellers and botanists drew the attention of other men of science too. Alerted by their testimony, Francis Bacon, Baron Verulam and Viscount St Albans, the great Renaissance statesman and philosopher, took an interest in the physiological effects of the coffee bean. After his forced withdrawal from political office in 1621, Bacon retired to his family estate at Gorhambury, about two miles from St Albans in Hertfordshire, where he was 'employed wholly in contemplation and studies'.[25] In the final years of his life he developed a series of works devoted to scientific study, publishing, in Latin, the first part of his natural history in November 1621, entitled *Historia Naturalis et Experimentalis ad condendam Philosophiam*. A few months later, in February 1622, the second part appeared, on the history of life and death, *Historia Vitae et Mortis*.[26] This was designed as a wholesale critique of medical science: rather than aiming simply to diagnose and cure a few diseases and conditions, Bacon directed physicians to the higher aim of prolonging human life. In this book he discusses the physiological effects of a range of natural products, grouping together four similar officinals, including coffee, tobacco, the opium poppy and betel (*Piper betle*), a leaf chewed as a mild stimulant.[27] Before Bacon died in April 1626 – halfway through an experiment with a chicken and some snow to establish if cold could preserve food – he wrote an English version of his natural history, published as *Sylva Sylvarum: or A Naturall Historie* (1627). Of coffee, Bacon wrote:

> They have in *Turkey*, a *Drinke* called *Coffa*, made of a *Berry* of the same Name, as Blacke as *Soot*, and of a *Strong Sent*, but not *Aromaticall*; Which they take, beaten into Powder, in *Water*, as Hot as they can *Drinke* it; And they take it, and sit in their *Coffa-Houses*, which are like our *Tavernes*. This *Drinke* comforteth the *Braine*, and *Heart*, and helpeth *Digestion*.[28]

Bacon's observations are unlikely to be from personal experiment: his phrasing in the book suggests that the most likely source for his knowledge is Sandys's *Relation*, a book he relied on elsewhere.[29] Coffee's curious physiological properties, shared with opium, betel and tobacco, urged further research. Together, they shared an ability to 'condense the spirits' or change the emotional state of the consumer, rendering them 'Strong and Aleger', or resourceful and lively.

Another reader much influenced by the travellers' accounts of coffee was the English philosopher Robert Burton. In the fourth edition of his seminal treatise *The Anatomy of Melancholy* of 1632, he recommended coffee as a cordial or 'alterative' capable of 'mending the Temperament'. Like 'Wine and strong drinke', which he observed 'have such vertue to expell feare and sorrow, and to exhilarate the mind', Burton thought coffee had potential as a cure of melancholy. A shy and retiring librarian of Christ Church college Oxford, he was impressed by the Ottoman reputation of coffee as an efficacious remedy. 'The Turkes', he remarked, 'finde by experience' that coffee 'helpeth digestion, and procureth alacrity' (sprightliness and liveliness).[30] Coffee also appeared in the major English herbals of the 1630s. Thomas Johnson's 1636 edition of Gerard's great herbal (originally published in 1597) included 'buna' or coffee among several of the 'exotics', the new simples discovered by travelers.[31] In 1640 the London apothecary John Parkinson derived a copious entry on coffee from various botanical accounts: '*Arbor Boncum fructu suo Buna*, The Turkes berry drinke', he noted, 'hath many good Physicall properties therein: for it strengtheneth a weak stomacke, helping digestion, and the tumours and obstructions of the liver and spleene, being drunk fasting for some time together.'[32] By the 1650s coffee was a recognised constituent of the London apothecary's *materia medica*.

Among the medical men alerted to coffee's properties was William Harvey, famous for his account of the circulation of the blood. Harvey was one of the first habitual drinkers of coffee in London, from perhaps as early as 1627.[33] A physician at St Bartholomew's Hospital in Smithfield, London, he came from a wealthy family of Levant merchants. His younger brothers Daniel and Eliab had been admitted members of the Levant Company in 1611 and 1616, and were among its principal traders (Daniel Harvey had the reputation of knowing more about trade than any man in England).[34] The Harvey brothers were well placed to import coffee for their own consumption. Much later in the century the antiquarian John Aubrey remarked of William, 'I remember he was wont to drinke Coffee, which he and his brother Eliab did, before Coffee-houses were in fashion in London.'[35] By 1630, then, it is probable that small quantities of coffee were being privately imported to England through Levant Company circles. The diarist John Evelyn wrote (in 1697) that he remembered that in 1637 a Greek Orthodox priest, Nathaniel Conopios, studied at Balliol College, Oxford, where he 'was the first that I ever saw drink *Caffe*'. As he remarked, coffee was 'not heard of then in England, nor til many yeares after made a common entertainment all over the nation'.[36] Merchants in Marseilles trading to the Levant also developed a taste for coffee, importing small quantities for their personal use as early as 1644, together with 'all the little implements us'd about it in Turkey', including 'very beautiful . . . *Fingians* or dishes . . . of old *China*', according to the recollection of the French traveller Jean de La Roque (writing in 1716).[37] When Harvey wrote his will in 1652, he left to his niece Mary West half his linen 'together with all my plate excepting my Coffey pot'.[38] Who got the coffee pot is not clear, though its existence suggests Harvey's love of its contents. Unlike Bacon, Harvey took little scientific interest in the drink and its properties. To him it was recreation.

Coffee took just over a century to make its advance through the Ottoman Empire, moving up from Yemen through Arabia to Egypt, and from there to Aleppo, Anatolia, Smyrna and Constantinople, slightly more time than the conquering armies of the Ottomans took to make the reverse journey. But coffee was not an army and had no general to direct its strategy. Rather, it was more like a plague, or virus. As all coffee drinkers know, it does not seduce by the flirtatious charms of sweetness but, rather, has a more insidious effect. It is not pleasant to drink for the first time; it is an acquired taste. But it does have rewarding effects and it is habit-forming. Coffee changes people. Moreover, it changes the way they interact with their friends, their fellow citizens and their community. The proliferation of coffee-house drinkers and the establishment of coffee-houses were the first signs of this change.

CHAPTER THREE

The First English Coffee-House

In 1650 Thomas Hodges was a wealthy man. Like his father before him, he was a member of the Grocers Company of London, a guild whose merchants had made fortunes importing spices, drugs and currants. The Hodges, however, had almost outgrown the city livery through their engagement in the even more lucrative trade of exporting English woollen cloth, gunpowder and tin to Turkey, and importing desirable commodities in their stead: 'raw *silkes* of *Persia*, *Damasco*, *Tripoly*, &c. *Galles of Mosolo* and *Toccat Chamblets*, *Grograms* and *Mohayrs* of *Angora*, *Cottons*, and *Cottonyarne* of *Cyprus* and *Smirna*, and sometimes the *Jemmes of India*, and *drugges of Egypt*, and *Arabia*'. Despite the troubled and distracted times, Hodges's wealth and power was undiminished. Like most merchants of the City, he was an enthusiastic supporter of the cause of Parliament during the Civil Wars of the 1640s. As one of 'the first persons of abilitie' of the ward of Walbrook, he was forced to pay heavy tax impositions by both the King in 1640, and Parliament in 1651.[1] Thomas Hodges was also influential in commercial circles: as well as serving on the Committee of the East India Company, he was a Court Assistant in the Levant Company.

With his wife and four children, he lived in some splendour in a large and imposing five-storey house in Walbrook, a street close to the commercial heart of the city. In the cellar, besides the kitchens, was extensive storehousing for precious Levantine cargoes. Above them, the merchant kept his principal place of work: his counting house, where his apprentices and fellow merchants kept their ledgers, and the warehouse, where packets of English broadcloth were parcelled up for export and Levantine luxuries displayed for resale to the retail market. Both rooms were busy with the comings and goings of messengers from the Exchange, fellow traders from neighbouring shops on

Cornhill and Cheapside, and sea captains seeking bills of lading. Above the public rooms were the private quarters for his grown family and, in the garret, rooms for his three apprentices, Marmiduke Wyfeild, William Rannales and Chris Boweman, and the five maids the family kept as domestic servants. The family's principal rooms displayed their wealth and prestige. The largest, used for entertaining friends and associates, were panelled with intricately carved wainscoting, hung with gilt-embossed leather wall coverings and decorated with the exclusive treasures of the Levantine trade: tables displaying intricate 'turkey-work' carpets of lustrous hue and geometric patterns in silk and wool, delicate Chinese porcelain and Ottoman dishes, polished marquetry floors in rare wood, richly embossed silver plate, delicate sarsnet silk curtains to screen the sun. The latest cartographic apparatus of maps, orreries and globes could be used to explain the provenance of these bewildering commodities. This display of magnificence proclaimed the creditworthiness of the family concern and advertised their wares. Rather than the usual ale or best canary wine, visitors to the Hodges household were served coffee and sherbet, with curiously spiced comfits.

In 1651 Hodges welcomed a young merchant, Daniel Edwards, to his household. Recently returned from Smyrna in Anatolia, where he had lived since the mid 1640s, Edwards was from a good family who were also wealthy Levant merchants. Hodges had it in mind to seal his alliance with Edwards's family by marrying his oldest daughter, Mary, to him. The Edwards family resided in a comfortable country house in the pretty village of Stratford Bow to the east of the city, although they also had a residence and warehouse in the city, in the parish of St Gabriel Fanchurch.[2] Daniel was a freeman of the Drapers Company and a member of the Levant Company.[3] The merchants of the Company of Merchants of England Trading into the Levant Seas were a special bunch, not least because they were so rich. When James I incorporated the Company in 1605, he had granted to them a monopoly on the trade between the Ottoman Empire and England. According to Lewes Roberts in 1638, the 'height and eminency' of the Levant Company in this period made them 'second to none other of this land'.[4] To facilitate their trade, they had negotiated the right to establish communities of traders, known as factories, in the principal markets of the Ottoman Empire: first Constantinople and Aleppo, then later in Smyrna and Cairo. Trade was strictly controlled: ships plied to Turkey in spring and

Aleppo in autumn, and imports had to be balanced against exports (each trader received the proportionate space on the returning ship as he occupied on the outgoing).

The Edwards family were the leading concern in the Anatolian port of Izmir, which they knew by its Roman name of Smyrna. The Turkish historian Evliyâ Çelebi described Izmir as 'a fabulously rich port city' whose houses 'cling to the slopes below the castle [. . .] among the airy gardens of various palaces and mosques'.[5] It was a remarkably urbane and cosmopolitan city: its population of Muslim Turks exceeded by a large community of mercantile outlanders, predominantly Greek Orthodox Christians (Greeks), Gregorian Orthodox Christians (Armenians) and Jews. The Franks, European merchants, were corralled together for their own protection on a long street that ran parallel to the sea. Along this wide boulevard the Franks' large villas overlooked their terraced gardens and the capacious warehouses that lined the quay. Their community was like a society of its own: a French visitor, Tournefort, remarked that life in Smyrna was like being 'in *Christendom*; they speak nothing but *Italian*, *French*, *English* or *Dutch* there'.[6] Joseph Edwards, the head of the Edwards family, was one the most important Franks in the factory, 'the leading English agency for foreign principals', looking after the interests of merchants engaged in the trade but not resident in Smyrna, such as Thomas Hodges. The house of Joseph Edwards was the social centre for the whole of Frank Street: hosting musical assemblies on most evenings, with dancing and magnificent suppers. One visitor to the city recalled attending sumptuous picnics – 'entertainments *Alla Turchesa*' – as well as noting the pleasures of 'a Dish of Caffe' at the baths.[7] Coffee became the centre of Frankish life in Smyrna: rather than a peculiar Turkish custom, the English themselves became habituated to it.

In Smyrna Daniel Edwards employed a young Greek man called Pasqua Rosee in the capacity of servant and when he returned to London he brought Rosee with him. To be a servant to a merchant in this period was not a demeaning employment: others worked in the household, waiting on tables, cleaning and cooking. Rosee's job was more like that of a personal assistant. Skilled in many of the languages of the city, he was an indispensable aid in negotiations with the traders and *dragomen* (middlemen) of the bazaar. He was a clerk of accounts, a translator and a social diplomat, using his knowledge of Turkish customs to smooth the path of commerce. He was also a valet, agent and coachman, rarely leaving his master's side. Paul Rycaut, English consul in Smyrna in the 1660s, advised that Greek or Armenian servants were both cheaper and better than English ones: a good man was easily worth his wages of 50 silver thaler a year (£11 in English money), with board, free bread and annual liveries or clothing.[8] Even though domestics served Edwards at table, only Rosee, his trusted valet, prepared his daily coffee. As a long-time resident of Ottoman Smyrna, Rosee was skilled in coffee preparation and also had knowledge of the local market for coffee beans.[9] Smyrna was well provided with coffee-houses: a register made by Ismail Pasha in 1657–8 counted more than forty establishments.[10] The French scholar Jean de Thevenot, when visiting Smyrna in the 1650s, remarked both on the numerousness and sociable nature of the 'Cahue-hane' or coffee-houses he encountered, which he called '*cabarets publics de cahue*'.[11] Although the cosmopolitan social life of Smyrna crossed seemingly insurmountable barriers of language, manners and religion, the English could not leave their troubles at home. In 1647 and in 1650, Daniel Edwards played a prominent role in resisting Royalist factions in the Levant Company: official dispatches mention his personal bravery in releasing some fellow merchants incarcerated by the bogus Royalist ambassador, Sir Henry Hyde, in a stinking dungeon in the castle at Smyrna.[12]

In 1651 Daniel Edwards left Smyrna and travelled overland to England, possibly to escape these troubles, or perhaps to avoid an outbreak of plague in the city.[13] Along with his manservant, Pasqua Rosee, Edwards brought some characteristic habits of Levantine merchants: hard work, Puritan politics and coffee drinking. In the domed church of St Stephen's Walbrook he sealed his allegiance to the Hodges family by marrying Mary Hodges on 31 March 1652.[14] There he entertained his family, his friends and his fellow merchants with tales of the Levant, of the squabbles among the factory and of meetings ending with daggers drawn. He brought with him a quantity of coffee and all the elaborate paraphernalia of coffee making: *ibriks* (the open-topped jugs in which coffee was boiled, with their characteristic opposed handle), rotary coffee roasters, long-necked grinders and delicate porcelain dishes called *finians*. Daniel Edwards was a prodigious drinker of the new beverage. His friends later recalled that he 'drank two or three Dishes at a time' of coffee, 'twice or thrice a Day'. Coffee became a regular occurrence in the house of Hodges. Their merchant friends, especially those who had served their time in the Company factories, gathered at their house to drink coffee together and in a short time, it 'grew more in use in several private Houses'.[15]

The distinctive custom of the Levant Company merchants in drinking this exotic and expensive comestible was in part habit, in part compulsion. There were also more local reasons for the growing vogue for coffee. The civic authorities in London in 1652, burning with Puritan zeal, inveighed against the 'growing evil' of taverns and ale houses, in which 'many lewd and idle persons are harboured, and many Felonies are oftentimes plotted and contrived [. . .] to the great losse of many mens lives and estates by disorders therein, to the great dishonour of God, scandal of the Government of this City, disturbance of the publicke peace, and to the ruine and destruction of very many people'.[16] In a similar vein gambling, Christmas, cockfights and football matches were suppressed as encouraging licentiousness and superstition.[17] Under this Puritan repression public pleasures were deserted, and the face of the city was melancholy and dejected. Behind the damask curtains, however, the divines discerned that many men continued tippling and gaming. The pleasing aspect of drinking coffee, the Levant merchants knew well enough, was that it did not make you drunk and, in fact, it made you feel better and brighter.

The trouble with this collective coffee drinking, Edwards realised, was that there were so many men coming to his house that it was impeding the family's work – the 'novelty' was 'drawing too much company to him'.[18] The cost of the coffee was presumably mounting up as well. Casting his mind back to the practice in Smyrna, he must have realised that although he had the coffee, what was missing from the equation was the coffee-house. In response, Edwards and Hodges resolved to open a public coffee-house, conceiving the venture as a business enterprise modelled on the Ottoman *cave-hane* Edwards had experienced in the Levant. Both Edwards and Hodges were too grand and too busy to open it themselves – especially as it was a condition of the Levant Company that they remain a 'mere merchant' engaged solely in wholesale trading, without retailing or refining products.[19] The solution was to sponsor Pasqua Rosee; setting him up in a small business selling coffee to the public.

Not only was this the first London coffee-house, it was the first in Christendom. Reliable evidence of when it opened does not exist, although it was certainly before 1654 and perhaps as early as 1652, the date asserted by many later authorities, for which there is some corroborating evidence. The picture is confused by a rival claim, which has very little credibility. In 1671, nearly twenty years after the events he describes, the Oxford antiquarian Anthony Wood stated that public coffee selling was initiated in Oxford in 1650. There is much reason to suppose this date imprecise. In the earliest version of Wood's diary, written up to the end of 1659 and now in the British Library, he merely claims that coffee was first consumed in private in Oxford in 1650, and at an unstated date between 10 August 1654 and 25 April 1655 adds that coffee was 'publickly solde at or neare the Angel within the East Gate of Oxon ... by an outlander or a Jew'.[20] In 1671 Wood redrafted his diary, now called his 'Secretum Antonii', a document held in the Bodleian Library. In this revision he claims that 'Jacob a Jew opened a coffey house at the Angel in the parish of S. Peter, in the East Oxon' and that 'When he left Oxon he sold it in Old Southampton buildings in Holborne neare London', a building first constructed in 1664. In the late nineteenth century this undated addition was conjecturally dated by Wood's editor Andrew Clark at 'March 1651', but there is no evidence to support this earlier date.[21] No positive evidence – such as building leases or licences issued by regulatory authorities – has come to light to back up these assertions, but nonetheless most authorities have accepted Oxford's claim. Much better evidence can be found for Pasqua Rosee's coffee-house in London.

A business start-up is always a precarious affair. In this case Rosee and his sleeping partners were going to trial a new product on a virtually untested market in what was probably a hostile regulatory regime, to a public that had almost no idea about the product. To mitigate these dangers they decided to open their business close to the one group they hoped might have a taste for it: the merchants. Although merchants lived all over the City, the one place where they congregated on a daily basis was the Royal Exchange, a noble building on Cornhill, built by Sir Thomas Gresham in 1566–8 as 'a Bursse, or place for marchants to assemble in'.[22] It was a splendid neoclassical building, with a large central trading floor in which merchants assembled to transact business, the whole surrounded by an arcade, above which were a series of small retail shops, known as 'the Pawn'. While the Royal Exchange was the epicentre of the City's commercial activity, the streets and alleys around the Exchange also bustled with traders, sea captains, and foreigners, while in the buildings above were the offices of a vast army of associated trades: stationers and booksellers, notaries and lawyers, victuallers and tavern keepers, toy men and barbers. They were now to be joined by the figure of the coffee-man.

The location chosen for Rosee's coffee business was St Michael's Alley, a narrow lane leading off the great thoroughfare of Cornhill, about a hundred paces from the entrance to the Exchange. Although this alley is now a quiet and retiring spot among the great buildings of the modern City, in 1652 it was a very desirable address. Alleys such as this one, or the nearby Pope's Head Alley, had become central to the City's commercial culture, akin to modern office blocks and shopping malls. The network of lanes and alleys between Cornhill and Lombard Street comprised a single integrated retail and business space. It was their narrowness, perversely, which made them ideal for this purpose, because they could not be encumbered and congested by the passing traffic of carriages and dray carts. They were paved with freestone, and lit with lanterns and lights from the shops and offices. The jettied architecture of the buildings, nearly meeting overhead in the narrower lanes, also offered some protection from inclement weather.

The alley was dominated by St Michael's parish church, described by John Stow in 1603 as 'fayre and beautifull', but 'greatly blemished' since the mid sixteenth century by a series of buildings erected around it. Various pressures, from the need to house a rapidly growing population to the desire to lock up the parish's wealth in bricks and mortar, led the Rector and Churchwardens to permit these buildings, first along the frontage to Cornhill, then later around the edges of the green and pretty churchyard. Though no more than six feet wide at points, St Michael's Alley was a thoroughfare, as it opened through passageways under houses on to several other alleys: George Yard leading to Lombard Street and Bell Yard leading to Gracechurch Street. The cloister had a beautiful internal courtyard surrounded with an arcade of columns supporting an arched ceiling round a peaceful central garden. From there, passers-by could walk through several gates into the walled churchyard, with its large wooden pulpit cross amid the grass and memorial stones. This was the spot on which they chose to open Rosee's coffee shop.

Their first enterprise resembled a market stall, occupying a shed in the churchyard next to the cloister. Such sheds were common in the London retail trade in this period: the main feature of which was a shelf – called 'the stall' – on which the goods were displayed for sale. Samuel de Sorbiere, visiting from France in 1664, observed that 'there is no City in the World that has so many, and such Fine Shops: the Stallage is not very rich, but the Sight is agreeable; for they are large, and the decorations are as valuable as those of the Stage; the Scene is new everywhere, which extreamly pleases and attracts the Eye as we go along'.[23] If Rosee's shed was like the others in the churchyard, it was made of deal boards: thin planks of pine or fir, painted and decorated to attract custom.[24] His shop sign, identifying his business, was said to be an image of himself, dressed in some Levantine clothing. Such market sheds were designed to be closed up at the end of the day, with highly decorated horizontal shutters covering the open window. In the morning the lower shutter would be 'unbuttoned' to form the counter or stall board. The upper shutter, called the pentice, extended over the counter to form a sheltering awning and cover to protect the stall and the customers from the rain and sun. Rosee's shed must have had some sort of hearth or brazier to heat water to make coffee.

His customers, having bought their coffee, assembled in groups under his awning, or took their coffee in the ambulatory of the nearby cloister. Although no business records survive of his venture, Rosee's enterprise was apparently successful. But exposed to London's inclement weather, offering no seated accommodation for customers, it was far removed from the elegant and comfortable structures the merchants remembered from their days in the Levant. The churchwardens, too, were concerned that their property was being defiled. Their meetings in the 1650s repeatedly called for the preservation of order in the churchyard, especially the 'annoyance' of hanging lines displaying 'ruggs, cloathes and other things', which occluded free passage in the alleyway.[25]

Among the throng of people attracted to the coffee-house was a young gentleman, William Brereton, an enthusiast for experimental science and novelties in trade. On 4 August 1654 he informed Samuel Hartlib that 'A cuphye-house or a Turkish – as it were – Ale-house is erected near the Old Exchange' in Cornhill. Hartlib was a Czech immigrant who from his 'office of intelligence' in Westminster operated the most extensive network of scientific correspondence in the decades before the foundation of the Royal Society. Through collaborators such as Brereton, Hartlib collected information, which he entered into his *Ephemerides*, a unique archive closest in form to what would now be called a database. This 'cophye-house drinke', Hartlib noted, was 'a Turkish-kind of drink made of water and some berry or

Turkish-beane. [. . .] It is somewhat hot and unpleasant but [has] a good after relish and caused some breaking of wind in abundance.'[26] This counts as important contemporary evidence, made by an eyewitness to the events at the time itself. Another early visitor to Rosee's coffee shop in these years was a young Levant merchant called Thomas Rastall, who had encountered coffee with Daniel Edwards during his seven-year apprenticeship in the Levant.[27] Rastall remembered meeting Edwards and Rosee on their way home to London in 1651 in the trading entrepôt of Leghorn (Livorno) on the coast of Tuscany. In the 1690s, more than forty years later, he recalled the early days of the London coffee-house for an antiquarian historian, John Houghton, who was writing his 'Discourse on Coffee' for the Royal Society. According to Rastall, the date Rosee established his coffee shop was 1652, but we only have his word for it. There is, however, an archival record of Pasqua Rosee and his coffee-house from four years later, 1656. That he left any record at all is due to the meticulous work of the churchwardens of St Michael's. When the vestry met in its regular wardmote court, minutes of their discussions were recorded in vast leather-bound folios, kept in a special wooden chest in the Quest-house chamber. The vestry minutes of St Michael's in Cornhill still exist, now safely stored in the Corporation of London's Guildhall Library.[28]

Rosee's English was not perfect: it was presumably his third language, after Greek and Turkish. English satirists found much to mock in his accent. In *A Broadside against Coffee; Or, the Marriage of the Turk* (1672), the anonymous satirist explains that the first coffee-man in London, Pasqua Rosee, was a lowly coachman in the service of Daniel Edwards, recording his strongly accented speech: '*Me no good Engalash!*' In this broken English Rosee promoted the beneficial effects of coffee, playing 'the Quack to salve his Stygian stuff', recommending his beverage as '*Ver boon for de stomach, de Cough, de Ptisick*'.[29] Within a few years, his coffee shop had overgrown the simple shed in the churchyard. The concourse of people drinking there attracted attention, not all of it supportive. His competitors in the drinks market were particularly displeased, especially the ale sellers. The City authorities strictly controlled the number of taverns and ale houses in each parish. In Cornhill the licence or recognisance was granted to only five permitted taverns, each of which had to obey a long series of orders and regulations.[30] Each of these licences was a jealously guarded business property. To the ale sellers it seemed that Rosee's coffee-house was an interloper invading their trade and stealing their livelihood, so they reported him to an alderman, who brought notice of his infraction to the Lord Mayor's office. This was, of course, a matter of interpretation: Rosee's was not an illegal tippling house selling 'ale, beer or other strong drink without licence', nor was it a disorderly house 'harbouring rogues or master-less men'.[31] But it was, equally, more than a little like such places. What his coffee shop shared with the tavern, it was plain to see, was a communal and convivial sociability.

Although there is no record of the success or failure of their petition to the Lord Mayor, the ale sellers found a simpler way to harass the business. Rosee, as everything about him proclaimed, was not an Englishman. More specifically, he was not a citizen of London, a legal status that could only be granted by being admitted to a livery company, one of the ancient guilds of the City that guarded the interests of specific crafts and trades. Daniel Edwards and Thomas Rastall were members of the Drapers Company, and Thomas Hodges was a Grocer. Only those made free of the City could gain permission to trade. Freedom was acquired by three methods: servitude (working out an apprenticeship), patrimony (being the son of a freeman born after the father was made a freeman), or redemption (applying to the Chamberlain, supported by two Guild members, and paying a fee). As a stranger and an alien, Rosee could do none of these things and had no permission to trade in the City. Daniel Edwards and Thomas Hodges, however, could see the commercial potential of coffee and were unwilling to let pass the opportunity Rosee's shop presented. It was clear to them that the habit of drinking coffee was a taking one for, once sampled, coffee had a way of drawing people back to try it again. They found the concourse of people at the coffee shop a pleasing sight: a good business that was itself good for business. The solution to their problem was to find Rosee a partner, someone who was free of the City.

They found their man in one of Thomas Hodges's former apprentices, Christopher Bowman. Bowman was the son of a farmer, a yeoman from Mymes in Middlesex (now South Mimms), a village on the road north from London. By 1641 Christopher was living at Hodges's Walbrook town house, where the boy had been taken on by Thomas Hodges as an apprentice in the 'Mistery of the Grocerie', presumably when he was fourteen years old. Each member of the livery company was permitted three apprentices: in return for their labour, and the profits from their labour, the master of each apprentice trained the boys in the 'mysteries' of the trade and provided for their welfare (food, clothing and lodging). In 1644, 'Xtofer Boman' was bound by indenture for seven years and his name was entered in the Register of Apprentices.[32] Most masters were harsh disciplinarians, seeing it as their duty to protect their charges from the dissolute pleasures of the city around them. After nearly nine years Bowman was admitted to the freedom of the Grocers, on 22 February 1654. As a Grocer, Bowman was now permitted to trade on his own behalf in the City of London and, like many apprentices, he received some assistance from his former master in setting up his business.

The partnership of Pasqua Rosee and Christopher Bowman set about improving their business. The first thing they did was to find more auspicious premises, moving out of the shed in the churchyard and into a house across the alley. It was true that this was a tumbledown wreck, but at least it had doors and windows. London houses were notoriously badly built: Richard Newcourt described in 1640 the 'obscure and base' construction of the city, with its 'multitude of bye-lanes, nooks and alleys hudled upp one on the neck of another, soe that some howses scarce ever saw the sun, And the inhabitants lived comfortless and unwholesome'.[33] The standard of construction was so poor because leaseholders were given short leases that gave them little interest in constructing long-lasting houses. As Richard Neve complained in 1703, 'The greatest objection against London-houses [. . .] is their slightness, occasioned by the Fines exacted by Landlords. So that few houses at the common rate of Building last longer than the Ground-lease, and that about 50 or 60 years.'[34] The building Bowman and Rosee moved to in St Michael's Alley was 'in and nigh unto the Churchyard' as the early leases said of it. It had been erected in 1604 and by 1656, when they took it over, it was in a state of disrepair. In those years it had housed various almost respectable businesses including a bookseller's warehouse and an upholder (a dealer in second-hand articles of clothing or furniture). But most recently it had been occupied by several tenants in quick succession, some of whom had been delinquent in paying the rent. It had even been left empty for some years. When Bowman and Rosee took over their shop from a man called Mr Marlborough the lease had only a year left to run.

The negotiations with the churchwardens for a new lease proceeded through the summer of 1657. The vestry formed a committee of churchwardens 'impowered to determine as they shall think good concerning the building and letting of the houses in the holding of Christofer Boman Pars Rosee and Mr Bladwill'.[35] The current rent of the shop was only £4 per annum. For the ward of Cornhill the ground plot was reasonably large, occupying a rectangle of land over twenty-seven feet long facing the alley and nineteen feet deep. It was divided into two dwellings, or 'messuages' in the lawyers' terms, and after some lengthy difficulties with the occupier of the other half, a William Bladwell, merchant of St Olave's parish, the whole building was let to Christopher Bowman. The negotiations for letting the building began on 14 July 1657, were concluded by the end of the month, and the lease granted and signed on 14 August, ready to commence at the next Lady Day, 25 March 1658, the traditional beginning of the legal year. At the start of the negotiations the churchwardens took note of Pasqua Rosee's role in the business, but by the end he was not mentioned in the lease and Bowman signed it by himself. The sparse record of the vestry minutes does not relate the reason for this. Perhaps there had been a power struggle between the two partners, with Bowman as the victor carrying off the prize; or perhaps Rosee dropped out of the picture when the wardens became acquainted with his alien status. Houghton remarked cryptically that some time after 1654 '*Pasqua* for some Misdemeanour run away, and *Bowman* had the whole Trade'. In any case, after appearing in the churchwardens' accounts for this year, issued in April 1658, Rosee is not mentioned again, although his name lived on in the coffee-house. Certainly, no record has been found of any 'misdemeanour' on his account, nor any sign, as is sometimes alleged, that he went on to open a coffee-house on the tree-lined boulevard of Korte Voorhout in the Dutch capital of The Hague in 1664.[36]

The lease Bowman signed suggests both that the churchwardens drove a hard bargain and that he believed it was a viable proposition. Bowman's lease was granted for thirty-one years, due to run out in 1689, at the rate of £10 per annum paid quarterly. In addition Bowman had to pay a fine (a single fee) of £40 on completion of the lease. These rates were typical for St Michael's Alley. But the lease did have some unusual 'Covenants and Agreemts on the Tennants part'. It required of Bowman 'That he will in the first 5 yeares bestow £300 upon the substantiall new building of the two messuages with all materials and workmanship fitt necessary' and have receipts to prove to the churchwardens that the work was done to this high standard. Once the new building was erected, the lease went on, he had to 'mayntayne support, susteyne, keepe and amend' it and its glass windows. Furthermore, in order to guarantee that he carried out this work, the lease demanded on him a bond 'of the penalty of ffive hundred pounds to pay the Rent and perform the Covenant'[37] This enormous sum was most unusual, although presumably it was only a surety to be paid if he did not meet the covenants and, certainly, he never paid it. Houghton relates that Bowman's move into this building was assisted by 'the Generosity of his Customers, who contributed Sixpence a piece, to the number of almost a Thousand'.[38] Although 1,000 sixpences is only £25, Houghton's story suggests that Bowman's coffee-house was a considerable commercial success, attracting a large and enthusiastic clientele. William Brereton reported to Hartlib that the 'keeper' of the Turkish 'cophye-house' 'gets 30 or 40 shillings a day' as the 'sellar of that drink'.[39]

Takings like this were a prodigious amount. If this were true, Bowman's business would have a turnover of almost £450 per annum, which even with the varied expenses of the trade, the cost of raw materials and so forth, suggests a considerable profit. Certainly, the churchwardens' Account Book records that he paid his rent on time in the next few years.[40] As his wealth grew, so did his prestige in the neighbourhood: he was requested to pay a tithe of 20 shillings a year in January 1659, and, like a good parishioner, subscribed to the fund to repair the steeple, although he never paid what he promised.[41] The Vestry minutes, calling him the 'Coffee-man in St Michael's Alley', even report him offering to pay for the repair of the limestone flagstones in the alley outside his coffee-house in May 1660.

No visual images of Bowman's coffee-house in St Michael's Alley survive. Nonetheless, archival information gives some idea of it. The Hearth Tax returns for 1663, levied at the rate of 1 shilling for each fire, hearth and stove in each dwelling, state that 'Christopher Bowman' was assessed at eight hearths, suggesting a large building perhaps ranged over four floors.[42] Bowman's lease required that he spend £300 on rebuilding the house, a sum which was typical for a London townhouse of three or four storeys.[43] The building was most likely to have been built originally in some version of the London vernacular favoured by the building trades: timber-framed structures, with lath and plaster or brick infilling, double-storeyed bay windows and jettied upper floors extending out over the passageway below.[44] A spruce renovation might have made the building look respectable again by patching paint and plaster. Of the interior little is known, although Bowman's aim was to provide a sociable environment. Walter Elford, a coffee-man himself, recalled visiting the coffee room at Bowman's as a schoolboy in the early 1660s. Elford's recollections were recorded by the Scottish anatomist James Douglas in the course of his research on the history and biology of coffee in the 1720s. 'The Coffee-Room', he remembered, where the assembly of men presided, 'was up one pair of Stairs.' From here the building had lights or windows into the green oasis of the old churchyard. He also recalled it was a sociable arena, where even in the early years of the coffee-house men conversed, gossiped and transacted business. Walter Elford recalls that this entertaining and educative socialising stopped abruptly in 1665:

> in the Year of the Plague, 1665, it was a Custom among those that frequented it, as soon as they went in, to look quite around the Room for some of their Acquaintances, and then to begin, by asking how all was at their Houses: If no body was sick, they join'd with them in Company; otherwise, or when they met with none they knew, all sat at a distance from one another.[45]

What Bowman achieved in his coffee-house, with its dedicated, specially furnished coffee room, with its fires and stoves for warmth and preparing coffee, was a retail revolution, although such places quickly lost their strangeness. But in the fanatical environment of the Interregnum and Restoration, the coffee-house to many was a haven of civility.

By the end of the 1650s further coffee-houses had been established. The Rainbow Coffee-House was in operation by 1657, when the Wardmote inquest book of the parish of St Dunstan's recorded that James Ffarr, a barber, was presented for causing annoyance to his neighbours from the 'evil smells' and fire associated with coffee making.[46] The coffee-houses were declared to be one of the signs of the depravity of republican London, according to John Evelyn. In *The Character of England*, published in May 1659, he contrasted the city with Paris, to which he had initially fled after Charles I's execution. Imagining a Frenchman viewing London for the first time, he said the city was provincial, dirty and poorly built: 'a very ugly Town, pestred with

Hackney-Coaches, and insolent *Carre-men*, *Shops* and *Taverns*, *Noyse*, and such a cloud of *Sea-coal*, as if there be a resemblance of *Hell* upon Earth, it is this *Vulcano* in a foggy day'. As well as a 'prodigious' number of ale houses, Evelyn further lamented there were other houses, even more 'deplorable, where the gentlemen sit, and spend much of their time; drinking of a muddy kind of *Beverage*'. Such luxuries as coffee and tobacco, he complained, have 'universally besotted the *Nation*' and 'consumed many Noble Estates'.[47]

Bowman's coffee-house continued to trade under Pasqua Rosee's signboard, presumably not only because it was a memorable name, but it was also an established brand. Bowman did what he could to keep the Pasqua Rosee story alive. He printed a one-page advertising handbill which he enclosed, folded in three, in the parcels of coffee he sold. *The Vertue of the Coffee Drink. First publiquely made and sold in England, by Pasqua Rosee* explained the authentic Ottoman method of preparing the beans and made a series of extravagant medical claims for the drink's properties. At the bottom of the page it explained that coffee is 'Made and Sold in *St. Michael's Alley* in *Cornhill*, by *Pasqua Rosee*, at the Signe of his own Head'.[48] This handbill was later copied by other coffee-house owners, each of whom placed the name of his own establishment at the bottom of the page. One enterprising coffee wholesaler, probably operating in Oxford, made a version which left a blank at the bottom of the page, so that any of his various retailers could add their own names as they saw fit.

By 1662, Bowman had become a substantial member of the parish community, with a named pew in the church: he sat at pew 21, while his wife, sitting with the women, had number 17. He took on apprentices: the first, John Painter, in 1658 or 1659, admitted a freeman in May 1666, and his second, Humphry Hodskins, a labourer's son from Spitalfields, in June 1661, admitted a freeman on 15 June 1668.[49] But this good fortune did not last long. In 1662 Christopher Bowman contracted consumption (tuberculosis) and died in October. His widow paid for a funeral befitting his new status: he was buried in the south isle of St Michael's, with a knell played on the church's famous bells. After Bowman's death his coffee-house seems to have gone into decline. Widow Bowman, probably assisted by the apprentices, continued to pay rent on the building in 1662 and 1663.[50] A survey of the coffee-houses in the City of London made in May 1663 listed Widow Bowman, but also recorded that there were six other coffee-houses in Cornhill ward, all competing for the same customers. In 1664 Widow Bowman remarried Jeremiah Jeneway, about whom little is known, and thereafter the churchwardens received the rent from 'Mrs Jenoway formerly Bowman'.[51] But already the fame of Bowman's coffee-house had declined.

In September 1666, of course, calamity struck. The Great Fire of London started in Pudding Lane on the morning of Sunday, 3 September and by Monday had consumed the whole of Cornhill, including St Michael's Alley. Thomas Vincent, a Puritan Divine, wrote in his diatribe *God's Terrible Voice in the City* (1667) that the fire demonstrated that the sins of the city were too hot to be extinguished:

> Now the flames break in upon *Cornhill*, that large and spacious street, and quickly crosse the way by the train of Wood that lay in the streets untaken away, which had been pull'd down from houses to prevent its spreading, and so they lick the whole street as they go; they mount up to the bottom of the lowest Vaults & cellars; and march along both sides of the way, with such a roaring noise as was never heard in the City of *London* [. . .]
>
> *Then, then* the City did shake indeed, and the Inhabitants did tremble, and flew away in great amazement from their Houses, lest the flames should devour them; *Rattle, rattle, rattle*, was the noise which the Fire struck upon the ear round about, as if there had been a thousand Iron Chariots beating upon the stones; and if you opened your eye to the opening of the streets, where the Fire was come, you might see in some places whole streets at once in flames, that issued forth, as if they had been so many great Forges from the opposite windows, which folding together, were united into one great flame throughout the whole street; and then you might see the Houses *tumble, tumble, tumble*, from one end of the street to the other with a great crash, leaving the foundations open to the view of the Heavens.[52]

The ancient wooden city of London was destroyed. Nothing remained of Bowman's house and although Jeneway rebuilt, the building was never used as a coffee-house again. Jeneway did not live long to enjoy his new house, as he died and was buried in the south isle of St Michael's on 5 March 1671.[53] After her second husband died, Widow Jeneway seems to have had no further interest in the house, and afterwards it was leased by a 'clerke and scrivener'. Houghton, writing in 1699, remarked that when Bowman died he 'left his Wife, who had been Alderman *Hodges*'s Cook-maid, pretty Rich, but she died Poor not many Years since'.[54]

The fame of Pasqua Rosee lived on, however. In 1952 the Corporation of London unveiled a blue plaque celebrating his 1652 'coffee-house', locating their memorial on the walls of the Jamaica Wine House built in 1888, standing on a part of the churchyard where Rosee's shed sold his coffee.[55]

CHAPTER FOUR

The Republic of Coffee: The Coffee Club of the Rota

The year 1659 was a busy one for the printers and booksellers of London. As the English republic lurched from crisis to crisis, the demise of each of the seven distinct governments of that year was followed by a tidal wave of publications. Each civic disruption in London produced volcanic eruptions of printed text and a heady revolutionary atmosphere in which politicians and commentators traded tracts of advice and policy, delineating rival schemes for the reformation of the commonwealth. One writer complained of 'this time of general scribling, and dayly impregnating the Press with no less seditious then ridiculous Pamphlets';[1] while another grumbled that in 'this Scribling age' the presses laboured under the burden of 'every wilde and brain-sick fancy of our Republican candidates'.[2] For each serious proposal for constitutional reform there was an even greater number of satires, squibs and lampoons, variously scabrous and pornographic, scurrilous and vulgar. These 'jeering books and pamphletts', remarked Thomas Rugg, a barber of Covent Garden in his *Diurnal*, showed the tide of opinion moving against Parliament and the army. As the city was engulfed by debate, discussion and dissension, the coffee-houses came into their own, the forum of republican deliberation. As Rugg noted, 'theire ware also att this time a Turkish drink to bee sould, almost in evry street, called coffee'.[3]

Such were the complexities of this parade of governments that even those who lived through these times found events hard to follow. After the execution of Charles I in 1649, England had found a secure political settlement difficult to achieve, first as a republic and then under the rule of the Lord Protector, Oliver Cromwell. After Cromwell died on 3 September 1658, power had passed to his son Richard. When his Protectorate Parliament met in January 1659, its divided and factional debates were disrupted by army officers and renegade MPs. After this Parliament's dissolution, the army persuaded the Lord Protector to recall the surviving members of the purged Long Parliament. These few men, never numbering more than seventy, were described by Major-General Richard Brown as the 'Rump'. By October the army were weary of their indecisive rule and they were deposed in a bloodless military coup. By December, even the officers' Committee of Safety had had enough and after a few riots by apprentice boys in London they quietly dispersed. For ten days at the end of December there was no legitimate government in being, until the Rump returned again on 27 December.[4] It was still not popular: one wit remarked, 'A Rump is the hinder part of the many-headed Beast, the Back-door of the *Devils Arse* a *Peake*, Tyranny and Rebellion ending in a Stink, the States *Incubus*, a Crab Commonwealth with the But end formost.'[5] At each turn of events the future of the English republican experiment seemed open to speculation and influence. Throughout 1659, and right up until mid February 1660, the outcome that seemed most unlikely was a restoration of the monarchy: as John Aubrey recalled, 'as to human foresight, there was no possibility of the King's returne'.[6] But March brought General Monck, a change of heart and the end of the republic: 'all those empty Nothings which seem to make such a fine and Gawdy shew' were suddenly revealed as 'meer ayr and bubble'.[7]

The tumultuous events of 1659 crystallised the political construction of the coffee-houses, establishing their unique discursive sociability in the public imagination. News reports, satires and diaries saw the coffee-house as the instinctive home of republicans, of political critics and of debate in affairs of state. This was to be a lasting legacy, although not all approved of the connection. The 'wantonesse' or popularity of 'the coffa-beane', argued the agricultural improver John Beale, demonstrated the injurious effect that 'vanityes & Luxury' had on the commonwealth, diverting English wealth 'to sustaine our forreigne brethren'. As he complained to Samuel Hartlib in December 1658, the 'Coffa-drinke will growe into generall use having already obtaind such a general reception by young & old in our Innes of Courts; & I should rather wish our supply from our owne plantations, than from Turkye'.[8] Satirists, too, wondered whether coffee suited the English constitution, querying whether the College of Physicians should examine the question 'Whether Coffee, Sherbet, that came from *Turky*, Chocolate much used by the Jews, Brosa by the Muscovites, *Ta* and *Tee*, and such other new-fangled drinks, will agree with the Constitutions of our *English* bodies'.[9] Aping both the matter of political debate and formal habit of asking questions, scandalous satires circulated gossip and innuendo in taverns and coffee-houses.[10] In *Select City Queries: Discovering several Cheats, Abuses and Subtilties of the City bawds, Whores and Trapanners* of 9 March 1660, the author asked, 'Whether Mrs *Huzzy*, a late Coffee-Merchant, has not more Rooms to let than Beds to lie in; and whether the East *India* Merchant could lodge in hers (during her husbands absence) and *Margery Spaights* blinde Chappel at one and the same time?'[11] The coffee-house, as the market for news, is scapegoated as a kind of brothel, or market for sex. A few weeks later, on 11 April 1660, this gossip sheet returned to the question:

> Whether Huzzy the She-Coffee-merchant in the Postern by Moorgate, must return to Turnbal-Street or Rosemary-lane, if she should be whipt as she deserves, from Constable to Constable, for keeping a Dancing-school; and whether Guzman the Spanish Rogue would not be a more fit Attendant than her modest husband, whose estate she has too much embezzled?[12]

John Garfield's obscene satire on the underworld of Restoration prostitution, *The Wandring Whore* (1660) further identified one 'Mrs. *G*—— neer the Coffee-house in the *Postern* by *More-gate*' – a 'tearing Girl' whose clothes, uncommonly, were adorned with silver lace and fine ribbons.[13] To contemporaries the innovative social world of the coffee-house, and the transgressive figure of the coffee-woman, placed the coffee-house at the centre of this period of social disruption.

As nearly all agreed that the monarchy would not be restored, the future form of government in 1659 was both unclear and open to innovation. One of the most brilliant proposals for the future of the Commonwealth and England's republican experiment was that advanced by the lawyer James Harrington, son of a gentleman, educated at Oxford, who had travelled extensively in Europe in the 1630s. Although he took no part in the first Civil War of the 1640s (a statement in itself) he was appointed a gentleman of the bedchamber to Charles I in 1647 and stayed with him until shortly before the King was executed in January 1649. After these events Harrington lived quietly until the publication of his political fable, *The Commonwealth of Oceana*, in September 1656, one of a series of important analyses of republican forms of government offered to the public during the discontented years of Cromwell's Protectorate. Considered as a book, *Oceana* is a work of fiction, a 'political romance' as Harrington called it, in which England appears as Oceana and the hero of the story, Cromwell, as Olphaus Megaletor. In his position as 'sole legislator' of Oceana, Megaletor calls together a group of philosophers to compose a new constitution providing for a government by the people. When the new order is established and operating smoothly, Megaletor returns to private life, leaving Oceana a flourishing and prosperous republic. Such is the story. Considered as a political philosophy, *Oceana* is a utopian theory of commonwealth government, offered as a model to engender debate. Oceana is ruled by the people rather than a king or sole legislator, but it is only a small elite (determined by property) that has any hand in government.[14] The spirit of faction, Harrington argued, would be avoided through the principle of 'rotation', by which one third of the representatives would be replaced in each year.

As Harrington had intended, his book attracted both support and criticism. One witness to these events was John Aubrey, the Oxford gossip turned antiquarian, who recalled that 'That ingeniose Tractat, together with his and Henry Nevill's smart discourses and inculcations, dayly at Coffee-houses, made many Proselytes'.[15] Capitalising on the manic deliberations of 1659, Harrington published a swarm of pamphlets and tracts, elaborating, clarifying and defending his model of the commonwealth, so that the coffee-house debaters might be persuaded to his point of view. One of the earliest, *The Art of Lawgiving* (1659), stripped away the elaborate fictional machinery of *Oceana*, indentifying the subject of the model republic as England and offering concise summaries of the constitutional proposals. In others the criticisms made by Harrington's opponents were addressed and countered. Harrington's numerous contributions to the war of tracts over the future of the commonwealth undoubtedly converted some to his cause, just as it annoyed others. His next move, however, was a significant change in direction. In addition to continuing the printed debate, he initiated a brilliant and unorthodox advertising campaign for his ideas.

In October 1659 Harrington and some supporters established a club to discuss his model of the commonwealth, holding the debates in the Turk's Head Coffee-House in New Palace Yard, a location in the vicinity of Parliament and the government offices at Whitehall. New Palace Yard was a large open space to the north of Westminster Hall, now subsumed under the approach road to Westminster Bridge, used for centuries for executions, state occasions and public festivals. Westminster Hall itself was an enormous medieval building at the centre of the parliamentary complex, home to several higher law courts and a range of shops. Around the edges of New Palace Yard were numerous eating houses, taverns and coffee-houses. This was an arena central to the political drama of the Interregnum and Restoration: a confluence of parliamentarians, soldiers, lawyers, controversialists and adventurers. It was also a place of work and residence: Samuel Pepys lived not far away in Axe Yard off King Street and worked (in 1659) in the Exchequer building next to Westminster Hall. Harrington's choice of the Turk's Head, then, placed him in the hub of the state drama of the republic's future. The notion of a club was well known: the Interregnum was the first great period of clubbing in London. A club was understood to be a meeting or assembly, held in a public space like a tavern, for the purpose of social intercourse and debate, in which the costs of the meeting were defrayed communally: Aubrey defined 'the word *clubbe*' as 'a sodality in a taverne', making use of the Latinate term sodality, an association of fellows. The sense of this older term was also retained in Samuel Johnson's definition: 'An assembly of good fellows, meeting under certain conditions'.[16] In the seventeenth century the club had become a central part of the associational world of English social life, as Peter Clark has phrased it.[17]

The proprietor of the Turk's Head was called Miles. According to John Aubrey, he provided Harrington's club with a unique piece of furniture, a table 'made purposely'. It was oval in shape and large enough for many men to sit around, and 'with a passage in the middle for Miles to deliver his Coffee'. Sitting at this table, conversation and discussion could continue without interrupting Miles's provision of coffee and pipes of tobacco. The table was a kind of machine for debate and was a stunningly original piece of political technology. 'About it sate his Disciples, and the Virtuosi,' Aubrey relates. Political debate in the 1650s had proved disorderly and incendiary, and in response Harrington proposed a highly regulated form of discussion. Towards the end of December 1659 he printed a summary of his proposals made in *Oceana*, reduced to a few numbered paragraphs in a cheap quarto edition and called *The Rota: or, A Model of a Free-State Or equall Commonwealth* (1660).[18] This short pamphlet announced that Harrington's model 'once proposed and debated in brief' in *Oceana* in 1656, was 'to be again more at large proposed to, and debated by a free and open Society of ingenious Gentlemen'. Harrington's club took its name, the Rota, from this text, perhaps derived from the Italian academies he had encountered in his travels.

The printed text of *The Rota* explained on its first page how the club was to function. Participants were to purchase and read a copy of the tract in advance. Each evening the members of the club would gather at the Turk's Head, and each evening another clause of Harrington's model would be debated. Meeting in the evening, it was reckoned, allowed those in employment or charged with affairs of state to attend. The clause to be discussed was agreed the night before and there was a specific injunction against pre-empting debate by discussing the clause during the day. If debaters thought fit, they might 'bring in their Quaeries upon, or Objections against the Clause in Debate, [...] in writing'. The club appointed Cyriack Skinner, 'an ingeniose young gentleman, scholar to John Milton', chairman of proceedings. Argument would be structured around these written questions and statements, so it would not be a cacophony of competing voices. At the end of the debate, when all points of view had been heard, the 'Judgement of this Society' on that clause would be determined by the 'Ballating-Box'. One royalist satire – supposedly published by 'Trundle Wheeler, Clerk of the Rota' and printed by Paul Giddy 'at the Sign of the Windmill in Turne-againe Lane' – ridiculed these arrangements as possessing a formality disproportionate to their importance. The 'usual custom' of the club, the satire mocked, was 'to dispute every thing, how plain or obscure together, by knocking Argument against Argument, and tilting at one another with our heads (as Rams fight) untill we are out of breath, and then refer it to our wooden Oracle, the *Box*'.[19] The satirist Henry Stubbe also had a low opinion of Harrington's oratory, complaining that he would 'hawk and hum' while sprinkling his discourse with arcane erudition from Roman and Jewish history.[20] To Harrington's enemies the club was nothing but an exercise in vanity and self-promotion.

In the long term, however, Harrington's model of a debating coffee-house may have been more influential than his 'Principles of Government'. The manner in which his model was debated established an important pattern for coffee-house discussion whose ramifications were felt extensively over the following centuries. By contrast, the cause of the commonwealth men was beginning to look doomed by the end of December 1659. The tide of publication and the ferocity of debate was consuming the republican cause. The coffee club of the Rota was an attempt to reorientate discussion: to render it rational, critical, civil, serious. This 'society of the Rota' is a response to satirical attack and popular discontent, a reformative model of popular politics. John Aubrey testified to high quality of debate in the coffee-house: 'The Discourses in this Kind were the most ingeniose, and smart, that ever I heard, or expect to heare, and bandied with great eagernesse: the Arguments in the Parliament howse were but flatt to it. [. . .] The roome was every evening full as it could be cramm'd.'[21]

The list of those who attended included some of the key political theorists of the period (such as Henry Neville and William Petty), as well as influential army radicals (Major Wildman, Major Venner), wealthy merchants, officers and soldiers. Aubrey recalled that the time was right for this kind of speculative, serious discussion. 'The Doctrine was very taking, and the more because, as to human foresight, there was no possibility of the King's returne.' But Harrington and his colleagues also encountered opposition. The great men of state, 'the greatest part of the Parliament-men' Aubrey says, 'perfectly hated this designe of Rotation by Ballotting; for they were cursed Tyrants, and in love with their Power, and 'twas death to them, except eight or ten, to admit of this way'.[22] Politicians, Aubrey suggests, grow to like the power they wield and would be unwilling to relinquish power simply because their allotted time in office had expired. The Rumpers especially had aggrandised themselves to the position of 'Senators-for-Life'. Other opposition was less well mannered. Aubrey remembers that one night 'Mr Stafford and his Gang came in, in drink from the Taverne, and affronted the Junto', tearing up the society's orders and minutes. 'The Soldiers offerd to kick them downe stayres, but Mr. Harrington's moderation and persuasion hindred it.'[23] It was a reminder, however, that the language of politics included idioms distant from Harrington's congenial world of discussion.

According to Aubrey, the coffee-house debating society was 'a philosophicall, or Politicall Club, where gentlemen came at night to divert themselves with Politicall discourse and to see the way of Balloting'.[24] That this entertainment occurred in a coffee-house may simply be because Miles was content to let it happen. But it seems more likely that the conversational turn of the coffee-house was more suited to this model of debate than the riotous drunkenness encountered in the taverns and ale houses of Westminster. A few years later the poet Samuel Butler, in his 'Character of a Coffee-Man' (written between 1667 and 1669), understood the importance of the physiological properties of coffee. The 'coffee market', he says, is 'where people of all qualities and conditions meet, to trade in foreign drinks and newes, ale, smoak, and controversy'. The coffee-house, he continues, 'admits of no distinction of persons, but gentleman, mechanic, lord, and scoundrel mix, and are all of a piece, as if they were resolv'd into their first principles'. The coffee-house is a social leveller, reducing all (or elevating all) to their essential quality, their first principle. And the coffee, it seems, is central to this social alchemy: 'all manner of opinions are profest and maintain'd' in the coffee-house, 'to the last drop of coffee', which, he says, is due to 'the sovereign virtue it has to strengthen politic notions'.[25]

One witness to proceedings at the Turk's Head Coffee-House was Samuel Pepys. In 1659 he was twenty-seven years old, employed in a junior position in the bureaucracy of government as a clerk to George Downing of the Exchequer, a post he had held for several years, and which at this time revolved around receiving Excise money and paying off soldiers. Pepys's office, in Exchequer Yard, was in a courtyard off New Palace Yard. On Monday, 9 January 1660, Pepys reports that over a breakfast with some fellow clerks of cold turkey pie and a goose at Harper's Tavern on King Street, he had been introduced to Henry Muddiman, a 'newes-book writer' for the parliamentary newspapers. Pepys remarks he found Muddiman 'a good scholar' and 'an arch rogue' who was happy to 'talk very basely' of the Rump politicians who paid him. It was this journalist who introduced him to the Rota: 'I went with Muddiman to the Coffee-house and gave 18d to be entered of the Club.' Given that this was a time of straitened financial circumstances for Pepys – he had been forced to borrow from the office cash account to pay his rent only five days earlier – Pepys's decision to spend the considerable sum of 1½ shillings to join the Rota club suggests its importance. After work the next evening, Tuesday, 10 January, Pepys returned to the Turk's Head. When he wrote up his diary he recorded his visit 'to the Coffee-house, where were a great confluence of gentlemen; viz. Mr Harrington, Poultny cheareman [chairman], Gold, Dr. Petty, &[c]., where admirable discourse till 9 at night'.[26] Impressed by the number and the quality of the audience for that night's debate, Pepys stayed late at the coffee-house. As well as Harrington himself, Pepys noted the presence of the wealthy property developer Sir William

Poulteney, Nicholas Gold, a prosperous London merchant, and William Petty, a gifted mathematician and administrator, whose activities in the commonwealth's Irish colonisation had netted him considerable rewards. Attending the meeting of the Rota club at the coffee-house, Pepys realised, not only placed him at the centre of political debate, but also made him important personal connections. For a man on the make, the coffee-house was a network of potential patrons.

The constant round of political changes in these months presented men like Pepys with an unparalleled opportunity for advancement. By keeping up with the news and maintaining contacts with different factions, he hoped to end up on the winning side. Going to the coffee-house and listening to the club debates were all part of this strategy. On the evening of Saturday, 14 January, Pepys went 'to the Coffee-house and heard exceeding good argument against Mr Harrington's assertion that overbalance of propriety [property] was the foundation of government'. This was an important debate for Harrington, going to the centre of his theory that property owners should form the core of the legislative function. Pepys returned after work the following Tuesday (17 January) to hear the debate resolved.

> So I went to the Coffee club and heard very good discourse; it was in answer to Mr. Harrington's answer, who said that the state of the Roman government was not a settled government, and so it was no wonder that the balance of propriety was in one hand and the command in another, it being therefore always in a posture of war; but it was carried by Ballat that it was a steady government; though, it is true by the voices, it had been carried before that it was an unsteady government. So tomorrow it is to be proved by the opponents that the balance lie in one hand and the government in another.[27]

Pepys reports that the coffee club was still debating Harrington's principles of government (which Pepys makes a poor job of describing). But he also describes how the debate was settled by the 'ballat'. On this evening the vote taken by vocal outcry was reversed by the ballot box. But the evening's vote also revealed a flaw in Harrington's plan, as the debate of the club could countenance no reversal. Having from the beginning established the agenda of the club's discussions in the printed pamphlet of *The Rota, or, A Model*, no deviation from Harrington's proposals was possible: while there could be debate,

Harrington could not imagine dissent from his view. Despite his commitment to the political process, the coffee club reveals his fundamentalism and that he is, in contemporary parlance, a 'phanatique'. Business – primarily Pepys's quest for advancement to the position of under-clerk to the Council of State – kept him from the coffee-house for several days. The following Friday (20 January), Pepys went 'to the Coffee club, where there was nothing done but choosing of a committee for orders'.[28] Seeing this evidence of how the club could waste its time on procedural matters reminded him more of the interminable wranglings of the Rump itself than any utopian model of a future commonwealth. He didn't go back for a month.

Events in the street were in any case making debating clubs irrelevant. The Rump Parliament's rule was doomed. On 3 February Pepys witnessed the march of General Monck's Scottish army down Whitehall, 'in very good plight and stout officers', effectively signalling the army's assumption of power. By Tuesday, 7 February Pepys gleefully reports that 'Boys do now cry "Kiss my Parliament" instead of "Kiss my arse", so great and general a contempt is the Rump come to among all men, good and bad'.[29] The possibility of a restoration was now openly canvassed, partly because it was the only option which offered stability. Commonwealth modelling was at an end. One Rump broadsheet satire, *Bumm-Foder or Waste-paper Proper to wipe the Nation's Rump with, or your Own* (1659), thought Harrington's model was a better example of the period's confusion than of its constitutional theorising:

> Youl find it set down in *Harringtons* Moddle,
> Whose brains a Commonwealth do so coddle,
> That t'as made a Rotation in his noddle:[30]

On 11 February General Monck demanded that the Parliament readmit the secluded members within a week, and call a full and free Parliament by May. Monck had finally overruled the Rumpers, for he knew that the secluded members would call a free election, which would more than likely restore the monarchy. The city erupted in joyful celebrations, bonfires, bell-ringing and drinking.

Pepys's final visit to the Rota club took place just over a week later, on Monday, 20 February. On that day he had sat in a tavern in Whitehall drinking with his fellow clerks and reading a 'pamphlet, well-writ and directed to General Monke in praise of the form of Monarchy which was settled here before the Warrs' – probably Roger L'Estrange's *A plea for a limited Monarchy* (1660), written as much against 'our Projectours of Common-wealths' as in favour of monarchy.[31] In the evening he went

> to the Coffee Clubb, where nothing to do. Only, I heard Mr. Harrington and my Lord of Dorsett and another lord talking of getting another place, as the Cockpitt; and they did believe it would come to something. After a small debate upon the Question whether learned or unlearned subjects are the best, the club broke off very poorly, and I do not think they will meet any more.[32]

Pepys absented himself and went to Will's ale house, Old Palace Yard, for a pot or two of ale. There is no record that the coffee club of the Rota ever met again. Nothing came of the plan to shift venues to the Cockpit, an abandoned theatre attached to Whitehall Palace. But despite the evident ruin of the commonwealth debating club, Harrington's question 'whether learned or unlearned subjects are the best' was an interesting one, suggesting that the form of discussion might outlast the particular topic at hand.

The next day, Tuesday, 21 February, Pepys witnessed the return of ninety of the ejected Members of Parliament, ushered secretly into the Commons by the very soldiers set there by the Rump to prevent them. The army, it seemed, obeyed Monck, not the Parliament. The restored Members immediately set about rescinding various measures passed between 1648 and 1660, freeing prisoners of the Parliament and appointing Monck commander-in-chief of all land forces.[33] After dining with one of the returned MPs (Mr Crew), Pepys returned to Westminster Hall, where he met by accident two of London's most eminent musicians.

> Here I met with Mr. Lock and Pursell, Maisters of Musique; and with them to the Coffee-house into a room next the Water by ourselves; where we spent an hour or two. [. . .]
>
> Here we had a variety of brave Italian and Spanish songs and a Canon for 8 *Voc*:, which Mr Lock had newly made on these words: *Domine salvum fac Regem*, an admirable thing.[34]

Occupying a room overlooking the river, these three men spent some time singing and playing music. Matthew Locke was one of England's leading composers and Mr Purcell was either the uncle or father of the famous Henry Purcell, the composer. Both were noted tenors.[35] Although this meeting testifies to Pepys's lifelong interest in music, what is doubly interesting here is that this is Pepys's first purely social visit to a coffee-house. The Turk's Head offers these men not only a location for serious discussion but also – as they sing their newly composed songs – artistic endeavour. Out on the streets the return of the secluded Members was greeted with bonfires and celebration. At every street corner in London the people built large fires and roasted rumps of beef and mutton, celebrating in a vast open-air political barbecue. From the coffee-house, Pepys recorded, 'Here, out of the window it was a most pleasant sight to see the City from [one] end to the other with a glory about it, so high was the light of the Bonefires and so thick round the City, and the bells rang everywhere.'[36] The political climate was changing, with astonishing rapidity, towards a royalist settlement.

The prospect of the return of the King was enough for old and would-be Cavaliers to recover their swagger. While the presses groaned under the productions of this new royalist politics, popular demonstrations of a newly found monarchist loyalism were seen everywhere. One manifestation of neo-royalism was drinking habits. While the Republicans drank their coffee, Royalists old and new drank bountiful healths to the King and his supporters in ale and wine. A mock-newspaper, *Mercurius Phanaticus. Or Mercury Temporizing*, of 21 March 1660, satirised this change in the drinking temperament of the people by giving notice of two imaginary books recently published.

> *In Cervitia salus*, A book wherein the excellency of Ale, is excellently examined and set forth; by the fluent pen of *Daniell Pepper.*
>
> *Mors in Olla*, The downfall of Coffee, an excellent tract of Morality, wherein by way of digression is proved that the great *Turk* was born of a Woman, and that *Bacchus* was a better Gentleman than he, by the Company of Vinters.[37]

The very first act of legislation issued by the King on his return to London was that of 13 May 1660, seeking to control the debauched drinking undertaken in his name (*A Proclamation Against Vicious Debauch'd and Prophane Persons*). The King explained that he was 'ashamed' of those of his supporters 'who spend their time in Taverns, Tipling-houses, and Debauches, giving no other evidence of their Affection for us [the King], but in drinking our Health, and Inveighing against all others who are not of their own dissolute temper'. He urged them to 'renounce all that Licentiousness, Prophaneness, and Impiety with which they have been corrupted, [. . .] and that they will hereafter become examples of Sobriety and Virtue'.[38]

After the end of the Rota coffee club, Harrington retired from an active engagement with politics. In April 1660 the irony of the Restoration was not lost on one satirist who drew an allusion to the Ottoman Empire. In 1622 Sultan Osman had been executed in a coup by his bodyguard of janissaries, who proceeded to install his son on the throne and so returned themselves to the tyrannical autocracy that had inspired their coup. The querist asked, 'Whether Coffee be not the most fitting Drink for the *English* Nation, since we have equalled, nay out-gone the *Turks* themselves, for though they murdered the father, yet they presently set up the Son?'[39] Coffee, a Turkish drink, is a richly ironic emblem for this republican allegory.

On 29 December 1661 Harrington was arrested and committed to the Tower of London, for 'treasonable Designs and Practices'. He was accused of having established a club in March 1661 in '*Bowstreet in Coventgarden*' and 'the *Mill Bank*', where twenty people debated the dissolution of Parliament and the bringing in of a new one. As a result of his confinement Harrington's health collapsed, after which his family petitioned to have him detained somewhere more favourable. On St Nicholas's Island near Plymouth, he was prescribed a physic by Skelton's doctor Dr Dunstan, comprised of 'a preparation of *Guaiacum* in Coffee'. Harrington 'drank of this Liquor in great quantitys, every morning and evening', despite the foul taste of guaiacum, the resin of the *lignum vitæ* tree, usually inspissated and dissolved in alcohol. The coffee-medicine seems to have driven Harrington mad: 'He was reduc'd to a Skeleton, not able to walk alone, slept very little, his imagination disturb'd, often fainted when he took his drink, and yet so fond of it that he would by no means be advis'd to forbear it.'[40]

On the Restoration of the King a club such as the Rota and printed models of commonwealths were suddenly seditious and proscribed. As John Aubrey noted, 'all these aierie modells vanished' on the arrival of General Monck's Scottish army: such meetings were suddenly treasonous.[41] The influence on the coffee-house was profound, however, for after this time the London coffee-house was firmly identified with radical causes, with republican discourse and with opposition to the crown. They were so closely associated with the republican cause that the end of the Republic looked like the end of the coffee-houses too. An anonymous satirist in 1665 explicitly tied the coffee-house to the cultural landscape of the English Revolution:

> Coffee and *Commonwealth* begin
> With one letter, both came in
> Together for a *Reformation*,
> To make's a free and sober *Nation*.[42]

At the breaking-up of the Rota, Harrington made a prophecy that monarchy would not last long. 'Well, the King will come in. Let him come-in, and call a Parliament of the greatest Cavaliers in England, so they be men of Estates, and let them sett but seven yeares, and they will all turn Common-wealthe's men.'[43]

The restored Stuart monarchy lasted longer than Harrington predicted. Nonetheless, less than two decades later the people and the parliamentarians had become so disenchanted with the absolutist tendencies of Charles II and his brother, James II, that in 1688 the house of Stuart was deposed in an almost bloodless coup: events in which the coffee-house played an important role. With hindsight it was possible to see that through the crucible of 1659 they had found a new role in the popular imagination, established as the people's forum, where ordinary folk met to debate affairs of state.

CHAPTER FIVE

Talking to Strangers

The *Diary* of Samuel Pepys provides the first extensive account of a single man's custom of coffee-house visiting. In his meticulous record of his life, Pepys detailed every notable activity that occurred to him, motivated by an intense desire to account for himself: his time, his money, his actions, and his secret thoughts and desires. Over the course of the diary, which runs for nearly ten years from 1 January 1660 to 31 May 1669, Pepys records ninety-nine visits to the coffee-house. At the beginning of the diary Pepys is an inveterate drinker in taverns, making only occasional visits to coffee-houses, such as that where Harrington's coffee club met. But for a few years, especially 1663 and 1664, the coffee-house became a central part of Pepys's daily routine, visited as much as two or three times a week, as time permitted. In a not untypical week in December 1663, for example, Pepys went three times to his usual establishment in Exchange Alley. At noon on Saturday the 26th he 'sat long in good discourse with some gentlemen concerning the Roman Empire'; he returned on the following Wednesday, where he met up with two Royal Society fellows, Captain John Graunt and Sir William Petty, 'with whom I talked and so did many, almost the whole house there' about Petty's new invention of a double-hulled sailing vessel. The next day he went back, his head aching after work, 'and sat an hour or two at the Coffee, hearing some simple discourse about Quakers being charmed by a string about their wrists'.[1]

Coffee-house conversations, Pepys had discovered, presented a fascinating panoply of philosophical puzzles. The attraction of the place was never simply the coffee, which Pepys did not seem to like much, but rather the potential he found there for social intercourse and companionship with one's fellows – what his age called 'sociality' or 'sodality', the quality of fellowship, brotherhood and company.[2] As one philosopher observed in 1681, in the idea of sociability humankind found the 'inclination to live together in company, Man with man', a principle which was the foundation both of the city and the state.[3] In the convivial space of the coffee-house Pepys found a microcosm of the ideal of sociability. As one satirist quipped in 1661, the coffee-house has 'Humane shape, where a Liquor made of an *Arabian* Berry called *Coffee* is drunk' – discerning that a coffee-house only really exists when it is full of people.[4] Pepys's diary records his enjoyment of the convivial fellowship he found there, sometimes noting the topics he heard discussed, always listing the men he met, so as to be able to recall their names if he encountered them again. 'I find much pleasure' in the coffee-house, Pepys said, 'through the diversity of company – and discourse'.[5] His visits cemented cordial and mutually beneficial friendships with his superiors from the Navy Office, with merchants and contractors, with vertuosi (scientists and scholars) and men connected to the circle of his patron, Edward Mountagu, Earl of Sandwich.

Pepys's coffee-house visits had become more regular just after he stopped going so frequently to pubs and taverns. Throughout 1662 his *Diary* shows him resolving repeatedly to work hard, live frugally and apply himself to the office, entertaining dreams of wealth and station, when he might 'be a Knight and keep my coach'.[6] Pepys realised that if he wanted to be a great man, he had to look and act like one. From this period he deliberately altered the way he socialised with other men, increasingly abstaining from the loutish interactions of the public house: not only because drinking made him unfit for business, but also because he realised that while pubs were appropriate for a young man at the start of his career, they were not the place great men socialised. Instead, he began to spend more on clothes, and to give elaborate and spectacular dinner parties at home.[7] In January 1663 he hit upon another way to signal his upward mobility, by visiting coffee-houses and cultivating the acquaintance of the sober men of business he encountered there. In January 1663 Pepys starting going to the coffee-house with more frequency: he even went twice one day, hearing 'discourse well worth hearing' but also noting that he had drunk coffee 'till I was almost sick'. Milton's nephew, John Phillips, observed a few years later that 'this setting up of Coffee-houses' was a 'happy Invention' for men of business, 'for to drink in Taverns was scandalous, to be seen in an Ale-house more unseeming; but to sit idling away their Time in a Coffee-house, [. . .] that's an Employment without the Verge of Reprehension'.[8]

By the winter of 1663–4 Pepys was visiting the 'the Coffee-house in Exchange-ally' more than three times a week, sometimes in the company of a friend or business colleague, and sometimes with the intention of meeting someone by arrangement. Nonetheless, Pepys had become so enamoured of the place that he made some visits on a purely speculative basis, in the hope of encountering men who would entertain him, or be useful to him in some way. In his diary he kept a record of some of his conversations, noting a brief summary of the topics he discussed or news he heard. Sometimes, however, his imagination was captured by the stories he heard there, as when he chanced upon some merchants of the Eastland Company in December 1663 and sat for several hours listening to their tales of life in Russia.[9] Merchants were of particular curiosity to Pepys at this time, as he was anxious to learn about business practices in the City, especially how the navy contracts were negotiated. The fact that the coffee-house was physically separate from where he worked at the Navy Office in Seething Lane allowed him the freedom to talk widely with these men. Having made the acquaintance of merchants on the Exchange, he made friends with them in the coffee-houses nearby. With the commercial knowledge he learnt from them Pepys transformed his job as 'Clerk of the Acts' to the Navy Board. Where he once simply kept records and correspondence, he now made deals and contracts with suppliers. Through the bribes and kickbacks he received from them the coffee-house made Pepys very wealthy. But as he got richer and developed more illustrious friendships at court, he had less need to go to coffee-houses to meet with merchants and vertuosi. By 1665, some months before the outbreak of plague in the city, he virtually gave up his coffee-house visits.

In the first decades of the Restoration the coffee-houses were the subject of an intense literary scrutiny, seeking to understand, and control, this innovative cultural space. The first satirical review of them was *A Character of Coffee and Coffee-Houses*, published – and perhaps written – in 1661 by the Anabaptist bookseller John Starkey, who kept a shop at the sign of the Mitre in Fleet Street by Temple Bar. Several coffee-houses clustered together in this locality, alongside taverns and booksellers' shops. As well as satirising the peculiar physiological qualities of coffee, his *Character* reflects on the nature of the coffee-house. Beginning with the declaration that 'A Coffee-house is free to all Corners', Starkey's satire examines how its uncontrolled and open quality determines the coffee-house's character. He details that 'Here is no respect of persons. Boldly therefore let any person, who comes to drink Coffee sit down in the very *Chair*, for here a Seat is to be given to no man. That great privilege of *equality* is only peculiar to the *Golden Age*, and *to a Coffee-house*.'[10]

Arriving in the coffee-house, customers were expected to take the next available seat, placing themselves next to whoever else has come before them. No seat could be reserved, no man might refuse your company. This seating policy impresses on all customers that in the coffee-house all are equal. Though the matter of seating may appear inconsequential, the principle of equality this policy introduced had remarkable ramifications in the decades to come. From the arrangement of its chairs, the coffee-house allowed men who did not know each other to sit together amicably and expected them to converse. In the anonymous context of the city, in which most people are unknown to each other, this sociable habit was astonishing. Furthermore, the principle of equality established by the seating arrangements recommended equality and openness as the principle of conversation. As another coffee-house *Character* published in 1665 said:

> Now being enter'd, there's no needing
> of complements or gentile breeding,
> For you may seat you any where,
> There's no respect of persons there.[11]

In the coffee-house, unlike all other social institutions of the period, rank and birth had no place. Of course, this was always a fiction as systems of respect were not abandoned totally. One of the attractions was meeting with men whose knowledge, interests, social position or trade might be of value to you, and to such men due deference was necessary. Nonetheless, if there is one thing that coffee-houses did to change the wider culture around them, a strong contender would be these egalitarian rules of seating.

There were, of course, no rules regulating such behaviour. In 1674 one coffee-man, Paul Greenwood, published a short, and ironic, poem called 'The Rules and Orders of the Coffee-House'. Greenwood, who operated a profitable establishment retailing 'the best Arabian Coffee-Powder and Chocolate' at the sign of 'the Coffee-Mill and Tobacco Roll' amid the boisterous meat and livestock market of Smithfield, published these rules as part of a one-page broadsheet advertising his business, entitled 'A Brief Description of the Excellent Vertues of that Sober and wholesome Drink, called Coffee, and its Incomparable Effects in Preventing or Curing Most Diseases incident to Humane Bodies'. In a parody of the 'Civil-Orders' or city laws which regulated the private life of its citizens, Greenwood's poem drily mocked the social practices of the coffee-house:

The RULES and ORDERS of the Coffee-House

Enter Sirs freely, But first if you please,
Peruse our Civil-Orders, which are these.
First, Gentry, Tradesmen, all are welcome hither,
And may without Affront sit down Together:
Pre-eminence of Place, none here should Mind,
But take the next fit Seat that he can find:
Nor need any, if Finer Persons come,
Rise up for to assigne to them his Room;
To limit Mens Expence, we think not fair,
But let him forfeit Twelve-pence that shall Swear:
He that shall any Quarrel here begin,
Shall give each Man a Dish t'Atone the Sin;
And so shall He, whose Complements extend
So far to drink in COFFEE to his friend;
Let Noise of loud Disputes be quite forborn,
No Maudlin Lovers here in Corners Mourn,
But all be Brisk, and Talk, but not too much
On Sacred things, Let none Presume to touch,
Nor Profane Scripture, or sawcily wrong
Affairs of State with an Irreverent Tongue:
Let Mirth be Innocent, and each Man see,
That all his Jests without Reflection be;
To keep the House more Quiet, and from Blame,
We Banish hence Cards, Dice, and every Game:
Nor can allow of Wagers, that Exceed
Five shillings, which oft-times much Trouble Breed;

Let all that's lost, or forfeited, be spent
In such Good Liquour as the House does Vent,
And Customers endeavour to their Powers,
For to observe still seasonable Howers.
  Lastly let each Man what he calls for *Pay*,
  And so you're welcome to come every day.[12]

These verses parody Ben Jonson's well-known Latin poem *Leges Convivales* (Convivial Laws, 1620), written to describe what his first translator called 'the sociable rules' of his club of drinking poets at the Apollo room of the Devil Tavern in Temple Bar in the early decades of the seventeenth century. Following Jonson, Greenwood adopts a pompous tone amusingly incongruous for the purpose and uses the repeated 'Let' construction, reminiscent of the Old Testament, to give rhetorical coherence to his law-making. But while Greenwood parodies or imitates Jonson's versifying, he advances a rather different argument about the sociability of the coffee-house.[13]

Greenwood's 'Rules and Orders' repeat the argument that the coffee-house encounter is founded on the openness of the discussion to all comers. No one should be excluded from the discussion, nor should anyone have precedence by a quality they brought with them from outside such as status, wealth, power, or strength of arms. All speakers are considered equal and within the collective fiction of the coffee-house hierarchy is erased. The cost of this equality of access, Greenwood suggests, is that all who enter agree to behave by his 'Civic Orders', the rules of discussion within the house. In reality, there were no regulations or rules governing the coffee-houses: Greenwood's satire ironises the very idea of regulating their behaviour.

What his satire advertises, in a way, is the subtle kinds of implicit regulation that coffee-houses created in their customers' expectations. When entering a man might expect to behave in a certain manner appropriate to the setting, conducting himself differently in a tavern, a private dwelling or in a church. As anthropologists have observed, in many societies people assemble habitually in particular places for unstructured social interaction: such as around a well in medieval France, or a tofu shop in post-war Japan, or the porch of a general store in Texas. In each of these places there are no rules governing their conduct for each participant knows the way to behave there and does not tolerate aberrant interlopers. The expected set of behaviour for each community location is in effect immanent in the practice of everyday life. For fear of looking odd, or out of place, people learn to obey the set of expectations established in each place. This fear of looking abnormal, odd or strange has been identified as one of the key ground rules for social behaviour in public and is especially associated with urban life according to the sociologist Erving Goffman. Behaviour in public places like the coffee-house, Goffman argues, is governed by the imaginative and creative ways people can act with propriety and with the appropriate level of involvement.[14] The comic charge of Greenwood's 'Rules and Orders' is that they make literal a series of unstated assumptions, which everyone proceeded to break anyway.

What many noticed about the coffee-house was the noise. As Starkey's *Character* concluded, 'all the Elements' were so 'confusedly mixt' that 'this House appears to him as a meer Chaos'.[15] The aural landscape was a complex mixture of human voices and clattering busyness. Snapshort, the apprentice-clerk in *The Maidens Complaint Against Coffee* (1663), grumbles that he could find no peace in a coffee-house in Lothbury because of 'the ratling noise of Kettles, Skim[m]ers and Ladles among the Brasiers'.[16] The murmur of conversation connoted a sense of business and conviviality, producing a peculiar hum or buzz, blending the background noise of coffee sipping, cup rattling, chair scraping with the sounds of conversation and talking. Starkey, too, noticed the confused 'murmur' of 'Insignificant Notes' as men sip their 'muddy water'.[17] The distant babble of voices was so characteristic of the coffee-house that one satirist made it a symbol for the moral climate of the Restoration city, in which individuals 'chop in with all in common'. In his *Remarques on the Humours and Conversations of the Town* (1673), he observed that in the coffee-house 'you will hear an unintelligible buzzing, and a noise of what you understand not: some snatches of occurrences, whose beauty you are not able to perceive without the knowledge of the whole'.[18] To this country gentleman, unused to the ways of the city, the active buzz of the coffee-house sound is rendered as an undifferentiated din, incomprehensible and foreign.

Coffee-house conversation was certainly not always civil, rational and ordered. Discourse was often disrupted by destructive and uncongenial tendencies. Satirists identified four particular qualities of ruined discourse: gabbling, gossip, wheedling and idleness. Starkey's *Character* argued that coffee-house debate most often degenerated into squabble and conflict, precisely because there were no polite limits. 'Very critical and very discerning is the Assembly here,' Starkey sarcastically noted. Coffee-house discussion was repeatedly represented as catastrophically heterodox and ill-disciplined, and given to pointless and intemperate debate, swapping 'diverse Monster Opinions and Absurdities'. Starkey's *Character* satirised this 'Garrulity', 'Talkativeness' and 'confused way of gabbling' as being emblematic of a deeper intellectual confusion. In his estimation, coffee-house debate was swayed by flattery, insinuation and bribery. Discussion is hopelessly unfocused: 'A Coffee-house, like Logick the Lawyer, [. . .] will maintain any Cause . . . Infinite are the Contests, irreconcileable the Differences.' At a coffee-house there are 'neither Moderators, nor Rules'. As a 'School', he says, 'it is without a Master. Education is here taught without Discipline. Learning [. . .] is here insinuated without Method.'

Even the greatest truths, Starkey opines, are rendered contemptible in the coffee-house: 'the Noblest Speculations, the Divinest Truths, becomes as Common [. . .] as Stones.' Coffee-houses are more entertained by a 'facetious or merry Story' than raw 'Philosophy'; and, like traders bearing worthless beads and mirrors, coffee drinkers vent 'strange and wild Conceits', 'impertinent Fancies and ridiculous Notions'. Because the patrons are all talk, Starkey concludes, coffee-houses have the peculiar power to render impotent almost any doctrine. 'How can any one in reason, think, that a Coffee-house is dangerous to the Government, that seeds of Sedition are here sown, & Principles of Liberty insinuated? A Coffee-house hath alwayes been as great a Friend to Monarchy, as an Enemy to Liberty.' As Starkey explains, with reference to Harrington's coffee club of 1659–60, the 'Principles of a Popular Government at the *Rota* were weaken'd, and rendred contemptible'.[19] *The Women's Petition Against Coffee* (1674) agreed that coffee-houses were politically emasculated: 'yet for being dangerous to Government, we dare be their Compurgaters, as well knowing them to be too tame and too talkative to make any desperate Politicians'.[20] Important matters get discussed there but they don't get done.

Nonetheless the 'clamour' and 'confused way of gabbling' of the coffee-house associates it with gossip, conventionally gendered as feminine. Starkey's *Character* noted that 'In this Age Men tattle more than Women' and that the company of men in the coffee-house 'have out-talk'd an equal number of Gossipping Women'.[21] In *The Women's Petition Against Coffee* the men of the coffee-house '*out-babble* an equal number of [women] at a *Gossipping*, talking all at once in Confusion, and running from point to point [. . .] insensibly, and [. . .] swiftly'.[22] Satirists argued that this gabble, the undifferentiated stream of opinions, was not only typical of the coffee-house but was also symptomatic of the moral emptiness of modern city life. The gabbling manner was taken to its extreme by the figure of the fop or gallant, a man who was defined by his passion for fashion and modishness, the man without substance. The '*Town-Gallant*' wrote one satirist, 'is a Bundle of *Vanity*, composed of *Ignorance*, and *Pride*, *Folly*, and *Debauchery*; a silly *Hussing* thing, [. . .] a kind of *Walking Mercers shop*, [. . .] valuable just according to the price of his *Suit* and the merits of his *Taylor*'. The coffee-house resounded to his empty opinions, similarly formed by listening to what is in vogue. By way of example, the satirist observes that the town-gallant affects to be an atheist, an outlook he imbibed from Hobbes, despite not having read his works: 'However the Rattle of it at Coffeehouses has taught him to Laugh at Spirits, and maintain that there are no Angels but those in petticoats.'[23]

Another coffee-house character said to be typical of the moral climate of the city was the wheedle or town-shift, who specialised in flattery and obsequity. Richard Head's mock treatise on the topic explained that '*The art of Wheedling* is a Science'.

> Advantage is the soul or center of this *Art*, regarding no other interest but its own, and subservient to none other. [. . .] *This Art of Wheedling*, which some would have called Complaisance, is in plain terms, nothing else but the *Art of Insinuation*, or Dissimulation, compounded of mental reservation, seeming patience and humility, (self-obliging) civility, and a more than common affability, all which club to please, and consequently to gain by conversation.

In practising his science, a wheedle persuaded his gullible victims to perform actions contrary to their own interests, that would personally profit the wheedler, either financially or socially, using the dark arts of dissimulation, flattery, humility, civility, affability and plausibility. The coffee-house was the natural habitat of this creature: 'A Coffee-house is this *Wheedles* Bubbling Pond, where he angles for Fops, singles out his man, insinuates an acquaintance, offers the Wines and at next Tavern sets upon him with high or low Fullams, Goads, &c. and so plucks my Widgeon and sends him home featherless.'[24] The wheedle, the long forgotten ancestor of the spin-doctor, rendered truth, loyalty and faithfulness contingent and conditional precisely at a time when Restoration political masters argued they needed to be solid and concrete.

Another important quality of coffee-house conversation, to satirists, was its ability to waste time. As Starkey's *Character* argued, 'at this place a man is cheated of what is, by far more valuable than Mony, that is, Time'. Taverns had long been associated with idleness, skiving and absenteeism, as drinking beer and spirits not only occupied the precious time of apprentices and artisans, but made them unfit for their work the next day. In contrast, the wakeful sobriety of coffee made the coffee-house the natural ally of this puritan ideology of work and labour. Historians have long argued that the sixteenth and seventeenth centuries saw 'important changes' within intellectual culture 'in the apprehension of time'. As the people became more time conscious, so too there was a 'severe restructuring of working habits', particularly around the discipline of timekeeping.[25] As Starkey's *Character* said, the coffee drinkers 'borrow of the night, though they are sure, that this drink taken so late, will not let them close their Eyes all night'.[26] The importance of thrift, sobriety and work discipline was further emphasised in a humorous advice book by Henry Peachum, first published in 1667, entitled *The Worth of a Penny, or, A Caution to keep Money.* Observing that want of money caused melancholy and misery, Peachum's book taught the industrious worker how to save money through practical advice about thrift in '*Diet, Apparel, Recreations*'. Wishing to be practical, the book supplied a list of things that cost only a penny, noting lozenges at the apothecary, entry to the animals at the Tower, having a dog wormed and a bread-roll at the bakers. Newspapers and coffee were both recommended:

> For a penny, you may have all the news in *England*, and other Countries; of Murders, Floods, Witches, Fires, Tempests, and what not, in the weekly News-books.
>
> For a penny, you may buy a dish of Coffee, to quicken your Stomach, and refresh our Spirits.[27]

A later edition in 1687, however, retracted some of these recommendations, for although these recreations were thrifty and sober, they were still profligate with regard to time. Peachum argues that those in want should be 'diligent and industrious' and should avoid all 'idle Society'. In particular he warns against 'those sober and civil Conventions, as at Coffee-houses and Clubs, where little Money is pretended to be spent but a great deal of precious time lost, which the Person never thinks of, but measures his Expences, by what goes out of his Pocket'. 'Consider', he continues, 'what he might have put in by his labour, and what he might have saved, being Employed in his Shop.' He instances his examination of the abrogation of work-time discipline in the coffee-house with an anecdote delineating an artisan's day:

> A mechanick Tradesman it may be goes to the Coffee-house or Ale-house in the Morning to drink his mornings Draught, where he spends two pence, and in smoking and talking consumes at least an hour: in the Evening about six a Clock he goes to his two Penny Club and there stays for his two Pence till nine or ten, here is four Pence spent and four hours at least lost, which in most Mechanick Trades, cannot be reckoned less than a Shilling, and if he keeps Servants, they may lose him near as much by idling or spoyling his goods, which his presence might have prevented, so that upon these considerations for this his supposed groat a days expence, he cannot reckon less then seven groats, which comes to fourteen Shillings a Week (Sundays excepted) which is thirty six Pound ten Shillings a Year, a great deal of Money in a poor Tradesmans Pocket.[28]

As Peachum observes, time occupied in the sodality of the coffee-house is also money spent: both were a prodigal waste.

Nonetheless, while there were no explicit rules governing behaviour in coffee-houses, the implicit rules were still powerful. Among the most potent was that which excluded women, a rule so potent it did not even need saying. There was no need formally to exclude them because it was assumed that no woman who wished to be considered virtuous and proper would want to be seen in a coffee-house. Women certainly drank coffee at home, in private, and in certain public gatherings. Pope's Belinda, for example, drinks it with the Baron in *The Rape of the Lock* (1714): 'From silver spouts the grateful liquors glide / While China's earth receives the smoaking tyde.'[29] Perhaps some transgressive women did participate in political discussion with the men in coffee-houses, but they have left no record and, despite some claims, there are no reliable records of respectable women attending a public coffee-house in the seventeenth and early eighteenth centuries.[30] The keynote topics of eighteenth-century coffee-house discussion – science, commerce, politics – established it as a space for men and men only. There were spaces for heterosexual encounters (parks, pleasure gardens, playhouses), but at these places such serious topics were not countenanced. In effect, coffee-houses were almost more than anywhere else male-orientated, gendered almost exclusively masculine. Something of their masculine orientation is indicated by the definition of the word in Francis Grose's *Classical Dictionary of the Vulgar Tongue* (1785): 'COFFEE HOUSE, a necessary house, to make a coffee-house of a woman's * * * *, to go in and out and spend nothing'.[31]

This is not to say that women were entirely absent from the coffee-house. Many were employed there and some were owners. A few isolated references exist to the presence of women in coffee rooms, but only to suggest they were prostitutes. Ned Ward's fiction *The London Spy* (1698) observed the working life of two prostitutes in the coffee room of the Widow's Coffee-House, perhaps the one of that name in Devereux Court, Temple Bar. Alongside coffee the proprietor, 'the Reverend Doctress of Debauchery', retailed a distilled liquor called 'Aqua Veneris', guaranteed to restore virility. In apartments above, the spy watches two 'Mortal Angels', 'airy' and 'mercurial' ladies, work the coffee room, displaying an 'accustomary wantonness' behind their 'feign'd modesty'.[32] An army officer called Thomas Bellingham records in his *Diary* that he was 'with several women att ye coffee-house' in Preston on 20 January 1689: but in such a way as to suggest he did not think much of their morals.[33] A libertine magazine of the 1770s, *The Covent Garden Magazine*, listed four prostitutes who worked at the Denmark Coffee House, Bridges Street in 1773: a 'seminary, though no nunnery', which boasted 'some of the most agreeable votaries of Venus anywhere to be met with'.[34] The prospect of women in the coffee-house was to other writers a kind of absurdity. The poet Ambrose Phillips, in his essay periodical *The Free-Thinker* (1718–21), related a dream, or nightmare, of a '*Coffee-House*, full of women' encountered 'somewhere near the *Exchange*', except their 'whole discourse was strangely vulgar; their language of the male kind, and very unpolite'. Explaining the 'meaning of this strange assembly', a fairy whispers to him that 'these ladies were a troop of bad house-wives, who were turned adventurers, and came there to seek their fortune'[35]

Later in the eighteenth century the notion of a women's coffee-house took on new life in the spa town of Bath. In the Assembly Rooms, the retail shops, the splendid paved streets and the Pump Room, Bath was provided with a number of spaces in which people of both sexes congregated and conversed. Even at the baths, men and women bathed together, albeit wearing voluminous canvas clothes. In this unusually heterosexual environment, Bath's coffee-houses, such as the Parade Coffee-House, fronting the North Parade,[36] were almost the only places where the sexes were segregated: the coffee-house was just for men. Nonetheless, Bath had one very unusual social space for women, which was described, not always sympathetically, as a female coffee-house. Next to the Pump Room was a room to which 'ladies' could subscribe, as Oliver Goldsmith said, 'for the advantage of reading the news, and for enjoying each other's conversation'.[37] Because of its resemblance to the gentlemen's coffee-house, in offering conversation, company and newspapers, Goldsmith ironically called it 'a female coffee-house', although it isn't clear that coffee was actually sold there. Tobias Smollett picked up on Goldsmith's joke in his novel *Humphrey Clinker* of 1771, where the room is described by Lydia Melford: 'Hard by the Pump Room, is a coffee-house for the ladies; but my aunt says, young girls are not admitted, inasmuch as the conversation turns upon politics, scandal, philosophy, and other subjects above our capacity.' Excluded from this room, Lydia has to make do with the novels and plays in the circulating libraries.[38]

The newsmonger's hall

Almost more than coffee and conversation, the attraction of the coffee-houses was news. On entering, customers were as likely to call out 'What news?' as they were to order a dish of coffee. This obsession with news gave the coffee-house a distinct quality, which satirists were quick to notice; perhaps because they thought it would get these upstart enterprises in trouble. In the broadside poem *A Cup of Coffee* in 1663, an anonymous satirist described the beverage as

> A loathsome Potion, not yet understood,
> Syrrop of Soot, or Essence of old Shooes,
> Dasht with Diurnals, and the Books of News?

It seemed as if coffee was made with newspapers and diurnals, a mixture of gossip and used ink. Asking 'what wonder drops . . . in the coffee shops', he depicts the coffee-house as a place catering more to the thirst for news than coffee:

> *Your Servant, Sir, what News from Tripoly?*
> *Do the Weeks Pamphlets in their Works agree?*
> Then Dame *Diurnal* goes to the Pot; if you
> But say she scoulds, she's duck'd in Coffee too.[39]

The coffee room made the provision of news quite literally central to its organisation. On the large communal tables of the coffee room the proprietor would leave copies of newspapers and newsbooks for the clients to read. Londoners were more likely to read the newspaper in a coffee-house than they were to buy their own copy. Coffee-houses were also centres for the circulation of unprinted news, both in handwritten manuscript form, and also in the oral forms of gossip, rumour and scandal. The association of coffee-houses with news did much to build their cultural association with debate, controversy and, in later decades, sedition.

Writing from rural Nottinghamshire in 1667, John Cooper complained that 'the itch of news' had 'grown into a disease'.[40] Although the English had emerged from the Interregnum with a profound love of news, it remained the case that the business of news reporting was new in this period. News – information about recent events – was an elastic category, stretching from salacious gossip about the King's mistresses, to rumours of Puritan republican uprisings, to accounts of events overseas. 'Nothing seems to have circulated so fast in Restoration England as news, gossip, rumour, scandals, scares, and the spoken word. The talk of the town was the most effective publicity available.'[41] Reading the news, discussing scandal and repeating gossip in coffee-houses, clubs and taverns made the populace articulate and politically aware.[42] The King, his government and the ruling elite assumed that news concerned the activities of the monarch, court and government, and was written by these authorities. Any intelligence that was not produced from these sources was routinely described as false news, even if it was true. But as the proliferating stories of court gossip proved, the government was not always in control of the news agenda. People in the coffee-houses continued to talk on matters of public interest, whether they were scientific experiments, spectacular murders, or political rumours. News had become a commodity, sold through news-sheets and consumed in coffee-houses.

When Pepys went to the coffee-house his ostensible purpose was often to find news, even when one suspects he was in search of companionship. After a terrible storm in February 1662, Pepys went with his lawyer friend Moore to the coffee-house. There, he wrote, 'among other things, the great talk was of the effects of this late great wind', such as a wondrous story of 'five great trees standing together blown down'. Coffee-houses were places where news was encountered first hand, in its raw state. But it was also the place for encountering printed news. On the same visit Pepys read an account of a scandalous trial 'in the news-booke', which had reprinted the deposition of 'Lord Buckhurst and his fellows' – a brief that left Pepys unconvinced.[43] Pepys repeatedly found the coffee-house, especially Elford's in Exchange Alley, a better source of information about naval business than the official information disseminated from Whitehall: both faster and more accurate. In almost a third of his visits in the winter of 1663–4, Pepys came away with news he thought worthy of noting in his diary. For example, on 30 March 1664, he heard important news of the court's war plans at the coffee-house by listening to the thoughts 'about a Dutch war' uttered by Captain George Cocke, a Baltic merchant and navy contractor. War, of course, meant a certain increase in the business of the Navy Office and further opportunities for profit. In his *Diary* Pepys noted that 'it seems the King's design is, by getting under-hand the merchants to bring their complaints to the parliament, to make them in honour to begin a war, which he cannot in honour declare first, for fear they should not second him with money'.[44] Pepys discovered that attending to news in the coffee-house discussions gave him an insider's understanding of political events.

In response to this explosion of interest in news the government moved to assert a tighter control of printed news. After the Restoration in 1660 Charles II continued the policy adopted by Parliament, allowing the publication of only two weekly newsbooks, which were mostly filled with anodyne foreign news. Reports of domestic news were kept to a minimum, mostly consisting of official announcements. Advertisements – for books, commodities and lost property – became one of the few items related to life in the metropolis. When in 1663 Roger L'Estrange was made Licenser of the Press, he was granted a monopoly on publishing the newsbooks. In the first issue of *The Intelligencer* L'Estrange announced that the King had granted him 'the *Priviledge* of *Publishing* all *Intelligence*, together with the *Survey*, and *Inspection* of the *Presse*'.[45] In early 1666 the Secretary of State, Joseph Williamson, replaced both these papers with one, *The London Gazette*,[46] which exercised a near-monopoly on English printed news from September 1666 to December 1678, challenged only by some advertising sheets, foreign news digests and trade publications. The government moved to license and control the press too. The Licensing Act of 1662 had established a system of censorship by a range of authorities (the church, the universities, the Lord Chancellor and the secretaries of state), enabled to license approved books before publication.[47] Those who published unlicensed books would be held accountable by the secretaries of state, with the help of a Surveyor of the Imprimery and a number of messengers. Roger L'Estrange was appointed to this office too in 1663, giving him powers to search the premises of suspected printers and seize seditious papers and books. But despite these controls the thirst for clandestine news continued unabated.

Alongside printed news, which was intended for a relatively wide audience, government officials operated a news service for a more privileged audience of local officials and foreign embassies, giving them confidential intelligence about state affairs. These newsletters were professionally written and comprised a regular (weekly or fortnightly) compendium of news derived from official and unofficial sources on foreign and domestic topics, for which a regular fee was charged in advance. Through the Paper Office of the secretaries of state (also called the Letter Office) a reliable and official news channel was established. Unlike the printed newsbooks, these handwritten newsletters contained extensive coverage of domestic news, including parliamentary debate and even opinion (or reports of domestic opinion), and occasionally criticism of government policy. Such letters were reproduced in relatively large numbers by professional copyists – Henry Muddiman's newsletter had a circulation of at least 150 – posted around the country with the printed newsbooks, reaching a wide and socially diverse readership, including postmasters, clergymen, booksellers and coffee-men. Vigilance was necessary, however, to keep the intelligence confidential. In 1667 John Cooper in Newark said that a disaffected man at Nottingham called Slater was receiving a copy of Muddiman's newsletter and, at meetings with disloyal men, was 'descanting upon their intelligence'. 'The meetings at his home', Cooper remarked, 'resemble London coffee-houses for liberty of speech.'[48]

Coffee-houses remained the most notorious location for the consumption of news and the spread of sedition. The numerous plots against the crown hatched by radical Protestant groups in the 1660s were repeatedly linked to the indiscriminate socialising of the coffee-houses. The French historian Sorbiere, who visited London in 1664, noted that coffee-house talk was dominated by complaints of high taxes and regrets at the passing of Cromwell's regime.[49] In August 1664 the Secretary of State, Henry Bennet, the Earl of Arlington, was alarmed by intelligence of rebellious talk 'at a meeting at a coffee-house in Lothbury', where Major Holmes, an officer of Cromwell's army, had been agitating for 'liberty of conscience', predicting that 'Quakers will be as forward as any to draw the sword' and claiming the rebels 'expect to get arms from Holland, through Benbow, a merchant'.[50] Contemporary satires continued to remark upon the historical connection of the coffee-houses to the political culture of the Interregnum. Through the 1660s, and increasingly in the 1670s, the coffee-house was accused of nurturing an unhealthy obsession with news. From discourse on news, many argued, it was a short step to sedition and rebellion. In 1668 a Florentine nobleman, Count Lorenzo Magalotti, who was visiting London, described how in the coffee-houses 'there are various bodies or groups of journalists where one hears what is or is believed to be new, be it true or false'.[51]

Coffee-houses, especially those around Temple Bar, offered an important nexus between the printing trade and the news gatherers. In the early 1670s, for example, Ffarr's coffee-house at the Rainbow gained notoriety for the number and variety of the clandestine and subversive books found there. Detractors derided it as a 'Wits-Commonwealth' frequented by rabble-rousers such as the poet Andrew Marvell. In 1673 Marvell wrote a bitter and witty attack on the poet John Dryden and the Anglican apologist Samuel Parker, defending the policy of toleration of dissenters.[52] The cavalier satirist Edmund Hickeringall described Marvell's 'cabal' meeting at the Rainbow in 1673:

> At the *Rainbow-Coffee-house* the other day, taking my place at due distance, not far from me, at another Table sat a whole Cabal of wits; made up of Virtuoso's, Ingenioso's, young Students of the Law, two

> Citizens, and to make the Jury full, *vouz avez*, one old Gentleman: his bald Pate cover'd with a huffling Peruke, without an Eye of gray in't, or one gray-hair. But I knew him to be be Old, because they all laughing heartily and gaping.[53]

Other satirists also rounded on Marvell's unlicensed satire, complaining that it was a vulgar form of railing whose natural home was the coffee-house. Richard Leigh protested that coffee-house habitués like Marvell were followed by 'the Disciples of Prattle', who incited the 'Coffee-men' to become stationers and booksellers. The coffee-men, Leigh continued, had demonstrated 'to the world the wonderful effects of an Education in their Academies', for there, the customers find seditious libels 'the best part of their Cheer, News and pleasant Tales'.[54]

As early as 1666 the King was becoming seriously alarmed at the political views being expressed in the coffee-houses, especially the 'Pasquils and Libels' censuring his conduct during the fire. Charles requested that the Lord Chancellor, the Earl of Clarendon, do something about it. The King, said Clarendon,

> complained very much of the Licence that was assumed in the Coffee-houses, which were the Places where the boldest Calumnies and Scandals were raised, and discoursed amongst a People who knew not each other, and came together only for that Communication, and from thence were propagated over the kingdom; and mentioned some particular Rumours which had been lately dispersed from the Fountains.

Clarendon comprehended the unprecedented 'Impunity' from the law assumed by the coffee-houses, 'where the foulest Imputations [. . .] laid upon the Government, [. . .] were held lawful to be reported and divulged to every Body'. In short, Clarendon concluded, 'people generally believed that those Houses had a Charter of Privilege to speak what They would, without being in Danger to be called in Question', and counselled the King to 'apply some Remedy to such a growing Disease'. Clarendon advised either a proclamation to suppress the coffee-houses, or the organisation of 'some Spies, who, being present in the Conversation, might be ready to charge and accuse the Persons who had talked with the most Licence in a Subject that would bear a Complaint'. Clarendon was given leave to propose the suppression of the coffee-houses to the Privy Council, but there he was opposed by Secretary of State Sir William Coventry, who argued 'that Coffee was a Commodity that yielded the King a good Revenue, and therefore it would not be just to receive the Duties and inhibit the Sale of it, which many Men found to be very good for their Health'. Furthermore, Coventry argued, the coffee-houses 'had been permitted in Cromwell's Time, and that the King's Friends had used more liberty of Speech in those Places than They durst do in any other; and that he thought it would be better to leave them as they were, without running the Hazard of Ill being continued notwithstanding his Command to the Contrary.'[55] The King persuaded, Clarendon found it politic to drop his proposal to suppress the coffee-houses. It was an idea, however, that did not go away.

CHAPTER SIX

Coffee with Wings: The Spread of the Coffee-House

By becoming synonymous with trade and news, coffee-houses in London established themselves as the natural home of merchants, men of science and intelligencers, providing a single location for the overlapping interests of commerce and politics. The advantage they afforded were clear to see and places like them were soon copied in other towns and cities. Oxford was probably the first after London. The apothecary Arthur Tillyard opened an establishment selling coffee on the High Street opposite All Souls in 1655 or 1656. The antiquarian Anthony Wood remarked in his Diary that 'He was encouraged so to do by som royallists, now living in Oxon, and by others who esteem'd themselves either *virtuosi* or *wits*', men who sought esteem as practitioners of the new experimental science.[1] As an apothecary, Tillyard was well placed to provide entertainment and instruction to these natural philosophers, and a room in his shop was used as the venue for the Chemical Club, an important precursor of the Royal Society.[2] But Tillyard's coffee room soon outgrew this narrow audience, and began to appeal to a wider clientele in the university and the city. By the Restoration there were several coffee-houses in Oxford. In 1665, when Parliament removed to Oxford to escape the Plague, one of the rooms in the Divinity School was set aside for 'a coffee hous for the parliament men'.[3]

By the end of the 1660s coffee-houses had been set up in numerous English towns. Just as it had in the Ottoman domains, the coffee-house idea spread along important routes of communication, both commercial and scientific. In Cambridge the university authorities thought the new coffee-houses distracted the attention of the students and in 1664 they passed a statute to the effect that all students who went 'to the coffee-houses without their tutors' leave shall be punished according to the statutes for haunters of taverns and alehouses'.[4] Roger North said that 'Whilst he was at *Jesus College*, Coffee was not of such common Use as afterwards, and Coffee-houses but young. At that Time, and long after, there was but one, kept by one *Kirk*. The Trade of News also was scarce set up; for they had only the public Gazette, till *Kirk* got a written news Letter circulated by one *Muddiman*.' Within a few years, however, the coffee-house had become central to social life of Cambridge scholars. North explained that it was 'a Custom, after Chapel, to repair to one or the other of the Coffee-houses (for there are diverse) where Hours are spent in talking; and less profitable reading of News Papers, of which Swarms are continually supplied from *London*'.[5]

In most provincial cities the coffee-house functioned as one of the chief points of dissemination for news, both commercial and political. In addition to the university cities, coffee-houses in Yarmouth, Harwich and York were operating by the end of the 1660s.[6] In Bristol John Kimber's Coffee-House at the sign of the Elephant advertised itself as being of particular utility to 'all wholesail and retail dealers who usually come to Bristol Fair'.[7] In Dublin the new coffee-house opened by Lionell Newman in 1664 issued a trade token stamped with a depiction of Sultan Morat on the reverse.[8] In Scotland John Row opened a coffee-house near the Parliament House in Edinburgh in 1673, and in the same year one was established in Glasgow by Colonel Walter Whytfoord, given liberty for 'making, selling and toping of coffie' by the Town Council, with a nineteen-year monopoly on the trade.[9]

Coffee-houses were firmly established as a British institution by the end of the 1660s. Nearly every English city of consequence had at least one, where men assembled to discuss the news and to prosecute their business. They also spread abroad, particularly to those cities with sizeable communities of English merchants, although they were typically operated by a coffee-man of Levantine origins. The English merchants in the Hanseatic port of Bremen established a coffee-house in 1669, as did those of Hamburg in 1670. The Dutch East Indies Company held its first coffee auction in 1663 and by 1665, according to one source, a coffee-house was opened in Amsterdam by a Greek called Demetrius Christoffel.[10] Court records in The Hague and Leiden suggest that coffee-houses were operating in those cities by 1670.[11] For English merchants, of course, one of the most profitable trade routes was that across the Atlantic to the British colonies in North America. One of the first coffee-houses outside Britain was that established for the merchants of Boston in the Massachusetts Bay Colony in 1670 – which was trading before their like had arrived in Paris, Venice or Vienna.

In 1670 Boston was the largest city in British North America and, with more than 7,000 residents, was equivalent in size to some of the principal provincial cities in England itself. Boston was closely connected by ties of culture, people and trade to British cities across the Atlantic. As the commercial hub of the American colonies, Boston merchants were in continual and close contact with their British counterparts, habituated to their manners and customs, moving between the two continents as frequently as their trade demanded. Familiar with the coffee-house culture of the London Exchange, Boston merchants agitated for permission to open their own. The Town Council of Boston issued annual licences to keepers of 'houses of publique entertainment', the great majority of which were taverns and ordinaries, selling beer, wine, strong water and cider.[12] At the meeting of 30 November 1670 the Selectmen of the council agreed that two women might keep coffee-houses, decreeing that 'Mrs Dorothy Jones the wife of Mr Morgan Jones is approved to keepe a house of publique Entertainment for the sellinge of Coffee & Chuculettoe. Jane the wife of Bartholomew Barnard is approved of alsoe to keepe a house of publique entertainment for the sellinge of Coffee & chuculettoe.' In February 1671 they further licensed 'Capt James Johnson & Abell Porter' to sell coffee.

These first coffee-houses in America flourished for some years, with licences being renewed annually in 1671, 1672, 1673 and 1674, and with only minor changes in personnel.[13] Although the record is patchy, some change in fortune may have happened by 1676, when 'severall Merchants & Gentlemen' felt it necessary to urge the Selectmen to allow a new person 'to keepe a publique house for selling of Coffee'. In October of that year John Sparry was licensed (and again in 1677, 1678, 1679, 1680 and 1682).[14] Sparry's establishment was near to the Town House, a 'fine Piece of Building' under whose wooden columns was the 'Walk for the Merchants', or Exchange, and around which clustered the colony's many booksellers' shops.[15] By locating the coffee-house next to the Exchange, Sparry intended that it would become the meeting place of merchants, replicating the pattern developed in London.

In September 1690 the Boston coffee-house scene was enlivened when the enterprising puritan bookseller Benjamin Harris persuaded the Selectmen of Boston to license him to retail coffee from a house near the Town House on King Street.[16] In London, Harris had kept a bookshop in Sweeting's Rents next to the Royal Exchange (a lane with several coffee-houses in it): he had emigrated to New England in 1686 because the Protestant flavour of his publications attracted the ire of James II's licensing authorities. His knowledge of London coffee-houses had taught him the powerful combination of coffee and print. In America he continued as a bookseller, retailing books imported from London, and publishing almanacks and other titles popular in Boston, which he sold from a counter in the London Coffee-House. In September 1690 he started a monthly newspaper – also a first in the American colonies – called *Public Occurrences*, which the Governor suppressed soon after as unlicensed. By the time Harris returned to London in 1695, a rival coffee-house was operating. Gutteridge's Coffee-House was connected to the printing house of Nicholas Buttolph, the publisher of the influential theologian Cotton Mather. Buttolph's brother-in-law, Robert Gutteridge, kept the coffee room in Buttolph's bookseller's shop on the corner of Washington and Court Streets in central Boston until a fire in 1711 destroyed the whole area.[17] By combining these new technologies of coffee-house and news, the bookseller coffee-men of Boston had successfully replicated in their cities the characteristic urban culture of London. As such, from the 1670s the coffee-house was a central aspect of Boston's civic government, its social life and its commercial prosperity.

It was not until 1696 that a coffee-house was opened in New York. A British immigrant, John Hutchin, established his Coffee-House at the Sign of the King's Arms on Broadway, just north of the churchyard of the first Anglican church in the colony, Trinity Church – a site now close to Ground Zero. Hutchin's coffee-house was modelled on those he knew from London, with a large upstairs coffee room, lined with booths screened with green curtains. Doors lead out to balconies affording splendid views of the river and harbour, giving the merchants early notice of ships arriving in the port. The new coffee-house quickly became the 'unofficial headquarters of English New York', providing a home for 'municipal and provincial officials, merchants and officers from the fort'.[18] Its opening was evidence of the city's growing Anglicisation under Governor Benjamin Fletcher, who sought to diminish the influence of the rebellious Calvinist settlers of Dutch origin who still dominated the city's population. As well as promoting the coffee-house among his followers and leading celebrations marking royal occasions, Fletcher invited a bookseller from Philadelphia to settle in the colony and encouraged him to publish a newspaper.[19] With a coffee-house and a newspaper, New York started to take on the appearance of a regular English colony.

By 1701 the new governor, Richard Coote, Earl of Bellomont, could boast that New York was the 'growingest town in America'.[20] In the convivial setting of the King's Arms, men of the 'English party' met, sometimes to discuss business and gossip about society, but more often to talk about news and politics. In 1702 John Hutchin got in trouble with the authorities after he collected signatures for petitions protesting about the oppressive government of the city: the line between conviviality and disaffection was a fine one.[21] Nonetheless, over the next decade, as the city became more English, Hutchin's coffee-house came to occupy a central role in its civic politics. As one of the principal public spaces of the city, his coffee room hosted meetings of the committees of the Common Council of the city and of the colonial assembly. Any colonial city that aspired to greatness soon had need of a coffee-house. Such places were opened in Philadelphia in 1703 (by the postmaster, Henry Flower, whose coffee room also served as the merchants' exchange) and in Charles Town, South Carolina in 1724.[22] The coffee-house, in the British colonies in North America, attracted but also defined a high-status clientele in search of coffee, companionship, commerce and communications.

In Paris, however, the coffee-house does not seem to have emerged out of this mercantile milieu. Instead, the technique of coffee preparation and the practice of drinking coffee were first advertised by the splendid embassy of Solyman Aga, sent by Sultan Mehemet IV to the King of France in 1669. Members of the ambassador's retinue brought with them large quantities of coffee, and served it to many people from the court and the city.[23] The first coffee-house was not established, however, until 1671, after they were already trading in North America and Holland. The early history of the coffee-house in Paris relies on the account given of it by Jean de La Roque (1661–1745) in 1716. The son of a Marseilles merchant, he published an account of his travels in Arabia between 1708 and 1710, entitled *A Voyage to Arabia Fœlix* (1716), which contained a natural history of the coffee tree, a guide to the preparation of coffee and an 'Historical Treatise' concerning 'its Introduction into

France, and the Establishment of the Use of it at Paris'. Like many a patriot, La Roque was keen to establish French priority in the trade, although seventeenth-century French scholars admitted that coffee had come into use in England almost twenty years earlier.[24] But in La Roque's account the French learn of coffee without reference to English practices. He suggests that Levantine merchants in Marseilles, including his own father, adopted coffee drinking in the 1640s, following habits learnt in Turkey, and that the first French coffee-house opened in Marseilles in 1670 to serve their needs.[25] As in London, the metropolitan and cosmopolitan character of coffee relates it to the sociable practices of a specific sector of the commercial elite of the city: La Roque specifies principal merchants, mariners (*gens de mer*) and especially the merchant-druggists.

Coffee-houses in Paris opened in a land-locked city with no direct trade with the Levant and, with no community of merchants and traders to make it their home, business was difficult. In 1671 Pascal, an Armenian, established a coffee-house in the St Germain fair in Paris, which later moved to the Quai de l'Ecole (Quartier du Louvre), mostly frequented by foreigners. After his enterprise failed, Pascal was reported to have fled to London, where such a trade was easier to pursue. In 1676 another Armenian, Maliban, set a coffee-house, initially in rue de Bussy (Quartier St Germain) and subsequently in other locations. A number of itinerant hawkers also sold hot coffee in the streets. The early coffee-houses of Paris were typically operated by poor Levantine coffee sellers and frequented by foreigners. As La Roque concludes, 'Gentlemen and people of fashion were ashamed to go into those sort of publick-houses, where they smoked, and drank strong beer: besides, their coffee was none of the best, nor the customers served in the handsomest manner'.[26]

The significant change in the nature of the coffee-house in Paris was initiated in 1676, when an Italian, Francesco Procopio dei Coltelli, established one at the annual St Germain fair. By 'setting off' his coffee room with 'tapestry, large peers of glass [mirrors], pictures, marble tables, branches for candles, and other ornaments', he was able to attract a much higher-status clientele. Success at the fair was translated into a more permanent establishment at rue de Tournon and, after 1686, in rue des Fossés-Saint-Germain, where the Café Procope still trades as a restaurant, advertising itself as the oldest in the world.[27] 'Being thus changed into well furnished rooms', La Roque comments, the coffee-houses 'were crouded by gentlemen who came thither to drink coffee, and divert themselves with good company; and men of letters and the most serious persons, did not shun these meetings, where they might so conveniently confer on matters of learning, and what subjects they pleased, without any constraint or ceremony, and only, by way of amusement'.[28] According to La Roque, these elegant interiors scoured the coffee-house of both vulgarity and orientalism: everything was henceforth of the best taste. The authorities were not convinced: in December 1685 the Secretary of State, Jean Baptist Seignelay, wrote to the Prefect of Police that 'The King had been informed that in several cafés in Paris, all sorts of people assemble, especially foreigners. The King wants you to send me a report on all those who run cafés and asks if you do not think it proper to prohibit them in future.'[29]

The victualling trades in France were highly regulated by licences granted according to the kinds of alcohol each establishment sold. Although the right to sell wine was restricted to members of the wine merchants guild, a variety of trades shared the right to sell beer. The arrival of coffee-houses in the early 1670s coincided with the introduction of a number of new alcoholic drinks, including brandy, eau-de-vie and fruit-flavoured liqueurs, which were hitherto considered rather medicinal, like coffee. In 1673 the King gave the right to sell both kinds of new drinks, coffee and the various eau-de-vies, to the newly formed guild of *limonadiers* (lemonade sellers). Three years later, in 1676, the *limonadiers* were merged with the distillers and brandy merchants into a single guild.[30] The right to sell eau-de-vie was a lucrative business, quickly finding a ready market, and this propelled the early coffee-house keepers to move their business upmarket. But this accidental turn in regulation permanently changed the sociability of the Parisian café. From their inception, the primary commodity sold in French cafés was alcoholic drink. Although coffee was the nominal difference between the café and its competitors (*guinguettes*, taverns and *cabarets*), it was essentially metaphorical. As numerous visitors to Paris noted, the café was not a coffee-house.

As the coffee-house had spread across Europe, its form and nature had been changed by its encounter with each society. In England it remained a masculine space, devoted especially to news, to reading and writing, to business, and to gossip and intelligence. As such it was especially appropriate for all men of business: not only merchants and traders, but also clerics, courtiers and critics. In each European city where a coffee-house was opened this English model was invoked. But though the London style prospered in America, it was not in the end the dominant model in Europe. The French model of the café, a hybrid institution between a coffee-house and a tavern that attracted a high-status clientele, proved very influential in Continental Europe, especially in Italy.

In Venice, for example, there had long been some knowledge of coffee. From around 1570 a sizeable community of Turkish merchants had lived there, in a house in the Rialto assigned to them by the Signoria. These men certainly drank coffee in the city, as is attested to by an inventory of the goods of a textile merchant, Huseyin Çelebi, who was murdered in Venice on 20 March 1575. Among the list of his personal belongings and goods, made after his death, was his tableware, which included his *finian* (*fincan* in Turkish) used for drinking coffee.[31] In the 1630s coffee beans were reportedly sold by apothecaries in the city, suggesting that the drink was consumed, at least by some, as a medicine. Nonetheless, the first coffee-house in Venice, retailing coffee to Christian Venetians, was not opened until 1683, in a shop under arcades beneath the Procuratie Nuove (the New Law Courts) in St Mark's Square.[32] The first coffee sellers met with hostility from the government, however, which was concerned that these establishments might provide encouragement to subversives and agitators. As one commentator noted in 1707,

> It is in conformity to this Advice, that the Venetians do not allow of any Coffee-houses in their City, that are able to contain great numbers of People. Their Coffee-houses are generally little shops, that will not hold above five or six Persons at a time, and perhaps there are not Seats for above two or three. So that the Company having no where to rest themselves, are gone as soon as they have made an end of drinking their Coffee.[33]

One of the early coffee-house keepers of Venice was Floriano Francesconi, who opened a small establishment in St Mark's Square, under the Procuratie Nuove, in 1720. Despite being nothing more than a few austere rooms, he called it *Venezia trionfante* (Venice Triumphant), perhaps ironically, for in these years the Venetian state did not prosper.

Floriano's business became better known as Caffè Florian, still trading today from the same location. The Venetian state continued to exert close and watchful surveillance on the coffee-houses, posting spies in every room and periodically ordering their coffee rooms to be closed after midnight. The State Inquisitors heard a report in 1754, for example, of a woman called Barbera, a 'balcony harlot', who went 'very lewdly dressed' to Cicio's coffee-house, under the Procuratie Nuove, in the company of a nobleman, the Marquis Teofilo Calcagnino of Ferrara.[34]

The coffee-house market in Venice was transformed in 1723 by Giuseppe Boduzzi's new Caffè Aurora, under the arcades of the Procuratie Nuove next to the campanile (bell tower). This was a coffee-house in the grand manner known in Paris, employing a high quality of interior decoration and fittings to redefine the coffee-house clientele. 'The bowls and saucers, the basins, and the plates, were made of solid silver, and the coffee-house keeper served the coffee to all in beautiful fine china.'[35] The other coffee-houses of St Mark's Square, feeling the competition with the Aurora, also improved the splendour of their decoration (although Caffè Florian's famous painted wall and ceiling decorations, with their extensive use of gilding and mirrors, date from the renovations of 1858). By the mid eighteenth century most of the shops around the piazza were coffee-houses.[36] The English agricultural writer Arthur Young, visiting Venice in 1788, suggested that St Mark's Square and its coffee-houses was 'the seat of government, of politics and of intrigue' in Venice.[37] Florian's is known to have played host to illustrious clients such as Jean Jacques Rousseau, Henri Beyle (the writer known as Stendhal) and the painter Giuseppe Guardi. Across the square from Caffè Florian a serious rival emerged in Caffé Quadri, which opened in 1775 and which remains in business. As in Paris, these establishments were more like restaurants than coffee-houses, in that they sold wine and spirits, served food and were frequented by women as well as men.

In Rome the most famous coffee-house was the Caffè Greco, which was already established by 1750. Rome was a premier destination for English *milordi* on the Grand Tour and, to meet their aesthetic needs, a horde of Northern artists, from Britain, Germany and Scandinavia, worked in the city. This coterie of painters, sculptors and antiquarians made the Greco their favourite. It was not a large establishment: even in the nineteenth century it only had three small rooms, when the caffè at the Palazzo Ruspoli had seventeen. Around 1752 the English artists quarrelled with their German colleagues and removed en masse to a coffee-house on the Piazza di Spagna, a few hundred metres away. There they established the Caffè degli Inglesi, or English Coffee House.[38] James Boswell used it as a letter office in 1765, asking his friend John Wilkes to write to him *'al Caffè Inglese'* while he was in Rome.[39] The young Welsh painter Thomas Jones recorded being taken there on his first day in Rome in December 1776, where he was delighted to find his 'Old London Acquaintance', listing eighteen friends, new and old, in his diary. The coffee-house, he noted, was in 'a filthy vaulted room', but decorated in the most exciting modern manner, 'painted with Sphinxes, Obelisks and Pyramids, from capricious designs of Piranesi, and fitter to adorn the inside of an Egyptian-Sepulchre than a room of social conversation'. Staying in uncomfortably damp lodgings during a cold Roman winter, Jones noted the only relief was to fly 'to the English Coffee house', where, 'seated around a brazier of hot embers placed in the Center, we endeavoured to amuse ourselves for an hour or two over a Cup of Coffee or Glass of Punch and then grope our way home darkling, in Solitude and Silence'.[40] The Caffè degli Inglesi did not survive the Napoleonic wars, however, and in the nineteenth century English, American, German and Danish artists congregated happily together at Caffè Greco.[41]

In Vienna the arrival of coffee has long been romanticised by the story of a Pole named Franz Georg Kulczycki (Koltschitzky in German spelling). In 1683 Vienna was besieged by a huge and well-equipped Ottoman army under the command of the Grand Vizir Kara Mustapha. After months of bombardment, and just as the fortifications seemed to be giving way, the siege was lifted by the arrival of forces under Prince Sobieski of Poland and Charles, Duke of Lorraine. In a remarkable reversal the besieging Ottoman army was routed and its entire camp captured, including virtually all its armaments and provisions. Viennese officials were amazed at the 'copious amounts of war materiel and foodstuffs' the camp contained, especially the prodigious stores of victuals that were so desperately needed by the starving city. In their inventory of the spoil the Viennese chroniclers listed coffee among the grain, flour, bread, butter, lard, rice, sugar, honey, cooking oil and kitchenware, as well as camels, buffaloes, mules, oxen and sheep.[42] In reward for Kulczycki's bravery during the battle, in which he had undertaken some dangerous espionage, he was rewarded with the bags of Ottoman coffee, which no one else could see any use for. With these copious supplies of coffee, Kulczycki hawked his drinks around the city, establishing a taste for the beverage among its inhabitants. Nonetheless the first coffee house was opened a few years later in 1685 by a merchant from the city's Armenian community called Johannes Diodato. In January 1685 Diodato applied for, and was granted, the sole privilege of preparing and offering for sale the 'Oriental drink' in Vienna, for a period of twenty years. The sale of coffee remained carefully controlled in the city, so that by 1729 there were still only eleven licensed concessionaires.[43]

CHAPTER SEVEN

'Freedom of Words': Charles II and the Challenge of the Coffee-House

At the gates of the Royal Exchange on Wednesday, 29 December 1675, passers-by would have noticed a flurry of activity. Messengers of the King's printers were fixing a Royal Proclamation to the pillars, its importance proclaimed by its ominous black letter typeface and royal coat of arms. Intrigued onlookers read, under the signature 'Charles R.', 'A Proclamation for the Suppression of Coffee-Houses'.[1] 'The Multitude of Coffee-houses of late years set up and kept within this Kingdom', it declared, were the 'the great resort of Idle and disaffected persons' and as such have 'produced very evil and dangerous effects'. In such places, the proclamation rumbled, tradesmen wasted valuable time when they should be employed about their 'Lawful Callings and Affairs'. More seriously, at their coffee-house meetings, 'divers False, Malitious and Scandalous Reports are devised and spread abroad, to the Defamation of his Majesties Government, and to the Disturbance of the Peace and Quiet of the Realm'. As a result, the King declaimed, it was thought 'fit and necessary, That the said Coffee-houses be (for the future) Put Down and Suppressed'. All coffee-house keepers were commanded to desist from retailing their 'coffee, chocolate, sherbet and tea' from 10 January 1676, only twelve days away. To the coffee-house keepers this was an unmitigated disaster, the ruination of their business. To the people of London too this was a calamity: a challenge to their liberty of assembly and free speech.

The proclamation was published in full in *The London Gazette* the next day, crammed into the last column of the back page, above an advertisement for two nags missing out of a stable in Birmingham.[2] On that morning Robert Hooke wandered down to Garraway's Coffee-House in Exchange Alley from his home at Gresham College, as he did every day. Ensconced in the Green Room at Garraway's, Hooke discussed the news of the proclamation with his fellow scientist Abraham Hill, Treasurer of the Royal Society. Having dined at home (where he cut the top off his thumb while working on one of his experimental flying engines), he returned to Garraway's in the evening, where he met Mr Newbold of the Old Bailey, before going on to Jonathan's Coffee-House next door. There, drinking hot ale with Mr Wild, he stayed until midnight, discussing 'my contrivance of flying' and getting into an argument with 'A company of 3 strangers' about the proclamation against coffee-houses.[3] Hooke made nothing of the irony of discussing the proclamation shutting the coffee-houses in a coffee-house.

Ever since the Restoration of the King in 1660 the coffee-houses had been accused of encouraging political dissent and rebellious attitudes. For most of Charles II's reign royal circles had entertained ideas of suppressing them. Clarendon had proposed a clampdown in 1666 but the action came to nothing. The only regulation of the coffee-houses was that of the Excise legislation. The Excise Act of 1660, modelled on the system established by Parliament during the Interregnum, had first extended the Excise to coffee.[4] The Excise was a tax on articles of English manufacture or consumption, such as beer, cider and other liquors. Unlike duty, it was not levied by the customs on importation but at the point of manufacture, where production was measured by the Excise officers, known as the gaugers. The Excise on coffee was set at 4 pence per gallon in 1660, while tea and chocolate was levied at 8 pence per gallon; increased to 6 pence and 16 pence respectively in 1670.[5] While such a system worked reasonably well with brewers, in the case of coffee the nature of the drink's preparation made the Excise easy to evade. To remedy this the Additional Excise Act, passed in 1663, required the coffee-house keepers to pay a bond of security for the Excise due upon their trade to the Office of Excise, who issued them with a certificate. With this certificate the coffee-house keeper applied for a licence from the magistrates, without which no 'persons shall be permitted to sell or retail any Coffee, Chocolate, Sherbet or Tea'.[6] The Excise certificate cost only 12 pence, but the fine for each month of trading without licence was £5.

This rudimentary form of regulation did not address the role of the coffee-house in the circulation of illicit news, rumour and sedition, which by the early 1670s was felt to be acute. An anonymous court satirist wrote in 1674 that coffee was

Bak'd in a pan, *Brew'd* in a pot,
The third device of him who first begot
The Printing Libels, and the Powder-plot.[7]

In January 1672 the Under-Secretary of State, Sir Joseph Williamson, noted that 'the great inconveniences arising from the great number of persons that resort to coffee houses' had led the King to ask the judiciary for their written opinion 'how far he may lawfully proceed against them'.[8] The judges identified no easy solution and instead a royal proclamation was issued on 12 June 1672, designed, as its title indicated, to 'Restrain the Spreading of False News, and Licentious Talking of Matters of State and, Government'. It warned that 'Spreaders of false News, or promoters of any Malicious Slanders and Calumnies in their ordinary and common Discourses', should 'presume not henceforth by Writing or Speaking, to Utter or Publish any False News or Reports, or to intermeddle with the Affairs of State and Government'. These 'bold and Licentious Discourses' had grown to the extent that

> men have assumed to themselves a liberty, not onely in *Coffee-houses*, but in other Places and Meetings, both publick and private, to censure and defame the proceedings of State, by speaking evil of things they understand not, and endeavouring to create and nourish an universal Jealousie and Dissatisfaction in the minds of all his Majesties good subjects.[9]

Identifying coffee-houses as the pre-eminent location of 'speaking evil' of the government, the proclamation urged those that heard such discourses to report them to Privy Councillors or Justices of the Peace within twenty-four hours. It did little good, for on 2 May 1674 a further proclamation was published, also titled 'A Proclamation to Restrain the Spreading of False News, and Licentious Talking of Matters of State and Government'. It promised to punish all 'Spreaders of false News, or promoters of any Malicious Calumnies against the State' by considering them to be 'Seditiously inclined'.[10] Everywhere the coffee-houses seemed immune to these measures. The King's equerry wrote in October 1673 that London was besieged by '1000 coffee-houss reports and libells sans number', each encouraging 'our Great Ministers' to be jealous of one another.[11] An anonymous tract written in 1673 inveighed against the coffee-houses, which 'allowed people to meet in them' and 'sit half a day, and discourse with all Companies that come in, of State-matters, talking of news, and broaching of lyes, arraigning the judgements and discretions of their Governors, censuring all their Councels, and insinuating into the people a prejudice against them'. The coffee-house debates, the writer warned, 'if suffered too long', would prove 'pernicious and destructive'.[12] In government circles coffee-houses had become a sort of shorthand for the malicious talk and rumour of 'the town'.

Paradoxically, the coffee-house also held an important part in the government's news-gathering machinery. The office of the Secretary of State had well-established networks of correspondents who functioned as domestic spies, reporting on the state of popular opinion. One of Secretary Williamson's correspondents was the victualler Richard Bower of Yarmouth in Norfolk. This town was not only an important trading port and fishing town, but was renowned for its concentration of Nonconformist Protestants. Soon after the Restoration, Bower had been employed as an intelligencer for the Secretary of State, sending frequent letters to Williamson describing the political condition in the town. At some time around 1667 Bower had established his wife in a coffee-house, 'for the better gaining of intelligence'.[13] By listening over the tables he gained confidential knowledge of town politics, reported on shipping movements to Holland, and collected what gossip he could from strangers and travellers in the town.

Through the coffee-houses the government gained a unique insight into the political feeling of dissenters. Government spies were endlessly attentive to what they heard there. After an indecisive naval battle in June 1673, for example, the Letter Office clerk Henry Ball reported that 'roguish seamen' on the ships had been writing letters which had appeared 'in some coffee houses, and does much prejudice in disheartening the people'. The Letter Office also made notes on rumours circulating in coffee-houses, even those known to be false. Ball complained to Williamson in September 1673 that popular feeling was running so much against the King's pro-French policy that 'I dare not write halfe what is spoken in publique in every coffee-house'. Another correspondent, Sir Thomas Player (Chamberlain of the Paper Office), wrote to Williamson in November 1673 that 'the common people talke anything, for every carman and porter is now a statesman; and indeed the coffee-houses are good for nothing else'. Coffee-houses were commonly held responsible for the unprecedented heat of public debate.

'It was not thus when wee dranke nothing but sack and claret, or English beere and ale. These sober clubbs produce nothing but scandalous and censorious discourses, and at these nobody is spared.'[14]

The King was propelled to issue the proclamation in 1675 in response to the increasingly fractious nature of political debate, but also because he felt reasonably confident that it might succeed, one of several measures of that year aimed at controlling the state in a more autocratic fashion. Through the 1670s the King's opponents, though not a political party in any modern sense, acquired some of the trappings of a self-conscious identity. The followers of the great opposition noblemen, Buckingham and Shaftesbury, were increasingly identified as the Country party, patriotic defenders of the country. Their enemies nicknamed them the Whigs, a term they in turn enthusiastically adopted.[15] The difference between the factions was represented in their different ways of life. The court party, centred on the pleasure-loving circles of the King, was naturally associated with Whitehall and St James's, where they made habitual use of the royal palaces, state offices and gardens of Westminster. The opposition party had no particular home of its own, but in the wider city a number of places became associated with their assemblies. The geography of opposition was distributed across the urban landscape in booksellers' shops, taverns, the Exchange and private homes, but the place that became synonymous with their assemblies was the coffee-house.

In Parliament, 1675 had turned out to be an awkward year. Opposition analysts detected in government policy a concerted effort to peel back the liberties of Parliament and the people. Piecing together the machinations of the ministry, the poet turned polemicist Andrew Marvell remarked with characteristic wit that 'he is an ill Woodman that knows not the size of the Beast by the proportion of his Excrement'.[16] In particular, Marvell identified a series of measures undertaken by the ministry of the Lord Treasurer, Thomas Osborne, Earl of Danby. The first of these was the new Test Act, which required all holders of political office to swear not to take arms against the King, nor to 'endeavour the alteration of the government, either in Church or State'.[17] Introduced into the House of Lords the act, if it had passed, would have established a doctrine of passive obedience which, Marvell argued, amounted to absolute monarchy. But in the face of a recalcitrant Parliament, in October and November 1675, unwilling to vote supply for the King, Charles unexpectedly prorogued Parliament until

15 February 1677, so that it would not sit again for fifteen months. (Unbeknownst even to Danby, Charles had secretly secured a subsidy for his own expenses from the French and had no need of Parliament.) The Test Act and the long prorogation set the scene for the proclamation against coffee-houses: all were evidence of the King's subversion of parliamentary government.

The newsletter writers of Sir Joseph Williamson's Paper Office observed on 30 December 1675 that 'great complaints [. . .] were made day by day to his Majesty of the license that was taken in coffee-houses to utter most indecent, scandalous and seditious discourses'. These protests, the clerk notes, 'at last produced this proclamation for the suppressing of them'.[18] Without Parliament sitting, of course, the only method the King had at his disposal was a proclamation. In constitutional terms, proclamations were issued on the authority of the executive as an expression of the King's prerogative. As an exercise of executive, rather than legislative, power, however, a proclamation was only capable of reinforcing existing legislation: there was no institution which could punish its breach. As a result, proclamations tended to be exhortations or warnings to obey pre-existing laws, such as those that encouraged law officers to fulfil their duty by, for example, prosecuting Sabbath breakers. Certain aspects of commercial legislation were regulated through proclamations: the price of some commodities, such as coal and wine, rates of conveyance and the post office. Both the circulation of news and the productions of the press were controlled and regulated through proclamations, through the Stationers Company and the Office of the Licensor – but these offices were backed up by legislation. However, in the case of the coffee-houses it was unclear whether legislation backed up the proclamation and, as such, the proclamation seemed to rest solely on the King's authority. The suppression of the coffee-houses went to the heart of the constitutional debate of the seventeenth century, probing the powers the King had to act in government outside his Parliament.

The proclamation was to be effected by the recall of those licences issued by magistrates under the provisions of the Excise legislation. It commanded the magistrates to 'recall and make void all Licences at any time heretofore Granted, for the selling or Retailing of any Coffee, Chocolet, Sherbett or Tea', and to punish those who traded without such licence £5 a month.[19] Having withdrawn the licences, the magistrates could prosecute coffee-men for carrying on their business without them. This was a cunning, if somewhat tortuous, strategy, designed to give teeth to the proclamation. But although it was confidently worded, this legal device was not at all secure, as subsequent events made clear. If the government was forced to back down, it would demonstrate that the people were more powerful than the executive. Writing on 1 January 1676, a private newsletter declared that the people were in 'a mutinous condition in this towne upon the account of coffee-howses', and that 'The suppression of them will prove a tryall of skyll. All wytts are at worke to elude ye Proclamation.' Shutting the coffee-houses was certainly not going to be straightforward. As the letter writer noted, 'if the Government shew itselfe to feare the people I suspect the people will hardly feare the Government.'[20] The contest over the proclamation, the letter writer argues, would be a trial of the relative strength of the court and its opponents.

But to the coffee-men the question was not one of politics but economics, for the proclamation threatened to devastate their livelihoods. By 1675 the greatest among them, such as Thomas Garraway in Exchange Alley, had become wealthy men and although their status was much below any of the parliamentary politicians or the great merchants of the City, they had supporters and acquaintances among them. Thomas Garraway (variously spelt Garroway or Garway) had strong family connections to the coffee traders in the Levant Company and had a cousin, William Garroway, MP for Chichester, who was influential in opposition circles. To many City merchants the coffee-houses were of more commercial than political importance, for their free sociability had become central to the commercial prosperity of the City. Alarmed by this direct attack on their trade, the coffee-house keepers began to organise their resistance. Under Thomas Garraway's leadership, they drew up a petition pleading their case to the Privy Council. On 6 January a newsletter commented, 'Our Coffeemen are intending a Petition to ye King & Councell tomorrow to pray 6 months tyme to prepare for ye Execution of ye Proclamation this I heare.' Perhaps through Garraway's parliamentary connections, the coffee-men persuaded a privy councillor, Sir John Duncombe, to present the petition.[21] Duncombe was Chancellor of the Exchequer, but was somewhat isolated and out of favour by this time, satirised for his excessive deference and obsequity.[22] When he agreed to present the coffee-men's petition his decision was seen as an attack on Danby. A newsletter writer commented, 'Methinkes this lookes lyke an opposition to the Treasurer [Danby], and such a one as seems to make desynes, to be brutal with you, to be ill.'[23]

The unfairness and illegality of the proclamation caught the attention of some of the court's most gifted opponents, including Andrew Marvell, the poet turned Member of Parliament. Marvell's case against the proclamation was made in a poem entitled 'A Dialogue between the Two Horses' (1676), which he was forced to circulate in manuscript to avoid censorship. Although he had come to popular attention with his early lyric poems, his literary compositions in the 1670s were dominated by biting satires. This poem was no exception, ridiculing Charles II through an uncomplimentary comparison with his father, the executed Charles I. It was conceived as a conversation between two horses from celebrated royal equestrian statues in London, who talk together after their royal riders have absented themselves in pursuit of pleasure. The horses run through a litany of complaints about the financial mismanagement of the country, the ruinous cost of wars, the immoral behaviour of the King and court, the influence of the King's mistresses and the bribery and corruption of great men. They lament that the ordinary pleasures of the people, coffee and tobacco, have been taxed – ''Tis they that brought on us this scandalous yoke / Of excising our cups and taxing our smoke' – while the pleasures of the Kings, particularly their courtesans, go unpunished. But such talk makes Charles I's horse nervous and he reminds his friend that they ought to 'bridle our tongue' as speaking the truth is punished as treason. Their dialogue ends with a rousing, and seditious, chorus: 'A commonwealth! a commonwealth! we proclaim to the nation, / For the gods have repented the King's Restoration.' The poem concludes with an address celebrating the speech of brute animals as a prodigious prophecy predicting the fall of the younger tyrant, just like his father:

> When they take from the people the freedom of words,
> They teach them the sooner to fall to their swords.
> Let the City drink coffee and quietly groan;
> They that conquer'd the father won't be slaves to the son.
> It is wine and strong drinks make tumults increase;
> Choc'late, tea, and coffee are liquors of peace:
> No quarrels nor oaths amongst those that drink 'em;
> 'Tis Bacchus and brewers swear, damn 'em, and sink 'em!

Then, Charles, thy edicts against coffee recall:
There's ten times more treason in brandy and ale.[24]

In these lines Marvell defends coffee drinking as a peaceable activity, unlike the riotousness associated with alcoholic beverages. This contrast recalls the historically enduring construction of Cavalier drinking practices. But in Marvell's hands a neat reversal takes place: royalists raising toasts in ale, wine and brandy are equated with treason and rebellion, while citizens drinking coffee, chocolate and tea are associated with free speech and peace. Marvell's rallying cry remained the defence of the freedom of speech ('the freedom of words'), won by the revolutionary period ('They that conquer'd the father won't be slaves to the son'), which he saw as embedded in the sociable practices of the coffee-house.

In the face of the coffee-men's petition, and the popular hostility to the move, the government began to panic. Danby and Jones knew that at some stage their actions would be accountable to Parliament, even if it was unlikely to be soon. The case had to be watertight: but faith in the device to suppress the coffee-houses began to waver. On Thursday, 6 January it became clear that their petition would be heard by the King and his Privy Council: the highest authority in the land.

The coffee-men's petition

Late in the morning of Friday, 7 January Thomas Garraway and another coffee-man, Mr Taylor, gathered in Whitehall with Sir John Duncombe. They presented the appearance of simple, honest and loyal tradesmen, a habit which suited their position of supplication. The coffee-men cast themselves as merchants who obediently, legally and merely sold coffee. It was for this purpose, they reminded everyone, that they held the 'licences' from the magistrates, guaranteeing the payment of their Excise duties.[25] The law, they reasoned, recognised their place within the commercial world. As they further observed, the coffee trade paid a great deal of money in taxes and their trade was a lucrative source of revenue for the King. All this, they argued, was jeopardised by the proclamation. Furthermore, the proposed suppression of their trade would leave these poor and hard-working tradesmen in some considerable hardship: they would have great stocks of coffee left unsold, the price of which would collapse.[26] What kind of reward was this for the loyal taxpayer? From Duncombe's rooms in the Treasury the coffee-men walked through Whitehall Palace to the Cockpit, overlooking St James's Park, to the Council Chamber. While the Lords entered from the Presence Chamber on the King's side, through the Privy Gallery, the petitioners waited in an ante-room. Duncombe left them to go into the Council Room. Their petition was the only business of the day.[27] When the council was ready a messenger called them in, reminding them to remove their hats. Around a long table sat the Privy Councillors, at the head the King, wearing his hat. The Councillors all remained seated while the coffee-men were ushered in. A fire hissed in the chimney, candles guttered in the draught. The clerks at their side table shuffled their papers in a businesslike manner. The coffee-men kneeled at the open end of the table and placed their petition reverently on the board.

And then it was over: without speaking, the coffee-men were signalled to withdraw. The discussion of their case would be heard in secret. Although the Privy Council clerks kept a record of the decisions of the Council, its members took notes as they thought necessary. Williamson, the Secretary of State, kept an especially close account, meticulously recording the debate, then filing his notes methodically among his papers.[28] After the coffee-men withdrew a clerk read out their petition, which was, in terms of law, a simple appeal for clemency: they wished for more time to sell their existing stocks of coffee. But they also launched a carefully worded defence of their licences to trade. The case was debatable. The discussion would focus on the proclamation's method rather than its purpose: that is, whether it was lawful for the government to recall the coffee sellers' licences. Councillors were expected to give their advice freely and openly: all were equals within the Council. But there were protocols to be observed. They spoke in order of seniority and only once unless permission was granted to speak again.

The first to speak was the Attorney-General, Sir William Jones, the architect of the proclamation.[29] Jones was a man in his mid forties, whose brusque manner had made enemies among some courtiers, who described him as 'a man of morose temper', with 'a roughness in his deportment, that was very disagreeable'.[30] In his broad West Country accent he explained how the proclamation was supposed to work and expatiated on the key problem, the nature of the coffee sellers' licences. If the licences merely gave permission for the coffee-men to trade, he argued, 'then they may be revoked'. He admitted, however, that some licences, such as those granted to wine sellers, were granted a specific period of time ('time certain') and in this case they could not be revoked before the end of that time. Jones was uncertain about the nature of the coffee sellers' licences because the law was unclear. The 'time certain' of the coffee sellers' licences was not stated in the statute, but was inferred from practice. Although he thought that all the coffee-house licences had expired in the county of Middlesex, he was forced to admit that in London 'they have licences for a time certain'.[31] If this was so, the recall of the licences was much more doubtful. Jones's enemies within the Council saw a weakness.

The Privy Council continued their debate. Consulting the law books in the Council Room's book press, it became clear that the nature of the licences was left obscure in the statute. The 'primary intent of this law was to secure the duty' rather than to regulate the coffee-house keepers or the behaviour of their clients. The senior judges in the room could add no further clarification. With the discussion going in circles it was decided to examine the coffee-men in more detail. Garraway and Taylor were brought back into the council chamber. Kneeling at the end of the table, their hats in their hands, the coffee-men waited nervously for the questioning to begin. As they were aware, non-cooperation could end with their imprisonment in the Tower. Taylor became florid in his sycophantic supplications, denying that he or any of the coffee-men had 'anything to object to the legality of the prohibition', adding a great many obsequious entreaties and pleas in his defence that they came merely to 'fly to the King's mercy', seeking his 'leniency to them'. To Williamson's gratification, things then took a surprising turn. Taylor came up with a proposal, that the coffee-men would accept stricter regulations: as Williamson's notes say, they 'Pray favour upon regulations, &c'. The coffee-men's proposal was that, firstly, the Excise men should give certificates 'only with loyal men' and secondly that they would 'take security to discover what they know or hear said prejudicial to the Government'. The coffee-men were offering to be spies and to pay for the privilege.[32]

The coffee-men having been sent out again, the Lords deliberated further. The device to recall their licences would not work, for the law was 'ill-expressed'. 'Reasoning out' the law, Williamson testily scrawled in his conclusion, 'the meaning of the Act is not to license or empower the vending of the commodity, and, though no time be specified in the licence, yet necessarily the licence ought to be construed to be of the extent of the certificate', which was three years. As such, it seemed unlikely that they could be simply withdrawn as Attorney Jones planned. This was, of course, a humiliating reversal and Jones sought permission to get further legal advice about the matter. The Privy Council broke up as dusk fell in the cold evening air. The waiting delegation of coffee-men were told the proclamation would be reversed and they would be given six months to prove their loyalty. As they jubilantly went home towards the City, Danby's enemies celebrated, recognising that this concession was a major retreat. Within hours, news of their discussions was being debated around the town. Richard Langhorne wrote to his patron, 'This day ye Councill satt only to consider ye Petition of ye Coffee sellers and have respyted ye Execution of ye Proclamation by giving tyme to sell Coffee for six months.'[33]

The next day Jones called an emergency meeting of all higher judges resident in London over the Christmas season: perhaps they could rescue his proclamation.[34] They agreed that the act did require the coffee-men to have a licence and the magistrates were permitted to refuse a licence at their discretion. But with regard to the key point whether licences could be revoked before their end, Roger North noted, they could 'not agree in opinion, but returned [. . .] that there remained some doubts'. As one judge observed, 'The intent of the Act is to raise a revenue, not to licence a trade.' The judges concluded that the recall of the licences was unworkable. But they were more optimistic about the proposed reforms to the licences. Williamson noted that they agreed 'That of those that have licences granted duly, security may be demanded for the good behaviour &c. and good order'. If such licences were issued an individual coffee-house could be closed, should seditious activity be detected there.

The judges all agreed that coffee-houses were a nuisance. Sir Edward Turnor, Chief Justice of the Court of Exchequer, complained, 'By the common law retailers of coffee may retail [coffee] as the shops do, i.e. for people to buy and go away, but to sit there and drink it, 40 or 50 in a room, may be a nuisance, and for that reason a licence may be refused.' North agreed: coffee-houses were in the 'Nature of Comon Assemblys to discours of Matters of State, News & Great persons, as they are nurserys of Idleness, & pragmaticallness, & hindred ye expence of ye Native provisions, they might be thought a Comon Nusance'.[35] North reveals here how ignorant the great men of the court were about the popular culture of the coffee-houses in the City. Rather than being focused on commerce and trade, in his estimation coffee-house conversations were a kind of idleness that could serve no useful purpose. In them, people talked together on matters of state, debating and circulating news and intelligence and, worst of all, evaluating the conduct of the 'Great persons' at court. To North, such discussions erased an important boundary between the rulers and the ruled and, as such, constituted the coffee-houses a common nuisance, against which the magistrates were bound to act. While licences could not be revoked comprehensively, conditions might be added to their regulations, which would serve to control the coffee-men's behaviour.

Williamson and the judges saw the advantage in the coffee-men's proposals for further regulation. Williamson began to draft some ideas, making a list of the desirable qualities or 'expedients' in a reform of the coffee-house, and the conditions they might ask of the coffee-men and add to the licences:

> Expedients: – 1. Not in common rooms. 2. Good behaviour from the master of the house &c. to the extent of those of alehouses. 3. On any information found of words spoken &c. in any coffee house and not discovered by the master whether he were present or no, he to forfeit his recognizance. 4. Printed or written libels &c., letters &c. that are publicly spread or uttered in their house, the master to be answerable on bond.[36]

The regulation of ale houses provided a model of how to proceed. Ale-house keepers had to sign recognisances which forbade the publican to allow any gaming, opening on the Sabbath, drinking of ale in silver tankards, 'tipling after nine o'clock', or 'harbouring rogues or master-less men'.[37] Williamson's first 'expedient' was the most far-reaching, but was not adopted. He proposed that coffee-houses should be forbidden to have common rooms, for he perceived that it was the promiscuous meeting of all kinds of people, their communal discussion and their collective reasoning, that was the source of their seditious power. The second, third and fourth of Williamson's expedients sought specifically to control the coffee-houses' circulation of printed and manuscript libels. All these provisions were enacted in some way. The Privy Council decided to add a set of conditions to the coffee-men's licences, preventing the circulation of 'libels, papers, scandalous &c.

and unlicensed books' in coffee-houses and requiring, as per statute, the coffee-men 'to give information within two days to a justice of the peace' if they heard any such scandalous reports.[38] The coffee-men would be Williamson's spies from henceforth.

The 'Additional Proclamation Concerning Coffee-Houses' was officially published on Saturday, 8 January 1676, although no news of it reached the coffee-houses until the Monday following. At Garraway's, Hooke discoursed with 'a one eyed travelling painter' about the 'proclamations tolerating coffee house[s] till midsummer and against Libellen'. The newsletters noted, 'Wee have this day had a Proclamation proclaimed for suspending a Proclamation which was Tenn days since proclaimed in relation to ye Coffee houses.'[39] In compassionate response to the 'humble Petition' of the coffee retailers, the preamble announced, the King gave his permission for the coffee-houses to trade for a further six months, until 24 June 1676. The proclamation noted the coffee sellers' humble confession of the 'Miscarriages and Abuses committed in such Coffee-houses', and their expressions of 'true Sorrow', and their promises of 'utmost Care and endeavour to prevent the like happening in the future'. To enact this, the coffee retailers were required to enter into recognisances for their good behaviour, with a surety of £500, the conditions of which were detailed on a form printed at the bottom of the proclamation:

> The Condition of this Recognizance is such, That if the above-bound A.B. shall at all times hereafter, so long as he shall be Permitted or Licenced to Sell and Retail Coffee, Chocolate and Tea, use his utmost endeavour to prevent and hinder all Scandalous Papers, Books and Libels concerning the Government, or the Publick Ministers thereof, from being brought into his House, or there Read, Perus'd or Divulg'd; And to prevent and hinder all and every person and persons from declaring, uttering and divulging in his said House, all manner of False and Scandalous Reports of the Government, or any of the Ministers thereof: And in case any such papers, Books or Libels, shall be brought into his said House, and there openly Read, Perus'd and Divulg'd, or in case any such False or Scandalous Reports shall be there openly declared, utter'd or divulg'd, if the said A.B. shall within Two days respectively next ensuing, give information thereof to one of his Majesties Principal Secretaries of State, or to some one of His Majesties Justices of the Peace, then this Recognizance to be void, &c.[40]

On the publication of this proclamation the magistrates were to use this form to ensure the loyal behaviour of the coffee sellers. The Privy Council also offered a reward of £20 for those discovering libel writers and private printing presses.[41]

After the second proclamation the coffee-men appeared to have been turned into domestic spies. Rather than allowing their common rooms to be the centre of the circulation of news and libels, they were to be at the forefront of the effort to control them. But the proclamation not only had to be issued, it had to be enforced, and in many locations the magistrates were likely to turn a blind eye to the coffee-men and their clientele. In the following decades the coffee-houses continued to be emblematic locations for debate on public affairs by those outside the higher echelons of political life. Through such discussions and debates, a new notion emerged that there could be such a thing as an unofficial knowledge of affairs of state, that the common people had an interest in evaluating how they were governed. Such a notion, however embryonic here, finds its legacy in the modern notion of public opinion.

Coffee-house sedition after the proclamation

After the second proclamation the authorities launched a crackdown on religious and political dissent. Magistrates were urged to take action against seditious libels, clandestine printing presses and dissenters meeting in conventicles. Williamson's newsletter announced on 18 January that 'Several persons have of late been taken into custody for holding seditious discourses and spreading false news, and some discovery has already been made upon the proclamation against libels'.[42] The Amsterdam Coffee-House, behind the Royal Exchange, was raided on 16 January in search of 'a scandalous treatise affirming the lawfulness of polygamy'. A coffee-house keeper of Sheer Lane was caught transcribing libels in the office of a Mr Petit of the Inner Temple, having been revealed to the authorities after an informant read 'the proclamation for the discovery of seditious libels'.[43]

Ironically, the proclamation was turned against one of Williamson's own coffee-house spies, Richard Bower of Yarmouth. After a particularly incendiary letter in June 1676 denouncing the Nonconformists who held high office in the town, Bower found himself brought before the Yarmouth magistrates for allegedly selling beer and cider as well as coffee. Using the provisions of the new coffee licences, they shut up his coffee-house and wrote to the Secretary of State protesting his 'scandalous letter, a libel we may call it, written to you by Bowers, a coffee seller' of 'uneasy and peevish humours'.[44] To prevent him trading, the magistrates seized the pewter vessels he used to brew coffee and denied him a new coffee licence, despite his payment of the bond for the Excise. Both sides in the dispute invoked the text of the proclamation in their battle: although the magistrates must have enjoyed the incongruity of using the proclamation to close down a government spy.

Reverberations from the proclamation fiasco were also felt among the elite. In 1676 the Earl of Shaftesbury and the Duke of Buckingham were busy in the coffee-houses organising their followers, so that they might be ready when Parliament was recalled. Williamson recorded that 'the coffeehouse where the Earl of Shaftesbury vents out all his thoughts and designs is John's coffeehouse', perhaps meaning Jonathan's in Exchange Alley.[45] With their supporters, Shaftesbury and Buckingham co-ordinated a spirited pamphlet war expressing opposition to the long prorogation, circulating copies printed on their clandestine presses around the coffee-houses.[46] In the summer of 1676, while Parliament was prorogued, both Shaftesbury and Buckingham moved their London residences into the City, where the great lords would be handily placed for the Exchange and the coffee-houses around it. Their move was widely interpreted as an attempt to broaden the opposition from its parliamentary base into a wider interest or party, including City merchants, Protestant radicals and *çi devant* republicans. From henceforth the opposition extensively cultivated the distinct sociability of the City coffee-houses as a defining base for their faction, physically removing themselves from the King's court at Whitehall.

By the middle of 1676 the City, political dissent and coffee-houses had become virtually synonymous. Agitation in the coffee-houses centred on the defence of Francis Jenks, a City linen draper who had been prosecuted for delivering a sensationalist speech in June calling for an election for a new Parliament.[47] The King's followers continued to regard matters of state as being above ordinary citizens, even though such topics were the talk of all the coffee-houses. A newsletter noted on Wednesday, 28 June that 'A paper has been throwne about in Coffee houses' reflecting on Jenks's persecution (noting 'by the way' that the coffee-houses were 'still in being notwithstanding Midsummer day is past').[48] On the evening of 14 September 1676 the Duke of Buckingham arrived at Garraway's Coffee-House where, in the upstairs common room, he met with a party of men (Hooke noted his presence in his *Diary*).[49] Buckingham's associates included the republican lawyer Major John Wildman, a veteran Leveller associated with several republican plots in the 1660s, and an important financier and goldsmith of the City, Alderman Backwell, one of the wealthiest men in the kingdom.

Such a meeting of republicanism and City money was portentous, suggesting that various disparate factions were coalescing. Holding this meeting in such a public place was a media spectacle designed to advertise their plans to everyone. According to later reports 'the Duke had taken a cup of tea and drunk a health to another Parliament or a new Parliament, and to all those honest gentlemen of it that would give the King no money'. Other reports made his discourse sound much more inflammatory, claiming that the Duke had drunk a health to Jenks and his party, and more generally to the 'confusion' of the court's aims. Among those listening to the Duke was someone in the pay of the government, for the day after, on Friday, 15 September, the manuscript newsletter produced by Williamson's Letter Office pronounced

> The Duke of Buckingham was last night in ye great Coffee house in the Citty in an excellent talking temper where he had a very full audience, before which he declared himself freely & aloud with out enjoyning any secrecy that he was absolutely for a new parliament upon which subject he enlarg'd himself very openly & with liberty & plainness enough in conscience.[50]

To Williamson's mind the Duke was declaring himself so freely, loudly and publicly that he placed himself in a state of near treason.

About a week after the event Garraway had still not reported it to the Secretary of State. He claimed, however, that when Buckingham visited he was away in Edmonton, a village north of London, from where he did not return until late at night. Garraway had examined his servants and his wife about what had been said, but none had heard anything particular themselves, although his wife admitted to hearing snippets from men coming down from upstairs. Until he 'heard tell where to fix' the libel, and he had reliable witnesses to what had been said, Garraway did not see what he could report to Williamson. But as the controversy grew about what had happened that evening, Garraway's nonchalance evaporated. Evidently in something of a panic, he realised that if this scandal got out of control his personal alibi might be insufficient to save himself or the coffee-house. In a hurry, he found a reliable witness to what was said in Anthony Parsons, a wealthy City merchant, one of the Farmers of the Excise, who was willing to admit that he was in the upper room of the coffee-house where the Duke was that night, although at another table and not of his party. There, he told Garraway, he had heard the Duke drink his health to the new Parliament, but he heard nothing about Jenks or other seditious causes.[51] Armed with this intelligence, real or concocted, Garraway hurried to Whitehall, where in Williamson's presence he gave an 'information' to this effect. As he spoke, Williamson recorded the three-page statement by hand, and had a clerk make a fine copy for circulation to the King and others. Through his careful melioration of Buckingham's words, Garraway got away with it this time.

Coffee-houses, however, continued to be troublesome, partly because the government wanted to use them for contradictory purposes, both the collection of intelligence and the suppression of sedition. Pepys got in trouble in October 1676 when he found strategically sensitive information about military orders openly displayed in a coffee-house. The subsequent investigation discovered that it was Secretary Williamson's own letter office who had provided the information in the coffee-house. A servant at the Rainbow Coffee-House in Fleet Street, Stephen Harris, was interrogated for saying that he had overheard a libellous statement as he was serving coffee up and down the room, to the effect that Parliament had been bribed to pass a piece of legislation.[52] In February 1678, Thomas Garraway informed Williamson that one of the servants in his coffee-house had been receiving letters containing 'proceedings of the House and other papers' from one Edward Sing of Brook's Wharf 'contrary to my will and without my knowledge'. As Garraway explained, 'sending any sort of news here in manuscript' would bring him under His Majesty's displeasure. The confession was 'somewhat hard', he complained, 'since almost all the coffee-houses about me have the confidence to take in all sorts of papers and especially those persons who by order of Council ought to have been bound to the contrary'.[53] Other coffee-men were not so fortunate: because he 'made it his dayly practice to expose to the view [. . .] diverse seditious pamphlets and libels', William Pearce, who kept a coffee-house at Warminster, was summoned before the Quarter Sessions and forbidden to sell coffee after 10 January 1682.[54]

What the coffee-men and newsletter writers understood, but the court and authorities did not wish to recognise, was that the coffee-houses were functioning as a gauge of public opinion. Taking their temperature, the newsletters implied, was a more reliable guide to the actual opinions of the common people than the assumptions stated by their political superiors. The court and ministry assumed that ordinary people did not need to know about the state and its affairs: but it was manifest that 'affairs of state' no longer simply concerned the deliberations of the King and his courtiers. The government's reliance on the coffee-houses suggests that rather than simply regulating coffee-houses and sedition (through recognisances and censorship) the government had engaged in a competition for their attention, using them to create gossip as well as report on it.

Through the 1680s the coffee-house remained firmly associated with the production and dissemination of seditious libels. After the expiration of the licensing system that controlled the press in May 1679, the coffee-houses were deluged by a torrent of newspapers, periodicals, pamphlets and satires.[55] Entering one, a commentator wrote, one would find 'a crowd of idle Pamphlets presented on the Tables to view'; and pamphleteers themselves were the 'Cumber and Pest of every Coffee-house'.[56] In 1679 the proposal for the suppression of coffee-houses was revived. A complaint lodged with the Privy Council alleged that 'scandalous and malicious discourses' were 'most frequently promulgated' there. Debating whether 'they should be put down or not', the council would have moved against them were it not for some coffee merchants pleading that such a move would ruin them.[57] Just as in 1675, the coffee sellers defended the lawfulness of their trade, pleading that it was a branch of honest commerce. In the following years the controversies around the 'Popish' plots, sham plots and conspiracies against the King brought forth propaganda from all sides, as did the events of the Exclusion Crisis of the early 1680s. Although Parliament would decide the weighty issue of the Succession, one pamphleteer noted, 'There is no Coffee-house, and few private houses, but their Table-talk is of these things.'[58]

The Tory periodical *Heraclitus Ridens* criticised the 'Coffee-house Statesmen, who think themselves wiser than the Privy-Council, or the Sages of the Law', and paired the 'Conventicle and Coffee-House' together, complaining 'there's no great difference, but that the Law allows one and not the other', for 'they are both full of Noise and Phanaticks'.[59] The Amsterdam Coffee-House especially became infamous as the location of radical Protestant opinion, the home of notorious controversialists such as Titus Oates. In September 1683 Tory propagandists were delighted to learn that he had been involved in a fight at the Amsterdam Coffee-House, when Oates's incendiary claims provoked a scuffle with another gentleman. While Oates hit him with his cane, his opponent, wedged in on the other side of the table, could not make him a better return than throwing a dish of warm coffee in his face. The symbolism of this 'ceremony' appeared endlessly amusing to the Tories.[60]

Charles II's attempt to suppress the coffee-houses cast a long shadow. That the proclamation failed was widely understood as a confirmation not only of the Stuart conspiracy against parliamentary government, but also that freedom of speech was deeply embedded in the British constitution. In the early eighteenth century the Whig historian, John Oldmixon, argued the proclamation gave evidence of Charles II's 'endeavour to subvert the Constitution, and subject this Kingdom to Arbitrary Power *Ecclesiastical* and *Civil*'.[61] The great Huguenot historian Paul de Rapin argued that the proclamation gave evidence of 'the lasting Opposition between the particular Interests of the King, and those of the *English* Nation'.[62] David Hume argued in his *History of England* (1757) that the coffee-house proclamation was 'an act of power [. . .] grounded entirely on the prerogative', against an institution 'for which the English have long retained a mighty fondness'. The proclamation, he concluded, was an incident that tended 'strongly to mark the genius . . . of Charles's administration, during this period'.[63] These historians kept alive the memory of these events, animating the privileged place of the coffee-house in the culture of the period as the meeting place between affairs of state and the common people. In a debate in the House of Commons on 20 March 1771 on parliamentary privilege, the Hon. George Dempster, MP for Forfar and Fife, argued that in abusing its privileges the ministry could 'get into the same sort of business as Charles the Second did, when he wanted to shut up Coffee houses'.[64] The defence of the coffee-houses, it was understood, was a defence of freedom of speech.

CHAPTER EIGHT

The Coffee-House Trade

In May 1663, when the magistrates of the City of London commissioned a survey to establish how many coffee-house keepers traded in the wards of the City, they found there were eighty-two keepers of such establishments.[1] Even though every adult could remember that only a little more than a decade earlier such places had not existed, coffee-houses had very quickly established themselves as an important trade in the City of London. As the magistrates recognised, at the centre of the coffee-house business was the coffee-man: part showman, part technician, part accountant, part entrepreneur. Entering a coffee-house, a customer would be greeted by its master:

> Then comes the *Coffee-man* to greet you,
> With Welcome Sir, let me entreat you,
> To tell me what you'l please to have,
> For I'm your humble humble slave.[2]

Although much of the social and sensory experience of the coffee-house was beyond their control, the coffee-men worked hard to shape their customers' expectations of the experience. In the 1660s and 1670s, all those involved in producing the coffee-house experience (coffee-house keepers, coffee suppliers, news vendors and, increasingly, coffee-house customers) co-ordinated a campaign to secure the cultural positioning of the coffee-house. Central to this process was building the brand, not just of coffee, but of the English coffee-house experience.

Like his coffee-house, the coffee-man, as a wholly new type of tradesman, became a focus of considerable curiosity. 'The coffee-man', the poet Samuel Butler declared in 1667, 'keeps a coffee market, where people of all qualities and conditions meet, to trade in foreign drinks and newes, ale, smoak, and controversy.'[3] According to R. Campbell's *The London Tradesman* (1747), an eighteenth-century business manual, 'The Coffee-House-Man is a kind of Publican; he sells Coffee, but most of them sell other Liquors, of which they make large Profits.' The trade of a coffee-man, Campbell argued, could be likened to that of a vintner, who 'buys neat Wines, and his Profits arise from the Differences between buying and selling'. Campbell's obvious point about the source of the coffee-man's profits was rendered more pointed by the fact that though the universally agreed price of coffee, from soon after its introduction into London, was one penny a dish, the price of raw coffee fluctuated according to quality and availability. Like the vintner, Campbell concluded, few coffee-men were 'contented with that reasonable Profit'.[4] Squeezed by tight profit margins, the coffee-man was often tempted to extend them by all sorts of tricks and subterfuges, including adulteration, dilution and reusing grounds. One wit who thought he was given a short measure joked in 1735:

> A Clergyman, who had a *Dish* of Coffee administered to him, ask'd the Master of the House if he was not bred a *Printer*. No, said he, *but I understand something of* Books. *I imagin'd so*, replies the Doctor, *because I never met with a handsomer* Margin *to a Coffee-Cup in my Life*.[5]

This was only one of many methods of skinning customers. The coffee-house was always a business: if the coffee-man didn't make a profit, bankruptcy or debtor's prison awaited him. The market for beverages was characterised by cut-throat competition, so that coffee-houses competed on price, quality and sociability, not only among themselves but also across the whole drinks and entertainment market.

Some successful coffee-house keepers used their Levantine or Mediterranean origins to establish their standing, in the manner of Pasqua Rosee. One noted early coffee-house keeper was a Greek, George Constantine, who had come to England as a young sailor. Having been raised in the Ottoman Empire, he was skilled in the preparation of coffee and, once in England, opened a coffee-house in Wapping.[6] A bustling maritime community, the riverside at Wapping was a thicket of docks and wharves, where ships from around the world unloaded their wares. The long, winding road of Wapping High Street next to the river was filled with seamen and dock workers, their families and followers, a population which made this a notably cosmopolitan region of the city. Despite this, by May 1663 he had moved his coffee-house to a better location in Threadneedle Street, next to St Christopher's Church, in Broad Street ward, close to the north entrance of the Royal Exchange.[7] Constantine's advertisement in *The Intelligencer* (23 January 1665), claimed that his coffee, made of 'the right *Turky* Berry' was 'as cheap and as good [. . .] as is any where to be had for mony', adding that 'people may there be taught to prepare the said Liquors *gratis*'.[8] He was noticed among the foreign merchants of coffee in the anonymous verses of *The Character of a Coffee-House* (1665):

> Constantine the *Grecian*,
> Who fourteen years was th'onely man
> That made *Coffee* for th'great *Bashaw*,
> Although the man he never saw:[9]

His business moved again after the Great Fire in 1666 to Devereux Court, just outside Temple Bar off the Strand. This tiny bow-legged alley, built by Nicholas Barbon on the site of Essex House in 1676, was thronged with lawyers and judges, for it served as an entrance to the Temple, site of two Inns of Court and thus a major residential and working space for the legal profession. Several famous coffee-houses were established there by the beginning of the eighteenth century. Constantine's coffee-house, known to all as the Grecian Coffee-House, was still kept by him in 1727, when James Douglas published his research on coffee-house history. 'To this Person, the oldest Coffee-Man now alive in *London*, and perhaps *Christendom*,' Douglas said, 'I am beholden for several facts here mention'd.'[10] The longevity of George's peripatetic business nonetheless suggests something of the profitability of the trade in this period.

Coffee-men were often the subject of satire, both for their trade and for themselves: depicted as mountebanks and charlatans, showmen who retailed luxurious trifles. Among the many impositions of Mr Black-burnt the coffee-man depicted in the satirical *Maidens Complaint against Coffee* (1663) is the charge that he makes extortionate profits. This kind of satire is a mock dialogue aping the legal form of the complaint (a charge that somebody has committed a crime): it is unlikely to have been written by a woman. The maidens' complaint is not only that the coffee-house keeps their men from their homes and wastes their time but, further, that the drying effect of the coffee makes them impotent. One of the complainants, Mistress Troublesome, the wife of a usurer, accuses Mr Black-burnt of driving so 'fine a trade' with his 'cursed liquor' that it amounts to extortion. In his defence, Black-burnt claims that his 'gain is but ten pence in the shilling, and I am as well contented with that as he that gets pounds'. For every shilling invested in his coffee-house, Black-burnt makes 10 pence profit: which, as Mistress Troublesome observes, is a healthy profit, equivalent to £83 6s 8p for each £100 invested.[11]

There were few trades that would offer profits so high: even a usurer could not make as much with his extortionate rates of interest. In reply to the maidens' satire, a pseudonymous defender of coffee replied with an apology for coffee called *The Coffee-Mans Granado Discharged Upon the Maidens Complaint Against Coffee* (1663), written by 'Don Bollicosgo Armuthaz' and designed to stoke the fires of controversy. Written in clumsy rhyming couplets, it takes the form of a 'Dialogue' between Democritus, a journalist-writer, and Mr Black-burnt the coffee-man. The verses describe how the coffee-man wishes to burn the maidens' 'Lying Pamphlet' in 'scorching fire', but the journalist persuades him that any publicity is good for his business, flattering him by observing that 'for health' coffee is 'beyond all Cordial drink'. Impressed by this canny line of argument, Black-Burnt accepts his proposal to write a book for £5, which will 'raise' his 'Coffee higher far then Sack' (sherry) so that even the gods will drink it. Democritus promises 'to make your Drink Infallible to all', so that despite being as black as ink it will seem crystal and helpful.[12] The blizzard of satires on coffee-houses in the Restoration period, which supposedly attack their product, customers and sociability, were a form of marketing that launched specious controversies to keep the product in customers' minds.

The satirist's attention was also attracted by the women who kept coffee-houses. In the magistrates survey in 1663 two women coffee-house keepers were identified: Widow Bowman in Cornhill and Widow Allen in Farringdon-within.[13] These two were by no means the only ones. Newspapers and magazines contain advertisements and notices from Anne Blunt, proprietor of Blunt's Coffee-House, Cannon Street, in 1672; Widow Wells, proprietor of Mrs Well's Coffee-House in Scotland Yard, between 1696 and 1712; Jenny Man, proprietor of Jenny Man's Coffee-House in Charing Cross, in 1712; Jane Rudd, who as proprietor of Widow Rudd's Coffee-House in the Haymarket was found bankrupt in May 1731; and Mrs Edwards, proprietor of Daniel's

Coffee-House in Temple Bar and later Edward's Coffee-House in Fleet Street, in 1739.[14] So although they were not expected as customers in the coffee-house, women's presence in the coffee room was nonetheless not unusual. Many wits, in fact, observed that they played a crucial part in the sociability of the coffee-house.[15] The male preserve of the coffee-house, its distinct masculine sociability, included a significant amount of flirtation across the bar. To male customers the serving woman was one of the attractions. Celebrating this flirtatious interaction confirmed the heterosexual interests of the clientele. The Grub Street satirist Tom Brown commented in 1702 that

> Every Coffee-House is illuminated both without and within doors; without by a fine Glass Lanthorn and within by a Woman so *light* and *splendid*, you may see through her with the help of a Perspective. At the Bar the good man always places a charming Phillis or two, who invite you by their amourous Glances into their smoaky Territories, to the loss of your Sight.[16]

Many depictions of the coffee-house show the coffee-woman surrounded by male admirers, as if she was placed there simply to entice customers into staying longer. Others saw her presence as a threat to moral order, arguing that her seductive charms were a threat to lead the coffee drinkers into vice. An anonymous pamphleteer complained that there was 'scarce a Coffee-Hut but affords a Tawdry Woman, a wonton Daughter, or a Buxome Maide, to accomodate Customers'.[17] In the early eighteenth century Laurence Eusden wrote to *The Spectator* about the beautiful coffee-women, or idols, of his time. 'There are in six or seven Places of this City, Coffee-houses kept by Persons of [the] Sisterhood' of Idols, apparently inspired by the female proprietor of the Widow's Coffee-House in Devereux Court, located off the Strand near the Temple. Eusden continues:

> These Idols sit and receive all day long the Adoration of the Youth within such and such Districts; I know, in particular. Goods are not entered as they ought to be at the Custom-House, nor Law-Reports perused at the Temple, by reason of one Beauty who detains the young Merchants too long near Change, and another Fair one who keeps the Students at her House when they should be at Study.

The adoration inspired by these coffee-women, Eusden elaborates, drives young men to suicide, distorts the proper operation of the market (as the love-lorn customers accept poor-quality coffee) and worse, 'poisons' the conversation of those 'who come to do Business, and talk Politics' – presumably because the 'Heartburnings' of love pervert the masculine discourse of the assembly.[18] Eusden sees coquetry, and women in general, as a poison or 'Ratsbane' to coffee-house sociability, which ought properly to be orderly, conversational, convivial and homosocial. Another moralist complained that this endless flirtation ruined the servants too, 'dizzied with these idle Compliments'. 'These Creatures being puffd up with the fulsome flattery of a set of Flesh-Flies, that are constantly buzzing about 'em, carry themselves with the utmost Insolence imaginable', until at last, by driving away 'Men of Sobriety and Business', their flirtatious behaviour makes the place 'a Den of Vagabonds and Rake-Hells'.[19]

In the eighteenth century a minor literary genre developed relating the histories of some of the more outrageous exploits of coffee-women.[20] A short scandalous biography, *The Velvet Coffee-Woman* (1728) celebrated the 'Gallantries and Amours' of Anne Rochford. Born the daughter of a servant, Rochford's early life showed promise as a property developer, but after an unexplained turn in her fortunes, referred to as the 'Vicissitudes of Female-Affairs', Rochford was forced to become a proprietor of a coffee-house and a prostitute, two occupations she saw as nearly synonymous. A celebrated beauty (described as 'the Pine-Apple of Great Britain' because she included the 'Flavours of all the delicious fruits in the World'), Rochford associated especially with rakes and libertines, gambling and drinking with the best of them.[21] Her coffee-house became a fashionable destination, if not quite a reputable business. Macky, in his *Journey Through England* (1714) mentions Mrs Rochford's as one of the coffee-houses where 'the Beau-Monde assembles' every day.[22] She earned her unusual cognonym, 'the Velvet Coffee-woman', after a notable public scandal, when she was introduced to the King, dressed in an expensive velvet dress, thereby giving the appearance of virtue, wealth and merit.[23] As purveyors of gossip and scandal, and as subjects themselves of rumour and innuendo, the coffee-women were dangerous sexual non-conformists.

As proprietor of King's Coffee-House in Covent Garden, Moll King was also the subject of a scandalous biography. Born the daughter of a shoemaker and a market seller, she married Thomas King, known as

'Smooth'd-Fac'd-Tom', a gentleman educated at Eton and at King's College, Cambridge, who ran away to London to enjoy the pleasures of the town by working in a 'bawdy-house'. As one of the 'gayest Ladies of the Town', a friend of the notorious courtesans Nanny Cotton and Sally Salisbury, Moll was an attractive catch. With the profits from a nut stall, Tom and Moll opened a small coffee-house in a single-storey shed on the south side of the market opposite Southampton Street, which Moll continued to run after Tom's death. Although unprepossessing in appearance, this little 'Hovel' grew rapidly, attracting huge crowds of people, especially very late at night. Because their main customers comprised their fellow market sellers, their coffee-house opened at one or two o'clock in the morning, especially on market days in the fruit season. It soon became the favourite 'Rendezvous' of 'young Rakes, and their pretty Misses', the principal office of their 'nocturnal Intrigues'. Its fame was commemorated in the prologue to Henry Fielding's *Covent Garden Tragedy* (1732), where the poet asks 'What rake is ignorant of King's Coffee-House?'; a question he answered with a witty footnote explaining it was 'A Place in *Covent-Garden* Market, well known to all Gentlemen to whom Beds are unknown'.[24] In its habits, Moll's coffee-house was very like a brothel, frequented by a remarkable variety of people, from the nobility wearing the 'Star and Garter', to footmen and market sellers, drawn hither to be ' sure of finding a Nymph in waiting'.

> Here you might see Ladies of Pleasure, who appear'd apparelled like Person's of Quality, not at all inferior to them in Dress, attended by Fellows habited like Footmen, who were their Bullies, and wore their Disguise, the more easily to deceive the unwary Youths, who were so unhappy as to Cast their Eyes upon these *deceitful Water-Wag-Tails*.[25]

Moll only defended herself from prosecution for running a bagnio or brothel by ensuring there were no beds on the premises. Well acquainted with 'low and genteel Life', Moll King's biography advertised both the coffee-woman's transgressive qualities, and the riotous, bawdy and vulgar sociability of her establishment.

Below the coffee-house keeper were several layers of employees. For the running of the business the most important were the serving staff, known at the time as drawers or coffee-boys, whose primary responsibility was, of course, to serve coffee. Their work extended further, however, to include many other duties for the master of the house, such as preparing coffee under his orders, cleaning and carrying, and for the customers, fetching pipes and newspapers, taking messages and running errands around the neighbourhood. The coffee-boys were officially registered as apprentices, bound to their employers and their City guild. Campbell's *London Tradesman* (1747) described the kind of boy who would be an appropriate apprentice to a coffee-man. Such a 'Lad', he said, 'must be an acute, active Fellow, quick of Apprehension, nimble in his Heels, ready handed and complaisant in his Disposition; he ought to read and write, and may be bound about Twelve Years of Age; some of them even as Drawers make very good Bread of it.'[26]

Campbell concluded, however, that the 'Trade of the Master' was scarcely worth learning, because as it was held in 'general bad repute', it 'is neither so large nor so certain as formerly'. Even by the late seventeenth century the guild system was in decline and the apprenticeship was often no more than a form of badly paid labour with long working hours, a fertile field for satirists. The first play set in a coffee-house, an anonymous five-act comedy, was called *Knavery in all Trades: or, The Coffee-House* (1664), performed by apprentices. It features four boys, each apprenticed to a master in the victualling industries: a vintner called Compound, an oilman called Pickle, a Grocer called Pepper and a victualler called Subtler. Much of the plot of the play turns on the spectacle of their apprentices, and their wives, defrauding their masters of commodities and labour by a systematic practice of work evasion and pilfering. In celebrating the apprentices' petty acts of resistance, the play satirises the corrupt nature of modern trade, in which every merchant lives on credit, cheats everyone else and avoids his creditors.

Knavery is the ruling passion. A nearby coffee-house, kept by Mahoone, a Turkish coffee-man, is the most extreme, and ridiculous, example of this. As Mahoone reveals, the coffee-house, which alone of all the businesses is full, retails a product which is nothing but a fraud and a cheat: a foul medicine invented by the devil and dressed up as a luxury. The coffee-house is the epitome of the modern world, in all its fallen wonder. The third act opens to find 'The Coffee-House discovered', described in the stage directions as having 'three or four Tables set forth, on which are placed small wax-Lights, Pipes, and Diurnalls'. The first to enter is Mahoone, 'trimming up the Tables, his Man ordering the Fire-pots and China Cups, his Wife in the Barr, his

Maid imployed about his Chocolet'. When some gentlemen enter, Mahoone asks 'Vat vill you drinc?' to which one replies 'Coffee, bring me a Cup of Coffee' and the others chorus 'And us the like. [. . .] Coffee, Coffee.' Even in the coffee-house, Mahoone complains, his servants destroy his trade by wasting their time and adulterating his coffee.[27]

Nonetheless, many 'ready-handed' boys and girls must have learnt their trade in the coffee-houses. Fragmentary remains of a ceramic tile panel from a coffee-house, preserved at the Museum of London, depict a coffee-boy, arrested in the moment of pouring a dish of his master's best brew from a simple tin or copper coffee-pot. Next to him is a table with a blue-and-white coffee dish, ornamented with foliage, alongside two clay pipes and a copy of a newspaper on which the letters AZET can still be seen (presumably *The London Gazette*). On the table, swathed by a long cloth, there is also a large delftware mug and a flagon of wine. Above the coffee-boy's head a legend proclaims 'Dish of Coffee Boy'.[28] The coffee-boy wears a coat loosely unbuttoned, with a cravat or necktie of some kind, and his badge of office, a long apron, while his long hair cascades down his back. In Thomas Sydserfe's play *Tarugo's Wiles* (1668), the impecunious trickster hero is able to escape the bailiffs on one occasion by swapping his fine clothes (his brocade vest, hat, periwig and sword), for a coffee-boy's brown coat and apron. When the bailiffs enter the coffee-house they are unable to perceive the disguised gentleman.[29] The gentleman, Tarugo, makes an amusing coffee-boy because, for a servant, he is unusually erudite. Dressed in Will's working uniform, Tarugo serves some customers, addressing them with the phrase 'You're very welcome Gentlemen, and as I may say, come in season to taste the best Coffee that e're wet purslin' – using an archaic spelling and pronunciation of porcelain. The customers respond by ridiculing the exaggerated claims Tarugo makes for his coffee, which they say is nothing more than 'warm water boyl'ed with burnt Beans'. Indignant, the Coffee Master gives them a copy of a 'Paper' with an 'Exact account of its qualities'. When he pompously reads aloud from his handbill, it is revealed as a travesty of Pasqua Rosee's advertising sheet, the *Vertue of the Coffee-Drink*, making ludicrously inflated claims for the properties of coffee, such as 'cementing the cracks and flaws of the Government' or dissolving 'the ligaments of Liberty' in the noddle of a Quaker.[30]

Some coffee drawers became famous in themselves as characters about town. At White's Chocolate House in St James's Street, a waiter called Thomas was nicknamed 'Sir Thomas' and 'Tom the Tyrant' for his peremptory manner with his fellow servants (giving 'his Orders in the most Arbitrary manner to the servants below him, as to the Disposition of Liquors, Coal and Cinders').[31] Humphry Kidney, the major-domo of the St James's Coffee-House for many years, gained some notoriety as an arbiter of taste and fashion, using his position to gain a kind of prestige among the wealthy and powerful customers of the coffee-house. In Richard Steele's periodical, *The Tatler*, Kidney was represented as an imposing personage whose decisions and opinion influenced all his customers. He was described as having 'the Ear of the greatest Politicians who come hither', having 'long convers'd with, and fill'd Tea for the most consummate Politicians'.[32] Kidney understood his role was not only to dispense tea and coffee, but also to converse with the customers about the news and gossip of the day. In *The Tatler* he is often depicted receiving and distributing letters and post to the customers, and organising the newspapers and foreign 'advices', but he was also described as 'Keeper of the Book-Debts of outlying Customers, and Observer of those who go off without paying'. In March 1711 he was succeeded by John Sowton, who had previously been 'Enterer of Messages and first Coffee-Grinder'.[33]

On making coffee in the seventeenth century

To a society with no history or habit of drinking hot beverages, coffee was a perplexing, and not entirely likeable, phenomenon. It was not much like beer, wine or brandy. The previously available hot drinks, the old English caudles, possets and punches – various kinds of heated wines and spirits mixed with cream, butter and spices – had not given much hint of the peculiar flavour and aroma of coffee either. To many an innocent English palate of the 1660s the new beverage was reviled as a 'Newfangled, Abominable, Heathenish Liquour'.[34] An exotic unknown, with an unsavoury appearance, this black, opaque and bitter drink provoked and annoyed those who tasted it. The varied attempts by satirists and wits to describe coffee express this indignant pique, indicating that to many coffee was, in some important but ill-defined sense, counterfeit, dissident and diabolical. In their words it was a drink 'as thick as puddle-water', tasting like 'boiled Soot', 'made with the scent of old crusts, and shreads of leather burn'd and beaten to a powder'.[35] Others said coffee was a 'black, nasty, Hel-burnt Liquor', a

'Syrrop of Soot, or Essence of old Shooes, / Dasht with Diurnals, and the Books of News?', 'a forraign Fart, / Mixt and miscall'd according unto Art', 'Piss and Cack? / Jumble't together', a '*Satanic Tipple*', 'The Sister of the common Sewer'.[36] Another described it as a 'Horse-pond Liquor' and advised, 'look but on the colour of the Liquor, and if it don't resemble *Stix* itself, and then the Scent on't does conclude it came from old *Gehenna*, *Lucifers* deep Furnace, a stench to stifle virtue and good manners.'[37] Coffee, concluded one, was a 'hot *Hell-broth*', '*Pluto's Diet-drink*; that Witches tipple out of *dead men's Skulls*, when they ratifie to *Belzebub* their Sacramental Vows'.[38]

Much of this excited response could be ascribed to the novelty of the drink, but there is also some reason to take seriously these claims that coffee tasted horrid. To understand why, it is necessary to know something of the method of brewing coffee in this period, but also to recognise that coffee-house keepers were always mindful of ways to extend their product and its profit margins. Searching for the most apposite phrase, satirists likened coffee to burnt toast, to soot, to shit, to ink, or to something satanic or hellish. In this extraordinary parade of wit it is possible to see the emergence of a new aesthetic language, describing a product for which there is no language, either of deprecation or appreciation. In *The Ale Wives Complaint* (1675), the ale-wife, with whose business the coffee-houses were in stiff competition, dismisses coffee as an interloper: 'It seems both by tast and smell', she says, 'to be no better than a Sirreverance, pulveriz'd and intermixt [with] soot.' A sirreverence was a common, yet polite, term for human excrement. The word derived, amusingly, from an altered form of the phrase 'save reverence', an apologetic way of introducing a criticism, or something offensive. As the ale-wife clarifies, both turd and soot are necessary for coffee, as the 'one gives it the Hogo [aroma], and t'other the colour'.[39] Here, then, the ale-wife's coffee aesthetic extends across two senses: 'Hogo' is an anglicised spelling and pronunciation of the French phrase *haut goût*, meaning a high or piquant flavour, or derogatively, a putrescent offensive stench. In a play acted, and perhaps written, by some London apprentices, called *Knavery in all Trades* (1664), the unpleasant taste of coffee allows the boys to make fun of the new fashion, and their masters. A coffee-man giggles when he discovers that the cat has shat in the coffee ('de cat sirreverence into de Caldron, faugh, faugh, fe, fe, fe'). In reply, his apprentice remarks it will improve the taste: 'Oh sir let it boyl well, a Dog or Cats Turd is as good as the

Berry itself, 'twill give a rare hogo sir, and make the drink the better.'[40] Many people were suspicious about this new drink, especially as it tasted so awful. Their suspicions about coffee, of course, manifested deeper cultural cautions about modernity. What they probably failed to recognise was that coffee was a habit-forming drug that changed its customers' taste to suit itself. People, in short, developed a taste for coffee: because of, as much as in spite of, the hogo of sirreverence.

The competitors for coffee in the market all point to a desire in this period for unusual bitter flavours – pungent, astringent and acrimonious, like medicine. These were often flavoured with officinal herbs listed in the pharmacopoeia. In *The Coffee-Mans Granado* (1663), the coffee-man is asked 'have you no other Liquor but Coffee?' and answers, 'Yes, we have Bracket, China-Ale and pure Cider.'[41] Bracket (or bragget) was a drink made of honey and ale fermented together, spiced with wort, while China-ale was beer flavoured with china root, a root of a shrubby climbing plant (*Smilax China*) related to sarsaparilla, with medicinal properties. Pepys was partial to China-ale, drinking 'a bottle or two' in Westminster at 'the China alehouse' on two occasions.[42] James Douglas (in 1727) wrote that the early competitors for coffee were 'a certain Composition call'd *Aromatick*, recommended by the Physicians', a drink made with wine, prunes, sugar, caraway and cinnamon, 'and a Liquor made with Betony'.[43] Betony (*Stachys Betonica*) was an officinal herb supposed to remedy maladies of the head and to aid digestion: it could be prepared as a hot infusion tasting something like tea. In James Lightbody's *Compleat Coffee-man* (1698), instructions were given for tea, sage tea, chocolate, as well as a '*Coffee-House-Liquor call'd* Content' (a kind of hot egg custard, not dissimilar to sabayon or zabaglione, flavoured with *rosa solis*, an alcoholic cordial seasoned with sundew (*drosera rotundifolia*), an insectivorous marsh plant whose juice was held to be efficacious in coughs and consumptions). One satirist depicted an ale seller accusing a coffee-man of deliberately making people fanatical by 'pernitious Inventions' of drink, causing them 'to affect as many several Liquors as sects'. In evidence the ale seller peevishly lists

> your back-recruiting Chocolet, your shortening Coffee, your Tea that will make one vomit that drinks it, your Lickorish Bracket, . . . your Aromatick, and your Cephalice, your Rosado's and Pomeroy's (words that sound more like names of Infernal Spirits than fit drinks for honest

> Mortals) what are they all but so many baits to inveigle wanton curiosity, and gratify proud Extravagancy.[44]

This was, then, a keenly contested market, in which the strongest drink would not necessarily be the one with the most, or the best, flavour.

The taste displayed in this period for a strongly stewed and bitter brew, redolent of stewed prunes, burnt beans and soot, should be understood as a positive preference for these distasteful flavours. Coffee was attractive because of its 'hogo'. The seventeenth-century writers were perplexed by it, unable to decide whether what made it interesting was its strong taste or its strong effect. In wine, beer and spirits, adulteration and dilution were widespread: drinks were watered down to extend them, spices and peppers were added to give them bite, and sugars and fruit juices added to make them sweet and potable. In such a market the hogo of the coffee was one of its attractive qualities: it was a drink best consumed when pungent, spicy and tangy.

Among the coffee-man's primary duties was roasting coffee beans, for it was this above all else that gave his coffee its character. Coffee beans were purchased from the importers 'green' (in fact they are a dull whitish colour), a state in which they were viable for sale for a year or two, long enough to make the long and slow voyage from Arabia Fœlix to the markets in Egypt or Turkey and on to London. Once roasted, coffee was viable only for a matter of weeks rather than months.

Coffee roasting was, and is, simple to do, yet difficult to get right. All it requires is that the coffee beans be exposed to heat for a certain period. But coffee roasting is also a complex chemical procedure that literally transforms the product, bringing out and developing volatile oils which are essential to its aroma and flavour. Green coffee beans are smaller and heavier before roasting. The coffee beans are heated in the roaster, where they begin to crackle and pop as the internal moisture is forced out. As they lose most of their moisture they expand in size, increasing in volume by half or more. When the bean's internal temperature reaches between 185 to 240 degrees centigrade, it undergoes a chemical process called pyrolysis or volatisation, in which the heat breaks down complex chemical substances into simpler ones. The same process causes the sugars in the beans to caramelise, and as the beans darken in colour the aromatic volatile oils develop and intensify.[45]

Longer roasting produces darker and oilier beans, as more oil is forced to the surface; but eventually longer roasting will cause the sugars and oils to carbonise and burn. In order to arrest the pyrolytic process at the desired degree of roast, the beans must be removed from the roaster and cooled quickly. In modern coffee roasting systems the whole process only takes minutes. In these commercial roasters considerable control can be exercised at each stage of the process, allowing particular roasts to be developed and repeated (so-called 'French' or 'Italian' roast, for example).[46] This kind of control was not available in the seventeenth century.

Techniques for roasting green coffee beans in the seventeenth century were learnt from Levantine sources. Many early coffee-house keepers (including Pasqua Rosee and George Constantine) made authenticating claims about their Ottoman training in making coffee. James Douglas reported that when coffee was first consumed in England, 'both Coffee-Houses and private Families roasted their own Coffee in a sort of Frying-Pan over the Fire'. These long-handled frying pans, derived from Ottoman models, were equipped with a close-fitting lid in which there was a revolving handle connected to a paddle to stir the roasting beans. More elaborate roasters were also used in the Levant, in which a purpose-built rotating drum, turned by a long handle, was fitted over a fire pit.[47] Douglas argues that such roasters were invented in London ('Mr. *Elford* the Father contrived the white Iron Machine, since much used, and which is turn'd on a spit by a Jack'), but it is more likely Elford copied a Turkish machine. Roasters like these were still widely used in the Mediterranean until the twentieth century: in Italian they are called *abbrustralaturo*. Douglas further relates that coffee was at first roasted over sea coal, a famously smoky and sulphurous fuel, that delivered a relatively cool temperature.

Only later, Douglas contends, did the English coffee roasters realise the superiority of charcoal, in terms of flavour and quality; an advantage, he concludes, that 'gave rise to the Publick Roasters' as the process was beyond domestic consumers.[48] Certainly, by the 1690s some coffee-men specialised in roasting coffee, developing businesses that supplied roasted coffee on a regular timetable to a series of coffee-houses, such as that of Thomas Twining at Tom's Coffee House in Devereux Court. Nonetheless, some private consumers preferred to roast their own coffee beans at home. When Jonathan Swift entertained Alexander Pope in July 1714, Swift prepared the coffee himself, talking all the while of politics and gossip. 'There was likewise a Side Board of Coffee which the Dean roasted with his own hands in an Engine for that purpose, his Landlady attending, all the while that office was performing.'[49] The ritualised drama of coffee making, from roasting, grinding to brewing, was catered for by elegant sets of domestic coffee-making equipment.

Extant seventeenth-century coffee-roasting instructions are derived from the Levantine method. Dr Bellingham, an English physician resident in Bremen in the 1670s, recorded the following instructions 'To make ye Coffee powder' among his 'Memoranda medica':

> Take any quantity of ye Coffee berry you please & put into a frying pan or like & hould it over an easy fire keeping it continually stirringly it burns not[.] the berry at first is white & after some drying will burne browne & at length be black[.] when you have thus well dryed it all the brownest of ye berry be turned in to perfect black then beat it in a morter & sift it through a fine sive & take ye quantity as above mentioned.[50]

These instructions give a perfectly adequate coffee, with a pronounced smoky flavour by today's standards. Dr Bellingham's recipe notes all the stages of the coffee-roasting process: the presence of a steady high heat, the importance of stirring the beans to ensure even roasting, their snap and crackle as they roast, the telling transformation of their colour from white to brown to black, and the need to cool the beans quickly at the end. Yet instructions like these produce a coffee that is imprecisely roasted to the modern taste, as the makeshift method of roasting introduces several imperfections: hand-stirred coffee is unevenly roasted (giving an unpleasant mixture of high- and low-roasted beans), and coffee roasted over a coal or charcoal fire is flavoured by the smoke. In the under-roasted beans the volatile oils have not developed fully, and the coffee is dominated by pasty, nutty and bread-like flavours, without much aroma. The over-roasted beans become blackened and burnt, giving the coffee a sooty, carbonised quality, with a thin, 'industrial' flavour and little aroma.[51] In the 1660s and 1670s when satirists searched for a language for coffee, they caught well some of these qualities, noticing both flavours typical of under-roasted coffee ('Burnt bread and pudle water', or 'burnt water and burnt beans')[52] and over-roasted, burnt coffee ('*Coffee* a crust is charkt into a coal' or 'this boiled Soot').[53] The satirists' descriptions of the flavour of coffee cannot be simply dismissed as satiric bites at this modish and exotic luxury, but also precise and intelligent observations of the flavours of imprecisely roasted coffee, containing beans that are both under-roasted and burnt.

To make their coffee the coffee-men followed the practice of the Ottomans. The French traveller Jean de Thevenot, who made several journeys to Constantinople and the Ottoman Empire in the 1650s and 1660s, and was a great afficionado of coffee, described the practice of the *cavehane* in the Levant. 'When they have a mind to drink of [coffee], they take a copper Pot, made purposely, which they call *Ibrick*, and having filled it with Water, make it boyl; when it boyls, they put in this Powder, to the proportion of a good spoonful for three Dishes or Cups full of Water, and having let all boyl together, they snatch it quickly off the fire, or stir it, else it would run all over, for it rises very fast'. When the coffee had boiled 'ten or twelve wambles'[54] it was poured into the drinking vessels so as to leave the residual sediment in the pot. The Ottoman *ibrik* was a specialised jug or ewer typically made of metal or pottery. Its conical or pear-shaped form had been found ideal for making coffee in the Levantine manner. It typically had a long spout set low on the side of the vessel, with a handle often set at right angles to the spout.

The Levantine method of making coffee was to seethe finely ground roasted coffee in recently boiled water. Levantine practice stressed the importance in maintaining the freshness of the brew, especially by reducing the time between roasting, grinding, preparing and drinking. J. S. Buckingham, travelling in Damascus in the early nineteenth century, noted that large coffee-houses there made a spectacle of roasting and grinding. Rather like the independent coffee roasters of the present day, he observed 'men constantly employed in roasting and pounding the berry, so as to have the beverage always fresh'. He commented that 'the only certain mode of retaining the pure flavour of the coffee is to roast, pound, and boil it all in quick succession, the roasted berries soon losing their flavour if laid by for a day, and the pounded coffee becoming insipid, even in a few hours'. The most extreme example of the freshness ideal that Buckingham encountered was that of the desert Arabs, the Bedouin. 'Even if they require only two cups of the liquid', he said, they roast 'a handful of the berries on an iron plate, pounding them in a pestle and mortar while warm, and the instant the water boils, which it will generally do by the time the other preparations are completed, so that no time is lost, putting the pounded powder into it, and suffering it to boil, stirring it at the same time for about a minute or two, when it is poured out to drink'.[55]

This concern for freshness was soon forgotten in England, as the surviving receipts for its preparation testify. An English correspondent (perhaps a coffee-man) called Kirk Bowen supplied a recipe 'To make Coffee' to Dr Bellingham in Hamburg:

> Take 5 quarts of water & when it boyles put into it 5 oz of ye powder of coffee & by ye time it boyles away a quart take it of ye fire & when it settles empty it into ye potts & sett it before ye fire so it may not boyle & in a little time standing it will be clearly fine: but at any time if you lett it boyle in ye potts ye bottome will rise & make it thick.[56]

In Bellingham's recipe the primary concern is securing a clear liquor to drink. After the coffee is added to the boiling water it is boiled for sufficient time to reduce the water by one fifth (about fifteen minutes). After this, the coffee is allowed to rest off the heat, so that the coffee grounds settle, and is then poured into the coffee pots. An anonymous seventeenth-century manuscript in the British Library also preserves a sheet of 'Receipts to make *coffe* and *chocolate*'. The 'Coffe Liquor', it advises, should be prepared using water in which the 'bottomes', or old coffee grounds, have been boiled for fifteen minutes. Only after this should the coffee powder be introduced and boiled for another fifteen minutes.[57] Some idea that quality mattered can be discerned in the suggestion made to Sir John Finch in 1678, that 'ordinary people' can make do with the coffee grounds (foots) boiled in water, while gentlemen should be served fresh powder every time.[58]

The first reform of the seething coffee-making practice was introduced in the early eighteenth century. In the new method, freshly roasted and ground coffee was placed in a cloth bag, over which boiling water was poured, and the liquor allowed to infuse. Edward Bramah, drawing on the evidence of surviving coffee pots, suggests this was a French innovation from around 1710, which was intended to keep the coffee clear of grounds, rather than to improve flavour, for the coffee bag was kept seething in the heated coffee for hours afterwards.[59] In the early nineteenth century the new technology of the coffee biggin introduced a screw by which the cloth infusion bag could be squeezed to release more flavour from the grounds. Another experimental path led to the drip method, developed especially for domestic use, in which boiling water was poured on to compressed coffee grounds, given some time to steep, then left to drip down to the pot below through a simple filter. These technological changes were driven by the desire to remove as much particulate from the liquid as possible. Nineteenth-century practice even recommended the addition of a few chips of isinglass, a transparent gelling agent made from the air bladders of sturgeon, giving it a sparkling crystalline quality.[60] This concern for coffee clarity served more to enhance the appeal of quality porcelain than the beverage itself.

Coffee was almost always consumed black, especially in coffee-houses. When it was first introduced, James Douglas explained in 1727, many people 'could not accustom themselves to the bitter taste [. . .]; for few People then mix'd it with either Sugar or Milk'.[61] When Pepys had sugar in his coffee one morning in March 1664 he thought it worth noting in his diary: on this occasion he was served coffee made by Lady Mennes, 'which was purely made, with a little sugar in it'.[62] In 1685 John Chamblerlayn argued that the therapeutic qualities of coffee were improved by sugar: 'many find this drink to be very profitable, taken in the Morning fasting, with a little Sugar, in a moderate quantity, and to very good purpose.'[63] The addition of sugar, which was also an expensive luxury, tended to remain the preserve of domestic coffee consumption. When milk was added to coffee it was usually for medicinal purposes, as milk was only recommended for the young and infirm. For this purpose, James Lightbody explained in his business manual *Every Man his own Gauger* (1698), the coffee-man was instructed that 'If you would make Milk Coffee, you must, to every Pint of Water, put a quart of Milk'.[64] In Laurence Sterne's comic novel *Tristram Shandy* (1759–67), the eccentric hero drinks something he calls 'milk coffee', believing it to be 'good for a consumption', advising that 'you must boil the milk and coffee together – otherwise 'tis only coffee and milk'.[65]

Tea and the coffee-house

One of the great competitors with coffee was tea, an equally exotic but even more expensive product that entered the English market soon after coffee. Men of science had been aware of tea since the mid sixteenth century and small quantities had been imported, for medicinal purposes, from as early as 1610. The Dutch, with their more extensive trade relations with South East Asia, had taken the lead in this trade and most of the tea on the English market in the seventeenth century was sourced through Amsterdam. It was still a rarity in London in 1657, however: Samuel Hartlib wrote enthusiastically to Comenius in Hungary on 28 December of that year, discoursing on '*de herba Theæ*', although Comenius replied testily that he had known of the substance for several years, without finding anything of interest in it.[66] The first notice advertising the public sale of tea was placed by the coffee-man Thomas Garraway in 1658, who promoted it in *Mercurius Politicus* on Thursday, 23 September 1658: 'That Excellent, and by all Physitians approved, *China* Drink, called by the *Chineans*, *Teha*, by other nations *Tay alias Tea*, is sold at the *Sultaness-head*, a *Cophee-house*, in *Sweeting's* Rents by the Royal Exchange, *London*.'[67] As Garraway made clear, he imagined his clientele would be drinking tea only on the recommendation of their doctors and apothecaries. Pepys notes that in September 1660 – by which time coffee was for him quite well known – a Spanish merchant of his acquaintance ordered for him 'a Cupp of Tee (a China drink) of which I never had drank before'.[68]

Tea was much more expensive than coffee and it remained a rarity long after coffee was ubiquitous in London. On the imposition of the Excise on coffee in 1660, tea was charged at 8 pence per gallon. At twice the rate on coffee, the Excise on tea imagined the commodity as a luxury product appealing to prosperous high-status consumers.[69] Elford advertised in 1662 that tea could be purchased retail from his Exchange Alley Coffee-House at a price between 6 and 60 shillings a pound, at a time when coffee ranged from 1s 8d to 6 shillings the pound.[70] The prestige enjoyed by tea led the East India Company of London to present Charles II with gifts of tea on two occasions: a two-pound canister in 1664 and a 23-pound box in 1666, both sourced on the Amsterdam market. The Company made its first order for the importation of tea in 1668, instructing its agents to 'Send home by these ships 100 lbs. weight of the best *tey* you can gett'. The first consignment of tea, amounting to 143 pounds, was received from Bantam in Java (now Indonesia) in 1669.[71] The contest between coffee and tea for the hearts and palates of English consumers was from this time also a contest between the great trading companies: the Levant Company defending coffee and the East India Company promoting tea. Nonetheless, imports of tea remained irregular until the eighteenth century, especially after the Dutch seized control of the factory at

Bantam in 1682 and excluded the East India Company from a direct trade with the Chinese merchants of South East Asia.

Tea drinking was more often associated with women, with consumption in the home and with luxury: and most often in a combination of all three. Richard Ames's satire, *The Bacchanalian Sessions: or the Contention of Liquors* (1693), imagined a contest between alcoholic drinks and the coffee-house liquors to decide which provided the most entertainment. The plea advanced by 'a drink much admir'd by the Ladies, called *Tea*' is rejected: the liquor was considered too trifling and foolish.[72] The expense of tea made it the ideal beverage for displays of conspicuous consumption and the favourite drink of the court, especially among the more fashionable aristocratic circles and the courtesans. Numerous poems written on tea in the early eighteenth century celebrated the commodity's association with women. In 1700 the Poet Laureate, Nahum Tate, wrote thirty-six pages of verse on the discovery and production of tea in his *Panacea: a Poem Upon Tea*; a subject of 'delicacy' and 'decency', he commented in his preface, suitable for 'an Entertainment for the Ladies'.[73] Another poet, Duncan Campbell, in his *A Poem upon Tea* (1735), commented that women are 'soberly inclin'd' and 'to one another affable and kind' when 'at Tea they sit', concluding that 'Tea is the School, at which they learn their Wit'. His poem too was addressed to the Fair Sex, with a preface for the Masculine Reader reminding men 'How insipid wou'd this World be, / Without some female Love, and Tea'.[74] Campbell's poem drew on the conventional analogy between the beauty and virtue of women, but extended it to include tea, whose virtuous properties, he declared, found their outward expression in the fragile beauty of porcelain teacups.

The East India Company transformed the market for tea in the mid eighteenth century. Tea imports had remained sporadic and uncertain until 1717, when the Company finally gained the right to trade directly with Canton. Thereafter, the Company's direct tea imports showed accelerating growth: from an average of nearly 900,000 pounds per annum in the 1720s to 3.7 million pounds per annum in the 1750s, with concomitant growth in sales receipts. Tea imports fell into two broad categories, green and black, both of which were sourced from China. Green tea was a delicate product made from the cut and dried leaves of *camellia sinensis*, mostly consumed with sugar or preserved lemon.

Black teas were prepared from the same plant, but manufactured so that the partially dried tea oxidised and turned black. The East India Company imported four main kinds of tea: the cheapest was Bohea, picked from the most mature and coarsest leaves. Progressively finer grades were called Congo, Souchon and Pekoe, the last made from newly formed leaf buds, commanding a high margin in price, but occupying a minuscule proportion of the trade.[75] As the expanding sales of tea suggested, more people in ordinary walks of life were drinking it in the mid eighteenth century. As an unknown writing master of Canterbury remarked in his poem *In Praise of Tea* (1736),

> When Tea was sold for guineas by the pound,
> The poor a drinking Tea were never found,
> Then only china dishes cou'd be bought
> Burnt in with gold, or else in colours wrought:
> Now Tea is cheap, so dishes are the same;
> Then pray wherein are they so much to blame.[76]

To some observers the growth in consumption of tea was an indication of the corrupting influence of luxury. In 1748 the Methodist John Wesley wrote against tea, pleading that 'What an Advantage it would be to these poor enfeebled People if they would leave off what so manifestly impairs their Health, and thereby hurts their Business also'.[77] The expense of this imported drug, Wesley lamented, might have been put to better advantage. The philanthropist Jonas Hanway also opposed the consumption of tea by the common people. 'I have long considered tea', he fulminated, 'not only as a prejudicial article of commerce; but also of a most pernicious tendency with regard to domestic industry and labor [*sic*]; and very injurious to health.'[78] Gin and tea, he reckoned, had led the plebeian orders into a general dissipation.

The cultural associations of tea and coffee remained distinct, and while they were often consumed in the same places, they were not considered and discussed in the same way. Both tea and coffee were available in many coffee-houses, and certain coffee-men were at least as famous for their tea as their coffee. Thomas Twining became the proprietor of Tom's Coffee-House in Devereux Court in 1706. From an early date he developed a retail trade in tea, which from 1717 onwards was sold from a shop next door to the coffee-house, at the sign of the 'Golden Lyon'.[79] The ledgers of his tea and coffee sales covering these years remain in the archives of R. Twining & Co., who continue a considerable trade as tea merchants almost 300 years later. Thomas Twining supplied tea and coffee to a number of other coffee-house proprietors. One of his most lucrative customers was Daniel Button, the keeper of Button's Coffee-House in Covent Garden. Between 1716 and 1722 Button purchased packets of roasted coffee almost every day, in one- or two-pound quantities, along with further orders for Bohea tea, Pekoe tea, green tea, spaw water, rum, arrack, snuff, sugar and chocolate. For the coffee Button paid between 5s 6d and 6s 8d per pound, and for Bohea tea between 16 shillings and 18 shillings per pound. Although he ordered nearly four times as much coffee as tea, his purchases suggest that tea was by this time a popular beverage at his coffee-house.[80] Nonetheless, the cultural associations of tea remained domestic and feminine: in the cultural imagination tea was consumed primarily in the home. So while coffee-houses sold both tea and coffee (alongside some wine and other alcoholic drinks), the public and masculine sociability of debate and business remained associated with coffee.

Dishes, cups, pots and bowls: the coffee service

To serve their product coffee-houses used utilitarian utensils made of base metals such as copper, brass and tin. Among the possessions listed in the will of a Lincoln coffee-man, William Peart, in 1682 was 'Copper and Tyn Coffee Pots and Coffee dishes' to the value of £1 6s 8d, found in the scullery adjoining his coffee room.[81] Blackened by the fire, battered by constant use, humble and rustic in its design, the coffee pot of the coffee-house was a decidedly quotidian item. It is not surprising, then, that the oldest known surviving English coffee pot is one made in silver, now in the Victoria and Albert Museum in London, probably made in London in 1681. An austere pot, it is about twenty-four centimetres high, modelled on the simple conical shape of a Levantine *ibrik*, with a serpentine handle covered in leather, a long spout emanating from halfway up the can and a small hinged conical lid. It is engraved with a coat of arms surrounded by billowing waves and the legend 'The Guift of Richard Herne Esq to ye Honorable East-India-Company'. Later coffee pots in this collection and others show considerable refinement and decoration. As both coffee and tea were expensive commodities, more luxurious sets of vessels came into demand for domestic use. The household of William Russell, fifth Earl and first Duke of Bedford, for example, first started making purchases of coffee for domestic consumption in 1670, when the Duke's gentleman of the privy purse, Mr Dixy Taylor, began to buy small packets of coffee worth a shilling for the particular use of individuals in the family. In 1670 he purchased a coffee pot, china dish and coffee, paying £1 2s 2d for the whole set. Later in the same year he paid 6 pence for a 'little coffee pot', purchasing a china cup to go with it for 1s 6d. Several other such coffee sets were purchased for individual members of the household over the coming year.[82]

The dishes used for coffee drinking in England were similar to those habitually employed in the Levant. In the Ottoman Empire coffee was consumed in small ceramic drinking bowls called *finians* or *fincans*. Ordinary coffee dishes in the Levant were cheaply produced using a coarse red earthenware clay, covered in a white slip with a simple lead glaze to render them waterproof. Such vessels were light and fragile, and were so cheap as to be virtually disposable. 'China is not half so dear here,' the Chaplain to the Levant Company factory in Constantinople wrote in 1677. 'Your little sherbet cups and coffee dishes are made often times of the same earth; they ring like a bell; the earth is darkish, but the outside glazed colour is greenish.'[83] These small bowls were only large enough to 'hold 4 or 5 Ounces' of hot coffee, reported Pedro Teixeira in 1604.[84] The Turkish practice, recorded in Ottoman miniatures, was to hold them between the foot and the rim using the thumb and the forefinger.[85] Some of the more elegant forms came with a matching flat dish underneath, a precursor of the saucer. More elaborate Ottoman domestic coffee sets were provided with purpose-made trays and sets of identical cups decorated to match a coffee pot. In the seventeenth century the Ottoman pottery market was dominated by wares produced in Iznik, across the Bosphorus from Istanbul, although others were made at Kutahya and Damascus. The most expensive and elaborate Iznik wares, highly coloured and elaborately patterned, were far superior to anything produced in Europe and surpassed only by the best Chinese porcelain. The Levant Company imported small quantities of these high-status commodities for the luxury market in London and England. In 1599 a Swiss traveller to London, Thomas Platter, admired the 'Turkish pitcher and dishes' he saw in the cabinet of Mr Cope, 'a citizen who spent much time in the Indies'.[86] Painted 'Turkey dishes' were in use in taverns and ordinaries in London in the 1620s.[87] But although coffee-drinking practice in London followed the Levantine model, the vessels were more commonly obtained from the Orient.

Very large quantities of Chinese porcelain were imported into Europe by the Verenigde Oost Indische Compagnie (VOC), the Dutch East India Company, in the mid seventeenth century. These shipments came by way of the VOC 'factories' in the city of Batavia in Java (now in Indonesia). From 1624 regular shipments of porcelain included hundreds of small drinking vessels, known even then as 'teacups', a kind of brand name, as there was no market for tea. Instead, they were used for drinking spirits and wine, and were prized for their delicate shape and ornamentation.[88] Evidence from European paintings and engravings suggests widespread domestic use of these imported pottery and porcelain dishes, continuing among the better sort even after porcelain manufacture began in Europe (in England, fine china akin to porcelain did not start production until the Chelsea factory opened in 1745). Cost, however, may have induced many coffee-houses to use coffee dishes of domestic English production. Cups and dishes were manufactured in metals such as tin and pewter, and even wooden cups were not unknown.

By the late seventeenth century, coarse earthenware cups of domestic manufacture were being advertised, chiefly by London potteries such as that established at Pickleherring Quay in St Olave's parish, Southwark.[89] According to a description of these potteries made in 1697, they had some ability with 'fine smale ware' such as 'Tea, Chocolate, and Coffee cupps', made with 'Tobacco pipe clay' imported from Poole in Dorsetshire.[90] Most domestic English 'Delftware' of this kind mimicked the imported Chinese porcelain tea bowl in design and decoration. Nonetheless, something like a modern coffee mug was sold by the 1690s: James Morley of Nottingham, a maker of salt-glazed stoneware, offered one called a 'capuchine' on his trade card of *c.* 1696–1700, examples of which are preserved in the Victoria and Albert Museum.[91] Intended for the consumption of coffee or chocolate, the capuchine was a tall, narrow cup with a slightly bulbous body and flaring mouth, a single handle, and decorated with stylised leaf motifs.[92] Little of this rustic folk pottery remains, partly because the thermal shock of hot drinks caused the tin-glazed earthenware to crack.

It is certainly possible to replicate the methods of coffee making outlined in this chapter. Using tools not much more complex than a suburban barbecue and camping equipment, it is not difficult to replicate the roasting techniques of the seventeenth century. After all, early coffee-making practice was developed using everyday equipment available in every kitchen. For several reasons this coffee is distasteful to the modern coffee drinker. Home roasting using a frying pan usually produces coffee which combines beans that are under- and over-roasted: especially when done over a smoky fire. Using Dr Bellingham's method to make up the drink also means the coffee is over-extracted: it is boiled too long, a process that destroys the fresh aromatic oils, making the coffee flat, bitter and stewed. These bitter flavours are intensified by the practices of reusing coffee grounds, adding fresh coffee to old and keeping it for long periods on a low heat. The closest analogy is a kind of coffee that can be found today: arriving at work in the morning, an unsuspecting employee pours a mug of coffee from the filter machine, only to discover, from its distinct hogo of sirreverence, that it had been left in the pot overnight and brought back to life, gently warming on the hotplate like some caffeine zombie, by an earlier arrival at the office. The full effect is achieved by using a cracked and unwashed mug.

CHAPTER NINE

Humours, Anti-Hypnoticks and Caffeine

Coffee, as it is now understood, contains a drug known as caffeine, which is generally regarded as a stimulant. In the seventeenth century there was no knowledge of caffeine, nor of its kind of complex vegetable alkali. Medical theory in this period was based on the traditional herbally orientated pharmacopoeia outlined in Galen, Hippocrates and Aristotle – a tradition of thought stretching back nearly two thousand years. The knowledge of the 'ancients', however, had been contested by 'modern' practitioners who followed the teachings of Paracelsus and, latterly, van Helmont. The enduring squabble between the 'ancients' and 'moderns' was reignited in London by the translation in 1662 of van Helmont's *Ortus medicinae* (1648), which brought his 'chemical' cures to a wider public. In November 1663 Pepys witnessed a debate on these different approaches in Elford's Coffee-House in Exchange Alley. He recorded in his diary that he

> heard a long and most passionate discourse between two Doctors of Physique [. . .] and a Couple of Apothecarys; these maintaining Chymistry against their Galenicall physic, and the truth is, one of the Apothecaries, whom they charged most, did speak very prettily; that is, his language and sense good, though perhaps he might not be so knowing a physician as to offer to contest with them. At last they came to some cooler term and broke up.[1]

Such a debate was typical of the public science of the coffee-house, which brought men of different philosophical traditions together in one shared space. The discursive contest that Pepys witnesses here is not only a battle between scientific approaches, but also between social codes, for the physicians had a much higher status than the lowly apothecaries. Nonetheless, all these men found in the coffee-house a place where a heated scientific squabble might be pursued on a more sociable footing. Pepys shows little grasp of what was at issue in this debate, for what he values is the 'pretty' rhetoric of the apothecary.

The first Western scientific treatise wholly devoted to coffee was that of the Welsh barrister and judge, Walter Rumsey. In 1656, aged seventy-two and in ill health, Rumsey was much troubled with phlegm and, to alleviate this, he invented an instrument called a 'provang' to give himself relief. His provang, made of a long piece of whalebone with a silk button on the end of it, was inserted down the throat into the stomach, where it was used to scrape out phlegm and induce the vomiting held to be efficacious in such cases. Rumsey instructed that before inserting the provang an 'electuary of coffee' should be ingested to prepare the stomach. He argued that the provang treated ill humours which arise in the stomach, where 'impurities obstruct the passages of life, poisoning and fermenting the whole moisture of mans body'. Rumsey believed that an excess of undigested meat poisoned the corporeal frame, forming corrupt humours in the veins and other parts of the body. The electuary (a medicinal paste) was made of 'Powder of Turkish Cophie', mixed with butter, 'sallet-oil' (olive oil) and honey, and was consumed in a ball about the size of a nutmeg. Coffee, Rumsey supposed, not only helped with vomiting, but also had the benefit of promoting farting, for as he warned, 'unless the fore-dore and the back-dore of the body be kept open . . . the body will be quickly destroyed.'[2] Not all were keen on the provang. John Aubrey said, 'I could never make it goe down my throat, but for those that can 'tis a most incomparable engine. If troubled with the wind it cures you immediately.' Aubrey's servant, he relates, 'used it incomparably', claiming that it was 'no paine, when downe your throate. He would touch the bottome of his Stomach with it.[3] Robert Hooke was still using his whalebone vomiter in May 1676.[4]

Rumsey's ideas sound crack-brained, but they make sense within the dominant account of the body in the period, in which well-being was understood as a precarious state of balance between four influences or 'humours', named as blood, bile, phlegm and melancholy (or black bile). According to the humoural system, which formed the basis for the Western tradition of medicine from ancient Greece down to the eighteenth century, illness was the result of some disturbance in the balance of the humours. Diet, lifestyle and a regimen of physic and purges were the primary means by which this humoural balance could be maintained. Every therapeutic product could be understood according to these four humours and their four qualities (the hot, the cold, the wet and the dry). In the case of medicines long known to physicians, such as *sal ammoniac* or rhubarb, there was a vast body of scholarship discussing their humoural properties. By contrast, coffee, as a hitherto unknown botanical simple, presented complex problems of definition and description, especially as it was seemingly possessed of powerful medicinal properties.

Rumsey became well known for his odd purging instrument and for his electuary of coffee. It was 'commonly sold at *London*, and especially at the long Shops in *Westminster-Hall*'. Rumsey's treatise, which was entitled *Organon Salutis. An Instrument to Cleanse the Stomach. As also divers new Experiments of the virtue of Tobacco and Coffee: How much they conduce to preserve humane health*, was published in 1657 by Daniel Pakeman, a bookseller 'living at the Rainbow, neer the Inner Temple Gate', a building which also housed James Ffarr's coffee-house. (Pakeman was among those who complained the coffee-house was a nuisance in 1657.) The first edition of *Organon salutis* was advertised in the weekly newspaper *Mercurius Politicus* for 11–12 June 1657 and, meeting with popular success, ran to further editions in 1659 and 1664. The book was dedicated to the travel writer Sir Henry Blount, who had 'brought the use of the Turks Physick, of Cophie in great request in *England*, whereof I have made use, in another form than is used by boiling of it in Turkie, and being less loathsome and troublesome'.[5] Rumsey secured two testimonials about coffee, one from Blount himself and the other from James Howell, the official historian of Charles I. These two testimonials established Rumsey's book (but perhaps not his provang or electuary) as the leading authority on coffee for at least two decades. In a letter to Robert Boyle, John Beale disparaged Rumsey's provang as a tool of no use but to 'drunkerds gluttens & such monsters', but he found the book interesting enough to send a copy to Henry Oldenburg in April 1663.[6]

Henry Blount was an enthusiastic supporter of coffee, recommending the 'rare efficacie' of this 'remarkable' simple. Referring to both coffee and tobacco, Blount observed 'how universally they take with mankinde, and yet have not the advantage of any pleasing taste wherewith to tempt and debauch our Palat, as Wine and other such pernicious things have, for at the first Tobacco is most horrid, and

Cophie insipid, yet do they both so generally prevail, that Bread it self is not of so universal use'. Lacking a precise language for addiction, Blount points to the curious taking quality of coffee, despite its horrid taste. James Howell, in his assessement of the 'rare pectoral Instrument' of the provang, also offered a defence of 'Cophie and Tobacco'. Declaring coffee to be 'salutiferous' (healthful), Howell magnified its properties: 'besides the exsiccant quality it hath to dry up the crudities of the Stomach, as also to comfort the Brain, to fortifie the sight with its steem, & prevent Dropsies, Gouts, the Scurvie, together with the Spleen, and Hypocondriacall windes'. This striking list of therapeutic effects was augmented by some other pertinent observations. Howell commented, 'this *Coffee* drink hath caused a greater sobriety among the Nations: For whereas formerly Apprentices & Clerks with others, used to take their mornings draught in Ale, Beer, or Wine, which the dizziness they cause in the Brain, make many unfit for business, they use now to play the Good-fellows in this *wakeful* and civil drink.'[7] But scientific curiosity about coffee was building. Soon after its foundation of the Royal Society in 1662, one of its fellows deposited some 'Discourses about Cyder and Coffee' into its growing archive,[8] possibly including *The Vertues of Coffee*, a compilation of extracts on the properties of coffee derived from the writings of Bacon, Sandys, Parkinson, Howell and Blount. As the unidentified compiler observed, he had 'often Drunk Coffa (as many other have done) for Company more then of any Knowledge I had of the Vertue of it'.[9]

As English scientists and travellers recognised, the best authorities on coffee remained the Ottoman researchers. Insight into the Ottoman work on coffee was gained in 1659 by the translation by the Oxford linguist and diplomat Edward Pococke of a treatise written in Arabic by the Turkish physician Da'ud ibn 'Umar Antaki (d. 1599, known also as David Antiochenus). Pococke was a noted scholar of Oriental languages, reported to be skilled in Hebrew, Persian, Coptic, Greek and Latin, as well Arabic.[10] He had twice visited the Ottoman Empire, once as Chaplain to the Aleppo factory between 1630 and 1636, and again in 1640 as chaplain to Sir Peter Wyche's embassy to the court at Constantinople. Pococke was appointed the first Professor of Arabic at the University of Oxford, the first chair of its kind in Britain. Pococke's translation was a remarkable document. Entitled *The Nature of the Drink Kauhi, or Coffe, and the Berry of which it is made*, it printed Pococke's translation next to a transcription of the Arabic text.[11] When it was published in early 1659 it immediately created a stir in scientific circles, although the four-page booklet was produced in very small numbers (only two copies survive today). From Oxford, Robert Boyle sent a copy to Samuel Hartlib in April 1659, commenting that 'he will suffer very few to be printed'. Hartlib thanked Boyle 'heartily' and commented that 'the printed paper of coffee, [. . .] will be gustful no doubt to your coffee drinkers, [. . .] who perhaps may add as many more good observations from their own experience, as the *Arabian* physician hath done'. Hartlib made a copy of Pococke's translation in his memorandum book, and passed on copies to other researchers, including the philosopher John Worthington, Master of Jesus College, Cambridge.[12]

Although these early scientific investigators came to no definite agreement about the properties of coffee, coffee-house men revelled in the extravagant therapeutic claims they could make about the effects of their product. They printed advertisements for their coffee on one-page handbills, which they wrapped up with packets of coffee and displayed on the walls of their coffee-houses. The 'vertues' or properties they delineated made coffee out as a veritable panacea, described below on a handbill produced for the Rainbow Coffee-House in Fleet Street 'between the two Temple-Gates':

> The quality of this drink, is cold and dry; and though it be a drier, yet it neither heats, nor Inflames more than a hot Posset.
>
> It so closeth the Orifice of the Stomach, and fortifies the heat within, that it is very good to help digestion, and therefore of great use to be taken about three or four of the Clock in the afternoon, as well as in the morning.
>
> It is very good against sore Eyes, and the better, if you hold your head over it, and take in the Steam that way.
>
> It suppresseth fumes exceedingly, and therefore good against the Headach, and will very much stop any Defluxion of Rhumes, that distil from the Head upon the Stomach, and so prevent, and help Consumptions, and the Cough of the Lungs.
>
> It is excellent to prevent and cure the Dropsy, Gout, and the Scurvy.
>
> It is known by experience to be better than any other drying Drink for people in years, or Children that have any running Humours upon them, as the King's evil. &c.
>
> It is very good to prevent Miscarryings in Child-bearing Women.

It is a most excellent remedy against the spleen, Hypochondriack Windes, or the like.

It will prevent drowsiness, and make one fit for business, if one have occasion to watch; and therefore you are not to Drink of it after Supper, unless you intend to be watchful, for it will hinder sleep for three or four hours.

It is to be observed that in *Turkey*, where this is generally drunk, that they are not troubled with the Stone, Gout, Dropsie, or Scurvy; and that their Skins are exceeding clear and white.

It is neither Laxative nor Restringent.[13]

Exaggerated claims such as these tried to identify coffee as a kind of physic (a dose of medicine), but also made them seem closer to a quack remedy.

The extravagant claims made for coffee by the coffee-men's handbills exposed the commodity to satire. The most notorious satire 'against' coffee is the six-page squib called *The Women's Petition Against Coffee. Representing to Publick Consideration the Grand Inconveniences accruing to their Sex from the Excessive Use of that Drying Enfeebling Liquor. Presented to the Right Honourable Keepers of the Liberty of Venus*, which was published anonymously under the pseudonym 'a Well-willer' in 1674. The tract presents a mock-petition addressed to 'The Worshipful Court of *Female-Assistants*' of the '*Liberty of Venus*', from '*several Thousands of Buxome Women*'. The satire argues that England, long '*A Paradise for Women*' due to the 'brisk *Activity* of our men', has suffered 'of late a very sensible *Decay* of that *Old English Vigour*'. The cause of this disaster is attributed 'to nothing more than the Excessive-use of that Newfangled, Abominable, Heathenish Liquour called *COFFEE*'. The travesty's vulgar humour, relying on pun and double entendre, jokes that the men are 'not able to *stand* to it, and in the very first Charge fall down *flat* before us. Never did Men wear *greater breeches*, or carry *less* in them of any *Mettle* whatsoever'. Coffee, the buxom petitioners go on to argue, has been 'Riffling Nature of her choicest *Treasures*, and *Drying* up the *Radical Moisture*, has so *Eunuch[ed]* our Husbands, and *Crippled* our more kind *Gallants*, that they are become as *Impotent*, as Age, and as unfruitful as those *Desarts* whence that unhappy *Berry* is said to be brought'.[14] The satire claims that the new sociable man of the coffee-house, with his endless talk and chat, is emasculated and impotent.

That coffee might have a deleterious effect on male virility was a theory accorded considerable scientific respect. It had first been suggested by the German physician, Simon Paulli, the professor of botany at Copenhagen. In a tract on tobacco and tea that he published in 1665, Paulli argued the seemingly therapeutic qualities of these foreign products would have harmful effects if taken in excess. In passing, Paulli condemned 'cahvvæ acqua' (coffee), a 'decoction' of which 'surprisingly effeminates both the Minds and Bodies of the *Persians*'. Coffee (like tea and tobacco), Paulli argues, 'so enervate the *European* Men, that they become incapable of propagating their Species, like *Eunuchs*, some of whom are highly salacious; but it is sufficiently known, that they are incapable of Procreation, tho' they emit something analogous to *Semen*'.[15] Although coffee drinkers may ejaculate, Paulli argues, the generative power of the semen will have been evaporated. His argument rested heavily on the observation of a German scholar, Adam Olearius, who had visited Persia in 1637 and who recorded that coffee there was widely deployed as a contraceptive. He noted that it 'hath a Cooling quality, and the *Persians*, think it allays the Natural heat. Whence it comes, that they often drink of it, inasmuch as they would avoid the charge of having many Children.'[16] Following Olearius, Paulli concluded that coffee had 'a Power of stimulating to Venery, but may yet induce Sterility'.[17] Later writers also considered the effect of coffee on sexuality. In 1771 the French doctor Bienville argued that strong coffee was one of the signal causes of nymphomania, as it boosted the 'tumultuous workings' of the female erotic imagination.[18] At the beginning of the nineteenth century the German Samuel Hahnemann reckoned that 'the monster of nature, that hollow-eyed ghost, onanism, is generally concealed behind the coffee-table'.[19] In these disparate opinions the argument is derived as much from coffee's continuing association with self-indulgence, exoticism and luxury as the effects of caffeine itself. Indeed, recent scientific research has shown there is no evidence that caffeine causes impotence and has suggested instead that it may enhance male fertility by increasing sperm motility.[20]

In any case the satirical target of *The Women's Petition Against Coffee* is not sexual prowess: rather it is the new urban manners of masculine sociability that coffee represents. The satirist accuses coffee-house habitués of being 'effeminate' because they spend their time talking, reading and pursuing their business, rather than carousing, drinking and whoring. By frequenting 'these *Stygian Tap-houses*', the woman petitioner claims, men 'will usurp on our Prerogative of *Tatling*, and soon learn to excel us in *Talkativeness*: a Quality wherein our Sex has ever claimed preheminence'. Men in the coffee-house '*out-babble* an equal number of [women] at a *Gossipping*, talking all at once in Confusion, and running from point to point [...] insensibly, and [...] swiftly'. In this way, their intemperate and uncontrolled discussions, swapping 'Monster Opinions and Absurdities', are also politically neuter: far from being 'dangerous to Government' such debates are 'too tame and too talkative to make any desperate Politicians'.[21] As a description of a coffee high the satire is remarkably accurate. According to the *Diagnostic and Statistical Manual of Mental Disorders* developed by the American Psychiatric Association (1994), after five or more cups of coffee the following signs are expected: restlessness, nervousness, excitement, insomnia, flushed face, and a rambling flow of thought and speech, not to mention diuresis, gastrointestinal disturbance, muscle twitching, tachycardia or cardiac arrhythmia and psychomotor agitation.[22]

The *Women's Petition* was swiftly followed by a reply, a visually similar six-page satiric travesty entitled *The Mens Answer to the Womens Petition Against Coffee, Vindicating Their own Performances, and the Vertues of that Liquour, from the Undeserved Aspersions lately cast upon them by their Scandalous Pamphlet* (1674). The satirist laments that women should be so ungrateful for men's efforts to please them. Invoking an historically enduring discourse of misogyny, the satirist complains that women's pleasure is exclusively sexual pleasure:

> Could it be imagined, that ungrateful Women, after so much laborious Drudgery, both by Day and Night, and the best of our Blood and Spirits spent in your Service, you should thus publickly Complain? Certain we are, that there never was an Age or Nation more Indulgent to your Sex; have we not condiscended to all the Methods of Debauchery? Invented more Postures than *Aretine* ever Dreamed of! Been Pimps to our own Wives, and Courted Gallants even to the hazard of our own Estates, to do us the Civility of making us not Contented, but most obliged Cuckolds.

The modern age of coffee-houses, the narrator continues, has afforded many things for women's pleasure too. Coffee he defends as a 'harmless and healing Liquor', which came into use as a 'Sober and Merry' remedy against the 'Fanatick Zeal' that had 'intoxicated the Nation' during the English republic. While ale and wine make a man both salacious and impotent, the narrator claims that coffee 'makes the erection more Vigorous, the Ejaculation more full, adds a spiritualescency to the Sperme'.[23] Paul Greenwood, who sold coffee in Clothfair in Smithfield Market, wrote in his advertising that 'the Ladies' (whores) have no 'reason to Complain':

> Coffee's no Foe to their obliging Trade,
> By it Men rather are more Active made;
> 'Tis stronger Drink, and base adulterate Wine,
> Enfeebles Vigour, and makes Nature Pine;
> Loaden with which, th'Impotent Sott is Led
> Like a Sowc'd Hogshead to a Misses Bed.[24]

Greenwood's one-page broadsheet enthusiastically named a range of diseases the 'rare Arabian cordial' of coffee would cure, including gout, dropsy, scorbutick humours, wind, rheums, palsies, jaundice, coughs, catarrh, consumption and venereal disease.

In 1671 a Maronite Syrian living in Rome, known as Antonius Faustus Naironi, published a tract in Latin on the healthful properties of coffee.[25] Having travelled widely in the Ottoman Empire in the 1650s, Naironi taught Chaldaic and Syrian at the College de Rome, where he gained renown as a defender of the Christian Maronite Church of Lebanon. Employing a knowledge of Ottoman practices and Arabic sources, and making good use of his extensive reading in travel narratives available in the Vatican library, Naironi fleshed out for the first time the history of the encounter between Western Europe and coffee, noting the bean's 'discovery' by a string of European travellers at the turn of the seventeenth century, including Jacob Cotovicus, Prosper Alpinus, John Veslingius and Peter de la Valle.

Naironi was an avid defender of 'this new Drink' called coffee, 'now diffus'd over most Parts of *Europe*, particularly this City of *Rome*'. Nonetheless, he writes of 'having met with some Discouragement' from people 'ignorant of its Qualities and good Effects'.[26] But he was not a scientist or physician, and his account of its 'Wholsomeness and Vertues', he states, relied on 'an Account of this Drink, printed first at *London*', probably N. D.'s compilation *The Vertues of the Coffee* (1663).[27] Expert opinion on the science of coffee, Naironi explained, was found among these English philosophers, where coffee use was more advanced. But Naironi's medical account of coffee is brief and confused: he cautions that coffee is still an unknown and cannot decide whether the 'different Vertues' of coffee means that it is hot or cold in its humoural properties.[28] Despite the poverty of its scientific enquiry, Naironi's little tract exerted a powerful influence over subsequent coffee science for the next century. Written in Latin, its scholarship was immediately available across the European scientific network. The book circulated in many different versions and adaptations. It was translated into Italian in 1671[29] and eventually into English in 1710, a translation 'made at the Instance of some of the Fair Sex; who being great Lovers of *Coffee*, were willing to read an Author who wrote so much in its Commendation'.[30]

Naironi's book became even better known in the versions published by the Huguenot physician and antiquarian Jacob Spon. In 1671 Spon used Naironi to put together a history and description of coffee in French (subsequently translated into English), which he placed alongside his translations of other works on tea and chocolate to produce *De L'Usage du Caphé, du Thé, et du Chocolate*, published in Lyons in 1671.[31] After the Revocation of the Edict of Nantes, as a French Protestant Spon was forced to seek refuge in Geneva, where he developed further his scholarship on coffee in his *Traitez Nouveaux & curieux du Café du Thé & du Chocolate*, which was published in Lyon and The Hague in French in 1685 under the pseudonym of his friend Phillipe Sylvestre Dufour,[32] and also in the same year, under his own name, in a Latin translation for the international scientific market (as *Tractatus Novi de Potu Caphé*).[33] In Spon's hands Naironi's little book had grown into a serious philosophical tract, bristling with footnotes and erudition, extensively illustrated and more than 400 pages in length. Spon's tract was reviewed enthusiastically by the great philosophe Pierre Bayle, who commended it for its successful mix of philosophy and commerce.'[34] The illustrated frontispiece showed an unlikely gathering of three men, wearing the typical costume of Turkey, China and America. Each drinks his appropriate beverage (coffee, tea and chocolate) from the appropriate dish, poured from the appropriate utensil. Opposite the first page of the section on coffee, a further engraving depicted the Turkish man, wearing flowing robes and a turban, seated cross-legged on the ground drinking coffee from a bowl, with a coffee pot next to him. An inset picture depicted a branch of the coffee tree, five coffee beans and a coffee roaster. In the various editions in French and Latin, and in translations in German, English and Italian, Spon's book and its illustrations became well known throughout Europe.[35]

In 1687 Nicholas de Blegny, the official doctor to the King of France, saw fit to appropriate Spon's work for his own treatise on coffee.[36] But although later editions considerably enlarged the sections describing the therapeutic efficacy of coffee on diseases of the head, heart and gut, the treatise, reliant on the humoural conjectures of the 1660s, remained unclear about the science of coffee itself. What is important about this blizzard of scholarship and plagiarism on coffee, in short, is not so much the scientific analysis on offer but the evidence they afford of a European-wide curiosity about coffee.

A more original analysis of the operation of coffee was produced by the English physician Thomas Willis, one of the foremost natural philosophers of the Royal Society. Resident in London since 1666, Willis had built up a lucrative medical practice and was renowned as one of the most skilled practitioners of the new arts of therapeutic medicine. Trained in classical Galenical medicine, he remained a defender of physic and purging, especially through vomits, enemas, laxatives and bloodletting, carthartic medicines that he believed expelled unwanted materials and purified the blood. But in the course of his research, Willis had emerged as a profound exponent of experimental science, making skilful and innovative analyses of the physiological effects of his therapies. In this way he became interested in the effects of those simples which seemed to operate on the brain and nervous system more than the stomach and its humours. Willis's thinking on coffee was first developed in a work on the operation of the brain, entitled *De Anima Brutorum* (1672), translated as *Two Discourses concerning the Soul of Brutes* in 1683. This was a ground-breaking study of diseases of the brain like epilepsy and madness, and argued that such conditions were subjects for medical study rather than theology or philosophy. Pursuing his study through careful comparative anatomy, Willis offered a polemically modern approach to psycho-physical problems, although his analysis retained much of the language of the humoural system. In an analysis of 'sleepy Distempers' – caused, he said, by an excess of 'subtil water' swelling the brain, so that the blood cannot wash the brain properly – he recommended coffee as part of his therapeutic regime. As a cure for somnolency, alongside bloodletting and purges, Willis prescribed 'At eight of the Clock of the Morning, and at five in the

Afternoon, let them drink a draught of *Coffee*, or the Liquor prepared of that Berry'.[37]

In his last work published before his death, *Pharmaceutice Rationalis* (1674), Willis again addressed the properties of coffee, which he considered an anti-hypnotick, 'highly efficacious for the driving away the *Narcosis* or stupyfyingness'. According to him, 'adust' particles in coffee (those scorched or burnt qualities introduced by roasting) freed the brain from the 'heavy oppletion and obstruction' of the blood that causes sleep. As a result, coffee has the welcome effect on the pores of the brain, 'laying aside their *torpor*, or drowsiness', and causing 'certain furies and provokings by which they are excited to the longer performing of their duties'. But drinking coffee in excess, he continued, could exacerbate 'Headach, *Vertigo*, the Palpitation of the Heart, the trembling or numness of the joints', so that imbibers experienced 'an unwonted *languor* in their whole Body'. Willis, however, advised that for nervous diseases, 'I do frequently prescribe this drink sooner than any thing else for their cure, and therefore am wont to send the sick to the Coffee houses sooner than to the Apothecaries shops.'[38] After he died in 1674, coffee was duly entered in his book of physic published for a popular audience, *The London Practice of Physick*, where it was recommended as a treatment for 'Head-aches, Giddiness, [and] the Lethargy', 'for being daily drank, it wonderfully clears and enlightens each part of the Soul, and disperses all the Clouds of every function'.[39]

Botanising for coffee

By the early 1670s coffee had became almost ubiquitous in London and well known across Europe. Bales of raw coffee were imported in London in very large quantities, to be roasted and ground in the coffee-houses across the city, or re-exported to provincial centres or cities abroad. No Londoner could have failed to note the number and variety of coffee-houses that had opened in the city. Any scientist interested in this remarkable commodity would need do no more to find a specimen of the coffee bean than walk across the street into a coffee-house. But almost nothing was known about the plant the bean came from. As one botanical historian has said, in 1685, 'ignorance was still almost complete' about the coffee tree (*coffea arabica*).[40] The most famous account, that of Spon–Dufour, was essentially a compendium of conflicting stories, twice-told tales and imprecise observations drawn from the conflicting disciplines of botany, medicine and even economics. Travellers' reports about the coffee tree were notoriously inconsistent, variously describing the plant as a tree, a low shrub, or a vine, and the bean as a berry, nut or fruit. Collecting rival accounts simply added further layers of inaccuracy and anecdote: even the great British botanist John Ray was unable to determine which story was the most accurate for the second volume of his supposedly definitive *Historia Plantarum* of 1688. From his house near Braintree, Essex, Ray systematically collected information about exotic plants. In the case of coffee it was clear that the state of botanical knowledge was scandalously confused. As well as the printed accounts of Levantine travellers and botanists, Ray had access to Rauwolf's herbarium of Levantine plants collected in the 1580s, in the course of which Rauwolf had made the first botanical description of coffee beans. But this famous herbarium had no sample of the coffee plant.

In March 1685, Ray wrote to one of his disciples, Tancred Robinson, asking him to pursue information on the nature of the coffee plant: as the son of a Turkey merchant, he had extensive connections in the region. Robinson's best source of information on Levantine plants was Dr John Covel, chaplain to the Levant Company factory in Constantinople in the years 1670–7. Although a keen collector of plant specimens and antiquities, Covel had no opportunity to encounter the coffee plant that did not grow in Constantinople.[41] Robinson's most confident reply to Ray, from London on 21 May 1685, related information gleaned from the French traveller and philosopher François Bernier, who had journeyed down the Red Sea in his voyage from Cairo to Persia in the 1650s. While in London in 1685, Bernier told Robinson some entirely incorrect information supposedly gleaned from Arab sources, 'that the coffee fruit was sown every year under trees, up which it did climb and run, from which he concludes it to be a species of Convolvulus. I think he might have well concluded it to be a *Phaseolus*, or some other scandent [climbing] Legume.' Bernier's misinformation also included the fable that the coffee beans were boiled before sale by the Arabs, so as to destroy their germinating faculty. Robinson set about his own observation of coffee beans in London, for as he observed, although most arrived decorticated (husked), the few entire beans allowed him to make a full description. He carefully described to Ray the skins or husks that covered the kernels, flat on one side and round on the other, 'on the flat side of the kernel there is always a slit, or a mouth, so that every kernel doth exactly resemble a *Concha Veneris* (Venus Shell)'.[42] Ray's description of coffee in Book 30 of the *Historia Plantarum* places it among a rather miscellaneous collection of foreign plants, including Camphor, Pistachio nut and Yucca. Without any better information the description relied on Spon's inconsistent account of coffee.[43]

In 1693 a specimen of the coffee tree was finally secured. A young English merchant, Edward Clyve, brought back ' a dryed Branch' of the Coffee shrub 'from *Moha* [Moka] in *Arabia Felix*' – 'the first who has brought any of its Branches and Leaves into these Parts'. Entrusted to the Royal Society, the branch was examined by the young botanist Hans Sloane, one of Ray's closest collaborators, and preserved in Sloane's herbarium, where it remains to this day.[44] His account was duly read before the Royal Society and was among the papers published in the Society's journal, *Philosophical Transactions*, when it was relaunched in February 1694. Accompanied by a detailed engraving of the specimen, Sloane's empirical observation of coffee established itself as the first definitive botanical description, appealed to as an authority throughout the eighteenth century in works by Bradley (1714 and 1721), Douglas (1727) and Ellis (1776).[45] But Sloane's account, taken from a pressed specimen, contained nothing on the cultivation of the coffee plant. For that, English botanists needed a live coffee tree, or a close look at someone else's.

In Europe, the undisputed leaders in coffee cultivation were the Dutch. In 1696 agents of the Dutch East India Company had succeeded in smuggling some saplings from Arabia Fœlix (Yemen) to Batavia (Java) in the Dutch East Indies, where they found the plant could be cultivated without difficulty.[46] From Java a live specimen was acquired by Dutch botanists at the Amsterdam Physic Garden, which they kept in a huge, purpose-built hothouse, under conditions of some security. James Petiver, an English apothecary and botanist on a tour of Holland in 1711, marvelled at the 'Coffee tree, which had near 2 pounds ripe fruit on it, a sight no less delightfull then amazing'.[47] At Petiver's urging another English botanist, Richard Bradley, ingratiated himself with the Dutch scientists in 1714 and in July managed to smuggle a live specimen back to London, where it was cultivated under glass in the nursery of Thomas Fairchild in Hoxton.[48] A further specimen was gifted to the Royal Physic Garden in Paris. From these specimens in collections in

Amsterdam, Paris and London, coffee cultivation was spread to the European colonies in the Caribbean. The botanical description of coffee was completed in 1737 when the eminent Swedish botanist, Carl Linnaeus, described the plant according to his binomial typology. In his system the plant was classified in the family *Rubiaceae*, as a separate genus *Coffea*, with one known species *Arabica* (its full name is thus '*Coffea Arabica* Linnaeus'). Since the second half of the nineteenth century more than a hundred more distinct species of *Coffea* have been discovered, ranging from low shrubs to trees more than thirty feet high. One of these, *Coffea Canephora* (var. Robusta), notable for its heavy cropping and large berries, was taken from Zaire to a nursery in Brussels around 1900 and, by being widely disseminated around the globe, has become the most common variety of coffee cultivated.[49]

The blessed fever of caffeine

Alongside this botanical research on the nature of the coffee plant, the Royal Society in London turned its attention to the problem of how coffee works. On 9 May 1687 the Dutch scientist Antonie van Leeuwenhoek wrote from Delft with the results of his microscopsy of the coffee bean.[50] Since 1677, using his advanced microscope, Leeuwenhoek's work had revolutionised the study of the cell structures of animals and plants. Read before the Royal Society at its meeting of 25 May, Leeuwenhoek's letter offered some conclusions on the 'growth and texture of the coffee-berry', namely that it was in the 'oil' contained in the berry that 'the principal virtue of the coffee' lay; and that this oil was present only after roasting. Accordingly, Leeuwenhoek 'gave direction for roasting the berry, and making coffee drink after the best manner'. His breakthrough discovery of the volatile oils of coffee was half understood by Hooke, who 'supposed, that the roasting of coffee is a sort of mailing thereof to make it give its tincture; and that without roasting it would not make coffee'.[51] Both Leeuwenhoek and Hooke point to the crucial pyrolytic (heat-driven) stage of the coffee-roasting process, which produces the typical, highly complex, bitter-sweet flavours and aromas of coffee.[52] Nonetheless, although this process brings about the typical flavour of coffee, this is not the cause of its habit-forming psychoactive properties, which reside in the chemical compounds identified as caffeine in the nineteenth century.

The agricultural writer John Houghton also made some

investigations into the physiological properties of coffee in his 'Discourse of Coffee' presented to the Royal Society in 1699. Although Houghton had attended university at Cambridge, he had spent many more years in trade as a coffee merchant, in a shop 'against the Ship Tavern in St Bartholomew Lane, behind the Royal Exchange'. As well as presenting some pioneering research on the history of the first coffee-house in England, he describes performing a '*Chymical* Analysis of Coffee', despite being a rather imprecise chemical experimenter. Houghton made a comparison between roasted coffee, horse beans and wheat, all prepared in a similar manner. The difference between these samples, he commented, was to be found in the amount of oil they contained, of which coffee produced twice as much as the other samples. Like Leeuwenhoek, he concluded that this oil enabled coffee to 'enliven and invigorate'. Invoking Willis, Houghton declared coffee was 'an Antihypnotick or Hinderer of Sleep', adding, 'Could I meet with a satisfactory Theory of Sleep, perhaps at this I might give some better guesses.'[53]

Throughout the lengthy debate in the eighteenth century on coffee's psychoactive properties, it remained clear that its effect on sleep and wakefulness were the most compelling. After a century of scientific enquiry, in which many medical theses and dissertations debated the therapeutic effects of coffee, there was no agreement as to how coffee worked. Consumers remained enthusiastic drinkers of coffee, even when they could not account for its efficacy. In 1802 the English poet Samuel Taylor Coleridge – his health ravaged by excessive consumption of opium – employed coffee as part of a strict dietary regimen, 'eating nothing at breakfast & taking only a single cup of strong coffee', sometimes with a teaspoon of ginger. Even though he abhorred tea as a 'pernicious stimulant', Coleridge believed coffee would prove a palliative to his nerves and stomach, 'tenderer, & more fluttery, & bowel-weak, than most'.[54] According to the German chemist Samuel Hahnemann, coffee transformed mental states, initiating a 'kind of blessed fever' in which 'presence of mind, attention, sympathy become more active'. Writing in 1803, he observed that a few hours after drinking, 'the coffee drinker smiles contented with himself [. . .] All external objects appear to excite a feeling of pleasure, they take on, if I may be allowed the expression, a joyous varnish [. . .]. All the agreeable sensations communicated are speedily increased to enthusiasm.' Only in this heightened state, he concludes, does the coffee drinker become 'completely alive'; and it is this 'property' that made coffee 'a social beverage'.[55] Hahnemann's unusually attentive observation of the coffee experience does not obscure the fact that he had no clear theory as to how coffee achieved this effect.

Already by 1803, botanists, using a new methodology derived from chemistry, had identified the active principal of opium – its power for somnolence – in an extract they later isolated and named 'morphine' in 1816. The active substance of coffee was in turn isolated in 1819 in Jena in Germany by the young chemist Ferdinand Runge, at the behest of the poet Wolfgang von Goethe, who had long evinced great curiosity about both chemistry and coffee.[56] Following the same route taken with opium, Runge succeeded in isolating a vegetable alkaloid from coffee beans with all the properties of the drink itself. The highly complex organic 'base' he precipitated was a bitter-tasting white crystalline powder which he called 'Kaffeebase'. When Runge's work on plant chemistry was published it attracted notice in both Germany and England: Coleridge was one of many who read his *New Phytochemistry* (1820) with great interest.[57] Nonetheless, French researchers were independently in pursuit of the compound too. Pierre Jean Robiquet and Joseph Pelletier independently isolated it in 1821, and it was they who gave the compound its name 'caffeine' (the -ine suffix indicating it was a vegetable alkaloid with powerful psychoactive properties akin to morphine and cocaine). By 1861 Adolf Strecker proposed the molecular structure of this 'trimethylxanthine' could be represented by the formula $C_8H_{10}N_4O_2$.

In the twenty-first century science remains undecided whether caffeine is good for health. Nonetheless, there is broad agreement about how caffeine affects the chemistry of sleep. When active and awake, brain cells produce a by-product called adenosine. Exported from the cell, adenosine binds to special adenosine receptors in the cell surface, where they slow down the transmission of neural signals. As levels of adenosine build up, the brain starts to work more slowly, an effect we understand as fatigue and drowsiness. In this way adenosine levels operate as a subtle 'thermostat' or 'brake' on the levels of activity in the brain. Caffeine has a broadly similar molecular structure to adenosine and can also bind itself to the adenosine receptors in the brain-cell surface. But unlike adenosine, caffeine does not slow down nerve-cell activity, with the result that the nerve-cells continue in a heightened state of activity, as if they are not fatigued. As the American neurobiologist Stephen Braun concludes, 'Caffeine can't stimulate anything.' It works as 'an indirect stimulant' that increases brain activity because it can no longer reduce speed. It is, he says, like putting a bit of wood under the brake pedal, so you can't slow down. As a result, the brain's own stimulants – dopamine, endorphins, adrenalin – increase neural activity.[58]

In pharmacological terms, the effects of coffee ingestion are comparatively slight, producing subtle changes that have proved difficult to study in everyday environments (studies show, for example, that most people have difficulty determining whether they have ingested caffeine or a placebo until quite high dosage levels, equivalent to three or more cups). Although many people report caffeine dependency, it is not addictive in the same way as nicotine, alcohol or narcotics.[59] Caffeine remains active in the body for a long time after ingestion (its half-life in the bloodstream is five hours) and has been shown empirically to disrupt sleep patterns. The day following coffee ingestion, consumers discover that their feelings of lethargy and fatigue can be temporarily alleviated by drinking more coffee. Though now awakened, the renewed dose of coffee repeats the interruption of sleep. A habituated pattern of consumption is established: coffee is needed to alleviate the symptoms of fatigue it has itself caused.

In the early nineteenth century Samuel Hahnemann eulogised the effects of coffee on the creative mind, claiming that to the coffee drinker, 'the ideas and pictures of the fancy flow in rapid succession and in a continuous stream before the seat of imagination'.[60] Extensive testing by the US Army determined in 2000 that caffeine was the best available dietary supplement to increase 'mental alertness and vigilance in situations of sleep deprivation', and recommended that caffeine supplements be made available in army rations.[61] But other recent studies have shown that although people believe themselves to be performing at higher levels after caffeine consumption, objective tests of performance show no improvement.[62] Scientists who research caffeine are increasingly coming to the conclusion that although it raises arousal levels, increases alertness and delays sleep, it does not, as many consumers believe, promote clearer thinking or greater creativity. Caffeine does not make coffee the 'think drink'.[63] The fact that so many coffee drinkers do believe this is not attributable to the psychopharmacology of caffeine, but rather to the cultural history of coffee, especially to that heady association between coffee, conversation and companionship encountered in the coffee-houses. In the seventeenth and eighteenth centuries, doctors, physicians and coffee-men actively promoted the 'vertues' of coffee as a potent medicinal physick. But, more importantly, satirists and poets, sometimes at the behest of coffee-house keepers, kept up a constant barrage of tracts, satires and verses that firmly established the role of coffee and the coffee-house in the new urban patterns of combinational socialising, discussion and news media consumption. Offering coffee in a bundle with companionship and conversation has so altered its cultural history that it is no longer possible to taste coffee and not be reminded of them. Coffee advertising continues to associate coffee drinking with the break from work, with reflection and insight, with conversation and companionship. Though it may not simply be the think drink, it is the talking cure.

CHAPTER TEN

The Free-School of Ingenuity

The emergence of the coffee-house transformed the social organisation of the city, bringing with it a new principle of convivial sociability based on conversation and discussion. From the first, coffee-houses attracted particular coteries of men, who enjoyed the opportunity presented there by the free and unregulated nature of debate. But though it was free and unregulated, it was not completely unstructured, because many coffee-houses became associated with specialised discourse on tightly defined subject matter. The Swiss traveller César de Saussure noted, 'Some coffee-houses are a resort for learned scholars and for wits; others are the resort of dandies or of politicians, or again of professional newsmongers; and many others are temples of Venus.'[1] As Saussure cautioned, although coffee-houses became the focus for assemblies of men engaged in particular concerns, not all those interests furthered their business or trade.

Many of the specialised allegiances between coffee-house and interest were determined by architecture and geography. The routines of everyday life in court and chambers brought lawyers, law students and clerks back to the same establishments located in clusters near the Inns of Court: both Nandos and the Grecian were noted for their legal flavour. In different periods, Child's Coffee-House near St Paul's Cathedral attracted clergymen, whereas the Chapter Coffee-House, nearby in Paternoster Row, was the haunt of booksellers and printers, and the hack writers they employed. Merchants, insurance agents and brokers met at Jonathan's and Garraway's coffee-houses in Exchange Alley. Particularising coffee-house conversation in this way enabled men with a singular curiosity to be sure of finding others of like interest, whose discourse was worth their attention. The coffee-houses, in short, became markets for specialised information, as well as places to drink coffee, stay warm and read the newspapers. To scholars, both of the arts and the sciences, coffee-houses became one of the most significant locations for debate and the exchange of ideas, evolving into an important research tool, somewhere between a peer-review system, an encyclopaedia, a research centre and a symposium.

For wits and poets an important concentration of coffee-houses emerged in Russell Street, a broad street leading off the crowded piazza of Covent Garden, close to the theatres. The first of these was Will's Coffee-House, which held the ascendancy from the Restoration to 1720, challenged by Tom's from 1700 and Button's from 1712, all located within a few doors of each other. William Urwin opened Will's Coffee-House, as it came to be known, at the corner of Russell Street and Bow Street shortly after the Restoration. From an early date the coffee room on the first floor was the favoured haunt of a group of writers who acknowledged John Dryden as their head, not only as one of the greatest poets of the age, but also as an influential critic and literary patron. Aspiring writers attended Will's at their peril, for to annoy the company there was certain to harm your prospects. On one occasion Pepys records meeting with this literary society, in February 1664, when he 'stopped at the great Coffee-house there' in Covent Garden, 'where I never was before'. There, he says, he found 'Draydon the poet (I knew at Cambridge) and all the wits of the town, and Harris the player and Mr. Hoole of our college; and had I time then, or could at other times, it will be good coming thither, for there I perceive is very witty and pleasant discourse. But I could not tarry and it was late; they were all ready to go away.'

Pepys was impressed by this group: as well as Dryden, he met William Howell (the historiographer royal), and the actor Henry Harris.[2] When Samuel Johnson was collecting evidence for a biography of Dryden, he was told that 'At Will's coffee-house Dryden had a particular chair for himself', set in pride of place by the fire in winter and on the balcony overlooking the street in the summer. Dryden's management of the coffee-house's space made his status within that assembly unequivocal: Johnson reports that Colley Cibber called him the 'arbiter of critical disputes at Will's', setting himself up as judge and jury on matters of literary debate and dispute. Cibber himself was estranged from Dryden, Johnson quipped, so he 'had perhaps one leg only in the room, and durst not draw in the other'.[3] The meetings at Will's gained renown, helping to establish the reputation of the celebrated poets and playwrights of the age, including William Congreve, William Wycherley, Thomas Southerne, the Earl of Rochester, the Earl of Roscommon, Nicholas Rowe, George Etherege, William Walsh, John Vanbrugh, Samuel Garth and Joseph Addison. Making the inner circle at Will's – famously signalled by the honour of being offered snuff from Dryden's own outsized snuffbox – established these men at the centre of their literary culture. As a boy, Alexander Pope was taken to see Dryden at Will's, as if a visit to the great man was equivalent to viewing the lions at the Tower.

The tables of Will's were covered in manuscripts and printed papers, not only newsletters and gazettes, but also poems, lampoons and verses of all kinds. One minor poet, 'Captain' Robert Julian, styled the 'Secretary to the Muses', took it upon himself to keep the coffee-house supplied with all the latest literary works, good and bad.[4] The great writers, William Wycherley estimated, made Will's into 'the Wits Coffee-house', for without them its society was given over to nothing but 'Puns, Couplets' and 'Quibbles'. In this period, 'wit' meant much more than mere humour, embracing a notion closer to the imaginative faculty: wits were noted for their ingeniousness, inventiveness with language and ideas, not just their jests and puns.[5] The critic John Dennis described Will's as 'the *Wits Coffee-House*', although during the summer, he once joked to Congreve, 'he must call it so by Antiphrasis, because there comes no Wit there'. In the absence of the great poets, he conceded that there were a few men who 'endeavour to pass for wise at the Coffee-house' only by remaining silent. 'Indeed the Coffee-house is generally the Exchange for Wit, where Merchants meet without bringing the Commodity with them, which they leave at home in the Ware-houses, alias their Closets, while they go abroad to take a prudent care of vending it.'[6]

In a letter from London written in 1701, a French gentleman equated Will's Coffee-House with the Academie Française in Paris, although unlike that august academy, the coffee-house was a place of 'Promiscuous company', open to all comers. Will's, he suggested, was 'consecrated to the Honour of *Apollo*, by the first-rate Wits that flourish'd in King *Charles* II's reign'. It was, he said, 'supported by men of great Worth; but it being accounted the Temple of the *Muses*, where all *Poets* and *Wits* are to be initiated, has given occasion to its being pester'd with abundance of false Pretenders, who rather darken, than heighten its former Splendor'. The 'Company which now generally meets at *Will's*', he suggested, 'may be divided into two Classes', which he dubbed 'the *Wits*, justly so call'd', and 'the *Would-be Wits*'.[7]

The company at Will's defined itself as an elite and, as such, attracted the opprobrium of those it excluded, who lambasted its inner circle as a sycophantic group of back-slappers and claqueurs. After a play, they imagined, the critics at Will's retired to the coffee-house, where, if the author was not one of them, they indulged in vituperative criticism. One anonymous satirist lampooned this 'Jury of Wit', composed of 'Painters, Fidlers, Poets, Minor Authors, Beaux, and the rest of the illiterate Blockheads', who 'retire from the Play' and 'over a Dish of Politick and Poetick Tea or Coffee', 'promiscuously dissect the poor Play, to be sure to the Author's disadvantage; how good soever, or whatever Success it met with'. Many satirists derided the 'Scene of the Wits' at Will's Coffee-House as a cesspit of pedants, punsters, and poetasters.[8] Aphra Behn, excluded by sex as well as inclination, derided their judgements as hypocritical and self-serving. In the preface to her comedy *The Luckey Chance* (1687), Behn characterised the critics at Will's as 'the Witty Few', who, motivated by 'Malice and ill Nature', censured her play simply because it was new, successful and by a woman. She found their hypocrisy particularly irksome: 'A Wit of the Town, a Friend of mine at *Wills* Coffee House, the first Night of the Play, cry'd it down as much as in him lay, who before had read it and assured me he never saw a prettier Comedy. So complaisant one pestilent Wit will be to another.' 'Every coffee-house', she complained in the prologue, 'still swarms with Fool.'[9] Behn had already written on coffee. In 1685, on the accession of James II, she had authored a broadside poem on coffee and tea called *Rebellions Antidote*, which tried to rewrite the historical allegiance of coffee with sedition. In the poem she imagines a dialogue between these two commodities, in which tea persuades coffee to abandon the rebellious supporters of the Protestant succession and loyally to support the King.'[10]

Some of these critical contests became quite heated. The publication of Dryden's poem *The Hind and the Panther* in 1687, which advertised his politically opportune conversion to Catholicism, provoked Matthew Prior and Charles Montagu to a stinging reply. They rewrote, or as they called it 'transversed', Dryden's fable of a deer (Christ) entertaining a panther (the Church) into a dialogue between a country mouse, an innocent milk-fed white creature, and a city mouse, a brindled and streetwise fop. In their tour through the town, the country mouse expresses a wish to visit Will's, the '*Wit's Coffee-house*'. Here, the town mouse assures her, she will see:

> Priests sipping *Coffee, Sparks* and *Poets Tea*; [...]
> And hear shrew'd guesses made, and reasons given,
> That humane Laws were never made in Heaven.

However, the chief sight is Dryden sitting in state:

> the *Poetic Judge* of sacred *Wit*,
> Who do's i' th' *Darkness of his Glory sit.*
> *And as the Moon who first receives the light,*
> *With which she makes neither Regions bright;*
> *So does he shine, reflecting from a far,*
> *The Rayes he borrowed from a better Star*:
> For rules which from *Corneille* and *Rapin* flow,
> Admir'd by all the scribbling Herd below.
> From the *French Tradition* while he does dispense,
> Unerring Truths, 'tis Schism, a damn'd offence,
> To question his, or trust your private sense.

Lampooning Dryden's role as the critical arbiter sitting in judgement over the poetical productions of the town, the town mouse argues that Dryden's neoclassical aesthetics were simply passive subservience to the French poetic rules of Corneille and Rapin; suggesting a further analogy with Dryden's new-found respect for the Catholic Church and political autocracy. Dryden was stung by the criticism: Tom Brown reported that he 'complained at Will's Coffee-House of the ill usage' he met with in the poem, observing that his own 'piece of Polemick Poetry' was published under his own name, while his attackers lacked the 'breeding and civility to do the like'.[11] Dryden had been the victim of a more robust form of criticism in 1679. In November of that year a poem satirising the King and his mistresses, *An Essay on Satire*, had attracted a lot of notice. It was commonly ascribed to Dryden, although its real author was the Earl of Mulgrave. Returning one night from Will's Coffee-House to his home in Long Acre, Dryden was seized by three men in the narrow alley of Rose Street and severely beaten with wooden staves. The paymaster of these thugs was probably Louise de Keroualle, Duchess of Portsmouth, one of the King's mistresses, although the Earl of Rochester was also suspected.[12] Rather than giving evidence for the 'democratisation of Wit,'[13] the exclusive sociability of Will's Coffee-House, with its cruel dismissal of new and unknown voices, suggests the professionalisation of wit into a tribunal of critics.

Upon Dryden's death in May 1700 the pre-eminence of Will's as the gathering place of the wits was challenged by Tom's Coffee-House, established at No. 17 Russell Street by Captain Thomas West in 1700. In 1714 the ex-secret-service agent John Macky described Tom's and Will's Coffee-Houses in Covent Garden as the haunt of 'the best Company' and 'the best of Conversation till Midnight'. Macky witnessed men of the highest orders of nobility, wearing the '*Blue* and *Green Ribbons* and *Stars*' that indicated their rank, 'sitting familiarly, and talking with the same freedom, as if they had left their Quality and Degrees of Distance at Home'. Macky's conditional 'as if' is crucial, of course: for these men were as careful to indicate their rank as they were to ignore it.[14] In 1712, at the height of the fame derived from his involvement in *The Spectator*, Joseph Addison established an ex-servant, Daniel Button, as master of a coffee-house opposite Will's. Alexander Pope reported that Addison went to Button's nearly every day, staying five or six hours at a stretch, sometimes far into the night. This was a regime that the frail Pope found too much, remarking 'it hurt my health so I quitted it'.[15] The circle of writers Addison assembled at Button's included Richard Steele, Eustace Budgell, Ambrose Philips and Charles Davenant. The rivalry between the Russell Street literary coffee-houses became intense, with each group claiming it stood for a markedly different set of values, both literary and political.

While belonging to a coterie of coffee-house wits reinforced the exercise of critical judgement and helped establish a poet's literary recognition, it could also expose him to attack and ridicule. Addison's enemies were underwhelmed by his group at Button's, believing that he self-consciously modelled his 'little Senate' on Dryden's, with the difference that both the members and the leader were less able. Literary debate frequently degenerated into bad-tempered quarrels. Rival translations of Homer's *Iliad* published in 1715 by Pope and Tickell provoked an abusive exchange of pamphlets and reviews between the rival coffee-house coteries. John Gay reported to Pope, 'I am informed that at Button's your character is made very free with as to morals &c.' As Pope commented, the wits, himself included, 'talk much of fine sense, refin'd sense, and exalted sense', but in their disputes, he concluded,

'Party affects us all.' He lampooned Addison, once his friend, as a man who acted as if he were the 'great Turk in poetry', sitting on his throne at Button's, surrounded by 'his Mutes too, a sett of Nodders, Winkers and Whisperers, whose business is to strangle all other offsprings of wit in their birth'.[16] The same portrait served to satirise Addison in the *Epistle to Dr Arbuthnot* (published in 1736), which depicted him as a hypocritical and vengeful critic sitting 'attentive to his own applause' in the coffee-house, surrounded by nobody but poetasters and flatterers.[17]

A later generation of writers in London found the Bedford Coffee-House a convivial home for their critics' circle. In 1751 Mr Town, the urbane conductor of *The Connoisseur*, found the Bedford, located under the arcades on the north side of Covent Garden Piazza, full of 'men of parts', almost every one a 'polite scholar and a wit'. Taking part in their energetic debate on 'almost every branch of literature', Mr Town declared, constitutes a 'school' to which he freely admits he is 'indebted for a great part of my education'.[18] The *Memoirs of the Bedford Coffee House* (1763) celebrated the place as the 'emporium of wit' and 'seat of criticism' – although the memoirist also suggested that critical judgements were nearly always partial and mercenary.[19] Reflecting its location next to the theatre, the walls of the Bedford were papered with playbills and the coffee room particularly associated with dramatic criticism. One wit announced in a newspaper that the critics maintained a '*Theatrical Thermometer*' to measure the critical notice of new plays. 'According to the Merit or Demerit of the Entertainment, the Liquor in the Tube rises or falls, as it does in Proportion to the degrees of Heat and Cold, in common Thermometers.' The degrees on the tube were marked from 'Excellent' to 'Pretty well' to 'So-so' to 'Execrable'.[20]

This sort of self-conscious fashioning of the image of a wits' coffee-house was an important contribution to the social function of literary criticism. Despite the vituperative enmity shown by the poets' circles at Will's and Button's, the differences between their coffee-houses do not now seem as remarkable as the similarities. The wits' coffee-houses were an architectural expression of an enthusiasm for collective sociability, which was mirrored by the manner in which groups of poets published 'miscellanies' or anthologies together, essayists joined forces in periodicals and even, in the case of the Scriblerian group, engaged in experiments in collective composition. Pope derided the 'modern

Custom of appearing in Miscellanies', which, although he also appeared in similar projects, he said were 'very useful to the Poets, who, like other Thieves, escape by getting into a Crowd, and herd together like banditti, safe only in their Multitude'.[21] Appearing in groups, in miscellanies, essay periodicals and coffee-houses, gave poetry and criticism an objectified institutional shape, freeing individual poets and critics from the need to invent or define their activities. Through this model of coffee-house sociability the modern notion of literary criticism came into being.

The sociability of the coffee-house proved attractive to natural philosophers and other scientists too. Meeting there, they found, was a fruitful way to transact their research, discover new facts and test hypotheses. Coffee-houses, in short, were a tool of the experimental method. Scientists' pronounced preference for the coffee-house over the tavern can be traced back to the Interregnum. In Oxford in the 1650s small groups of scholars, physicians and clerics associated with the circles of Robert Boyle, Christopher Wren and John Wilkins met in the coffee room of the Oxford apothecary Arthur Tillyard, in his shop on the High Street opposite All Souls College in 1655. In their 'Chemical Club' they discussed matters of current scientific enquiry, finding in their discourse a profitable refuge from politics. After the Restoration these men formed the core of the Royal Society for the Improvement of Natural Knowledge by Experiment, which was to meet weekly to debate, experiment and record investigations into all kinds of natural knowledge. The weekly meetings of the Royal Society at Gresham College were in the early years never as popular as their customary assemblies in the coffee-houses around the Royal Exchange, where they met on a daily basis. Reporting on the experiments tried at the College in a letter to Robert Boyle (6 October 1664), the Society's Secretary, Henry Oldenburg, explained that 'before our Philosophicall meeting' he had been 'at a Coffee Club', where he had heard 'not only State News' (of military preparations for the war against the Dutch) but also 'Philosophy, Whereof I must send you one or two particulars which were new to me'.[22]

The coffee-houses became one of the key spaces in which the New Science could be debated by the wider public. As Thomas Hobbes and others complained, the Royal Society only admitted as members men who already believed in the results and the methodology of the experimental philosophy. The opponents of their method, such as Dr Henry More, who retained a role for the divine in physical phenomena, or Sir Matthew Hale, who defended the authority of the ancients, were excluded from debates at the Royal Society. To Hobbes this exclusiveness meant that their meetings failed to meet the requirements of their own methodology for proving the truth of claims.[23] By contrast the coffee-house was genuinely open to all: ideas that could be proved true there could be proved anywhere. Science in coffee-houses was always more public, more debated, less abstract and more demonstrative. It is in this sense that they have come to be known as the penny universities (although the phrase was not used at the time). Describing the '*Character of a well-regulated Coffee-house*', the author of *Coffee-houses Vindicated* (1675) said 'with no less truth than plainness' that it is

> The *Sanctuary* of *Health*
> The *Nursery* of *Temperance*
> The *Delight* of *Frugality*
> An *Academy* of *Civility*,
> AND
> *Free-School* of *Ingenuity*.[24]

In the coffee-houses men of science, learning and scholarship found they had unprecedented access to all kinds of knowledge: commercial, literary, mechanical, theological. Unlike the narrow confines of the Schools, whether university, church or club, the coffee-house opened the whole world of learning to its clientele. To a seventeenth-century mind, entering a coffee-house was like walking into the Internet.

The valuable role of the coffee-house in the trade of science in Restoration London is revealed by the richly detailed diaries of Robert Hooke, one of the key players in the first decades of the Royal Society. Appointed Curator of Experiments in 1662, Hooke was a maverick genius of the theory and practice of the New Science – skilled in physics, mathematics, chemistry, optics and astronomy, as well as engineering, architecture and instrument building.[25] According to the *Diary* he kept in the 1670s, Hooke went to a coffee-house nearly every day – including Christmas Day – frequently visiting two or three in a day, and once spending the whole day traipsing between five. Although he wasn't a great fan of coffee, complaining once that 'Drinking coffee gave me stoppage of stomack', between 1672 and 1680 he visited more than sixty different establishments around London, attracted by the company of like-minded men and the information they retailed. He went several times a week to Man's Coffee-House in Chancery Lane near the gate to Lincoln's Inn, convenient for the College of Physicians, and the great recourse of doctors and medical men. Another regular stopping point was Child's Coffee-House in Warwick Lane, near the ruins of St Pauls Cathedral, convenient for the printers and booksellers of the area.[26] But two coffee-houses were his favourites.

Nearly every day Hooke visited Garraway's, about five minutes' walk from his lodgings in Gresham College and close to that great mart of news, the Royal Exchange. Sometimes Hooke's diary simply records he was 'At Garways', without saying whom he saw, or what he drank. Indeed, that he drank coffee seems to be assumed, for what was notable was when he didn't, as on 16 May 1674: 'Drank noe coffee. Slept pretty well.'[27] Hooke used Garraway's for meetings with fellows and officers of the Royal Society more often than anywhere else. Thursday, 11 June 1674 was typical: he met at Garraway's with Lord Brouncker, Henry Oldenburg and Abraham Hill, the president, secretary and treasurer, noting 'Noe meeting of the Society, nor noe Lecture nor noe Club'. Instead, Hooke gave a demonstration at the coffee-house: 'At Garaways I shewd [John] Collins [the mathematician] and Mr. Hill [the treasurer] my way to trace the way of a Bullet by the help of a transparent glasse plate or Rete.'[28] Meetings like this occurred almost every day. The pattern was altered only in 1675 when another grand coffee-house opened across the alley and thereafter, Jonathan's ('Joes') appears nearly as often in the diary. Unlike the intense atmosphere of austerity and hierarchy at Gresham College, Hooke discovered that coffee-houses 'allowed business and pleasure to be conducted under the same roof'.[29] Enjoying the constant procession of useful and notable meetings there, Hooke found the coffee-houses to be the crucial social space where the business of the Royal Society, and by extension the new experimental science, could be conducted. What made the coffee-house unique for Hooke was that it allowed him to meet, converse and transact business with artisans and craftsmen of the London scientific instruments trade, as well as physicians, surgeons, medical men; lawyers and politicians; writers and painters; great men and ordinary citizens.

In its rooms in Gresham College the Royal Society demonstrated both their own discoveries and their empirical method by performing experiments in natural knowledge in public. Attendance was often low at Hooke's Gresham lectures on Thursdays: indeed, he repeatedly notes that no one came at all.[30] By contrast, public scientific demonstrations in the coffee-houses reached out to a much wider audience and were a frequent occurrence by the 1670s. As public displays, the audience for these demonstrations was drawn widely, although they often seem to have been directed at the learned men already gathered at the coffee-house. For Robert Hooke, especially, the coffee-house experiments had an element of showmanship, as he presented work which he knew would succeed. On Thursday, 28 August 1679 the geologist John Beaumont 'shewd his starr stones' to a group of onlookers, for example, while Hooke explained the principles of magnetic attraction.

Some displays of the Society's experimental knowledge were spectacular indeed. On Friday, 14 November 1679 Hooke and his friend John Houghton encountered a dead porpoise, displayed at Ulbars, perhaps a fishmongers in the City. Specimens of strange sea creatures were regularly brought into port by fishermen, where they would be displayed and perhaps eaten. As the ancients were aware, sea creatures like porpoises and dolphins were anomalous, for they had the outward form of a fish, yet the internal organs of a mammal. At Jonathan's coffee-house Hooke told some fellow scientists of his discovery, including two young men (Nehemiah Grew and Edward Tyson). The next morning Hooke and Tyson paid 7s 6d for the porpoise and at three o'clock that afternoon performed a public anatomy of the creature at Garraway's: 'Opend fish (at Garways) at 3, fat skin, etc. drew figure.'[31] The spectacle was a great success and the specimen was judged so interesting that Hooke had the carcass brought back to Gresham College. The following Monday Hooke drew a second 'figure' of the porpoise, and he spent all of Tuesday and Wednesday with Tyson, John Beaumont and Abraham Hill 'about porpesse', performing a thorough dissection and making elaborate drawings of the animal's internal organs and skeleton. Subsequently, the physician Edward Tyson read a report on the porpoise to the Society (8 January and 27 May 1680)[32] and wrote a detailed monograph on the animal and its anatomy, which when it was published in the following year went a long way towards clarifying the mammalian status of the Cetaceous genus. Tyson was careful to give his thanks to his 'ingenious friend Hook'.[33]

But although the coffee-houses allowed an unusually open exchange of ideas, Hooke was often anything but friendly. His public demeanour was frequently abominable, picking fights with his opponents and competitors, boastfully claiming ownership of ideas, or slighting the contribution of others. He was, even his friends admitted, arrogant, argumentative and overbearing. The astronomer John Flamsteed recounted a story of meeting him in Garraway's in the early 1680s, where they debated recent advances in telescopes. Hooke's style of argument, Flamsteed lamented, was aggressive: 'it is his nature to make contradictions at randome, and with little judgement, and to defend them with unproved assertions.' Hooke tended to 'magnifie or assert some stupendious invention of his owne', even if he had 'only the conceite not the experiment, which he dares talke of not put to triall'. In their discussion, Flamsteed complained, Hooke 'bore mee downe with words enough and psuaded the company that I was ignorant in these things which that hee onely understood not I'.[34] So although coffee-houses were places of open exchange of ideas between men of differing origins, allegiances and stations in life, these were also often bad-tempered, rude and dangerous.

It was important, nonetheless, that coffee-house debates on science were not restricted to those who agreed with the agenda of modern science. An important early success for the Royal Society was its experiments conducted on air pressure, using the celebrated 'air pump' made by Hooke for Robert Boyle.[35] The public debate on the nature of the vacuum, and the experimenters' scientific method, lasted for decades. In May 1674 Matthew Hale, the Lord Chief Justice, published a reasoned, but unconvincing, account of this experiment, defending a rival argument, derived from Aristotle, that nature abhors a vacuum.[36] Hooke records buying Hale's book in May 1674 and by November the Society was ready to reply. At a meeting of the Society on Thursday, 12 November 1674, with 'Neer 40 of the Society', the mathematician Dr John Wallis, Savillian Professor, read *A Discourse of Gravity and Gravitation* (1675), before the group retired to Garraway's. That night a debate ensued at 'Powell's *Coffee-House in Wilde-street*' between the Society men, and Hales and his supporters. After the debate, as if to proclaim his victory, Wallis left a copy of his book in the coffee-house to prove his contention 'for all to peruse'. This aroused the ire of Hale's supporters, who printed a bad-tempered reply to be left with Wallis's book, arguing the opposite case:

> And these things, and many more, which the Book makes out plainly, are what the *Demi*-Doctor was pleased to call Nonsense; with a Noise and a Bawling, to keep others from hearing and acknowledging the Truth [. . .]. And because an Ass braying makes more Noise than ten wise Men, the Author hath thought it fit to put this Epitome of the Book in writing, and to leave it with the Book itself, at the Coffee-house in *Wilde-street*, where the Dispute was held; for every Man, that hath his Eyes in his head, to read and judge by himself, on which side lies the Nonsense.[37]

Here, then, the space of the coffee-house allowed the bad-tempered debate between the ancient and moderns to be tracked and followed as if in an archive, permitting other men in the coffee-houses to follow and assess their conclusions for themselves.

The Astronomer Royal, John Flamsteed, took a rather dim view of Hooke's coffee-house scientising. A 'dour unhappy man', Flamsteed distrusted the urbane sociability required of coffee-house banter.[38] To his mind science was produced by putting in the hours behind a telescope, painstakingly collecting data that only then might be used for hypothesising. Somewhat isolated in his Observatory at Greenwich, Flamsteed was repeatedly embroiled in quarrels with scientists who he felt (probably correctly) were conspiring against him in coffee-houses. In 1686, in the course of a heated disagreement with Edmund Halley, he claimed that his character was being traduced at Boden's Coffee-House by a certain Mr Dee, who made fun of Flamsteed's notorious parsimony. His friends pointed out to him that scientists could be encountered in coffee-houses all over town, explaining that 'it is impossible to be at Child's Coffee-House, and not meet' one of the 'clashing parties in the society, [. . .] for there some do lead their lives almost'. Flamsteed, who hardly ever went to the Royal Society, let alone the coffee-houses, objected that men like Hooke, who go to coffee-houses every morning, were idle wastrels. Flamsteed was, he said, 'too good an husband to squander his morneing hours in such Idle places'.[39]

From the mid 1670s the gathering of scientists at the coffee-house began to take the form of a regular club, in competition with the Royal Society itself. Hooke's club was supposed to be a congenial meeting place, in which experiments in science could be discussed and evaluated. But at the same time his aim was primarily to find and secure allies, and to exclude those like Halley and Flamsteed whose work or personality he found inimical. Meeting at Man's Coffee-House in Chancery Lane in January 1676, Hooke wrote in his diary, 'We now began our New Philosophicall Club. and Resolved upon Ingaging ourselves not to speak of anything that was reveald *sub sigillo* [in secret] to any one nor to declare that we had such a meeting at all.'[40] Saturday night meetings continued for most of the year, either at Child's Coffee-House or Wren's house, and in later years at Jonathan's Coffee-House. When Hooke resumed his diary between 1688 and 1693, he was still regularly meeting on Wednesday evenings at a club of Fellows at Jonathan's.[41] The coffee-house, with its convivial sociability and its range of sober drinks, was the established home of scientific clubs. In Hooke's diary these meetings are both scientific think-tanks for brainstorming new ideas and summits between allies in the interminable disputes that racked the scientific world.

The coffee-house proved to be a remarkably hospitable habitat for the New Science. In their convivial and amenable coffee rooms, networks of exchange and correspondence could be maintained between men of similar interest and dissimilar station. Coffee-houses became the home for a variety of 'private, unofficial and unchartered groups, clubs and voluntary associations of men . . . devoted . . . to some branch of scientific investigation as a matter of personal interest, recreation or both'.[42] One such group was the Temple Coffee-House Botany Club, formed by a nucleus of Royal Society gentlemen (Hans Sloane, Tancred Robinson, Nehemiah Grew) as an opportunity to meet and debate with the unlettered practitioners of 'the Recreative Science of Botany', not only amateur botanists but also nurserymen and gardeners.[43] One among these men was the apothecary James Petiver, the son of a haberdasher with no 'Academicall Learning' beyond a few years at Rugby Free School. After serving his apprenticeship to an apothecary, Petiver had developed a thriving trade in the 1680s, for which a thorough knowledge of the officinal (medicinal) herbs was necessary. Brought into contact with the natural philosophers of the Royal Society through the Superintendent of the Apothecaries Garden, Petiver became a keen member of the club at the Temple Coffee-House. The combination of men in the coffee-house club was 'a testimony to the egalitarianism of the Republic of the New Philosophy – or, at least, the absence of impenetrable social barriers'.[44] Despite Petiver's lack of social polish and sophistication, his enthusiasm, practical botanical knowledge, and his willingness to undertake arduous detailed projects made him central to the botanists' club and earned his election to the Royal Society in 1695. The club, 'unofficial, probably without formal organisation, and certainly social as well as scientific', mingled social conversation with the exchange of botanical information, specimens and communications from a wide range of correspondents in Britain, Europe and the colonies.

By the 1690s the popularity and influence of the coffee-house science clubs confirmed their status as a key location of the New Science. But as well as being used for the exchange of information, they were also used to popularise science itself. The mathematician John Harris showed considerable 'entrepreneurial talent' in 1698 when he began delivering lectures on mathematics, and later physics, at the Marine Coffee-House in Birchin Lane, hard by the Exchange Alley. These lectures found a public hungry for digestible knowledge about the glories of Newtonian physics, which were widely touted as evidence of British ascendancy. To cater to the demand, other lecturers discoursed on physics, astronomy, navigation, geometry and chemistry, sprinkling their prepared monologues with spectacular demonstrations and experiments.[45] This model of coffee-house science was still current in 1780, when a club began meeting fortnightly at the Chapter Coffee-House in Paternoster Row, bringing together a diverse group of experimental scientists, medical practitioners, industrialists and instrument makers to discuss all kinds of experimental philosophy (chemistry, physics, engineering, meteorology, ballooning). Though their conversations ranged broadly, their staple topic between 1780 and 1787 was so often the new chemistry of gases, especially the debate on phlogiston and inflammability, that they became known as the 'Chemical Society'.[46]

By the eighteenth century it was clear that the coffee-house had transformed the life of the scholar and scientist, whose work no longer kept him in studious isolation, like a magus or alchemist, but brought him into convivial communication, as a focus of collaborative research activity. Going to the coffee-house was not a distraction from work, but a part of scholarly work itself. In his essay for the *Philosophical Transactions* in 1699, John Houghton concluded that the 'Coffee-house makes all sorts of People sociable, they improve Arts, and Merchandize, and all other Knowledge; a worthy member of this Society (now departed) has thought that Coffee-houses have improved useful knowledge'. Through diligent and conscientious attention to coffee-house discussion, Houghton said, a well-prepared man might pick up the 'pith and marrow' of the best current research and thinking. Coffee-houses could be a short cut to learning and wisdom. One of the most popular publications of the 1690s, John Dunton's *Athenian Mercury*, published a weekly set of questions and answers on topics of public curiosity, especially science, sexual reproduction and social mores. Dunton defended the place of the learning and scholarship in the coffee-house.[47] By reading his journal in the coffeehouse, Dunton argued, '*Youth will learn to be sober* and drink Coffee, on purpose to make use of these Opportunities, which will make 'em disputants, and fit Company for their Seniors'.[48]

Coffee-house learning, however, was also commonly derided as shallow, credulous and unstructured. In a letter written in July 1670, John Evelyn derided the 'Universal Intellect' of the science writer Henry Stubbe, because it was derived not from experiment and observation, but from what he had 'pick'd up by Reading and Meditation, and the Coffee-houses'.[49] In the course of little more than twenty years between 1661 and 1683, the Master of Trinity College in Cambridge, Dr John North, noticed a complete transformation in the social habits of college Fellows. In the 1660s coffee was not in 'common Use', but by the 1680s North lamented the coffee-house-going habits of the Fellows, for it was, he thought, 'a vast Loss of Time grown out of a pure Novelty, for who can apply close to a subject with his Head full of the Din of a Coffee-house?'[50] Even Houghton, the enthusiastic defender of coffee-house learning, cautioned that a man needed some education to make the most of the opportunity. 'I must confess that he who has been well educated in the schools [universities], is the fittest man to make good use of the *coffee-houses*, and am fearful that too many make ill uses of them.'[51] Without the appropriate scholarly background, Houghton cautioned, the knowledge peddled in coffee-houses might be more dangerous than enlightening.

CHAPTER ELEVEN

The Concourse of Merchants

Passing through the columns at its main entrance, visitors to the Royal Exchange in Cornhill found themselves in a large courtyard full of merchants and traders of every nationality. In its commodious internal courtyard, lined with royal statues, traders from across Europe and round the globe met to set prices, arrange cargoes, settle bills and make deals. 'Each nation has its own quarter, so that those who have business with them can find them more easily.' From these separate 'walks', merchants could not only exchange contracts but also 'hear news of other countries and regions, which is a great convenience for those who traffick in merchandise across the seas'.[1] In each corner of the courtyard, stairs ascended to a 'merchants' seraglio', where in dozens of tiny pinfold market stalls, 'fair lady' shopkeepers sold an astonishing selection of ready-made luxury goods, from tortoiseshell combs to Belgian lace, from Turkish cambric to fine silk gloves, from silver watch-chains to mathematical instruments. In 'all Cities and Towns of Traffique', a merchants' manual of 1671 noted, the Exchange was the place 'where Merchants and Tradesmen do assemble and meet at certain hours, and limited times of the day, to confer and treat together, concerning Merchandizing, Shipping, Buying or Selling, and the like'.[2] On the exterior walls, arcades of shops and warehouses lined the streets, while underground vaults stored vast quantities of spices, wines and other commodities.

In the streets and alleys around the Royal Exchange, numerous ancillary traders found a lucrative niche: not only booksellers, printers and stationers, but also the trades necessary to equip a gentleman, including tailors, outfitters, hat makers, shoemakers, hosiers, sword makers, and toyshops (which sold luxury knick-knacks for gentlemen, such as gold snuffboxes, tortoiseshell cane handles and silk cravats).

The area also catered for the shops of some of London's most prestigious scientific instrument makers, selling the latest telescopes, astrolabes, globes, cameras obscura and microscopes. Legions of lawyers, scriveners, notaries and copying clerks were available for hire, allowing contracts to be signed and delivered in the shortest possible time. The Exchange was the epicentre of a vast and dense network of commercial activity, teeming with merchants. In *The London Spy* (1698–1700) the Grub Street satirist Ned Ward described how he had to push his way into the crowded trading floor, where he was jostled by 'a parcel of Swarthy Buggerantoes [. . .], a Crowd of Bum-firking Italians', a throng of Dutchmen, 'strait-lac'd Monsters in Fur and Thrum-Caps', as well as traders from France and Spain, Jews and snuff-taking fops. This microcosm of global trade became one of the great sights of the city. Its noise was remarkable: Ned Ward described its sound as 'an incessant Buzz, like the Murmurs of the distant Ocean'.[3] Merchants heard this buzz of trade with awe and curiosity.

The coffee-houses of Exchange Alley were the direct beneficiaries of this temple of commerce. In 1720 John Strype remarked that as the vicinity of the Exchange was 'crouded with Merchants, and Tradesmen' the area was noted for its 'Taverns, Coffee-houses, Eating-houses, and other such like Places of public Reception, as they make considerable Gains, so they pay vast Rents'. Strype marvelled at 'the Great Coffee-houses (*Jonathans* and *Garways*) that stand there', making Exchange Alley 'a Place of very considerable Concourse of Merchants, Seafaring Men and other Traders', frequented especially by 'Brokers, and such as deal in buying and selling of Stocks'.[4] By 1745, when the whole winding alley was consumed in a disastrous fire, there were no less than eight coffee-houses: Jonathan's, Garraway's, the Jerusalem, Baker's, Sam's, the Sword-Blade, Tom's and the Rainbow.[5] From its inception Exchange Alley had been conceived to take advantage of the traffic of merchants in the area: it had been opened up in 1662 as a speculative property development by a consortium of goldsmiths, bankers and merchants, who purchased contiguous plots of land in order to exploit this new and prestigious passage between the busy high streets. The initial leases (for more than thirty shops and seven substantial buildings) suggest that the magnificent scope of this retail development was on a scale that prefigures the arcade or shopping mall.[6]

At the centre of the developers' plans were coffee-houses, and by December 1662 'the new Coffee house in *Exchange Alley*', 'at the Signe of the Great Turk' on the south side of the alley, was advertising its prices in the newspaper *Kingdom's Intelligencer* and making a special offer of free coffee to attract custom: 'all Gentlemen that are or will be Customers are invited (the first day of the next new year) at the Signe of the Great Turk at the new Coffee house in *Exchange Alley*, where Coffee will be on free cost, and so may be to the worlds end.'[7] The commercial focus of the new coffee-house was signalled by the fact that by 8 January 1663 it was the venue for auctions of imported cloth to be sold 'by an inch of candle'.[8] The proprietor was Walter Elford, a girdler, granted a lease for 'the Coffee-house scituate in Exchange Alley' on 27 May 1664 at an extraordinarily high price, paying a premium of £200 and a rent of £100 per annum for twenty-one years. Rent this high indicated the site's potential for profit.[9] Elford's Coffee-house in Exchange Alley was probably the first grand coffee-house in London. Hitherto, coffee-house keepers had kept their businesses in small shops and stalls, often hastily converted by the addition of a few chairs and a table, a bar for the staff to use and a fire to keep the coffee hot. The coffee-house in Exchange Alley was by comparison large and elegant, housed in a new brick-faced building in the new development. But, like the rest of the City, it was consumed in the Great Fire of 1666, and through some fairly shady dealings Elford was unable to reach agreement with the owners of the alley when they were rebuilding, and as a result he was forced to reopen about a hundred yards away at a less prestigious site in George Yard off Lombard Street.

After the fire Exchange Alley, and the Royal Exchange itself, were rebuilt on an even grander scale than before. Elford's lease was taken by Thomas Garraway, who had hitherto operated a small coffee-house in Sweetings Rents.[10] Garraway's Coffee-House, too, was built on an impressive scale on a prestigious corner site, commanding a vantage point over the alley crammed with merchants and traders. On the ground floor it had several entrances on to the alley. Although no evidence remains of its interior decoration, it is likely that is was carried out in a high style, perhaps in the elegant neoclassicism favoured by the period, with panelled walls, gilded ornamentation, moulded ceilings, heavily carved chairs and tables. From the coffee-room windows, built using the latest sash technology, customers had a view over the action in the alley below. On the ground floor in later decades were several small rooms, including the kitchen in which coffee and other drinks were prepared. The main coffee room was up one flight of stairs. The refined and modern quality of the furniture and fittings of such a place made an important contribution to its sociability. As Lorna Weatherill has noted, because the 'furnishings were of a rather better quality than those found in many private houses', drinking in the new coffee-houses 'was not necessarily disreputable'.[11] Interiors were often quite luxurious, decorated with paintings, elaborate wainscoting, panelling, painted panels and mirrors. Interior decoration of this scale and sophistication attracted custom for itself. A rare colour image of *A Coffee-house Interior* gives a taste of this opulence. Alongside a number of notices or proclamations on paper, the walls are hung with three substantial paintings, depicting a somewhat lubricious fancy picture of a couple kissing, a swaggering portrait of a gentleman in armour and a full flowing wig and, finally, a landscape. All three are in ornate wooden and gilt frames.[12] The pictures are of sufficient interest to attract the attention of two men, who are observed inspecting the pictures using a candle for extra illumination. The point is clear in both: the interior of a coffee-house was a place for the display of art and aesthetic appreciation, even though the congested space of the coffee room was not always conducive to this activity.

The proximity of the Exchange Alley Coffee-House to the Exchange was always intended to enable its use by businessmen and merchants. The coffee-house became an extension of the trading floor of the Exchange itself, offering a warm and dry place where business could continue after the official hours had finished, becoming by this means the most celebrated aspect of the network of commercially orientated facilities of the Cornhill alleys. Thomas Rastall, the Secretary to the Company of Adventurers Trading into Hudson's Bay, made a habit of being in 'Mr. *Garraway's* Coffee-house . . . every Tuesday and Thursday . . . from Twelve to One a Clock', and advertised his habit to other merchants in *The London Gazette*.[13] Under Elford's management the Exchange Alley Coffee House encouraged this connection with merchants by becoming itself a market place. The great coffee room was used for auctions regularly from December 1662. On 8 January *Mercurius Publicus* advertised an auction 'at the Coffee-house in Exchange Alley near the Old Exchange *London*' of 'one hundred and fifty bags of Spanish Cloth wools', which could be viewed at a warehouse before had.[14] On 7 March 1664 an advertisement appeared in *The Intelligencer* for an auction of '78 Bales of *Coffee*, right *Turky Berrie*, good and fresh as possible'.[15] Other records also note ships and their cargoes being sold at the coffee-house in these years, especially at Garraway's and Lloyd's. In the late seventeenth and early eighteenth centuries, newspapers contained innumerable advertisements for auctions in coffee-houses: London's first daily newspaper, *The Daily Courant*, carried one or more every day. The Hudson's Bay Company used Garraway's for auctions of furs, such as the sale of 3,000 pounds' weight 'of beaver coates & skins at Mr. Garway's Coffeehouse upon Tuesday the 5 October [1671] at two a clocke afternoon.'[16] Advertisements announced the goods to be sold and, as the coffee-house was the location only of the auction itself, in which warehouse they could be viewed. All kinds of commodities were vended, including manufactured goods, luxury commodities, entire ships and even African slaves.[17] In September 1710 an advertisement in *The Tatler* proclaimed a sale of fine claret:

> For sale by the Candle on Thursday next being the 5th Instant [5 October 1710], at Garraway's Coffee-house in Exchange Alley, at Four in the Afternoon (only one Cask in a Lot) viz. 55 Hogsheads and 8 half Hogsheads of excellent French (Margaux and Obrion [Haut Brion]) Clarets, deep, bright, strong, and of the true Flavour, neat and entire, perfect fine, and fit for bottling; lying in a vault under Clothworker's-Hall in Mincing Lane. [. . .] To be sold by Thomas Tomkins, Broker, in Seething-Lane, between Tower-street and Crouched-Fryars.[18]

Satirists in the 1670s found the prevalence of coffee-house auctions an opportunity to poke some ribald fun at the royal court and its libertine morals. One of these gave notice that 'On Thursday May 29th is to be sold at a publicke sale by an intch of Candle at ye Royall Coffy house, neer Charing Cross. These following Goods – in small Lotts': and then listed thirty-five lots including '1 whole piece of the Duchess of Clevelands honesty, willow-green, valued at a Crown a yard' alongside '24 Ells of Nell Gwyns Virginity, in 3 peeces' and '200 weight of the Lord Arlingtons best sweet scented cut & dryed policy'.[19] Many auctions were conducted 'by an inch of candle', in which a section of wax candle was lit, and bidding continued until the flame went out, with the final bid carrying the lot. When Pepys witnessed such an auction for the first time on 6 November 1660 he 'observed how they do invite one another, and at last how they all do cry' as the candle gutters out. In September 1662, having been to another, he 'observed one man cunninger than the rest, that was sure to bid the last man, and to carry it; and enquiring the reason, he told me that just as the flame goes out the smoke descends, which is a thing I never observed before, and by that he do know the instant when to bid last – which is very pretty'.[20]

For many London merchants, attendance at the coffee-house was at least as important as their performance on the Exchange itself, for the two were one horizontally integrated network of gossip and news. Samuel Pepys was one young man who had to learn by experience that a successful performance in the market depended upon the knowledge and information he could collect. Pepys had discerned that traders in possession of the most up-to-date news could turn a healthy profit. It was also clear that as market information was not distributed evenly, it needed to be collected, and interpreted, to be of use strategically. In the commercial world of London the coffee-houses came to have a crucial role in the dissemination of financial intelligence and rumour. Its sociable habits, its open-ended conversations between strangers, made it an ideal location for encountering news, undertaking analysis into its value and credibility, and for the performance of strategy and deception.[21] Select City coffee-houses such as Jonathan's, Garraway's and Lloyd's became central to the spatial organisation of the commercial activity of the London financial markets. In this period, too, the market was expanding rapidly, especially after the Glorious Revolution of 1688. London itself had become the largest port and market for international trade in the world: the economy of London and Britain was undergoing a transformation that economic historians have described as 'a financial revolution'.[22]

The London market had long been home to joint-stock companies, in which investors clubbed together to finance large-scale long-distance trading expeditions, expecting to spread the risk and share the profits at the end of the voyage when the goods were sold in London (the dividend). In 1689 there were six major joint-stock companies, such as the Royal African Company, the Hudson's Bay Company and, by far the largest, the East India Company. By 1695 the number had grown to around fifteen, whose field of operation covered not just foreign trade but also domestic projects such as the Bank of England, founded in 1694, and the supply of water to the city. In the speculative mania of 1720 – the so-called South Sea Bubble – over 190 new joint stock-companies were launched. The market in shares in this trade had also been transformed. In 1693 the government permanently funded its increasingly large debt through the Bank of England, which raised a stock subscription, whose rent or interest was paid annually by the Crown at 8 per cent interest. Government stock was transferable, comparatively safe and remunerative, and, as extended by other joint-stock companies, vastly increased the market in securities.[23] As the financial market grew in these years, the experience of the coffee-houses in the vicinity of the Exchange came to play an important part in constructing the public image of the securities market – that which is now often called the stock market.

By the end of the seventeenth century the number of coffee-houses in London had grown considerably, although exactly how many existed is difficult to estimate. One certain figure is the eighty-two coffee-house keepers discovered by the City of London magistrates in 1663, although their survey did not extend to the metropolitan areas of Westminster or Southwark. In the early eighteenth century Londoners thought there were a great many. Anthony Hilliar's fictional visitor Ali-Mohammed Hadgi remarked in 1730 that 'there's a prodigious Number of Coffee-Houses in *London*', but he did attempt to not count them.[24] John Macky also remarked that coffee-houses were 'innumerable' in 1714, before going on to make the 'modest Computation' that there were 'above Eight Thousand of them, [. . .] in and about *London*'.[25] In his *Cyclopædia* of 1727, Ephraim Chambers 'computed' that there were 'three thousand Coffee-houses' in the capital alone, as had Edward Hatton in 1708.[26] Most twentieth-century historians have estimated the number of coffee-houses in London at the beginning of the eighteenth century as either 2,000 or 3,000 – hardly a helpful difference.[27] These figures are in any case an exaggeration. A more realistic estimate would be closer to 400 or 500, which is, of course, still a substantial number.[28]

The most accurate survey of the number of coffee-houses undertaken in the eighteenth century was that of the indefatigable topographer and historian William Maitland for his *History of London* in 1739. For eleven months this industrious man walked over every square inch of London, meticulously recording – with 'unwearied Application' and 'incredible Pains' as he said himself – the names of all the streets, squares, lanes and alleys he encountered. In addition to noting the distinguished public buildings (such as churches, mansions and prisons), Maitland recorded the number of houses, breweries, taverns and coffee-houses in each street. He counted a total of 551 coffee-houses. This is indeed a large number for a city of about half a million people.[29] But Maitland's survey reveals that coffee-houses were not evenly distributed across the city, but were concentrated in comparatively wealthy districts, especially the City, St James's and in the corridor between the two around Covent Garden and Fleet Street. There were far fewer in Wapping, Southwark and the area outside the walls between Moorgate and Whitechapel, where large conglomerations of poorer people lived. Furthermore, although the number of coffee-houses was broadly similar to those of taverns and inns, both were vastly outnumbered by brandy houses, the low shops that sold cheap liquor such as brandy and gin. While there were 551 coffee-houses in London, there were more than 8,000 gin shops. In poor areas like Wapping and Southwark there were more than eighty gin shops for each coffee-house.[30] London was one of the most caffeinated cities in the world in 1739, but the coffee-houses served an elite sector of the market. Those in the City, especially in and around Exchange Alley, were increasingly the home of men engaged in highly specialised trading in stocks and shares.

The coffee-houses, which had of course long been associated with the provision of news and newspapers, began in the 1690s to develop specialist news services for financial information. In 1692 John Houghton reported that merchants in Garraway's Coffee-House could consult a list which displayed 'what Prices the Actions bear of most Companies trading in Joynt-Stocks'. He proposed that his weekly periodical would henceforth report them to the 'whole Kingdom'.[31] Coffee-houses maintained specialised books listing commodity prices, rates of exchange of foreign coin and the prices of government stocks. These were published, in various forms, in several newspapers and journals, including the market 'currents', which printed the prices of commodities on each local market (commodity price currents, exchange rate currents and stock exchange currents). Other publications specialised in overseas trade, listing the goods imported at the Custom House. Mr Bridge's Coffee-House in Pope's Head Alley, next to 'Change Alley, advertised in 1681 that the Custom House Bills of Entry, listing in manuscript a daily account of the goods imported through the Customs Office, could be seen at the coffee-house 'any day they come forth'.[32] Another single-sheet serial publication was the marine list, which reported the arrival and departure of ships at English and foreign ports. The earliest marine list was established by Edward Lloyd, the keeper of a coffee-house in Lombard Street, who began to publish his shipping list at least as early as 1692. Lloyd's publications depended on the information collected in and through his coffee-house; and in turn, his coffee-house thrived as the value of his proprietary information became known.[33]

The sociability of the coffee-house, especially its convivial accessibility, also lent itself to the activities of these new financial markets, bringing potential buyers and sellers together in the coffee room to meet and agree terms. Conversation, chance encounter and gossip all played a crucial role in the setting of market prices.[34] Such face-to-face encounters relied on deeply held cultural notions of personal display and appearance, and made much of the fact that an individual's credit and honour were manifested on the trading floor and the coffee room. But the increasing variety of securities after the 1690s mitigated against a system based simply on the haphazard chance of coffee-house acquaintance. The market began to take on increased levels of organisation, using the space of the coffee-house to define the parameters of the trade. The existing coffee-house practice of auctions suggested one solution, as this was a system in which all interested parties could bid for securities. But while auctions were good for the vendor, who found a purchaser for what he had to sell, they did not allow a potential purchaser to make known his requirements. Another solution was intermediation, using individuals who were entrusted with the task of finding buyers or sellers on behalf of clients who wished to dispose of or purchase securities. These men were known as brokers. By 1700 men from many walks of business were acting as stockbrokers in the coffee-houses. In addition, certain specialised dealers – who became known as jobbers – bought and sold securities on their own account. These men made a ready market by facilitating buying and selling, because if someone wanted to sell, jobbers ensured they could always find a buyer.[35]

The spectacle of the jobbers' continuous buying and selling amazed, and worried, contemporaries, who could not see any purpose or design in their trade except self-interest. In January 1692 Sir Christopher Musgrave complained in Parliament, 'The trade of stockjobbing is now become the sole business of many persons, which has ruined great numbers of tradesmen and others.'[36] Ned Ward was only one of many who detected fraud and deception at the heart of the coffee-house jobber. 'At last I went to *Jonathan's Coffee-house* by the Change,' he says in *The London Spy*, 'where I saw a parcel of Men at one Table Consulting together' with 'Malice, Horror, Anger and Despair in their looks'. At another table he sees 'a parcel of merry, hawk-look'd blades, laughing and pointing at the rest'. In these fractious combinations, the spy related, the jobbers advanced 'unlucky projects' which, by their 'unexpected ill-success', drew 'a few fools' deeply into debt. '*A Stock-Jobber*', he concluded,

> Is a Compound of *Knave*, *Fool*, *Shop-keeper*, *Merchant* and *Gentleman*. His whole Business is Tricking: When he Cheats another he is a Knave; when he suffers himself to be Out-witted he's a Fool; he commonly keeps a Visible Trade going, and with whatsoever he gets in his Shop, he makes himself a Domestick Merchant upon Change, by turning Stock Adventurer, led on by the mighty Hopes of advancing himself to a Coach and Horses, that he may Lord it over his Neighbouring Mechanicks.[37]

The market in stocks appeared incomprehensible and was repeatedly represented as a mystery, conspiracy or deception. Bolingbroke's periodical *The Craftsman*, narrated by the spy Caleb D'Anvers, reported that in Exchange Alley he found 'that *mysterious Emporium* . . . a meer *Babel* of Noise, Hurry and Confusion. Some were mad with Success, and others frantick with Despair'.[38]

As the focus of the stockjobber's trade, the coffee-houses of Exchange Alley attracted particular attention. Few people at the time, if indeed any, really comprehended the nature of the market in Exchange Alley, especially of the function of the securities market or the role of the brokers and jobbers. The chaotic form of 'Change Alley, especially the mêlée of people crowding into the coffee-houses, gave the market some semblance of reality. In Defoe's hostile estimate,

> The Center of the Jobbing is *in the Kingdom of Exchange-Alley*, and its Adjacencies; the Limits, are easily surrounded in about a Minute and a half (viz.) stepping out of *Jonathan*'s into the Alley, you turn your Face full *South*, moving on a few Paces, and then turning Due *East*, you advance to *Garraway*'s; from thence going out at the other Door, you go on still *East* into *Birchin-Lane*, and then halting a little at the Sword-Blade Bank to do much Mischief in fewest Words, you immediately face to the *North*, enter *Cornhill*, visit two or three petty Provinces there in your way *West*: And thus having Box'd your Compass, and sail'd round the whole Stock-Jobbing Globe, you turn into *Jonathan*'s again;

> and so, as most of the great Follies of Life oblige us to do, you end just where you began.[39]

During the South Sea Bubble in 1720, the constrained boundaries of the area were notorious for the crush of speculators. (In 1847 this spectacle was made the subject of a celebrated painting by Edward Matthew Ward called *The South Sea Bubble*, which at the time was one of the most popular 'modern' paintings in the National Gallery.)[40] To its defenders, the particular sociability of the coffee-house allowed the market to operate, for its easy, free and open access allowed all kinds of buyers and sellers to come together to negotiate their deals. To those less enamoured of the securities market, those same easy and open principles of access made 'Change Alley, and 'the Hemisphere of a Coffee-House', appear like a jungle inhabited by ravening beasts.

These complaints about the disturbingly hermetic obscurity of the coffee-house stockbrokers reflected the fact that their social world had developed its own distinct language and code of behaviour. The very reason why stockbrokers found the coffee-house conducive to trade had served to render it unintelligible to outsiders. In Susanna Centlivre's successful marriage comedy *A Bold Stroke for a Wife* (1718), a key scene takes place within 'Jonathan's Coffee-House, in Exchange Alley'. The scene opens with four stockjobbers hard at trading, all carrying rolls of paper (South Seas Company stock), shouting incomprehensible prices ('*South-Sea* at *seven Eighths*! who buys?'), and talking in their incomprehensible jargon ('I have a good Putt for next week'). Around them the coffee-boys compete by bellowing 'Fresh Coffee, gentlemen, fresh Coffee? ... Bohea-Tea, Gentlemen?' It is no accident that the scene also depicts a masterly deception, perpetrated by the hero, Mr Freeman, against the foolish and conceited broker Mr Tradelove.[41]

Thomas Mortimer also thought the language of the stockjobbers at Jonathan's remarkable. When business opened at twelve midday, the brokers, the merchants, the waiters, the speculators and the spectators, he said, held forth 'almost all at once':

> Tickets – Tickets – South Sea Stocks for the opening – Navy-Bills – Bank Stock for the rescounters – Long Annuities – (here the waiter calls) Chance – Chance – Chance *Mr. Chance not here Sir, he is over at his Office* – Here Tickets for August – Omnium Gatherum for September – Scrip for the third payment – 3 per Cent. consolidated, gentlemen [...]

> Here Bank Circulation, who buys Bank Circulation – Tickets for the drawing, gentlemen – Well, what have you to do in Tickets for the drawing, Mr. Mulberry. – I am a seller of five hundred, Sir – and I am a buyer, Sir, but at what price? – Why, as you are a friend, Mr. Point-royal, I shall give you the turn, you shall have them at 14. The turn, Mr. Mulberry, why, do you think I do not know what I am about? they are all sellers at 13. – Well then, you shall [have] them at 13. – I will take them at 12, and no otherwise. Well, you shall have them, put 'em down.[42]

Mulberry and Point-royal conclude their deal, but to outsiders their encounter, albeit intended ironically, remains obscure, if not mysterious. In the chaotic spectacle of the open-outcry system, the brokers and jobbers at Jonathan's sold lottery tickets, government stock, insurance and other financial instruments. The abbreviated linguistic forms, 'invented to save the gentlemens breath', the huge sums of money involved, the speed of the transactions and the hyperbolic bravado of market masculinity all conspired to make the stockjobber's coffee room deeply inhospitable to outsiders. The influence of this system, however, has been long-lived. The market structure adopted by stocks and commodity exchanges to this day follows the institutional patterns developed in the sociability of the eighteenth-century coffee-house. In his anthropological study of Wall Street in the 1990s, Mitchel Abolafia found that open out-cry futures trading floors retained their resemblance to the coffee-house culture of the eighteenth-century stocks market. Even in markets where the trading floor had become electronic, the institutional structures of the coffee-house could still be discerned. In the tumult of the pit, described by Abolafia as a 'structured anarchy', the formal rules of market regulation and oversight are augmented by rules of conduct enforced by group pressure and intimidation, just as in a coffee-house situation.[43]

Proprietors of coffee-houses realised that identifying one's establishment with a particular branch of trade served to guarantee a clientele: merchants would be more likely to visit regularly if they could rely on meeting others of the same trade or interest. In the eighteenth century this tendency to niche orientation became more pronounced, as a number of well-known coffee-houses moved towards more highly organised exclusive systems of social management. The victualler Edward Lloyd had first opened a coffee-house in 1687, in Tower Street, near the Navy Office and the Thames. In the early years of the reign of William and Mary his business had relocated to Lombard Street, strategically close to the Post Office and 'Change Alley. Like Garraway's, Lloyd's Coffee-House staged many auctions, but also developed a unique range of financial publications (a single-page list of shipping movements from 1692 and a marine newspaper, *Lloyd's News*, for five months in 1696–7), which made the coffee-house the centre of the London shipping world. In the big, rather sparsely furnished coffee room on the first floor, Lloyd constructed a raised lectern for auctions and announcements. *The Spectator* found the reverential attention of the traders gathered around Lloyd's lectern an object of ridicule, satirising it as a kind of commercial pulpit.[44] The shipping information Lloyd so carefully collated was disseminated in a manner that made the merchants' presence in his coffee room essential: when it arrived it was read out by the waiters from the pulpit, then posted on noticeboards, before being printed for resale around the city, nation and globe. Through this system Lloyd made sure that those merchants who stayed in the coffee room all the time had the most up-to-date information, giving them an advantage over absent competitors. The procedure made his coffee-house the centre for shipping news, 'the chief commercial Saleroom in London', and the market leader in marine insurance.[45] By the time Edward Lloyd died in 1713, his coffee-house had become a brand, retaining the name of Lloyd's through frequent changes in proprietor in the following decades. Lloyd's was already both a real place to drink coffee in London and a variety of reliable shipping news.

The provision of extensive shipping intelligence made Lloyd's Coffee-House the obvious location for the marine insurance business, both for underwriters who accepted the risks and the intermediaries, known as office-keepers, who brokered them as agents for merchants and shipowners. In 1734 the coffee-house's shipping list was revitalised under the title *Lloyd's List*, the name it carries to this day. Much skill and money was invested in the system of correspondence for accumulating this commercial intelligence, utilising (in 1792) thirty-two designated correspondents in twenty-eight British ports and paying £200 per annum for a bulk postage arrangement with the Post Office. By the 1740s, with a virtual monopoly on reliable shipping news, the reputation of Lloyd's had grown so much that to many it seemed as if the entire marine insurance business was conducted in this one coffee-

A palace courtier serving coffee to Sultan Osman from a Chinese porcelain cup. English merchants first learned the habit of drinking coffee in Ottoman Turkey and brought the practice with them on their return to London.

Engraving from Jacob Spon's 1685 treatise on the three new beverages: coffee from Turkey, tea from China and chocolate from America. Each man wears the typical costume of his country and drinks from a distinctive dish or serving pot.

The earliest known image of an English coffee-house. This woodblock print of 1674 is from Paul Greenwood's one-page advertising broadsheet on 'the Excellent Vertues of that Sober and Wholesome Drink Called Coffee'.

Newspapers, smoking, conversation, and business were central to any successful coffee-house in seventeenth-century London.

A gentleman, outraged by another's opinion, throws a dish of hot coffee in his adversary's face. Coffee-houses were famous for their free and open debates, but such discussions were not always polite and friendly.

A map of 1748 showing damaged and destroyed property after a fire that began near the Royal Exchange in the City of London. The numerous coffee-houses in this area were at the epicentre of England's late seventeenth-century financial revolution.

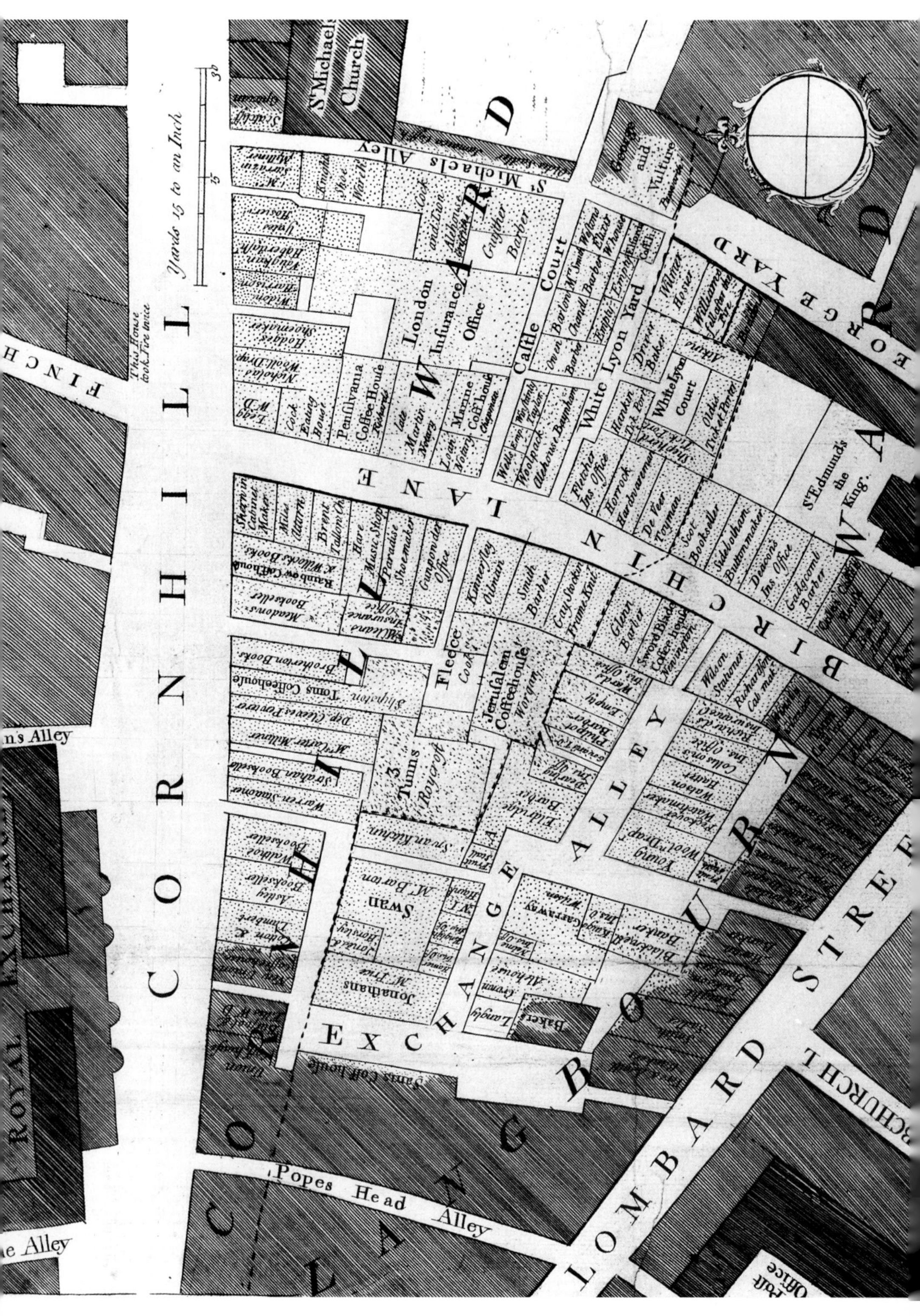

MOLL KING.

Moll King was proprietor of King's Coffee-House in Covent Garden Market in the early eighteenth century, a notorious location where gentlemen mixed late at night with market traders and ladies of pleasure.

Stockbrokers, carrying scrip in their hands, conduct a furious trade in stocks and lottery tickets at Jonathan's Coffee-House in Exchange Alley, while Britannia (on the far left), assailed by serpents, swoons away.

Coffee-house politicians, said Hazlitt, were a set of people who 'spend their time and their breath in coffee-houses hearing or repeating some new thing… with a paper in their hands in the morning, and a pipe in their mouths in the evening'.

By the early nineteenth century the coffee-house had lost its unique appeal: rather than engaging in conversation and discussion, the men in the Auction Mart Coffee Room sit alone, as far apart as possible, in a vast and echoing chamber.

The Café Royal, acknowledged centre of London's intellectual and artistic life from the 1870s until the 1950s. William Nicolson, George Moore, Augustus John, Alfred Rich and the artist, Sir William Orpen, sit beneath its gilt caryatids and mirrored walls.

The crush of teenagers and socialites at The Mocamba in Knightsbridge in 1954, one of the first of the new espresso bars in post-war London: 'a fabulous creation of bright décor, concealed lighting and lovely ceramics'.

The coffee-bar movement owed its success to its modernist design and decoration, inspired by the space-age styling of Italian espresso machines, whose signature frothy coffee attracted a new clientele, including young women, to café society.

Too much coffee goes to your head. The phenomenal growth in branded coffee-house chains in the 1990s has transformed the market for gourmet coffee, although their product lines are dominated by the flavour of milk.

house, although there was no regulation to prevent the trade happening elsewhere. But by the 1760s the underwriters had become dissatisfied with the negligent manner in which the then proprietor, Thomas Lawrence, conducted his business, in particular his tolerance of illicit gaming in life insurances. In 1769 a committee of these men decided to take their business elsewhere, but rather than simply moving to another coffee-house, they decided to establish a New Lloyd's Coffee-House for themselves in Pope's Head Alley, almost across the road. The cramped and decrepit building they secured there did not prove suitable, however, and in 1773 they moved again to two large rooms in the upper floor of the Royal Exchange on Cornhill. At the same time the habitués of New Lloyd's, as they called it, introduced an even more significant change by deciding to reorganise the coffee room. Henceforth, they concluded, entry to the coffee room, with its privileged access to shipping news, would only be available to those merchants, underwriters and brokers who had paid a subscription and been accepted as members. These more formal market arrangements closed the coffee room to outsiders and formalised the exclusivity of the underwriters' sociability. As a coffee-house Lloyd's was closed, but as a business it was just beginning.

The model for these changes was the behaviour of the stockbrokers at Jonathan's Coffee-House. In the 1750s they had become dissatisfied with the overcrowded, noisy coffee room there. Because it was open to the public, the stockbroking fraternity found that outsiders encroached on their business. As Thomas Mortimer explained in *Every Man his Own Broker* (1761), anyone might walk in 'to do business there', pay 6 pence and be entitled to 'pen, ink, paper and a small cup of chocolate', and 'if he understands the business' be his own 'Broker for that day'.[46] In 1761 150 brokers joined together into a combination to exclude the casual interlopers and made an agreement with the proprietor for the exclusive use of the coffee room for three hours a day for £1,200 per annum, during which time the coffee room would be open only to members paying an annual subscription of £8.[47] Tested in law by one of the men they ejected, however, the stockbrokers were told, in Lord Mansfield's judgement, that this exclusivity was incompatible with the nature of the coffee-house, for 'Jonathan's had been a market (time out of mind) for buying and selling government securities'. As the *London Chronicle* declared, 'Jonathan's Coffee-House is now a free and open market, and all combinations there destroyed.'[48]

Faced by this reverse, the brokers conspired to leave Jonathan's and to establish their own place of business. Lengthy negotiations between 1765 and 1771 led to their acquisition of a lease on a site at the Threadneedle Street end of Sweetings Alley, where in 1773 their new building was completed. The three-storey neoclassical building, initially called New Jonathan's but soon renamed the Stock Exchange, contained the dealing room in a large high-ceilinged room on the ground floor, with a coffee room on the floor above.[49] As before, the brokers paid 6 pence a day (or £7.80 per annum) to gain access to the room; but in 1801 a committee of proprietors succeeded in closing the room to all but those who had been accepted as members and paid a subscription. The effect on 'Change Alley was profound. *The Morning Chronicle* reported that after New Jonathan's opened in Sweetings Alley 'the old house is now totally abandoned, and 'Change-alley, lately the den for thieves, may now be passed through without danger of being robbed; but the people in that neighbourhood are all in mourning, as those gentry were their principal support'.[50] The foul-mouthed porters, who frequented the doorway of Jonathan's and whose scandalous behaviour was long the object of complaint, decamped the next day.[51]

In America too, coffee-houses played a central role in the institutionalisation of financial markets. Coffee-houses in Boston and New York had hosted auctions of commodities and real estate – called *vendues* – since the seventeenth century. From at least 1729 there was a coffee-house next to the merchants' Exchange in New York, located in a building on the corner of Broad Street and Water Street. The Exchange itself was a simple wooden shelter, open at the sides to the weather. In 1752, when a handsome new exchange was constructed, the building included a large room over the trading floor. From 1754 this room was opened as the Exchange Coffee Room, where it soon became an important rendezvous for men of commerce. Another coffee-house which attracted the commercial interest was the Merchants' Coffee-House, located at the end of Wall Street in the Meal Market, a public square where African slaves and indentured servants from Europe were exposed for sale. The Merchants' coffee room was the location for frequent *vendues* of merchandise and commodities, ships and their cargoes, real estate and horses, as well as slaves. Newspapers carried numerous advertisements for such sales, such as *The New York Gazette,* or *Weekly Post Boy* in 1750, which announced, 'Just imported, a parcel of likely negros, to be sold at public vendue to-morrow at Ten o'clock at the Merchant's Coffee House.'[52] The utility of such coffee-houses to the commercial life of the colony was evident for all to see.

In 1754 an enterprising resident of Philadelphia, the printer William Bradford, set about exploiting the synergy between coffee, companionship and commerce. Bradford, already the publisher of the *Pennsylvania Journal*, petitioned the Governor to 'keep a Coffee House for the benefit of merchants and traders'.[53] With subscriptions from over 200 merchants and traders, he took over a large and well-appointed coffee-house at the corner of Front Street and Market Street in the heart of the city (first opened by John Schubert in 1734). The London Coffee-House was conveniently next door to his booksellers' business and printing shop, from which he provided the coffee-house customers with copies of newspapers, magazines and public notices from London and the American colonies, detailing news of shipping movements, commodity price currents and political events. In the large rooms in the upper storey regular exchanges were held every day at noon to set prices, auction cargoes and arrange marine insurance. For the benefit of his customers and for visitors to the city he operated a postal collection service, promising to keep in safety all mail until its addressees called to receive it. Pens, ink and paper were at hand for any that called for them. Through Bradford's determined policy the London became the city's 'center for business, public affairs and the news'.[54]

After the American revolution the independent republic of the United States of America required a new set of independent commercial institutions. In New York, the proprietor of the Merchants' Coffee-House, Cornelius Bradford, found the city's economy in ruins when he returned after the British occupation ended in October 1783. Reanimating the coffee-house, he reasoned, would help kick-start the republic's fledgling economy. Bradford promised to make good his intention to take all the papers for the use of his patrons, having announced, 'Interesting intelligence will be carefully collected and the greatest attention will be given to the arrival of vessels, when trade and navigation shall resume their former channels.'[55] Following the example set by his brother William in Philadelphia, Bradford initiated the full panoply of commercial coffee-house technologies. He maintained a book to record the names of vessels arriving in the port, noting their origin and cargoes, and under the title of Bradford's Marine List this mercantile intelligence appeared in newspapers. Bradford further established a register of merchants, a precursor to the first city directory of New York businesses. Under his keeping, the Merchants' Coffee House soon regained its following among the commercial elite of New York.

Bradford's coffee-house was the obvious location for a meeting called in February 1784 by a group of prominent financiers to discuss proposals for a bank to provide credit for the fledgling republic, modelled on the Bank of England. The coffee-house meeting drew together the principal merchants and citizens of the city and by June the Bank of New York was in business, having drawn in over $500,000 in capital, held in gold and silver.[56] Emboldened by the success of the bank, the coffee-house merchants met again in April 1784 to re-establish the Chamber of Commerce, first founded in 1768 under British rule. The association for the encouragement of business continued to meet in the public rooms of the coffee-house for many years. For the period in which New York was the seat of government for the republic, the Merchants' Coffee-House occupied an important place in New York society. Elegant dinners were held there for the President and for the members of Congress. Social and philanthropic organisations used it for their meetings, such as the Society for the Manumission of Slaves, the Freemasons, the Friendly Sons of St Patrick and the St Andrews Society. The coffee-house meeting of the Manumission Society in January 1785 attracted thirty-two prominent citizens from across the political spectrum, including radical and conservative Whigs, as well as Tories. Under the Society's influence the New York legislature passed a bill for gradual abolition of slavery. As the Manumission Society meeting demonstrated, the coffee-house continued to function as a non-partisan public space, more identified with progress and civic reform than with any party or faction.

Economic expansion in the United States brought prosperity, but also concerns about the new market in American stocks. The securities market was organised after the model of London: stock transactions were concluded by brokers, acting as middlemen between specific customers, or by stockjobbers, who bought and sold for themselves. The traders met for stock auctions three times a week, with afternoon and evening sessions, in the Long Room at the Merchants' Coffee-House. Between sessions the brokers could be found in the coffee-house or, in summer, outside under the spreading boughs of a button-wood (sycamore) tree in Wall Street. In the early 1790s the trade in bank stock in New York had begun to get out of control, exacerbated by the launch of rival subscriptions for a bizarre range of new banks and companies. James Madison reported to Thomas Jefferson that during the 'bancomania' of 1791 the talk of stockjobbing drowned every other subject and the coffee-house was 'an eternal buzz with the gamblers'.[57] When the bubble finally burst in 1792 business languished and dozens of leading merchants were ruined. In May 1792 a meeting of twenty-two brokers and jobbers sought to give the securities market a more robust structure, giving preference to each other and outlawing uncontrolled stock auctions. Under these arrangements they moved in early 1793 into an elegant upstairs room of a new coffee-house built on Wall Street, the Tontine Coffee-House.

The Tontine was situated on the north-west corner of Wall Street and Water Street. The building, and its coffee-house, was named after – and financed by – a tontine, a financial arrangement pioneered in the 1730s by an Italian merchant called G. Tonti, in which a pool of members invested in a fund together, sharing the profit among surviving members at the end of a set period. As the site for auctions of commodities and cargoes, for gambling on stocks, for organising life and property insurance, it was soon named 'Scrip Castle' by wits of the town. For its time, the Tontine Coffee-House was an imposing building, designed to give a sense of permanency to the chaotic and unpredictable securities market.[58] In 1796 it became the headquarters of a tontine of moneyed investors trading under the name of the New York Insurance Company. This organisation was the predecessor of the New York Stock and Exchange Board, formed on 8 March 1817 and now called the New York Stock Exchange, the principal securities market in the United States. Operating as a call market, the name of each stock was read out in turn, allowing brokers to bid one security at a time.[59] Like Jonathan's Coffee-House in London, the subscribing stock traders introduced new regulations that excluded the day traders, exiling them to the unofficial kerb market on the street.

In seeking to close the coffee room to outsiders, the underwriters and stockbrokers in London and New York were motivated by what they saw as a desire for increased control over their own affairs, which they believed they could achieve by excluding spectators and day traders. In particular, they perceived the advantage, gained by their new closed environments, that they were henceforth able to set rules for personal conduct and business practice, prohibiting those who reneged on deals or who had been bankrupt. But the peculiar vivacity of the open conversations of the coffee-houses was ended, and thereafter Lloyd's, Jonathan's and the Tontine were simply places of work for the drones of capital. The Stock Exchange in London and New York obliterated their coffee-house origins, seeking greater glory under other names. The marine insurance market at Lloyd's, however, continued to gesture to its coffee-house origins. Even to this day, when Lloyd's of London is the world's largest insurance market and is housed in an elegant steel-and-glass building designed by Richard Rogers, the trading floor makes architectural reference to the coffee-house tables around which the underwriters gathered in the early eighteenth century and the building's porters are called waiters.

CHAPTER TWELVE

The Philosopher in the Coffee-House

'Man is said to be a Sociable Animal,' remarked Joseph Addison in the ninth issue of the periodical paper *The Spectator*. Written with his long-time friend, Captain Richard Steele, *The Spectator* argued that the sociable instinct was both the first cause and the greatest effect of modern city life. At every opportunity, Addison observed, men take the chance of forming themselves 'into those little Nocturnal Assemblies, which are commonly known by the Name of Clubs', joined together in friendship and mutually rewarding discourse. This rage for associative friendships, suggested Addison and Steele, epitomised a new and wholly original philosophy of urban life. Rather than the isolated and solitary existence experienced by the savage, or the bonds of domination and obligation in feudal society, modern urban life was comprised of civilised and refined social relations with fellow citizens, united as equals under the ties of trust, credit and friendship. The best examples of the associative principle at work in everyday life, they reasoned, were the coffee-house and the club, and accordingly they modelled their journals on them both. All around them, however, the crowded and bustling life of the city gave evidence that the society they lived in was not harmonious and balanced. If only, they mused, society could be more like the coffee-house, with its spirit of fellowship, mutual trust and conviviality.

The periodicals they wrote and edited – first *The Tatler* and later *The Spectator* and *The Guardian* – were designed to bring about a general reformation of manners. As Addison suggested in *The Spectator*, No. 10, 12 March 1711, his plan was in some sense to urbanise philosophy: 'It was said of Socrates, that he brought Philosophy down from Heaven, to inhabit among Men, and I shall be ambitious to have it said of me, that I have brought Philosophy out of Closets and Libraries, Schools and Colleges, to dwell in Clubs and Assemblies, at Tea-Tables and in Coffee-houses.'[1]

In this way *The Spectator, The Guardian* and *The Tatler* were at the forefront of what historians have called the 'culture of improvement', which championed a new paradigm of politeness and civility in literature and society.[2] They argued that human nature might be improved, cultivated, refined and reformed, investing the term 'politeness' with a range of important meanings: not only identifying an elite stratum of society ('the better sort', 'the Quality', supposedly practitioners of polite behaviour), but also delineating a process for achieving proper behaviour.[3] Urban life, and coffee-houses especially, brought people into close proximity, where they might be rubbed and jostled together, smoothing rough edges and polishing manners.

Addison's and Steele's essays both depict and teach the reader how to lead a polite life. They censured the rough aspects of society, castigating duelling, rowdiness in the streets, libertinism, immorality in plays, vulgar language, Frenchified fashions, love of praise, hooped petticoats and big wigs. Further essays actively praised virtue, honour, good nature, true worth and beauty. Samuel Johnson described the miscellany as comprising 'precepts of criticism, sallies of invention, description of life, and lectures of morality'.[4] But as well as describing the vices and virtues of the age, the style and form of the essays themselves were hailed as the epitome of elegance and felicity. Although their journal had many precedents, Steele's and Addison's essays were praised for their easy and conversational form, which successfully avoided both obscure moral squabbles and passionate rhetoric. They would, it was thought, inculcate the values of politeness and civility by improving the reader's ability to make refined judgements of taste. Of the 'several Methods for Cultivating and Improving' the 'intellectual Faculty' of 'Taste', Addison proposed that reading of 'Polite authors' and 'Conversation with Men of a Polite Genius' were chief among them.[5] As Dr Johnson observed, they offered an *'arbiter elegantiarum'* or 'judge of propriety', which removed the 'thorns and prickles' that encumber 'daily conversation'.[6] The natural home of this refined model of conversation was the urban environment of the polite coffee-house.

Both Addison and Steele were veterans of the coffee-house world. They had first met as schoolboys in London's Charterhouse School in the 1680s and had continued firm friends at university in Oxford. In 1692 Steele abruptly left university and took a commission in the King's bodyguard, the Life Guards. His return to civilian life in 1705 was hastened by the prospect of marrying a rich and elderly widow, Mrs Margaret Stretch, who owned a prosperous sugar plantation in Barbados (with over 200 African slaves). Having already gained some fame as a dramatist while in uniform, Steele came to London in search of a place in Queen Anne's court, a process that required 'sitting in great men's anterooms, associating with fashionable people at fashionable coffee-houses, saying the correct things and dressing in the correct manner'.[7] By 1707 Steele's first heiress had died and he was courting another, the younger and more beautiful Mary Scurlock. With a town house in Bury Street, St James's, and a court sinecure, Steele cut a fine figure around town although, despite his sizable income, he was almost always in debt, due to his penchant for expensive clothes and pastimes.

By the turn of the eighteenth century London was renowned across Europe as the biggest city in Europe and the pre-eminent city of coffee-houses. Even compared with ancient Rome, capital of the greatest empire the world had ever seen, London was believed to be superior in extent, populousness and wealth. Among London's advantages, the Huguenot writer de Souligné observed, was the 'abundance of Diversions' it afforded, 'far better than theirs' in ancient Rome. 'The Conveniency alone of our *Coffee* and *Chocolate-Houses* goes beyond all the common Diversions they had *at Rome*.'[8] Coffee-houses were emblematic of what was unique and modern about London. In 1699 the patriotic pen of another Huguenot, Guy Miège, observed that the drinking of the 'two sober Liquors' coffee and tea, were 'now so prevalent in *England*' that people desisted 'considerably from drinking of strong Liquors', especially among 'Men of Learning and Business, who know best the Virtue of 'em' to 'settle and compose'. 'To improve Society, the life of Recreation,' Miège continued, 'the *English* have, besides their usual and friendly Meetings called *Clubs*, the Conveniency of *Coffee-Houses*, more common here than any where else. In which all Corners intermix together, with mutual freedom; and, at a very easy Rate Men have the Opportunity of meeting together, and getting Acquaintance, with choice of Conversation, besides the Advantage of reading all foreign and domestic News'.[9] Coffee-houses represented the democratic foundation of the English constitution, for in their confines the indigenous spirit of liberty had been nurtured during the dark days of Stuart autocracy.

To Addison and Steele nothing could have seemed more usual or natural than the urban culture of coffee-houses and clubs. When he was courting his heiresses, Steele would sit writing love letters from the coffee-houses of St James's, complaining the paper they provided was not fine enough for the job at hand. 'I am forc'd to write from a coffee-house,' he protested on 30 August 1707, 'where I am about businesse. There is a dirty Croud of Busie faces all around me talking of *money*; while all my Ambition, all my wealth is Love!'[10] Such places were his office, his drawing room and his study. Both Addison and Steele cheerfully adopted the coffee-house as one of the central metaphors of their urbane philosophy. Steele came to journalism through his lucrative appointment as writer of *The London Gazette*, the official government newspaper. In April 1709 he inaugurated *The Tatler*, which comprised a folio sheet of paper, printed on both sides and folded once to create four pages, like a newspaper of the time. It appeared three times a week and cost a penny. The masthead claimed it was written by one 'Isaac Bickerstaff, Esq.', a subterfuge that successfully concealed Steele's identity for many months. The first issue announced it was 'principally intended for the Use of Politick Persons, who are so publick-spirited as to neglect their own Affairs to look into Transactions of State'.[11] As these coffee-house politicians would discover, *The Tatler* delivered not news but a gentle, ironic form of satire, poking fun at society and its follies. Bickerstaff declared, 'The general Purpose of this Paper, is to expose the false arts of Life, to pull off the Disguises of Cunning, Vanity and Affectation, and to recommend a general Simplicity in our Dress, our Discourse, and our Behaviour.'[12]

In pursuing this new simplicity, *The Spectator* redefined forms of social behaviour according to a new model of social bonds: the appropriate set of behaviour of the gentleman was modified from a primarily courtly and aristocratic code, given to the display of power and wealth, to a more bourgeois, commercial and feminised code, given to the display of benevolence, and sensibility.[13] The ideal citizen of *The Spectator*, Steele argues in No. 346, is 'frank in his Kindnesses, and abhors Severity in his Demands; he who in buying, selling, lending, doing acts of good Neighbourhood, is just and easy; he who appears naturally averse to Disputes, and above the Sense of little Sufferings, bears a nobler Character, and does much more Good to mankind than any other Man's Fortune without Commerce can possibly support'.[14] Steele does not attempt to fix the values of one particular social class as the desideratum of all society; rather, he mobilises a new model citizen from the interaction of many different social orders. The coffee-house was exactly the kind of arena where this social mixture and affective mobilisation could occur.

Bickerstaff himself was imagined as a tall skinny gentlemen of sixty-four years, something of a pedant, with spectacles, old-fashioned clothes and a penchant for Dick's Coffee-House in Fleet Street. In *The Tatler* the essays were supposed to be written in the coffee-houses. As Bickerstaff says, in pursuit of interesting 'Action or Discourse' about the town, he would not print 'musty Foreign Edicts' and 'dull Proclamations' (as did Steele's other publication, *The London Gazette*), but would range through the coffee-houses of the city collecting gossip, amusing anecdotes and telling insights. From White's Chocolate House in St James's Street, a noted assembly of town gallants, Bickerstaff promised to provide 'Accounts of Gallantry, Pleasure and Entertainment'. From Will's Coffee-House in Covent Garden, he promised accounts of 'Poetry' and all things literary, as was appropriate to that gathering of wits, poets and critics. From the Grecian Coffee-House in Devereux Court, the favoured haunt of the scientists, lawyers and scholars, he undertook to give accounts of 'Learning'. 'Foreign and Domestick News' – usually the staple of a newspaper – was to come from St James's Coffee-House, located on the corner of St James's Street across the road from the chief royal residence, St James's Palace. This coffee-house was thronged with courtiers, politicians and other assorted sycophants, and was a great source of news and court gossip. All 'other Subjects', Bickerstaff said, were to be dated from his 'own Apartment'. The cost of attending the coffee-houses alone, he argued, justified the penny price of the paper: he estimated Will's would cost 2 pence a day and White's at least 6 pence; while for the Grecian one needed some knowledge of languages to comprehend the debates, and as for the St James's, 'a good Observer cannot speak with even Kidney', the head waiter, 'without clean Linnen'.[15] As *The Tatler* continued over the months and years following, Steele repeatedly recalled the social space of the coffee-house around Bickerstaff: depicting him calling for ink and paper, perusing a poem left upon the common table, reading the news in a foreign correspondent's letter and, most commonly, repeating gossip overheard in the room.

In this selection of coffee-houses Steele had made a careful but partial choice. Despite the differences between them that Bickerstaff listed, they were all locations of a relatively exclusive and elite culture.

Such places demanded much of their customers in the way of money, learning and power. Their high status is reflected topographically: all were located in the socially exclusive West End of London (three are in Westminster and the fourth is just inside the western extremes of the City). None of them was associated with commercial interests or radical politics; indeed, those in St James's Street were the polar opposite. White's Chocolate House had been founded in 1693, and was soon notorious for attracting feckless nobility and idle gamblers round its Faro tables. 'At White's', one commentator sneered disapprovingly, 'we see nothing but what wears the mask of gaiety and pleasure; powder and embroidery are the ornaments of the place, not to forget the intolerable stink of perfumes [. . .]. Conversation is not known here.'[16] The St James's Coffee-House, founded in the early years of the eighteenth century, had established a close association with the royal court on account of its location across the road from the entrance to St James's Palace. It was a political house, later associated with Whig politics, but in this period especially concerned with the internal gossip of sinecures, bribes and preferment at the Queen's court. When describing the social world of the coffee-houses in St James's Street in 1730, the Prussian nobleman Karl Ludwig, Baron de Pollnitz celebrated their exalted status. He described how 'the fine Gentleman' rises late, and after dressing carefully in his ornate frock-coat, walks in St James's Park ('the Exchange for Men of Quality'). Afterwards, Pollnitz says, he

> saunters to some Coffee-house or Chocolate-House, frequented by the Person he would see; for 'tis a Sort of Rule with the *English*, to go once a Day at least, to Houses of this Sort, where they talk of Business and News, read the Papers, and often look at one another without opening their Lips; and 'tis very well they are so mute; for if they were as talkative as the People of many other Nations, the Coffee-houses would be intolerable, and here would be no hearing what one Man said, where there are so many.

White's Chocolate House, Pollnitz continues, 'is always so full that a Man can scarce turn about in it. Here are Dukes, and other Peers, mixed with gentlemen; and to be admitted, there needs nothing more than to dress like a Gentleman. At one o'Clock, they go to Court, to the King's Levee, and from thence to the Queen's Apartment.'[17] While such coffee-houses were large establishments, the elite and exclusive clientele they attracted effectively rendered them inaccessible to the great majority of ordinary Londoners from the middle stations of life, let alone the lower echelons of society.

Such 'polite coffee-houses', Lewis Theobald remarked in 1717, possessed their own code of behaviour, quite distinct from coffee-houses lower down the social order. The 'Assemblies of the *beau Monde*' that gather each day 'at the *Coffee-houses* in Vogue', seemed to him to be the best examples of social folly in his age. 'I take care to resort to those Rooms, where the Society is compos'd of the *gay* and *fashionable*; and where frequent Pannels of Glass seem to multiply the *embroider'd Customers*.' There, seated at a table scattered with papers, nursing a cup of half-cold coffee, Theobald's Mr Censor studied the elite society around him. To him it seemed their conversation was puerile and superficial, concerned only with the ostentatious display of luxury and the affectation of overly refined manners:

> To these *Polite Coffee-houses* the Members flock merely to see, and be seen; and they are Places of Rendezvous to the brocaded *Narcissi*. [. . .] Reciprocal Civilities are the chief Things to be remark'd, Grimaces of Satisfaction forc'd from the Conceit of a Courtier's Wit, and Addresses of Compliment instead of Applications of Weight or Moment. The Flutter of these fine Figures makes all common Objects used with Disrespect, and served with Leisure.[18]

Politeness in such coffee-houses was not civic but privileged, exclusive and patrician. In seeking to model the reformation of society on this elite pattern, Steele reveals his allegiance to a conservative and reactionary complacency, and demonstrates his failure to comprehend the challenging cultural transformations of the political economy of early eighteenth-century England.

For the two years during which *The Tatler* was published, in 1709 and 1710, the periodical dominated the London literary scene, commanding an enormous readership that extended well beyond its imaginative home in the London coffee-houses. Collected together into volumes, it sold well in the provinces, in the colonies and in Europe, as it did in numerous editions for the rest of the century. Only three months after *The Tatler* finished, however, on Thursday, 1 March 1711, the public were pleased to find that Steele and his friend Addison had begun a replacement, *The Spectator*. It too was in no sense a sheet of news, even though it was published six days a week like a newspaper. Levering itself upon its predecessor's popularity, *The Spectator* sold in even greater numbers (more than 3,000 per issue) and ran for 555 issues until 6 December 1712. As both a business and a cultural enterprise, *The Spectator* was also a stunning success, unmatched in the eighteenth century.

The Spectator dispensed with the conceit adopted by *The Tatler*, that the coffee-house was the site of its production. Instead of a medley written from four coffee-houses, it took the form of a single unified essay on a topic of exemplary or moral concern, each one supposedly written in turn by a club of men (an old-fashioned country squire, a student lawyer more interested in literature and the stage, a wealthy merchant, a retired army officer, an elderly beau and a clergyman), under the loose leadership of a ghostly man called Mr Spectator, a 'spectator of men' who seems to blend, chameleon-like, into almost all parts of town and all scenes of society. 'Sometimes I am seen thrusting my head into a Round of Politicians at *Will's* [Coffee-House]. Sometimes I smoak a Pipe at *Child's* [Coffee-House]; and whilst I seem attentive to nothing but the *Post-Man* [newspaper], overhear the Conversation of every Table in the Room.' As he goes on to say, he also frequents the St James's, the Grecian, the Cocoa-tree and Jonathan's coffee-houses.[19] Mr Spectator is an observer who isn't observed: a spy on the morals and follies of the age, all of which can be seen and noted by attendance at the coffee-house. In his subsequent journal *The Guardian*, published daily from March to October 1713, Addison proposed that the coffee-house customers themselves might furnish their own material for the journal. In the coffee room of Button's Coffee-House in Covent Garden, which he promoted as the place of the wits, Addison installed a large letter box in the shape of a Lion's head, 'holding its paws under the chin'. 'This head', he said in *The Guardian*, no. 114 (22 July 1713), 'is to open a most wide and voracious Mouth, which shall take in such Letters and Papers as are conveyed to me by my Correspondents. [. . .] Whatever the Lion swallows I shall digest for the Use of the Publick.' Through the open mouth of the letter box, readers in the coffee-house were invited to contribute 'intelligence' to the journal. At least thirteen issues contain letters claimed to have been received through the Lion's head at Button's.[20]

The Spectator imagined that the coffee-house was the centre of a gentleman's life in London. One essay, containing a mock diary of an ordinary man, depicts the 'sober Citizen' and 'honest Man' going there four times in a week, using his time to read the newspaper and discuss the news of the day.[21] As well as these tangible benefits, the coffee-house appealed to such a man because it offered the possibility of meeting strangers, observing their traits and learning from their characters. Addison's essay in *The Spectator*, no. 31 (Thursday, 5 April 1711) warns about a dangerous kind of man he calls a projector, whom Mr Spectator meets in a coffee-house in St James's: 'I diverted my self for above half an Hour with overhearing the Discourse of one, who, by the Shabbiness of his dress, the Extravagance of his Conceptions, and the Hurry of his Speech, I discovered to be of that Species who are generally distinguished by the Title of Projectors.' A projector was a schemer and promoter, a visionary and an entrepreneur, one who entertains hopes for the realisation of some grand yet ridiculous project.

On this evening in the coffee-house the projector is raising money to stage a plan for an opera entitled *The Expedition of Alexander the Great*, to be sung in ancient Greek, combining within it a compendium of all the 'strange Sights' and wonders of the city, including a Rary-show, a ladder-dancer, dancing monkeys and a moving picture – a ridiculous confusion of high culture and vulgar entertainment. To Mr Spectator's consternation, the projector singles him out for a particular harangue ('catching me by the Button of my Coat'), until the man is distracted by another victim, upon which opportunity, 'laying down my Penny upon the Bar' Mr Spectator 'retired with some Precipitation'.[22] As his adventures reveal, the coffee-house is the kind of place where you are as likely to meet social deviants as well-mannered gentlemen. His essays detail his encounters with quacks (peddlers of fake medicines), libertines (retailers of lewd stories), enthusiasts (passionate defenders of pet projects and hobby-horses), pedants (given to ostentatious displays of fragments of learning) and, worst of all, critics (tenacious maintainers of ludicrous or insignificant opinions). In such essays *The Spectator* warns its readers about the worrying promiscuity of coffee-house sociability – and suggests that only a thorough reform of manners could refashion this sociability into the controlled and stable politeness it desires. As Samuel Johnson was to observe later, *The Spectator* played an important role in reinforcing 'the minuter decencies and inferior duties', regulating the 'practice of daily conversation' and correcting 'those depravities which are rather ridiculous than criminal'.[23]

Although *The Spectator* essays purport to observe their urbane model of sociability in the coffee-house, in fact they manufacture one. The most significant analysis of Steele's revision of the cultural politics of the coffee-house appeared in *The Spectator*, no. 49 (Thursday, 26 April 1711). Mr Spectator begins by exploring the dynamics of coffee-house conversation: 'It is very natural for a Man who is not turned for Mirthful Meetings of Men, or Assemblies of the fair Sex, to delight in that sort of Conversation which we find in Coffee-houses. Here a Man, of my Temper, is in his Element; for, if he cannot talk, he can still be more agreeable to his Company, as well as pleased in himself, in being only an Hearer.' The coffee-house appeals to a man of Mr Spectator's own 'Temper': not only reflecting his quiet and reflective presence, silently observing the life that surrounds him, but also signalling his residence within a reformed mannered civility. The essay's main project is to chart the ebb and flow of coffee-house sociability through the hours of the day, as one group after another dominates the conversation. 'In the Place I most usually frequent, Men differ rather in the time of day in which they make a Figure, than in any real Greatness above one another.' Although Mr Spectator's coffee-house testified to an egalitarian respect for all kinds of people, he nonetheless observes that at different times of the day, different kinds of men associate there. Rather than reducing all men to an undifferentiated homogeneity, Mr Spectator observes how the neutral and receptive space of the coffee-house encourages a series of overlapping but distinct masculine sociabilities to come into contact with each other.[24]

Venturing to a coffee-house near the Temple early one morning, Mr Spectator observes a studious group gathered around a certain Mr Beaver the Haberdasher (a portrait that reminded contemporaries of the figure of James Heywood, a wholesale linen draper of Fish Street Hill). Expressing their contempt for business hours, these coffee-house politicians swap opinions on government policy in serious tones, each with 'a News Paper in his Hand'. After eight in the morning they are interrupted by the arrival of the law students from the nearby Inns of Court: some dressed seriously for court, and others whimsically wearing 'a gay cap and Slippers, with a Scarf and Party-colour'd Gown', gathering 'with no other purpose than to publish their Laziness'. When 'the Day grows too busie for these gentlemen', Mr Spectator observes that the students are supplanted by 'Men who have Business or good Sense in their Faces, and come to the Coffee-house either to transact

Affairs or enjoy Conversation'. Among these sort he finds men suited to his moral project. Such men are content 'to be happy and well pleased in a private Condition', seeking neither advancement in political office nor avarice and greed in commerce, while not neglecting 'the Duties and relations of Life'. 'Of these sort of Men', Mr Spectator says, 'consist the worthier Part of Mankind; of these are all good Fathers, generous Brothers, sincere Friends, and faithful Subjects. [. . .] These are the men formed for Society, and those little Communities which we express by the Word *Neighbourhoods*.' Identifying them as the best of men and the rightful inhabitants of the midday coffee-house, Steele consciously revises the coffee-house sociability in his own reformative image.[25]

In this essay Steele shows how the coffee-house has become a 'Place of Rendezvous to all [. . .] thus turned to relish calm and ordinary Life'. Over this charmed group presides an ideal man, whom he names Eubulus, of perfectly tuned virtue in a society ravaged by the corruptions and compromises of luxury and commerce. Eubulus is a rich man, yet he lives modestly; a man of wisdom and influence who holds no political or judicial office; a man who generously lends money at low interest to his friends rather than seeking the highest rate of return on the market. 'He does not consider in whose Hands his Money will improve most, but where it will do the most Good.' Steele's great insight here, making Eubulus one of the most remarkable achievements of *The Spectator*, is that while Eubulus is an ideal portrait, he is also an object of emulation. He does have an 'Authority' over all in 'his little Diurnal Audience' in the coffee-house, but it is founded in internal respect, not outward regulation. Eubulus's own virtuous behaviour encourages others to follow his course: each in turn becomes his own Eubulus. The 'Veneration' of the coffee drinkers towards him is 'so great', Mr Spectator observes, 'that when they are in other Company they speak and act after him; are Wise in his Sentences, and are no sooner sat down at their own Tables, but they hope or fear, rejoice or despond as they saw at the Coffee-house. In a word, every Man is *Eubulus* as soon as his Back is turn'd.'[26] From Eubulus's virtuous example, the forum of the coffee-house allows other men to emulate his civic-minded behaviour, a process sociologists have called self-fashioning.[27] The 'Eubulus effect' provides a powerful engine for *The Spectator*'s project of the moral reform of public culture.

Mr Spectator envisages and proposes that a coffee-house on

Eubulus's model would be dominated by rational and quiet discussion:

> Their Entertainments are derived rather from Reason than Imagination: Which is the cause that there is no Impatience or Instability in their Speech or Action. You see in their Countenances they are at home, and in quiet Possession of the present Instant, as it passes, without desiring to Quicken it by gratifying any Passion, or Prosecuting any new Design.[28]

In Mr Spectator's ideal coffee-house, debates will not raise men's passions, there will be no floating of hare-brained schemes, no sudden acts of creative imagination, no outlandish flights of discourse. In other essays Steele exhorts his fellow citizens to 'Modesty' and 'Moderation'.[29] In *The Spectator* as a whole, Addison and Steele counsel that reason should govern passion, vice and superstition, proposing that the 'Excesses which Men are guilty of', such as 'Usury, Stock-Jobbing, Extortion and Oppression', are all 'below the Pursuit of a reasonable Creature'[30] In coffee-houses the philosophical potential of polite culture will be made concrete and real. As Lawrence Klein proposes, 'their works represented London as a field of skirmishes on which the battle for politeness was won or lost.'[31] In Addison's and Steele's hands, the light and conversational genre of the periodical essay bears the weight of philosophy and the enlightenment project.

As Londoners at the time recognised, *The Spectator*'s ideal of a polite coffee-house was available only to a narrow and elite sector of society, although the argument claimed to address everybody. As few years later, in *The Censor* in 1717, Lewis Theobald dismissed the 'polite coffee-houses' as the home of a facile and affected elite, and defended what he called 'another Rank of Coffee-houses, a little subordinate to these'. As 'the Customers are not so abstracted a Sett', he says men of differing ranks are still able to sit together and talk as equals. Theobald's narrator, Mr Censor, reported that he 'often sat with pleasure to hear the nation settled, and the wits arraign'd' by gatherings of men containing both city gentlemen and country squires. He continues that he was

> as fully entertain'd sometimes with descending to Coffee-houses of less Note, and which are situated in Private Streets; where the Neighbouring *Mechanicks* meet to learn a little News, and, from their Politicks, to procure an Opinion of their Wisdom: It is pleasant to observe the

> Concern and Thoughtfulness that dwell on each face upon the Arrival of an *Express*, the coming in of the *Votes*, or the publication of the *Session's-Paper.*

The behaviour of tradesmen in these low coffee-houses impressed Theobald's Mr Censor, as it gave evidence of the seriousness with which the citizens treat government affairs, even though he confesses that 'it is provokingly ridiculous to hear a *Haberdasher* descant on a *General's* Misconduct, and talk of an *Army's passing a River* with the same facility as he himself could go over the *Fleet-bridge*'. Nonetheless, he went on,

> These are a Set of Men that are precise in their Coffee-house Hours, where they by Custom are intituled to a certain Seat, and are the *Oracles* of the Company. [. . .] It is frequent with these Gentlemen to keep up their Harangue in a Stile and Tract of Thought as absurd, as unintelligible. Their Method of explaining Things is different from that with Men of common Reason; and the Substance of their Oration as Foreign from the Point as it is pompous and affected.[32]

Without regulation and order, then, the plebeian coffee-house politicians – these 'Political *Oracles*' and 'declaimers in politicks' – are nothing short of a 'provocation'.

Many writers agreed with *The Spectator* that the coffee-house polished the manners, knocking off the rough edges of discord, smoothing the rudeness of party and faction. After the civil unrest of the seventeenth century this was a lesson that many desired the nation to learn. Some ventured a more prescriptive version. In 1737 Erasmus Jones wrote a conduct book to guide upwardly mobile men as to the behaviour expected of them in high society. His *The Man of Manners: or, Plebeian Polish'd* offered his grateful readers, he said, 'Plain and Familiar Rules for a Modest and Genteel Behaviour, on most of the ordinary Occasions of Life'. One place where the uncouth behaviour of the wealthy plebeian would expose him to 'contempt and ridicule' was the coffee-house. Jones cautioned,

> 'Tis vastly rude to whisper, either at the bar, or any other part of a Coffee-Room, with one's Eyes turn'd towards the Party spoken of; I

> have seen such Indecorum raise a Blush, even on the Cheeks of an Attorney.
>
> There are some people of moderate Fortunes, that lead their Lives mostly in Coffee-Houses, they eat, drink and sleep (in the Day-time) in them; their chief Employment being only to receive their Stipends or other Incomes, and to lay them out again; so that having no other Business on their Hands, and scarce knowing what to do with themselves, they idle and saunter about, like a Colonel with his two Subalterns, on a *Kensington* or *Hampton-Court* Guard.
>
> A Stranger cannot put his Head into a Coffee-Room, but these curious Gentlemen are immediately at the Bar, asking as many Questions, as a Country Vicar on his Induction into a new Living, does with his Parishioners.[33]

Likewise, in a set of 'Rules of Behaviour . . . Much Disregarded in this Populous City', *The London Magazine* in 1780 advised readers: 'In a coffee-house, never to use that unjust and provoking practice of keeping more papers than one in hand; for that is an arrogant encroachment upon the common right of *all* the company.'[34]

Addison's and Steele's argument about coffee-houses was enormously influential, confirming their role in the reformation of civil society. The legacy of *The Spectator* has coloured the perception of the coffee-house in the centuries that follow. Elaborated in other essays, and reinforced by other writers and satirists, its view of the coffee-house as a haven of rational and polite conversation open to all citizens has come to dominate discussion. At the time it was written, however, it must have seemed a partial account, with more than an element of wishful thinking. *The Spectator* sets out an argument about what society should be like, not what it is like: like many satires, it is both critical of the present state of affairs, and reformist and utopian about the future it desires. In reality, few if any coffee-houses reached the state of refinement and reformation outlined by Mr Eubulus and his followers. *The Spectator*'s coffee-house is in this sense an imaginary space, an argument made in defence of a vision of a civil Utopia.

Many writers following in the wake of *The Spectator* argued that Addison and Steele had overestimated the reformative effect of the coffee-house. For every man who was improved there was another who moved in the opposite direction. 'The mixed conversation at Coffee-house', John Hill commented in his journal *The Inspector* in 1753, was 'of the most advantageous kind' only 'if it could be restrained within any bounds of order and regularity'.

> How instructive it must be, to hear the observations of a number of different people on the variety of objects that have occurred to them in the course of the day? how agreeable to meet with the essence of a multitude of conversations, heard at the several parties the different people who make up the company have been engaged in, collected, separated from its superfluities and redundancies, and delivered to us concentrated as it were, and with all its merit, in the compass of a few periods!

Hill warned that the greater number of men's conversations evinced no such desire to inform their audience, but were content merely to attack the person of their enemy, or were aimed 'at no farther joy . . . than the triumph of deceiving' their audience 'into a belief of [their] ingenuity and candour'. As he concludes, this 'vice of conversation' was never 'at so exorbitant a height as at present'.[35] Samuel Johnson also argued that a coffee-house was as like to teach incivility, rudeness and hooliganism as virtue. In his essay periodical *The Rambler*, Johnson related the story of a young nobleman introduced to 'the knowledge of the town' through his coffee-house acquaintance. This man went 'every day to a *Coffee-House*, where he met wits, heirs, and fops, airy, ignorant and thoughtless as himself, with whom he had become acquainted at card-tables, and whom he considered as the only beings to be envied or admired'. Under the influence of the fops, the nobleman is first taught to disrespect his tutor, then instructed in the arts of drama criticism (disrupting the theatre by yelling catcalls), and finally initiated as a Mohock or rakehell, roaming through the town, drinking to excess, street-fighting and gambling.[36]

Even as he was writing his reforming essays, Steele must have been well aware of the coffee-house's continuing attraction to troublemakers and seditionaries. Zeal for religious causes, and the bitter debates thereby incurred, had not left London coffee-houses, whose tables continued to groan under the weight of tract and counter-tract, newspapers and pamphlets, as they had in the seventeenth century. In March 1710, for example, while Steele was writing essays for *The Tatler* serious rioting broke out in London in response to popular dissatisfaction at the politically motivated trial of the Tory clergyman Dr Henry

Sacheverell.[37] Debate on Sacheverell's arrest and trial dominated the news agenda, and the conversations in coffee-houses. Steele, however, assiduously avoided being drawn into a party dispute. In *The Tatler* of 4 March 1710 he wrote that 'the Attention of the Town is drawn aside from the reading us Writers of News'.[38] While London was swamped by the bitter exchange of pamphlet and libels, Steele's *Tatler* kept up its polite essays on social follies (snuff taking, formalities of the tea table, eavesdroppers). Many Tory supporters enjoyed the irony that the mob, usually seen by the Whig establishment as expressing the will of the people, were marshalled in support of the High Church faction (akin to rioting at a Countryside Alliance march).

This irony was not lost on Ned Ward in his long satirical poem *Vulgus Britannicus: or, the British Hudibras* (1710), modelled loosely on Samuel Butler's poem *Hudibras* (1661–3), itself an attack on Puritan cultural politics. In Ward's estimation the inner sanctum of Presbyterian support was found around the coffee-house tables, where the 'Paper Wars came on a pace':

> *The Coffee Tables* now were spread,
> With all the worst that could be said;
> And the two Good old *Cause Asserters*
> Read most by *Coblers* and by *Porters*
> Were by the Saints kind *Intercession*,
> Received again on this Occasion.

In coffee-houses men from low stations in life read pamphlets and newspapers which engaged them in political debates on Church and State – a situation which conservative thinkers of this time continued to believe was improper and confused. Whig coffee-houses especially were whipped by the 'Trappings of *Falsiloquence*' into a lather of indignation.

> Each *Coffeehouse* where the *Saints* were wont
> To read dull News, and Preach upon't;
> Was now into a *Bedlam* turn'd
> Where one side Laugh'd, and t'other Mourn'd.[39]

Persecuted by the Whig 'Saints', Sacheverell's trial ended in farce on 17 March, when he escaped with a light punishment despite being found guilty. The mob greeted these events with bonfires and illuminations.

In Ward's estimation the coffee-house is the place where scribblers both produce and consume the products of the paper war. Of the 'Dunces' gathered around the 'Prints on *Coffee-house Table*', he remarks that 'O'er their *Coffee* for a Penny', they 'Ferment their Zeal in *Case* they've any'. 'Men's Deportment in the Coffee-Houses' comes under particular scrutiny:

> Now Warm debates were carry'd on,
> In ev'ry *Coffee-House* Pro and Con;
> Where *Whigs* of ev'ry sort and size,
> Began aloud to *Tyrannize*.

An engraved frontispiece, entitled 'The CoffeHous Mob', depicted the lineaments of this coffee-house debate. The characteristic conventions of the scene are depicted: long tables around which a variety of men have assembled, talking, reading and smoking. Around them, almost oblivious to their customers, the waiters or coffee-boys serve coffee, spectacularly pouring it from their tall conical coffee pots into the dishes from a great height. Behind the bar the woman proprietor sits with a po-faced look of disinterest. Against this backdrop a vociferous dispute has broken out between two men, one of whom has been caught here in the moment of throwing a dish of coffee over another (quarrelling over the controversies and scandals of sectarian and factional differences, as Ward's verses explain). As he comments, the coffee seems to heat their discussions:

> Yet these will o'er their *Jewish* Liquor,
> About *Religion* Jar and *Bicker*;
> And rave till grown as *Piping Hot*,
> As the dull *Grout* o'er which they sot.[40]

In this sectarian coffee-house debate, coffee sheds its reputation for sobriety, and instead becomes a drink of rebellion and dissent. Coffee-houses continued to be likened to conventicles (the Protestant meeting houses repeatedly suppressed during the Revolution) in the opening decades of the eighteenth century. Defoe's *Lay-Man's Sermon* (1704) on the Great Storm of 1703 was delivered at 'an Honest

Coffee-House-Conventicle' – noting that the idea was 'not so much a Jest as 'tis thought to be'.[41]

In America the coffee-house was also associated with news and rebellion through the eighteenth century. In the disturbances that led up to the American Revolution, and in the revolution itself, it was a central arena for the civic drama of rebellion. In New York, both the Exchange Coffee-House and the Merchants' Coffee-House were home to the 'Sons of Liberty', as the rebel colonists styled themselves. The Stamp Act of 1765, which had introduced a form of business taxation levied on the American colonies by the British Parliament, had met with considerable resistance. The principal coffee-houses of the city served as the meeting places for politically engaged merchants and artisans fulminating about their liberty and calling for 'no taxation without representation'. In October 1765 a mob of disgruntled sailors and labourers staged a mock funeral for 'Liberty' outside the Merchants' Coffee-House. Inside, in the coffee room, an English officer, Captain James Montresor, noticed the change in atmosphere, observing that the backgammon sets were in mourning, 'covered with black, and the dice in crape'. Meetings of the Sons of Liberty organised against the Stamp Act were held at coffee-houses, which were placarded with 'Insolent Advertisements' threatening the property and persons of the English revenue authorities. At one demonstration in April 1766, sheets of the stamped taxation paper were burnt at the coffee-house. After protests against another royal monopoly, the Post Office, the Liberty Boys organised their own letter delivery service, so that 'the letters [that] are left at the coffee house [. . .] are distributed by the news carrier'. When the news of the Stamp Act's repeal finally reached New York in May 1766, Montresor commented that the Governor of the colony 'condescended to wait on the people of the City at the Coffee House to relate them the news'.[42]

The coffee-houses continued to be closely identified with the American rebels during the revolution in the 1770s. In May 1774, at a riotous public meeting at the Merchants' Coffee-House, a Committee of Correspondence was established to maintain a constant exchange of views and intelligence with the like-minded rebels in Boston and Philadelphia: Paul Revere was the most famous of these flying intelligencers. In their meetings at the coffee-houses, the New York rebels debated their protests against British policy and expressed their support for the foundation of the Continental Congress. To the Sons of Liberty, the egalitarian coffee-house seemed an especially welcoming location for their debates, as a neutral ground in which both wealthy merchants and labouring mechanics might meet together.[43] But during the Revolution, and until 1783, New York was the headquarters for, and was garrisoned by, British troops. In these years the Merchants' Coffee-House was better known as the principal place of resort of the English officers of the army, who gathered there to drink coffee and read the newspapers, as they had in London.[44]

The polite coffee-house of Steele's *Spectator*, as was apparent to all Londoners of the time, was not a real place. Even his own examples furnished him with ample evidence that coffee-house society did not actually cohere with this utopian vision. It was always an argument, and an idea, not a reality. Steele uses the coffee-house as the focus of discussion, forging a consensus about how to speak politely, how to be modern, urbane and civil. He writes philosophy, not journalism, even though his philosophising is journalistic. The importance of *The Spectator*, argues Michael Ketcham, is that 'it creates a language that can articulate this model of society. It creates a vocabulary and a set of conventions which are vehicles for this model; it formalises a particular perception of society through the shaping power of language, through the power of discourse to shape what we see in the world.'[45] The essays do not attempt realistic descriptions of the coffee-house. *The Tatler* and *The Spectator* deploy a rhetoric that addresses all of society and continually champion egalitarian ideas of social inclusion. Yet it remains a socially exclusive vision of moral reform, extending only to other men like Steele, to property-owning men of similar outlook. Nonetheless, to later generations this argument is understood to mean that coffee-houses were indeed open to all comers from all stations of life, even the poor and the disenfranchised.

All over Europe the English coffee-house was the most celebrated example of a new form of polite socialising, based around conversation and newspaper reading, conducted between equals. But the English model was also thought to be a somewhat exceptional institution, rarely, if ever, encountered outside Anglo-Saxon society. The sociability encouraged by the café in Paris, for instance, was quite different. An English traveller to Paris remarked in 1701 that the 'coffee-houses' there were unlike those he was used to in London, for there were only a few of them, they were much more expensive, they sold strong liquors alongside coffee and chocolate, and they were decorated in a luxurious manner unknown in England: 'All their Tea, Coffee-Pots, and other Utensils are Silver: There's one Coffee-House near the Pont-Neuf, where there are no less than 34 Marble Tables: I have seen another with Looking-Glass all about it.'[46] Historians of the French café in the eighteenth century, such as Thomas Brennan and Robert Isherwood, argue that their luxurious interiors attested 'to the elite's determination to gather separately from its social inferiors'.[47] The cafés' social identity was established by their copious use of marble, crystal and mirrors, expensive finishes which appealed to an elite audience. Without the pronounced interest in news, politics and commerce, Parisian café sociability in the early eighteenth century was celebrated as a less serious form of entertainment, more at home in the carnival and the fair than the exchange or law courts. At the annual fairs the cafés made use of 'great coffee and chocolate-pots of silver', and 'the ladies make no scruple in the fair-time to go into these places, where besides coffee they meet with all sorts of liquors, sweetmeats, and several other kinds of refreshment'.[48] As Brennan notes, however, the association of the café with the polite culture of the upper levels of society in Paris was deeply mediated by literary and artistic depictions in numerous plays, poems and novels. Diderot, for example, located his novel *Rameau's Nephew* in the Café Regence of the Palais Royal. Yet evidence from the criminal courts, and from police records, demonstrates that the poorer sort drank at cafés too, though less often.[49] Nonetheless, the cultural construction of the European café associated it firmly with propriety, politeness and the cultural elite.

Historians of *ancien régime* France have suggested that the social role carved out by the coffee-house in London was occupied in Paris by the salons, by Masonic lodges, and by the academies and debating clubs.[50] In the salons of Paris, French *philosophes* practised their sociable arts and refined their theories of public sociability. The polite conversation they found there was both pleasurable and instructive, and, they thought, both distinct from and opposed to the elaborate forms of politeness and deference required at the royal court. In the 1760s and 1770s many of the leading men and women of intellectual Paris held a weekly salon in their homes, where invited guests would assemble to talk and debate about literature, science, religion and politics. One *philosophe*, the Abbé Morellet (a writer on economics), went on Mondays to the salon of Madame Geoffrin, on Tuesdays to that of Helvetius, on Thursdays to Holbachs and on Fridays to the Neckers. From about 1765 he even began holding his own salon, on Sunday nights, so as not to conflict with the others.[51] In the salons, Morellet's opinion was valued as a man of letters rather than because of his rank or birth and he could venture critical opinions that it was impossible to publish in print. The salons were also thought to be distinctly friendly to women, whose opinion was treated with respect there.

The English traveller on the Continent out of habit turned to the coffee-house as the natural place to find information and the company of progressive thinkers. Thomas Nugent, visiting Wismar in Mecklenburg in 1768, remarked that he 'was surprised not to find a coffee-house [in the city], and no more than one book-shop; but they have several taverns where they meet in clubs, much after the English manner'.[52] Without a coffee-house, Nugent thought, the residents of this town lacked modern civilisation. Nonetheless, coffee-houses alone were not a necessary cause of this new sociability. Arthur Young, when travelling in provincial France in 1788, found the poverty of the newspaper press most annoying. In Moulins, he said, he went to the coffee-house to read the newspapers, 'where I found near twenty tables set for company, but, as to a newspaper, I might as well have demanded an elephant. Here is a feature of national backwardness, ignorance, stupidity, and poverty!' Young reasoned that it was the combination of coffee-houses and newspapers that created the polite and civic sociability of progress: without the discussion thereby engendered there could be no reform. As he said, 'That universal circulation of intelligence, which in England transmits the least vibration of feeling or alarm, with electric sensibility, from one end of the kingdom to another, and which unites in bands of connection men of similar interests and situations, has no existence in France.'[53]

Another measure of the connection perceived between coffee-houses and enlightenment progress was seen in Milan in 1764. A group of young reformers, led by Pietro Verri, Alessandro Verri and Cesare Beccaria, established among themselves a coffee-house club called the Accademia dei Pugni. Between June 1764 and April 1766 these men issued a journal, modelled on *The Spectator* of Addison and Steele. They called it *Il Caffè*, invoking not simply the place of business that sold coffee, but also the whole concept of the coffee-house revolution. The first essay not only recapitulated the history of coffee (drawing on La Roque's account from 1715), but also invoked the precedence of Steele, Swift, Addison and Pope as writers whose cultured essays had delighted and reformed their readers.[54] All over Europe, groups of young reformers clubbed together to produce progressivist 'Spectatorial' essays, designed to be read in the coffee-houses for entertainment and instruction.[55] There were many routes to enlightenment and the rule of reason in the eighteenth century, but the English one – moderate, civic and middle class – was understood to be through the doors of a coffee-house, armed with a newspaper.

CHAPTER THIRTEEN

The Passing of the Coffee-House

When the American novelist Henry James wrote about the public diversions of London in the summer of 1877, he was struck by the absence of any kind of café society in the city. In this 'mighty metropolis', he remarked, there are 'a thousand sources of interest, entertainment and delight'. For the 'inferior sort' there were gin palaces, each of which came equipped with a 'detachment of the London rabble'. But for the 'better sort' London was 'scantily provided with innocent diversions', such as those offered by the cafés he recalled from his time in Paris, with their little round tables on a pavement or a gravel walk. 'In France and Italy, Germany and Spain, the count and countess will sally forth and encamp under a row of coloured lamps, upon the paving stones.' In Europe the café provided a public space for socialising among the 'people of "refinement"'. But in London no gentleman would be prepared to 'sit down, in his own country, at a café door', for to do so would be to enter into all the 'participations, contacts, [and] fellowships' that such a place would presume between the different stations of life.[1] Yet less than a century earlier, London had been home to the greatest coffee-house society in the world. What had happened?

The passing of the great English coffee-house had not gone unlamented. As early as 1817, Isaac d'Israeli had noted the decline of the coffee-houses:

> The frequenting of coffee-houses is a custom which has declined within our recollection, since institutions of a higher character, and society itself, has so much improved within late years. They were, however, the common assemblies of all classes of society. The mercantile man, the man of letters, and the man of fashion, had their appropriate coffee-houses.[2]

D'Israeli (father of the novelist and prime minister) had himself once been a habitué of the St James's Coffee-House. Researching the history of coffee-houses in the Reading Room of the British Museum, he recognised that their passing was an important change. By the early nineteenth century nostalgia for *The Spectator*'s coffee-house sociability was pronounced. Leigh Hunt, writing under a pseudonym designed to recall *The Spectator*, 'Harry Honeycombe', remarked in the *New Monthly Magazine* (1826), 'As I never pass Covent Garden [. . .] without thinking of all the old coffee-houses and the wits, so I can never reflect, without impatience, that there are no such meetings now, and no coffee-room that looks as if it would suit them.' Instead, he complains, 'society' now congregates in the pew at church and the box in the theatre, both places in which Hunt finds only a kind of confinement. He regretted the passing of the old coffee-house, where 'there was a more humane openness of intercourse', and where 'Hostility might get in, but it was obliged to behave itself'.[3]

Many blamed tea, and the passing of the coffee-house was certainly accompanied by an unprecedented rise in tea drinking among the British people. Yet this change in affections, one hot caffeinated beverage for another, was not in itself the cause of the coffee-house's demise. Rather, since it had always been as much an idea as a building or a business, it was as an idea that it had lost its grip on the imagination of the people. Paradoxically, while coffee-houses waned in Britain, various Contintental rivals – the French café, the Italian *caffè* and the Viennese *Kaffeehaus* – prospered, both in reality and in the mind even of the British. While English gentlemen increasingly eschewed the old coffee-houses of London, they enthusiastically enjoyed the bohemian and intellectual mélange they experienced in Paris, Venice and Vienna.

As early as 1750 coffee consumption in Britain had been eclipsed by that of tea. The contest between these two beverages for the hearts and minds of the British consumer had been going on since the mid seventeenth century, with coffee in the ascendancy for the first hundred years after 1652. In seeking an explanation for the unprecedented rise of tea drinking in Britain, and the relative stagnation of the coffee trade, a long-term macroeconomic view must be taken. In the 1720s coffee produced in the Dutch colonies in Java and the West Indies began to appear on the English market, in competition with the higher-quality Ottoman beans from the markets in the Yemeni towns of Mocha and Beit-al-Faki. In 1737 the first Jamaican imports reached London, after the plant was introduced there in 1728. The open competition between importers from these different producers drove the coffee price down, which might have encouraged the market had it not also driven down quality. Coffee planters in the West Indies remained poor relations of the great sugar magnates, with little political influence in the islands or in Britain.

By contrast, as the economist Simon Smith has argued, the tea trade was monopolised by the East India Company, who kept very close control over the quality and price of tea on the market. Moreover, the East India Company was able to use its political influence to manipulate the system of tariff preferences to distort the trade. Even as production of coffee in the British colonies of the West Indies increased, the tea importers managed to manipulate taxes and tariffs to make the coffee trade less profitable. A vicious spiral resulted: falling consumption of coffee led to a lower price, to which growers responded by using high yield-low cost cultivation techniques, which further drove down the quality of the coffee on the market.[4] The fiscal bias towards tea on the British market made coffee taste increasingly unpleasant to the consumer, even though it remained competitive on price. In 1784, the year Pitt's government reduced the tea duty from 100 per cent to 12.5 per cent as a method to reduce smuggling, tea imports to England and Wales surged to 16.3 million pounds, while coffee imports were 7 million pounds.[5] Moreover, Britain dominated the world tea market, importing more tea than the rest of Europe together, whereas its share of the coffee market was small. The level of coffee consumption did continue to rise up to 1850, but that of tea rose even faster, so that by the early nineteenth century almost six times as much tea was drunk per capita as coffee.[6] Nonetheless, tea remained a drink that was primarily consumed in the home.

Tea suited the new domestic markets for hot beverages. It was simpler to make in the home: the leaves simply required boiling water to be poured over them, while coffee needed careful roasting and grinding before use. Studies of probate inventories of household goods – made for the executors of wills – suggest that by the mid eighteenth century more homes had tea-making than coffee-making utensils.[7] By the 1750s, commentators around Britain noted that tea drinking had become ubiquitous, not only among the highest echelons of the aristocracy, delicately sipping the finest Hyson from Bow porcelain teasets, but also among the lowest stations of the common people, drinking a weak brew of cheap Bohea in chipped earthenware mugs. Political reformers became concerned that the poor were wasting their hard-earned income on the unnecessary luxury of tea. The eccentric philanthropist and pamphleteer Jonas Hanway complained in 1767 that 'it is amazing how the people are tea-bitten, and become as tenacious of drinking this infusion, as a mad dog to avoid drinking at all'. The consumption of tea, he argued, 'must multiply wants and impoverish', a problem that was worsened, he felt, by the loss of time wasted on drinking it.[8] Arthur Young, the agricultural reformer, also became concerned that the labouring poor threatened the welfare of the kingdom through their 'idleness, drunkenness, and tea drinking'. To his mind the poor 'would have no cause to complain of the high prices of provisions, were they to be persuaded to use less expensive, though not less wholesome and nutricious food; and the same time totally to desist from that pernicious practice, the *drinking of tea*'.[9] In Hanway's estimation a typical poor woman, whose income might be only 3 pence a day, was spending a quarter of it on tea, 'the infusion of a drug, which from *the badness of its kind*, or *the disorders of her body*, is but a remove from poison'.[10] Historians suggest Hanway was exaggerating but nonetheless conclude that manual workers' families typically devoted 10 per cent of their expenditure to tea and sugar at this time.[11]

The new social practices of tea drinking in the eighteenth century produced no social revolution in public culture equivalent to the coffee-house. As the sale of tea expanded, there was no corresponding development of tea houses in the city. Only the pleasure gardens around London, such as Vauxhall and Ranelagh, and in the spa towns like Bath and Bristol, had places of resort called 'tea houses' or 'tea pavilions'.[12] In the confines of these unique and circumscribed establishments, self-consciously dedicated to pleasure, women and men of the higher stations of life came together to drink tea (or coffee, if requested). In general, though, as Virginia Woolf noted, 'the tea table [. . .] was the centre of Victorian family life'. From the 1830s, the social historian Jane Pettigrew argues, the higher echelons of society used increasingly elaborate rituals of afternoon tea as a way to display conspicuous consumption, both of expensive tea and of tea equipment.[13] Woolf described how in her own childhood at 22 Hyde Park Gate, a cul-de-sac off Kensington Gore, the tea table was 'the very hearth and centre of family life, [. . .] round which sat innumerable parties; on which, when Saturday came [. . .] pink shell plates were placed, full of brown Sunday buns, full of very thin slices of white and brown bread and butter'.[14] Public consumption of afternoon tea was of course possible in the tearooms of large hotels and in new kinds of tea shop. In 1894 the food industry entrepreneur Joseph Lyons opened his first tea shop in Piccadilly, London. Catering to the market for afternoon tea, the tearoom restaurants of Lyons Corner Houses created spaces where unchaperoned young women could meet together while maintaining respectability. The Lyons tea shops – which were serving over 300,000 customers a day by 1909 – cultivated an image of genteel propriety, but were priced and located to appeal to a new mass market of lower-middle-class women consumers.[15] The tearooms carried associations of femininity and the domestic virtues central to Victorian ideals of civil society, contesting the masculine, political and commercial values associated with the coffee-house.

The coffee-houses lost their grip on English culture gradually, of course. In late eighteenth-century London, gentlemen continued to make frequent use of the coffee-houses, to read the newspapers, eaves-drop on conversations, meet with friends and to take the temperature of the city. As a young man in London in 1762, Boswell had been delighted by Child's Coffee-House in the shadow of St Paul's Cathedral, which he had read about in *The Spectator*. 'It is quite a place to my mind; dusky, comfortable, and warm, with a society of citizens and physicians who talk politics very fully and are very sagacious and sometimes jocular.'[16] As a student in Cambridge, then subsequently in London, Horace Walpole had made a habit of going to the coffee-house to read the latest newspapers and scandalous verses, which he carefully transcribed for the benefit of his friends in the country. Later in his life he was more sanguine about the quality of information he read there. To his cousin, General Conway, he wrote mockingly in August 1768, 'One should lead the life of a coffee-house politician, the most real patriots that I know; who amble out every morning to gather matter for lamenting over their country.'[17]

The attitude towards the coffee-house of these two eyewitnesses, James Boswell and Horace Walpole, the great social observers of late eighteenth-century urban life, is revealing. In describing their experiences they were no longer animated by the kind of excitement and enthusiasm for the coffee-house that Mr Spectator had admitted to earlier in the century. As an urban ideal, the coffee-houses had become something of a dead metaphor: an accepted part of social life in the city, but unremarkable and commonplace. Although visitors to London in the final decades of the eighteenth century continued to note their ubiquity, they also complained that their tell-tale vivacity had evaporated. A German Lutheran clergyman travelling in England in 1782, Charles Moritz, arrived expecting much of the coffee-houses, but found that 'there generally prevails a very decorous stillness and silence. Every one speaks softly to those only who sit next to him. The greater part read the newspapers, and no one ever disturbs another.'[18] Though still unchallenged in the public market for hot drinks, the coffee-houses were losing their distinctive sociability.

As the eighteenth century came to its end, the great age of the British coffee-house was clearly over. Nonetheless, they did not entirely disappear in the nineteenth century. They became increasingly stratified, with very different kinds of establishment serving different social classes. The nature of these places was so transformed, however, that they no longer conformed to the coffee-house ideal. At the lower end of the social spectrum a plebeian clientele continued to find some of them amenable. Research into the ultra-radical underground between 1790 and 1830 by the historian Iain McCalman suggests that these circles gathered in convivial political clubs in coffee-houses for reading, singing and debating, attracting an audience of revolutionaries, artisans and minor tradesmen. Lunt's Coffee-House in Clerkenwell Green, for example, hosted an underground gathering called the British Forum five times a week, led by the debating barber John Gale Jones, where discussions on agrarian reform, the abolition of slavery, atheism and republican campaigning were enthusiastically followed. As coffee-houses were more easily established and relatively free from the control of the licensing judges, coffee-house keepers were more prepared to admit such clubs to their premises.[19] It wasn't a straight road, however. One radical, John Thelwall, complained bitterly that everywhere he went, government spies followed him: 'every tavern and coffee-house has been haunted', he said, 'by spies and sycophants.'[20] Nonetheless, radical coffee-house debating clubs were able to evade the government repression of other forms of assembly in 1795–1803 and again in 1819–21, and provided a lasting model of sociability for underground radicals.

The working poor, of London and the industrial cities, were further catered for by coffee stalls and coffee taverns. The former usually consisted of a simple barrow of two or four wheels, on which the proprietor stood several large cans of coffee, kept warm by charcoal braziers. As well as coffee and tea, they vended sandwiches, cake and bread rolls. 'From these', Henry Mayhew reported in 1849, 'the poor man mostly obtains his breakfast.'[21] There were a great many such stalls, Mayhew noted, and those with the best pitches were considered very lucrative. 'Wherever there is a public thoroughfare frequented by working people, on their way to their day's labour, there a coffee-stall keeper is sure to be seen.' Early in the morning, in all weathers, crowds of working men stood around them, drinking mugs of coffee, which sold for 1 penny (the same price as a dish of coffee cost 200 years earlier). A different kind of working-class coffee-house was found in the establishments of the Coffee Tavern movement, active between the 1840s and the 1890s. Championed by middle-class Temperance associations, the coffee taverns were conceived as a solution to the proclivity for alcoholic drinking among the working class, offering the temperance men who pledged themselves to abstain from the use of intoxicants and shunned public houses a place to socialise in the evening. At a Coffee Public House, the reformers hoped, a working man would find tea and coffee, as well as conversation, smoking and newspapers, but no gin, beer or dissipation.[22] By buying and converting public houses to coffee rooms, the Coffee Tavern movement had more than 1,200 premises by 1884, although the movement itself depended heavily on the financial interest of middle-class charities.

For the polite classes the tendency of coffee-houses was to adopt increasingly explicit regulation, excluding non-members from their sociability. In the world of commerce many City coffee-houses followed the model offered by Jonathan's and Lloyd's, whose coffee rooms were available only to recognised members of the trade who paid a subscription. Merchants engaged in the Baltic and Virginia trade had since the seventeenth century congregated in the Baltic Coffee-House, where the proprietor provided a focused commercial intelligence and a postal clearing house, even though it was an 'open house' with no regulation on its sociability or clientele. However, after unscrupulous speculation by dealers in Russian tallow in the early 1820s, the clients of the coffee-house moved to a more regulated regime, deciding that they would admit only those willing to pay a subscription for the privilege and putting a strict limit on numbers, so as to exclude speculators and ensure trade to those admitted to the closed shop.[23]

A similar move towards social exclusiveness was noticeable in St James's too, where many of the most famous coffee-houses of the eighteenth century were closed to the public. In these the regular clients transformed the open coffee rooms into gentlemen's clubs, whose subscription membership was strictly controlled. White's Chocolate House was transformed in 1736 into a private club catering to a high-status clientele engaged in no-limits gambling.[24] Other coffee-houses in St James's, such as the Cocoa Tree, were remodelled along this elite male-only model of gentlemen's clubs, some of which (White's, Brooks, Boodles) continue to exist to this day. The French novelist and socialist Flora Tristan remarked in 1830, when making her inspection of London life, that the sociability of these clubs was characterised by dining, drinking and gambling, without the 'intellectual results' once associated with the coffee-house. 'What do these two or three hundred club members do? Do they sincerely strive to acquire an understanding of important social questions? Do they discuss business and politics, letters, theatre and fine arts? No. They go to their clubs to dine well, to drink good wine, to play cards and escape the boredom of married life.'[25] Henry James was delighted by the clubs of London, revelling in their exclusive membership and luxurious decoration. Soon after his arrival in the city in 1877, he was put on the honorary list of the Athenaeum Club in Pall Mall and thereafter he was elected to the Reform Club next door. In one of his letters home, James enthused about the sociability of the club: 'all the great chairs and lounges and sofas filled with men having afternoon tea – lolling back with their laps filled with magazines, journals, and fresh Mudie books [popular fiction], while amiable flunkies in knee breeches present them the divinest salvers of tea and buttered toast!'[26] Here, then, was the inheritor of the coffee-houses whose absence he noted in the street outside.

The stratification of the coffee-houses into distinct and separate institutions for the leisured elite and the working class segmented and atomised the celebrated coffee-house sociability of Queen Anne's reign. In the City of London, indeed, the pressure on real estate meant that all the famous establishments were closed and demolished in the mid nineteenth century. A retired stockbroker commented in 1845 that the change had begun around 1815, when the City merchants removed their residences from the City, which thereafter became only a place of work for them, leaving their dwellings in the City itself to clerks and the poor. The effect on the coffee-houses, he complained, was unavoidable: their coffee rooms were now quiet, without conversation, and empty of customers before and after working hours.[27] When in 1873 Garraway's Coffee-House in Exchange Alley was demolished, the event was noted by newspapers as the passing of a landmark in the life of the City.[28] In 1888 a City businessman wrote that the

> golden age of coffee-houses, as depicted in the light literature of the last century, has passed away for ever. Whether we are more dull than our forefathers or only more 'exclusive', whether time is in these days of progress too short for such dawdling enjoyments as theirs – whatever the reason, certain it is that the representative of the nineteenth century does not take his pleasure as his grandfather did in a coffee-house.

The age of the coffee-house had ended. Even though it was still possible to go out into the city to purchase a cup of coffee, the idea of the coffee-house as a collective conversational experiment was finished. 'Self-absorption' and 'Selfishness' found 'no better exponent than the demeanour of one who takes his meals in a coffee-house', commented one Cambridge don.[29]

Europe and the world of the cafés

Across Europe in the nineteenth century, however, the idea of the café continued to excite both customers and commentary. In many cities the café, and the distinctive society it attracted, caught the attention of writers and artists as the source of entertaining anecdotes of an exotic and bohemian life. To such commentators it was the café, rather than the coffee-house, which now seemed quintessentially urban and modern. At the Caffè Florian in Venice in 1850 the French historian, Hippolyte Taine, painted a glowing picture of café life:

> Taking a seat in the café Florian, in a small cabinet wainscoted with mirrors and decked with agreeable allegorical subjects, one muses with half-closed eyes over the imagery of the day falling into the order of and transformed as in a dream; odorous sorbets melt on the tongue and are rewarmed with exquisite coffee such as is found nowhere else in Europe; one smokes tobacco of the Orient and beholds flower-girls

> approaching, graceful and handsomely attired in robes of silk, who silently place on the table violets and the narcissus.[30]

In this dreamy but temporary world of luxury, Taine is intoxicated by the café's exotic sensuality: coffee, tobacco, sorbet and flower-girls all seem to melt together. At the same time, however, the café's pleasures are rendered into a list of commodities, as if everything beautiful were for sale, including the flower-girl. In perceiving it as a paradigmatic institution of modern life, poets and painters were attracted as much to its drawbacks as its advantages.

In the late 1870s, for example, both Edgar Degas and Eduard Manet worked on an innovative series of drawing and paintings concerned with the café life of Paris. Manet's *Interior of a Café* (1880), now in the Burrell Collection in Glasgow, depicted the enticing world of a café in the Place du Théâtre-Français, with its mixture of women and men, wealth and poverty, beauty and distress. Amid this room of gilt and mirrors, the painter depicted a woman nursing a glass of absinthe, staring into the distance, while a man smoked a cigar, his back to the viewer and his companion. While Manet seems to celebrate café life, works like *Interior of a Café*, *The Café Concert* (1879) and *Corner of the Café Concert* (1878) also suggests a powerful sense of anomie: in the sociable spaces of the city few people seem to connect with each other.[31] In Baudelaire's prose-poem, 'The Eyes of the Poor', a new café at the corner of one of Haussmann's new boulevards, with its dazzling gas-lights, gilt caryatids and expanse of mirrors, is the scene for a confrontation between a middle-class courting couple and a poor family, who look on at this splendour in servile wonder. To the young man's disgust the woman he is courting, to whom he has been making expressions of love and devotion, is not moved but horrified by the spectacle of the poor, asking that the proprietor have them moved on. In the poem Baudelaire evokes the attractions of café life, but sees it also as a space that made all too apparent new urban segregations of class, sexuality and power.[32]

The social world of the café was in other respects less accessible and open than these depictions suggest. In the 1880s official statistics declared there were as many as 40,000 in Paris alone. In his work on the cafés of Paris the historian Scott Haine has identified a wide spectrum of café subcultures, often existing side by side in the same neighbourhoods, from grand cafés attracting an elite clientele on the new boulevards, to mean establishments frequented by thieves, artists or poets, to those acting as fronts for brothels, and others hosting clubs devoted to literary and political debate. Yet he also argues that each kind of café kept its clientele safely contained, isolated from each other, as there were few, if any, which allowed men from different classes to mix together as equals.[33] Middle-class women, too, were rarely expected in the cafés unchaperoned: art historians estimate that the women depicted in Manet's café scenes, for example, would have been understood to be prostitutes by contemporary viewers.[34]

In working-class life, Haine argues, the café provided a unique place for small-scale face-to-face encounters, allowing friendships to develop in an urban environment, where there was insufficient space or money in the home for entertainment. All kinds of cafés were under intense surveillance, however, with special detachments of police spies for every establishment, ready to report anyone voicing revolutionary sentiments. As a result, police records in Paris from the late nineteenth century contain an enormous wealth of detail about the social life of the café. Police sources, as might be expected, concentrate on the deviant, criminal and subversive activities encountered there – and as records of the lived experience of the café they might be seen to be as biased as those of the poets. To the police, any kind of group socialising was nearly always suspicious, redolent of rebellion or delinquency. Yet café socialising played an important role in making the industrial city feel like home, creating bonds of affection between migrant workers from different backgrounds, whether from the provinces or abroad. Labour organisations made use of cafés during strikes, not only as headquarters but to disseminate propaganda and influence opinion.[35] As Haine reminds us, however, the sociability of the Parisian café was powered by alcohol and, despite some similarities with the old English coffee-house, its closest analogy in England was with the tavern or public house.

In fin-de-siècle Vienna the *Kaffeehaus* offered another evocative model of urban and artistic modernity. Viennese cafés, which served wine and dinners as well as coffee and patisserie, occupied a special place in Austrian society and culture by the end of the nineteenth century. Their grandly decorated coffee rooms were especially attractive to writers, artists and intellectuals. From within it, seated at a table with a cup of *mélange* (half coffee and half milk), the wits and poets constructed the *Kaffeehaus* as the topic and emblem of their work. As Harold Segel has argued, 'Austrian literary modernism and the Vienna coffeehouse form an inseparable entity.'[36] These *Kaffeehäuser* were built on a grand scale: the Café Griensteidl on the ground floor of the Palais Herberstein across from the Hofburg, was lined with gilt mirrors and filled with marble-topped tables, and the Café Central, in the Herrengasse, had a central court with a high glass roof, originally constructed to serve as an exchange for the merchants. Fin-de-siècle Vienna witnessed a period of great creativity in arts and ideas. Painters such as Gustav Klimt, Egon Schiele and Oscar Kokoschka, architects such as Adolf Loos, and writers such as Alfred Polgar, Joseph Roth and Arthur Schnitzler, together with countless journalists, lawyers, schoolteachers, tradesmen and merchants, made the *Kaffeehaus* not simply a place to socialise over coffee and read newspapers, but also a central location for their intellectual life. As houses in Vienna were generally small and cramped, and few had telephones, the *Kaffeehaus*, warm, spacious and inviting, took on the role of a home away from home. Alfred Polgar's 'Theory of the Café Central' (1926) celebrated the *Kaffeehaus* as a leisured space in which people could become their true selves by casting off their work-time identities, precisely by doing nothing:

> The Café Central thus represents something of an organization of the disorganized. In this hallowed space, each halfway indeterminate individual is credited with a personality. So long as he remains within the boundaries of the coffeehouse, he can cover all his moral expenses with this credit. [. . .] The only person who partakes of the most essential charm of this splendid coffeehouse is he who wants nothing there but to be there. Purposelessness sanctifies the stay.[37]

The literary *Kaffeehaus* came to be understood as the central stage upon which an urbane and cosmopolitan Viennese modernity could be displayed. Such an atmosphere, of course, was brutally repressed under Nazi rule.[38]

Henry James had been right to remark that England had no equivalent of these continental cafés and *Kaffeehäuser*. But there was one exception, many people thought. In 1865 an enterprising French immigrant, Daniel Nicholas Thévenon, having taken flight from bankruptcy in Paris as a wine merchant, opened a small restaurant in a converted oilcloth merchant's store at 19 Glasshouse Street, which he called the Café-Restaurant Nicols. When Thévenon had arrived in London in 1863 he had only £5 to his name. His little restaurant prospered, especially after he secured the lease of the shop behind his, which had a frontage on to the grand boulevard of Regent Street. Combining the two spaces, he renamed the business the Café Royal. From his experience among the café society of Paris he had seen the potential for the grand café, which competed for customers with ever more opulent interior decorations. After further acquisitions, the Café Royal occupied a very large site between Glasshouse Street, Air Street and Regent Street, becoming one of the most renowned restaurants in London. Its lavishly appointed interior, with its profligate use of red velvet, gilt-framed mirrors, shiny brass fittings and electric lights, was only matched by the extravagant dinners it served, accompanied by the best wine list in London.[39] Osbert Sitwell described the ravishing effect the Café Royal had on customers, 'with its smoky acres of painted goddesses and cupids and tarnished gilding, its golden caryatids and its filtered, submarine illumination, composed of tobacco smoke, of the flames from the chafing dishes and the fumes from food, of the London fog outside and the dim electric light within'.[40] The Café Royal was not a coffee-house in the English sense, but a restaurant. Its success, however, confirmed the Continental model of the café in the English imagination.

From an early date, refugees from Europe found a home at the Café Royal. French exiles of varying political hues (Royalists, Orleanists, Imperialists) became well-known visitors. Notorious exiles like General Georges-Ernest Boulanger and the Marquis de Rochefort-Luçay plotted and connived in the restaurant against their possible return to France. Giuseppe Garibaldi and Alexander Kerensky were both, in their time, habitués. The most famous customers, however, were the artists and writers who made the brasserie at the Café Royal their favourite destination. In the 1890s both James McNeill Whistler and Oscar Wilde were regulars. Wilde dined at the Café Royal nearly every day in the early 1890s, especially with Lord Alfred Douglas: 'luncheon with its *liqueurs* lasted usually till 3.30,' he later recalled in a letter from Reading gaol.[41] They met there with their friends, who formed a distinguished group of aesthetes and decadents, including the artists Max Beerbohm and Aubrey Beardsley, the Symbolist critic Arthur Symons, as well as the leading lights of the Rhymers' Club, including Ernest Dowson, Frank Harris and William Butler Yeats. In his eulogy to the Café Royal, Symons wrote of it as a 'luxurious, convenient, unconventional Café', an island of bohemia in the heart of London.[42] In their public and private declarations these writers and artists constructed the Café Royal as a place synonymous with bohemian London, an equation that remained powerful for over fifty years, until the inevitable disruptions of the Second World War.

It was this louche and artistic reputation that drew London's modernists to the Café Royal in the first decades of the twentieth century. The brasserie was the intellectual home of the coterie centred on the artists Wyndham Lewis, Augustus John and Jacob Epstein, who met there with poets such as Ezra Pound, Nancy Cunard and T. S. Eliot, and philosophers such as Henri Bergson and T. E. Hulme. The place of the Café Royal in defining the associative culture of early twentieth-century intellectual life in London was recorded in Adrian Allinson's painting *The Old Café Royal* (dated 1915–16), which depicted artists and critics mingling together, reading books and newspapers, and talking over carafes of wine.[43] According to some reports, the Italian poet F. T. Marinetti had one of his Futurist Manifesto readings at the Café Royal, where it was duly signed in public by himself and the English artist C. R. W. Nevinson.[44] What was remarkable about it at the time was not only its scintillating concentration of bohemia and talent, but that it could simultaneously host grand dinners, albeit in private dining suites, for royalty and senior politicians. To its admirers it seemed that the Café Royal was London's common room. By the post-war period this bohemian intensity had largely evaporated, although the Café Royal continued to trade in a sanitised form. John Betjeman's poem 'On Seeing an Old Poet in the Café Royal', written in 1958, stands as an epitaph:

> I saw him in the Café Royal.
> Very old and very grand,
> Modernistic shone the lamplight
> There in London's fairyland.[45]

The coffee-house and the myth of Queen Anne's England

The success of restaurants like the Café Royal, the grand cafés of Paris, Vienna and Venice, or the gentlemen's clubs of St James's merely underlined how much the coffee-house itself had been erased from social life by the end of the nineteenth century. But, paradoxically, as they were erased from life, coffee-houses took on a new meaning as a memory, as history, as myth. In the nineteenth century, as historians and novelists imagined the social life of 'Old London', the coffee-houses painted a compelling picture of the period: warm and cosy refuges of politeness and rationality, bulwarks against sectarian troubles and political dissent. In this nostalgic, mythologised view, the coffee-house was a plangent reminder of a simple, less complicated England, dutifully compared with the hideous smoky world of industry and exploitation of the late nineteenth century.

In his great *History of England*, Thomas Babington Macaulay argued that the coffee house was 'a most important political institution', 'the chief organ through which the public opinion of the metropolis vented itself'.[46] Macauley's enthusiastic description of coffee-houses in 1685 was derived from his research in the pamphlet culture of the Restoration and early eighteenth century, mainly using literary and satirical material as evidence. Later nineteenth-century historians of the eighteenth century pursued Macauley's idea, eschewing the more radical phases of the coffee-house history and elaborating a vision of their social life during the reign of Queen Anne. In the coffee-house, they argued, it was possible to identify the origin of important principles underpinning the English constitution, especially nascent notions of egalitarianism, freedom of speech and liberty of conscience. It had become a sort of shorthand sign, an emblem, for the great virtues of liberty and common sense in English politics.

In the coffee-house mythology, Addison's and Steele's *Spectator*, and more generally the literary culture of the reign of Queen Anne, loomed large as the fullest and most complete expression of the culture of politeness. Newly published editions of *The Tatler* and *The Spectator* were read widely. Long out of copyright, they appeared in complete editions, selections and anthologies in almost every year of the nineteenth century, especially in the final decades. Cheap editions were prepared for schools, for missionaries, for teachers of writing and journalism. To many it seemed as if *The Spectator* and its avatar the coffee-house were the clearest expression of what was good about English morality and culture. The historian W. H. Davenport Adams argued in his *Good Queen Anne* (1886) that her reign 'witnessed a remarkable development of intellectual activity, which permanently affected the tone and character of our literature. It witnessed the evolution of our constitutional system, and the greater definiteness of ministerial responsibility'. Coffee-houses, which he discussed at great length, played a prominent part in 'the literary life of London *sub tempore Annæ*'.[47] Investigating 'the spirit of the age', the Victorian critic Leslie Stephen argued in his Ford Lectures on Eighteenth-Century English Literature and Society, delivered at Oxford in 1903, for the 'necessary connection between the social and the literary departments of history'. The 'number of coffee-houses', he said, facilitated 'the characteristic fraternization of the politicians and the authors' in the crucial period after the Revolution of 1688.[48] Having brought the world of politics to the world of literature, the coffee-houses comprised 'the literary organ of the society', in which the wits and writers who comprised 'the "town"' made and displayed their judgements on literature and politics. In this way, Stephen suggests, a new and important sense of public opinion had been born. In Stephen's rehabilitation of the early eighteenth century the coffee-house was a notable beneficiary of the 'sweetness and light' of the Queen Anne style, for here was a prime example of the work of ideas in society.

The history of coffee-houses was celebrated in a number of specialist books written in the final decades of the nineteenth century. The most influential among them, such as those by the antiquarian and journalist John Timbs and the amateur historian Edward Forbes Robinson, paired the coffee-house with the gentleman's club, an alliance that sealed their allegiance to genteel high culture.[49] The scholarship of the coffee historians and the Whig historians like Macaulay secured for the coffee-house an important role in twentieth-century ideas. The definitive account of English social history in this period was that of Macaulay's nephew, George Macaulay Trevelyan. First published in the 1930s, his enormously popular histories continued the celebration of the Queen Anne era, and its flourishing coffee-house culture, as the originary moment of fundamental concepts of the English constitution and its supporting values of liberty, tolerance and humanity. Trevelyan argues that coffee-houses were at 'the centre of social life', cheap and informal places which allowed admission to a wide audience hungry for news and conversation, producing 'a levelling influence' in a society much given to rank. Quoting John Macky in 1714, Trevelyan declared patriotically that 'the quintessence of Coffee House life' was 'The "universal liberty of speech of the English nation" uttered amid clouds of tobacco smoke, with equal vehemence whether against the Government and the Church, or against their enemies, had long been the wonder of foreigners'.[50] Whether read in the early 1930s, or when repeated almost verbatim in his *English Social History* of 1942,[51] Trevelyan's defence of the egalitarian spirit of coffee-house 'liberty of speech' compared well with the repressive dictatorships governing most of Europe.

After the Second World War, new generations of scholars in war-shattered Europe found attractive weight in the myth of the rational and egalitarian coffee-house of Queen Anne's England. Hans Speier, a German refugee from Nazi oppression who had found a home at the University in Exile at the New School for Social Research in New York, published in 1950 an academic article on the emergence of notions of 'public opinion' in the democracies of 'middle-class civilization'. Speier theorised that coffee-houses and literary salons had played a key role in the development of public opinion in the eighteenth century by broadening the appetite for reading and debate. He adapted the argument of Macaulay's school to a new theoretical paradigm, using the research of Robinson and a German study of the literary coffee-house from Dryden to Addison to add specific detail.[52] Defining public opinion as 'free and public communication from citizens to their government on matters of concern to the nation', Speier argued that it was in coffee-houses, 'popular as centers of news-gathering and news dissemination, political debate, and literary criticism', that 'the English middle classes began to accomplish their own education'.[53]

This view of the coffee-house found a wide audience in the last half-century among a range of highly regarded and influential philosophers, sociologists and critics in a broadly left tradition: Jürgen Habermas, Richard Sennett, Terry Eagleton, and Peter Stallybrass.[54] Habermas, for example, famously proposed in 1962 that the early eighteenth century witnessed the transformation of notions of public opinion (the untranslatable German term he uses, *Öffentlichkeit*, means something like 'publicness' but is usually given as 'public sphere').[55] This change, Habermas argues, was brought about in new social institutions that allowed ordinary people in the middle stations of life to participate in political life. The paradigmatic example for him was the English coffee-house, although he also saw a role for salons, clubs and the periodical press. The historical evidence he relied on was profoundly invested in the mythology of the Queen Anne period, being derived from Trevelyan,

Timbs and some German studies of Addison and Steele. In the 1950s and early 1960s there was an intriguing resonance between Habermas's argument that civil society, and modern participatory democracy, emerged from the coffee-house and the post-war effort to rebuild European democracy. These resonances were intensified by the coffee-house culture of espresso bars and cafés, which had transformed European culture in Habermas's own time. Perhaps for the first time since the early eighteenth century the idea of the coffee-house could be once again credibly associated with a reforming and convivial sociability.

CHAPTER FOURTEEN

Angry Young Men and the Espresso Revolution

Greeted with bonfires and dancing, the end of the Second World War held the promise of plenty and prosperity. But for years after there was no release from the austerity of wartime, from 'the small, dull, makeshift meals, from darkness and drabness and making do, from the depressing, nerve-aching, never-ending need to be careful'.[1] Entering a restaurant in London in the early 1950s, the hero of John Wain's novel *Living in the Present* (1955) was resigned to a menu full of 'dishes that were "off"', of 'platefuls of twice-cooked inferior food' and nothing to eat but 'corned-beef rissoles, a spoonful of greens boiled to rags and tasting of soda, and perhaps a chunk of waxy ice-cream to follow'.[2] Nearly a decade after the end of the war, food shortages remained common in Britain, and the habits of scarcity continued to be felt through all parts of social and cultural life. A lead article in the *Times Literary Supplement* opined in 1957 that 'we live in a muffled age' characterised by a 'mood of rather damp and grey moderation'.[3] Despite the confected excitement that had surrounded the Festival of Britain in 1951, the cultural landscape remained dreary. Supplies of almost all major foods, including coffee, were strictly regulated by rationing and price controls.

Coffee rationing had been introduced across Europe at the very beginning of the war: in Germany and Italy in December 1939, and in Britain in January 1940. To all intents and purposes, coffee disappeared off the market for more than a decade, to be replaced by foul-tasting, adulterated imitations and substitutes made from roasted chicory, beans and acorns (mixtures to which people became curiously habituated). After the war, production of coffee failed to keep pace with demand and rationing continued across all Europe, from Denmark to Germany, France and Britain, and in Eastern Europe. The domestic market for coffee in Europe and America was dominated by instant soluble products and by ersatz coffee manufactured from chicory and other sources.[4] In 1953, for example, Nestlé was continuing to find a ready market for a brand called 'Ricory', an instant coffee and chicory drink, sold alongside its other instant preparations such as Nescafé.[5] Yet demand for coffee in Britain had increased significantly during the war. Although low by European standards, by 1950 per capita British consumption had risen to triple what it had been before the war, while consumption on the Continent fell to well below pre-war levels, especially in Germany and Italy. Although tea was still celebrated as the British 'national drink', in January 1953 even *The Times* proposed that the rise in coffee consumption meant that it had become 'an amenity enjoyed at all levels in the welfare state'.[6] However, coffee prices rose steeply on the international market in the early 1950s, and, in 1950, not only was the ration cut by 20 per cent but the price was increased by 6–8 pence per pound. In Britain the Ministry of Food sought to secure coffee imports from the Empire (Kenya, Uganda and Jamaica especially), but the quantity produced there was insufficient.

On 20 August 1952 the British Ministry of Food finally removed coffee price controls, hoping that the trade association, the Coffee Buyers Association, would be able to import on the open market sufficient coffee from South America to meet demand. The first open trade coffee auction since 1941 was held in Mincing Lane on 9 January 1953, heralded in *The Times* as the return of private trade, although the editorial observed ruefully that almost all offerings were from the Ministry of Food's own stocks. By 1953 the crisis in coffee production was global, with very high prices maintained through 1954, as the Brazilian crop was decimated by drought. Coffee prices jumped too: the spot price for Brazilian Santos reached 90 cents a pound in New York in April 1954, up from 60 cents the year before.[7] High prices effectively placed even low-grade coffee in the luxury sector. On 26 January 1954 *The Times* reported that New York housewives were leading a 'strike' or boycott against the high price of coffee. There was widespread outrage, even in Congress, that some establishments were charging as much as 15 cents for a cup of coffee. Under headlines reading 'Coffee crisis in America', a Federal Trade Commission investigation was launched to investigate whether coffee prices were being maintained at artificially high levels.[8] The British Parliament similarly debated the reintroduction of coffee price controls.

The return of a free market for coffee, and its record high prices, effectively repositioned coffee as a luxury commodity. Whereas tea was generally priced at 3 pence a cup, coffee was now 6 pence. Keen entrepreneurs, liberated by the end of rationing, discovered that in the right environment, as much as 9 pence or even 1s 6d a cup could be charged for coffee. But demand at this price was narrow, requiring a high quality of service and environment. It was for this niche market that a Milanese dental mechanic, Pino Riservato, began importing the newest coffee-making technology, manufactured by the Societa' Brevetti Gaggia in Milan, Italy. Espresso machines were described as a technological 'advance', although they were derived from early nineteenth-century pressure percolators. Prototypical espresso machines had been patented as early as 1902 by Luigi Bezzera,[9] and his company was using the term *caffè espresso* by 1906.[10] In these early espresso machines individual cups were made by forcing boiling water under pressure through coffee grounds and a filter. However, the system used the extreme heat of the water in the machine (at a temperature considerably above boiling point) to maintain the pressure needed to force the water through the grounds, which meant that the coffee grounds were over-extracted and the resulting liquor bitter. Nonetheless, the speed of the service and the theatre of its production, amid clouds of steam, found favour with customers all over Europe. In 1946 the Italian engineer Archille Gaggia patented a revision to this system: the water was heated to a temperature below boiling point (approximately 90° Celsius), and then forced through the coffee grounds by pressure supplied by pistons powered by the waiter operating the machine. The resulting liquor extracted considerable flavour from the coffee but was much less bitter. Gaggia's revolutionary machines were quickly followed by others adopting similar solutions from Pavoni, Faema and Brasilia in Italy, and Rowenta and WMF in West Germany.

On a sales trip to England in 1951, Pino Riservato had been appalled by the quality of English coffee, which was typically made in large urns and kept hot for hours. Riservato hypothesised that a market for the Gaggia machines might be found in England. In these straitened times, however, import licences were impossible to obtain, and his first five machines had to be smuggled in by way of Dublin and the Isle of Man. He set up one in his flat in Jermyn Street, but the catering industry was unimpressed: to their eyes there was no market in Britain for a machine so wasteful of coffee. Riservato's solution was to circumvent the catering trade and, in effect, to reinvent the coffee-house. He established the Riservato Partners Ltd at 10 Dean Street, in the heart of Soho, the centre of the Italian community in London, proudly proclaiming the business to be Gaggia's 'sole agents for UK and the British Empire'.[11] In the basement beneath his offices Riservato started the Gaggia Experimental Coffee Bar, known also as the Riservato, in the summer of 1953. Modelled in some ways on an Italian *caffè*, the Riservato's novelty was confirmed by the shiny chrome styling of the espresso machine, and the light and modern architecture of exposed stone, recessed up-lighters and modern art.[12] Other 'coffee bars', as such institutions came to be called, followed quickly, all notable for their distinct modern aesthetic.

The Moka Bar, in Frith Street, Soho, may have been the first independent enterprise to take on Riservato's Gaggia machines. In a converted bomb-damaged laundry, the Scottish proprietor Maurice Ross employed the architect Geoffrey Crockett to design a contemporary modern interior, making copious use of Formica, the hard-wearing, glossy surfacing material at the forefront of contemporary design. Within a year a legion of exotic new espresso bars had opened across London and the provinces: *The Times* noted 'the mushroom growth of espresso coffee bars in London' in October 1955.[13] Their names are a roll-call of competitive imitation and innovation: Il Capuccino (George Street), the Rocola (Piccadilly Circus), the Gondola (Wigmore Street), Boulevard (Wigmore Street), Arabica (Brompton Road, Knightsbridge), Sarabia (Onslow Crescent, Kensington), Las Vegas (Old Brompton Road, Kensington), the Coffee-House (Haymarket) and the Orrery (King's Road, Chelsea). Within five years they had spread all across Britain: in May 1956 Martha Gellhorn reported 475 in London alone, and in 1960 Edward Bramah estimated 500 in London and more than 2,000 around the country.[14] The Coffee Publicity Association estimated there were over 130 coffee bars in Lancashire and the North-West by the end of 1956, 'usually ultra-modern, often with a Continental theme'.[15] Bertram Young joked in *Punch* that 'we have reached the stage when virtually the entire population of these islands goes in hourly danger of opening a coffee-bar'.[16] There was even a monthly trade journal, enticingly called *Coffee Bar and Coffee Lounge*, advertising all the modern paraphernalia of espresso machines and Cona coffee sets, jukeboxes, cigarette machines, automatic dispensers, individually wrapped sugar, shopfitters, crockery supplies, kitchen equipment, furniture, as well as branded coffee supplies.[17] At the annual Soho Fair, organised by the local trade association, a beauty competition sponsored by the Coffee Publicity Association searched for a 'Miss Cappuccino'. The first 'perfect coffee girl', selected from women who worked in coffee bars across the country was Andria Loran, a model ('no nudes').[18]

The rest of the world was soon to follow: in 1957 Italian migrants to Australia were opening coffee shops called 'espresso bars' in Sydney and Melbourne, 'attractive tubular places where old and new Australians alike drink cappuccino and eat pizza'.[19] In Wellington, New Zealand, the modernist Austrian architect Ernst Plischke designed an espresso coffee shop (Harry Seresin's Coffee Gallery) in the bookshop of Roger Parsons, which opened in 1957 on Lambton Quay.[20] Even America, home of the diner and the refillable cup, took to espresso. In San Francisco's North Beach an Italian immigrant opened Café Trieste in 1957, whose back room was famously inhabited by the Beat poets Allen Ginsburg and Bob Kaufman.[21] In 1956 Lillian Shaaf reported in *Esquire* that a new wave of European-style espresso bars could be found in New York at Orsini's on West 56th Street, and Serendipity 3 on East 58th Street:

> If you are currently 'in the know', your big evenings wind up in the chic little coffeehouses springing up all over America. [. . .] New Yorkers flock to the little espresso rendezvous in Greenwich Village after an 'off-Broadway' evening at the theatre. These little rooms often are startlingly reminiscent of a Charles Addams cartoon: cracked mirrors line the walls, a piece of dusty statuary peers at you from a corner, deep yellow paper masks the light bulbs. Then, as you grope your way to a table, your eye catches a sight of the pride of the establishment – the one imposing, sparkling, glowering feature, the monstrous Espresso machine. You order your Espresso or Cappuccino and then fearfully watch the monster produce same. Like a proud engineer the man behind the monster turns his steam levers; the great machine begins to throb and hiss, and just as you begin to think the explosion is inevitable, it starts to drip the brown nectar gently into the tiny white cup awaiting it. You sip the delicious brew, sigh appreciatively and think, 'What a show for the money!'[22]

But although the United States accounted for about two-thirds of the world's supplies of coffee, American consumers generally proved resistant to the stronger flavours of espresso.[23]

Early commentators on the espresso-bar scene were impressed by the crowds and the profits. Although espresso machines were expensive (between £100 and £450), the simple food and service of the coffee bar made them extremely economical to run. 'Many bars appear to be run by catering amateurs,' *Architectural Design* noted, 'but making a professional job of this new type of establishment – and a good income.'[24] In an examination of the trade in the American *Tea and Coffee Trade Journal* (March 1955) a British correspondent, Jack Brooks, noted the 'substantial profits' for 'operators of the modern coffee bars that have sprung up here in the last year', explaining that each cup was made individually on the espresso machines and sold 'at a price per cup of 8d to 1s.' One proprietor boasted, 'We can ask any price we like to ask. [. . .] Coffee drinking is catching on. They've been wanting something like this for a long time.' Without much experience of the catering trade, these new entrepreneurial coffee-bar proprietors – 'catering freelancers' in the opinion of one commentator – had created a new kind of coffee-house.[25] Central to the design of the espresso bar were the espresso machines, which were notable for their very expressive, over-styled front aspects. One architect advised that 'Machines are often fixed to the counter with service to one side, the operator usually hidden behind a battery of chromium cylinders'.[26] Ambassadors of modernism, the machines were instantly recognisable. 'There's that same machine', the novelist Marghanita Laski enthused in the *Architectural Review* in 1955, with '"Milan" at the top . . . balanced by "It works without steam" on both sides'.[27]

In addition to making espresso coffee, Riservato's machines introduced some new tricks with hot milk. Italian *caffè* proprietors had discovered that using the steam pressure in the machine to heat milk created a creamy foam. Deposited decoratively on top of a caffè latte the resulting drink became known as a cappuccino, supposedly because of its similarity to the brown habit of the Capuchin monks, topped with a shock of white hair. The froth on a cappuccino is a happy by-product of the heating process. When the steamer pipe is inserted into the milk it produces multitudes of bubbles, foaming the milk as it heats. The heat denatures the milk proteins, causing them to bond together in a network around the bubbles of air, preserving the foam.[28] The foam was a novelty to Jack Brooks. 'We sampled the coffee here served in glass cups and saucers. It was delicious, with a sort of whipped cream head on it. "How come?" we asked. And they said the milk is boiled by a special process that brings the fats to the surface. Some of the prosperous-looking customers appeared to be enjoying two, and even three, cups of this brew.'[29] Incredulity among the established coffee trade was matched by the customer's nervousness about these exotic beverages: one reporter overheard a new customer ask his friend, 'Do you think I dare say cappuccino?'[30] But the frothy coffee novelty gained acceptance as a part of this new social scene: as Bertram Young's spoof song-sheet sang in *Punch* in 1957, 'We really have a beano on a cup of Cappuccino.'[31]

The espresso bar launched a new kind of playful, hyperbolic Modernist design style. At the time purists derided it as 'Theatrical' and 'Fake', arguing that it was more like interior design than architecture. The young architect Stephen Gardiner complained in March 1955 about their styling as 'fake modern, fake Eastern, fake Indian, fake night-club, the whole box of tricks in one, a bizarre, sinister, ravishing bedroomy set-up'.[32] The first such coffee bar was the Mocamba in Knightsbridge, built in 1954 by the interior decorator Douglas Fisher: 'a fabulous creation of bright décor, concealed lighting and lovely ceramics', with walls lined with bamboo, mahogany tables and a leather bar. The exotic and elite clientele of such coffee bars was soon legendary, 'madly gay "chaps" and their girls returning from theatres and parties'.[33]

Fisher opened an even more histrionic coffee-house later the same year: El Cubano in Brompton Road, soon proclaimed one of the most notorious nightspots in Europe. The interior made extravagant use of luxurious and exotic furnishings: the ceiling was lined with bamboo matting, tropical house plants concealed the lighting, and the banquette seating was covered with a wild black and yellow textile. Looming over the bar was an enormous curvaceous espresso machine and at the end of a room was an aviary containing a toucan. 'The jungle had come to London.'[34] One commentator breathlessly reported that 'The first reaction is surprised delight. It's quite extraordinarily nice to walk into a place of refreshment in England where taste, both gastronomic and visual, is employed to please. How clever, how pretty, what fun, we say.'[35] Although architecturally El Cubano gave you 'nothing', Gardiner protested, it did deliver 'lavish décor, mystery, excitement, and a sense of unreality: it is completely escapist – an exhibition designer's opium dream. It is impossible to put one's finger on any single idea and say why it's so successful: the toucans in their cages, the exotic chair covers, the bamboo screens, the misshapen sugar pots, orange juice [served] out of coconuts.' If El Cubano was a success, he concluded, it was because it was 'vulgar, flashy and a fake'.[36]

Not all the new espresso bars were as extravagantly ornate as these. Gardiner identified an 'Authentic English' style: 'architect (or semi-architect) designed, severe, sensible, "tasteful"'. Terence Conran's Orrery was one; the Gondola on Wigmore Street (designed by Helen Low and Humphrey Spender) another: 'a simple, nicely designed room, with a delicate, if devitalised, mural . . . on one wall, a counter and tables with photostated tops and an acoustic tile ceiling: it gives you "honest-to-goodness" design without any fun . . . appropriate as a setting for the casual day-time coffee-drinker.'[37]

The espresso bars were a powerful sign of the changing times. As the *Daily Mirror* advised mothers in 1957, 'Never be contemptuous about coffee-bar society.'[38] Architecturally, the espresso bars were the among the first signs of the popular adoption of the modernist aesthetic showcased at the Festival of Britain in 1951. The extravagant newness of such designs helped to liberate the clientele from their expectations of the established catering industry. The espresso style 'means well', Gardiner argued, because 'it uses (and, therefore, displays) modern furniture, curtain and wallpaper designs; it shows off old materials (in particular, hardwoods) in new situations and new materials (aluminium, plastics, etc.)'.[39] 'The coffee-bar movement owes most of its success', the broadcaster John Pearson suggested, to its modernist design and decoration, which 'exactly suited the mood of post-war younger England. There was greenery and lushness and warmth and an emphasis, in the décor and dishes, on places like Italy and Mexico where life may be supposed to be hotter and fuller.' The espresso revolution, he argued, also represented a shift away from the slavish following of American tastes, 'for however popular the U.S.A. may once have been with the young, it is no longer fashionable'.[40] The element of protest in the coffee-bar scene, Laski suggested, was 'against the corrupted adaptation of an American way of life. The coffee-bar is essentially European.'[41] According to her, the espresso bar re-fashioned the coffee-house experience along models both modernist and European.

The 'espresso revolution', as Pearson called it on BBC radio in 1956, changed more than just the appearance of coffee retailing, reintroducing some of the sociability once associated with the coffee-house. Recalling an evening out in 1952, he established how much the coffee bars had changed London: he remembered 'how few were the places where younger people could go for a cheap night out. Compared with almost every other entertainment the coffee bars were convenient and wonderfully undemanding.'[42] In the coffee bars there was little of the formality, ritual and expense of dining in restaurants; and unlike public houses and taverns, there were no licensing laws regulating the age of customers and hours of business. They stayed open until midnight or later every night of the week. Their clientele was young, fashionable and, most notably, comprised both sexes, men and women. 'In scenes of varying charm', Martha Gellhorn noted, 'young people . . . can have company and warmth, from morning until midnight or later, at the minimum outlay of ninepence for a cup of foamy, milky coffee.' To her mind the young seemed to 'talk a great deal about the pleasures of good coffee', although it seemed lukewarm and watery to her. But as she observed, 'The young like it; beer is no longer a symbol of being free and grown-up.'[43]

Almost every commentator on the espresso bars noted the composition of the customers, a mixture that seemed conspicuously new and different. They observed how apparently prosperous working-class men and women, often notably young, mingled with the higher echelons of the middle classes: a provocatively promiscuous mixture for the period. The espresso bars also catered to a strikingly cosmopolitan crowd, composed of people of different races and cultures, again mixing freely and in equality. Journeying around the London 'Espressos', Martha Gellhorn met with 'foreign youth' in every quarter: two blond Dutch girls doing crossword puzzles at Les Enfants Terrible in Soho, Italians and a North African Arab at the Moka in Soho singing happily of *amore*; the Grenada 'favoured by negroes, which makes it exotic right off'; the famous West Indian waiters, dressed in batik shirts, at the Cubano, and an 'impossible to place Chinese-Javanese-Siamese' girl at the Orrery, talking inconsequentially to a Spanish-Arab-Cuban girl and a beautiful boy of 'unknown nationality'. This hallucinogenic parade of exoticism was matched, Gellhorn related, only by the 'enchantment' wrought by the décor. The espresso bars 'feel romantic, feel like distant places' with their 'bull-fight posters, bamboo, tropical plants, an occasional shell or Mexican mask', or 'tom-toms, masks and witch-doctors'.[44]

The modern movement magazine *Architectural Design* proclaimed the new coffee bars as 'the greatest social revolution since the laundrette' in 1954. In their estimation these espresso bars signified the 'revival of the Coffee House'.[45] The magazine invoked the historical significance of the seventeenth-century coffee-house by reprinting an illustrated frontispiece to a coffee-house tract of 1672, showing, it said, an 'interior of a coffee house' and an 'early type' of coffee machine.[46] Although *Architectural Design* was fascinated by the modern fashion of their design, the espresso bars also recalled for them the historical legacy of the coffee-house, especially their egalitarian accessibility to a mixture of people across the divides of class and race, and the renewed opportunities they presented for conversation and associations of friendship in a congenial environment. The modernist styling, they concluded, allowed a distinctive and new sociability to develop, but one that was redolent of the sociability made famous by the coffee-house in the seventeenth and eighteenth centuries.

Not all commentators were enthusiastic about this 'espresso revolution'. The shallow and standardised nature of its use of the modernist aesthetic was soon apparent: it was becoming 'a stereotype, a cliché'.[47] In an article wittily titled 'Coffee-Bar Theory and Practice', *Punch* satirised the stereotypical characteristics of an espresso bar, whose 'necessary constituents' were 'the india-rubber plant (*Ficus elastica*); the onion (*Alliam cepa*) the bamboo; and fish-net'. With these elements, in whatever order they were deployed about a room, *Punch* argued, the result would be a coffee bar, 'even before the electric coffee-engine has been installed or the transparent unbreakable cups and saucers purchased'.[48] The ubiquity of coffee bars, and the sameness of their design, also mitigated their revolutionary sociability for Laski, who suggested that many of the coffee-bar habitués would be as happy in a traditional tea shop. She observed acerbically that 'there's no new social habit here. Coffee for tea, somewhere to sit down with decent interesting décor, this doesn't add up to a new way of life.'[49] To others, though, merely the opportunity to socialise was a powerful corrective to the levelling uniformity of post-war life. 'Slick, polished, modern', the coffee bar offered grateful Londoners 'a shelter from bad weather, dull homes, bed-sitters and ourselves'.

Others took a darker view of the espresso revolution. To older generations the new sociability found in the coffee bars seemed frivolous and insincere. To the Left, such places lacked authenticity: Richard Hoggart, in his ground-breaking study of working-class culture, *The Uses of Literacy* (1957), bemoaned them as 'tawdry and gimcrack'. Compared with 'traditional' working-class culture, with its values of solidarity, home and community, the espresso bars seemed to him an empty and vapid expression of mass culture. Cafés and milk bars 'indicate at once, in the nastiness of their modernistic knick-knacks, their glaring showiness, an æsthetic breakdown'. The superficiality of this new cultural formation, its reliance on the fake, the imported, the spectacular, seemed to him to be an expression not of a European but an American origin:

> This is all a peculiarly thin and pallid form of dissipation, a sort of spiritual dry-rot amid the odour of boiled milk. Many of the customers – their clothes, hair-styles, their facial expressions all indicate – are living to a large extent in a myth-world compounded of a few simple elements which they take to be those of American life.[50]

Older voices on the Right were also dismissive. Writing in 1956 in the *TLS*, George Sutherland Fraser lamented the changed social scene in Chelsea. 'The whole place is too full of Espresso bars, antique shops, girls with jeans and pony-tails, and young men in duffle coats. Are these young people wholly serious? Do none of them do any work?'[51] But despite their fogeyish irascibility, both Fraser and Hoggart agree that espresso bars were a powerful emblem of the cultural and sexual revolution of 1950s youth culture.

The term 'teenager' had surfaced in American slang in the 1920s, referring to an age group (thirteen to nineteen years of age) and their characteristic clothes and forms of association. The emergence of teenage 'youth culture' in this period, the historian Eric Hobsbawm has argued, was one of the most dramatic political developments of the post-war period: 'a revolution in manners and customs, in ways of spending leisure and in the commercial arts, which increasingly formed the atmosphere that urban men and women breathed.[52] This view was widespread even by the end of the 1950s. The leading theorist of the new teenage market in the late 1950s was the economist Mark Abrams, a pioneer of market research in England. In 1956 he presented a 'portrait of modern British youth' in the left-leaning monthly *Encounter*, arguing that their numerical increase had been more than matched by an increase in the income and the time they had available for leisure.[53] The espresso-bar scene, especially in Soho, Chelsea and Mayfair in London, was frequently taken as emblematic of this cultural revolution. In his 1969 study *The Neophiliacs*, Christopher Booker suggested, 'By 1955 there was an unmistakable restlessness in the air. [. . .] In the West End of London the first Espresso coffee bars were appearing, giving the young a distinctive and "contemporary" meeting place.'[54]

When teenage problems became front-page news in the late 1950s, commentators mapped the most exaggerated forms of youth culture, such as espresso bars, Teddy Boys and skiffle music, on to the historically enduring locations of vice and sedition. Soho in particular was the focus for Establishment anxiety about youth culture. It had long been regarded as 'the square mile of vice'.[55] 'With its labyrinth of narrow streets and alleys, its underground clubs, and its eternal fascination for all those who are criminally inclined', Soho was despised by moral conservatives as a 'breeding ground of crime and hotbed of vice'.[56] Coffee bars were central to the imaginative geography of Soho. In the 'spicy' novel *Soho Street Girl*, which was successfully prosecuted for obscene libel in 1954, a nineteen-year-old prostitute Eve Parsons frequented 'The Etna Café' in Soho, socialising with 'a mixed crowd' of 'spivs, small time crooks, prostitutes; and odd shady characters that lived precariously on the fringe of the underworld'. To such people, the novel suggested, 'the café was a sort of no-mans-land where they could eat, drink copious cups of coffee, and talk'.[57]

The new urban coffee bar – the space, its clientele, their sociability – was frequently cited as the origin and centre of refractory youth culture. For the most part the Establishment distrusted youth culture. A series of Giles cartoons in the *Daily Express* in 1958 pictured espresso bars as the hangouts of fashion-conscious teenagers and Teddy Boys, given to exuberant hairstyles and clothes amid the modernist trappings of the espresso bar.[58] The Lord Mayor of Birmingham 'attacked [the] "aimless juvenile café society" which . . . led young people into the paths of crime'. Drinking coffee and soft drinks in espresso bars, and buying popular music, he fulminated, was wasteful of time and money.[59] Newspapers identified coffee bars as corrupting influences that led innocents towards vice, especially random violence, sexual promiscuity and intemperance. Consternation was caused in 1960 when the independent TV channel ITV aired a documentary called

Living for Kicks, directed by Daniel Farson, legendary habitué of Soho's bars and clubs. In his programme Farson interviewed teenagers at the Whisky a Go-Go espresso bar in Brighton, including the nineteen-year-old bearded beat poet Royston Ellis. While young couples kissed openly in the background, teenagers gave candid accounts of their views on sex and morality, making lurid claims (perhaps true) of pervasive premarital sex among their group.[60] Parents' groups across the country were horrified: the *Daily Sketch* ran a banner headline the next day proclaiming 'Sexpresso Kids in TV Probe'.[61] Teenage lives remained shadowy to adult investigation, visible only through the camera obscura of the coffee bar.

Men, Angry and Young

A rebellious cultural mood was to be found in high culture as well. Contemporaries argued that a spirit of outraged rejection permeated the work of the new young writers of the period, such as John Osborne, Colin Wilson, John Wain and Kingsley Amis. Moulded by manifestos and symposia, some superficial resemblances between their work was made to represent a group identity. The 'typical new hero' of their works, griped George Sutherland Fraser in the *TLS*, is 'the "angry young man" driven forward through a series of ludicrous and disastrous adventures by what seems a largely unmotivated fury and disgust'. Despite the reasoned voices and good manners adopted by these 'young intellectuals', Fraser concluded the alienation manifested in their work was a response to the 'intolerably galling' drabness and shabbiness of modern British life.[62]

Perhaps the angriest of the group was Colin Wilson, nicknamed the 'coffee-bar philosopher' by the press.[63] His first book, *The Outsider*, was enthusiastically reviewed when it was published in 1956 and sold more than 20,000 copies in its first six months. The book itself was non-fiction, a tract of domestic existentialism examining the figure of the outsider, which he defined as those writers, artists and fictional characters that questioned the conditions of life around them. A young man of twenty-four years, Wilson's own story was as fascinating to journalists as his book. He cultivated an 'outsider' image, proudly relating how he had spent the summer of 1954 sleeping on Hampstead Heath in a waterproof sleeping bag and writing during the day in the British Museum Reading Room. As winter came on he moved into a bedsit in New Cross, working as a dishwasher in a coffee bar in the evenings to make ends meet. He viewed himself as being like many of his literary heroes: 'alone in my room, feeling totally cut off from the rest of society'.[64] Wilson's sense of alienation, however, did not stop him from enjoying the working environment of the coffee bar, and its bohemian sociability: it turned out he was alienated only from the unquestioning philistinism of bourgeois existence, as he called it. Wilson was employed at the Coffee House in Haymarket, designed by Antoine Acket, a colourful room, with red leatherette banquette seating round the sides, pink-patterned Formica tables and a central water feature made of sheets of coloured perspex mounted on steel tubes with water trickling over them.[65] This was an 'enjoyable' place, Wilson later admitted, 'the conditions were clean and pleasant', and 'the place was staffed by out of work actors and pretty drama students from RADA'.[66]

In the imagination of the press, espresso bars were associated with thinking and the life of the mind. To the *Daily Mail*, Wilson was the original of a type they called the 'espresso evangelist', a 'seer of the Soup Kitchens', a 'messiah of the milk bars'.[67] Cartoonists depicted Wilson, with his mop of thick black hair, dark-rimmed spectacles, roll-neck sweater and duffelcoat, as the archetype of the coffee-bar philosopher, moodily followed by hundreds more. Angus Wilson, to whom Wilson had dedicated the book, cruelly satirised him in his 1957 short story collection *A Bit Off the Map*. The central character of the title story is a psychopathic Teddy Boy called Kennie Martin, a coffee-bar habitué ('You have to learn to make one coffee last'). At 'the Italian coffee house' in Soho, he meets a charismatic autodidact philosopher and mystic called Huggett, who is surrounded by a group of fashionably distressed disciples collectively known as The Crowd. 'The Crowd sat at two long tables in the far corner of the window', under the 'polished yet wilting rubber plant . . . once after all, a modish exotic'. 'They always met at the Italian coffee house, and they drank Cona. They were as always talking; or rather the men were talking and the women were seeming to listen.'[68] Populated by angry young men and coffee-bar philosophers, the coffee-house had atavistically returned to the unfettered intellectual debate of the seventeenth and eighteenth centuries.

The most searching analysis of the homogeneity between teenage rebellion and the coffee-houses was that launched by the 'New Left', a cadre of young intellectuals recently graduated from Oxford, clustered around the editorial committee of their journal, the *Universities and Left Review.* The *ULR* was a journal of 'socialist theory', 'left arts criticism', and 'university opinion'. When the first issue, with its brightly coloured modernist cover, and a mixture of political analysis and cultural commentary, had appeared in the spring of 1957 it had sold out both its initial run of 2,000 copies and a reprint of a further 6,000, despite receiving no publicity or reviews, even among the sympathetic left-leaning press. This reception suggested to the editors that a hunger existed for intellectual debate that took the issues of youth seriously. Later that year the avant-garde film maker Lindsay Anderson suggested the *ULR* was a sign that 'it is no longer seriousness that is felt to be a bore (particularly among young people), so much as obsessional flippancy and the weary cult of the "amusing"'.[69] One historian of their experience argued that the *ULR*'s signal innovation was its 'belief that decoding youth culture might provide the key to unlock the creative energies of the contemporary social system'.[70] The editors described their efforts as trying 'to find a language in which to map an emergent "new world" and its cultural transformations, which defied analysis within conventional terms of the left while at the same time deeply undermining them'.[71] The realignment of their analysis away from the arcanum of Soviet theory to the politics of their own youth culture was initially expressed geographically. Although the first issue had been produced in Oxford, in early 1958 the editorial committee moved en masse to London, in search not just of urban life, but also of some insight to the perplexing experiences of post-war politics and culture. The city, and especially Soho, was to be their education and their laboratory.

The editors were four young men, Stuart Hall, Gabriel Pearson, Raphael Samuels and Charles Taylor, all recent graduates of English, classics, philosophy and history at Oxford. Their politics were motivated by the widespread rejection of the Old Left institutions that had occurred after the death of Stalin, especially the 1956 crisis announced by Khrushchev's revelation of the extent of the Stalinist terror and the Soviet invasion of Hungary. Their analysis of British politics was sharpened by the fiasco of the Anglo-French invasion of the Suez Canal, which seemed to them (as to many) to demonstrate inherent weaknesses in the power and intelligence of the 'Establishment'.[72] From the start these angry young men wanted their journal to reach out beyond the converted, to regenerate the 'tradition of free, open, critical debate' by drawing into political discussion alienated young people, 'the vigorous, and active minds of the community'.[73] The first issue announced meetings of the Left Review Club, held 'in comfortable surroundings' at the Royal Hotel in Woburn Place, Bloomsbury, where authors of *Review* articles hosted discussions and debates with readers. The first 'readers' meeting', on a Sunday afternoon, was to be addressed by one of their distinguished contributors, Isaac Deutscher. It was much more popular than they expected: 'The four editors arranged the room in the Royal Hotel in what Raphael Samuel assured us was the intimate manner of the Berlin political cafés of the thirties and went off to have a meal. When we returned, there were seven hundred people waiting outside the building.'[74] Further meetings regularly attracted 300 or 400 people to discussion and debate, although their appeal was mostly to young middle-class Londoners.[75] By the summer of 1957 their activities had expanded to include Club Skiffle Social evenings.[76]

Their most interesting *coup de main* was a coffee-house. The ULR Coffee House, soon renamed the Partisan Coffee House, opened at 7 Carlisle Street in Soho on 22 October 1958, nearly a year after it was first proposed and several months late. Advertised as London's 'First Anti-Espresso Bar', the opening party was attended by the *Observer*, who printed a photograph entitled 'Scenes at the Partisan: an artist, a poet and a girl'.[77] In the first few months, 500 to 600 people visited each day, overwhelming the largely volunteer staff. On the floor above the *ULR* housed the Left Book Centre, selling books, pamphlets and periodicals. Open seven days a week until midnight, the Partisan announced itself as 'a coffee-house for the Left', serving 'Vienna coffee', 'café filtre' and 'Russian tea', served in specially commissioned pottery mugs.[78] Alongside these anti-espresso drinks was a studiously Left bill of fare, including boiled Breconshire mutton, Whitechapel cheesecake, borscht and frankfurters. Mingling authentic English food with East European dishes was a calculated rebuff of the Italianate menus of the espresso bars. The Partisan's interior was designed by the socialist architect Max Neufeld (who later worked for the LCC) and built by a volunteer craftsman, Ernest Rodker. Unlike the 'Fake Theatrical' styling of the Mocamba, the design of the Partisan strove for a warm, human and organic modernism, using natural materials such as wood and brick in unfussy honest configurations.

Promotional photographs of the inside of the Partisan show the light-filled interior decorated with paintings and furnished with modern-movement chairs designed by Alvar Aalto (Chair 611, with its characteristic cross-woven webbing). The clientele depicted in the photographs include sensibly dressed women and men, almost the only socialist women in the *ULR*, drinking and eating round large communal tables on which books, magazines and newspapers are strewn.[79] In this communal seating, and the respect for news and discussion, the Partisan recalled the coffee-house of the late seventeenth century. The historical reference was probably self-conscious. Christopher Hill, the Oxford historian and *ULR* contributor, observed in 1960 that the Restoration coffee-houses were 'centres of seditious activity', preserving a 'popular republican tradition' in a hostile political culture after 1660.[80] The historical connection was reinforced by the name of the enterprise: it was a 'coffee-house' not a café or coffee bar. They reiterated this difference in advertisements that announced that the Partisan was 'an Anti-espresso bar', driving home its distinction from the pop-culture sociability of the Soho espresso-bar culture all around them. This heritage was recalled in the term 'partisan' too: the word's older meaning of a zealous adherent of a particular political party or cause had been subsumed more recently by a secondary definition of a guerrilla army working behind the lines in enemy-occupied territory, such as the Russian and Yugoslavian partisans in the Second World War. The Partisan was the New Left's irregular army in the hostile terrain of Soho.

Initiatives such as the Partisan coffee-house reflect the *ULR*'s continued interest in reaching out to the lived experience of working-class youth. They argued that, unlike official institutions of the Left like the Labour Party, they took seriously the new realities of a consumer society, including the problematic aspects of youth culture. Issues of the journal in 1958 turned to the theme of alienation and the poverty of intellectual life in the period, and continued to evince great curiosity about the revolutionary potential of adolescents and teenager pop culture. The fourth issue of *ULR* used a photograph by Roger Mayne of a young Teddy Boy and his girlfriend on the cover, and included sociological observation of teenagers in the New Towns of Crawley and Harlow, and street gangs in Glasgow. Such work suggested that the actual lives of young working-class adolescents remained a mystery to be investigated and researched. Readers asked, 'What has this got to do with socialism?'[81] The final issue in autumn 1959 contained a long review essay by Stuart Hall called 'Absolute Beginnings' on the 'teenage problem', reviewing both Abram's market research report *The Teenage Consumer* and Colin MacInnes's novel *Absolute Beginners*, illustrated with more of Mayne's photographs of youth on the streets. As Raphael Samuels recalled in 1989, the *ULR* 'became increasingly preoccupied with "youth culture" and the popular arts, [and] prided itself on being streetwise. "ULR-ers" dressed sharply and danced coolly. In the idiom of the day, they were "hip".'[82] Their own analysis at the time was less rose-tinted. Michael Kullman's 'The Anti-Culture Born of Despair' had argued that teenage pop culture was unusually vibrant and vigorous, and that it had effectively supplanted active political engagement in the young. Unfortunately, Kullman concluded, to these young people New Left intellectuals were 'square' and therefore 'posh', uniformly 'hated for not "getting in the groove"' with Elvis Presley.[83] In Derek Allcorn's searching self-analysis at the time, the *ULR'S* work on the 'youth culture' of street gangs, hooliganism and skiffle clubs primarily had the effect of neutering these new form of working-class sociability, just like that of the Establishment.[84]

The Partisan coffee-house, then, ought to be seen as part of a continuum of responses to the 'youth problem'. The *ULR*'s research on youth culture was part of, rather than separate from, the debate on this problem by the Establishment. The late 1950s saw an enormous effort by a wide range of bodies to dissect, understand and regulate the teenager. There were more than thirty separate reports published between 1956 and 1960 by a wide range of official sources: government departments, political parties, non-governmental organisations and newspapers. Stuart Hall was among those who made submissions to the Labour Party's report on the teenage problem, *The Younger Generation*, published in August 1959, which suggested the party must resist its habitually dismissive and condescending attitude to the young, but which then proposed little more than tinkering with existing policies on schools, employment and the Youth Service.[85]

A section of the Department of Education, the Youth Service was also the subject of a parliamentary Committee of Inquiry in 1958, led by Diana Keppel, Countess of Albemarle, and including Richard Hoggart on the committee. Known as the Albemarle Report, it homed in on the problem of juvenile delinquency, the outward forms of which, 'an act of wanton violence, a bout of histrionic drunkenness or a grasping at promiscuous sexual experience', masked a 'general malaise, a sense of emptiness, a quiet rejection of social responsibilities'. The brightest spot in the juvenile scene, the report argued, was teenagers' own propensity to association in clubs and societies, even if only for skiffle evenings and Sunday football in the park. The report urged that more 'experiments' should be made 'to cater for their special needs in the unconstrained way which they appear to seek. We have in mind the coffee bar sited strategically at the sort of place where they tend to congregate, the "drop-in" club, [or] the experimental youth centre or workshop.' The Youth Service was urged to offer 'club-like' spaces modelled on those of 'a college union', with 'good decorations in good colours; modern appearance; a coffee bar rather than a canteen; reading room; listening or viewing room; games room, and small rooms where self-programming groups can meet'. Such spaces, the report argued, would compete more effectively with commercial entertainments such as skiffle clubs and espresso bars, and allow the Youth Service to enhance the personal and civic development of teenagers.[86] In response, various official bodies, such as the catchily titled National Association of Mixed Clubs and Girls' Clubs, and the Education Committee of Brighton Town Council, experimented with 'Coffee Bars for "Teenagers"', modelling their 'youth clubs' on the coffee bars to attract 'young people between the ages of 15 and 18 to come and drink coffee, talk, and perhaps to make music and dance'.[87]

Intellectual responses to the espresso-bar revolution met with varying degrees of success. Throughout 1958 and 1959, the Partisan coffee-house attracted large numbers of customers, but by the end of 1959 the commercial management of the organisation collapsed and it had to be rescued by a private benefactor, Nicholas Faith. Advertisements for the coffee-house ('a meeting place and eating place for Socialists') appeared in the *New Left Review*, the new journal formed after the merger of the *ULR* with the *New Reasoner*, the journal of E. P. Thompson's rival new left group.[88] But trading conditions continued to be difficult and, as badly paid volunteer labour proved unreliable, the management structure of the coffee-house had to be repeatedly revised. One habitué, Leone Gold, reported that by 1960 the Partisan

> got nastier and nastier. One didn't even want to go in there for a cup of coffee, it got so bad. At one point it got taken over by drugees; it had a beautiful basement where there were little caverns. In our romantic

> way we thought how lovely this was for a coffee house, but in fact what happened was that really nasty things happened in those caverns; they were all rather dark and so on.[89]

Many on the Old Left were scathing about the Partisan. Despite being on its management board, the Communist historian Eric Hobsbawm derided it as a 'lunatic enterprise', a 'utopian' and 'hare-brained project' that was 'not a serious business proposition'. The 'austere' décor, which reminded him of a 'station waiting room', was suitable only for 'demoralised bums and fringe hangers-on', who spent their time, according to Hobsbawm, taking drugs and wasting time 'drafting thesis chapters' and engaging in 'long debates on tactics', rather than paying for their food and drink.[90] In 1961 the Partisan ceased trading amid mounting debts and the building was taken over by the *New Left Review*, which under Perry Anderson's ownership turned its back on the populism of Raphael Samuels's group. Despite its claims to be an 'anti-espresso bar', the Partisan turned out to be a coffee shop much like any other, beset by all the usual problems of running a small business. But though it closed, the twenty-four-hour party that was Soho continued unabashed.

The espresso-bar revolution had 'exploded like a bomb' in the mid 1950s.[91] Importing an idea and some technology from Italy, it was transformed by London's particular forms of urban sociability, by jazz and skiffle, by teenage fashions and migrant expectations. Repudiating conventional politics in favour of consumerist hedonism, the espresso bars were auguries of the new politics of later decades. At the time, however, they posed an intriguing problem both for political parties and the official institutions of youth culture. A diverse range of bodies and organisations – from town councils to the Youth Service, from the YMCA to the *ULR* – anxiously examined their purpose and effects. Coffee bars represented the extremes of modern anomie: they were an emblem of the rootlessness, moral vacuity and alienating superficiality of post-war culture. In this mode, coffee bars were an intensification of other youth-culture phenomena like Teddy Boys, motorcycle gangs and skiffle clubs, an illuminating sign of youth's distaste for the values of those in authority, a symptom of the rising tide of juvenile delinquency. Yet in the coffee bars, as report after report noted, the young came together in moments of free and civic association, in the only places open to receive them in public, away from the influence of alcohol, where they were freely participating in the consumption of the products and commodities of the new cultural industries of music and fashion. To authority, coffee bars confusingly looked like both the cause and the solution of the problems of teenage delinquency. The 1950s witnessed a concerted contest to control the representation of the espresso bar, to declare it to be definitively one of these paradoxical constructions.

The coffee bars seemed to represent a place where people of all kinds could socialise together: richer with poorer, migrants with metropoles, women with men, creating a space that seemed to reject the values of official discourse on class, gender and race. The coffee bar was not simply a home for working-class or middle-class culture, but a space where young people of different social stations mixed freely, confusing the hierarchies of value both of Marxist and conservative analysis. Moreover, the kind of social interaction was new and as such, did not follow, or even aspire to follow, the prevailing notions of 'middle-class' propriety and manners. For many reasons, built on expectations of long historical formation, this could not happen anywhere else: youth clubs, pubs, tea shops and the Café Royal all had particular cultural resonances that excluded this new crowd. The espresso 'bomb' proclaimed its revolutionary ambitions through its gleaming modern style, but it was not contained by it. Like the coffee-house of the seventeenth century, the espresso bar had forged a new social space which allowed the assembly of a hitherto proscribed mixture of people. In these new associative spaces, a new public consciousness was forged by the free and subversive discussion of the issues that concerned them. Like the seventeenth-century coffee-houses, this space was not foreseen or understood by political theory or Establishment culture: the space itself seemed subversive and exotic, begging regulation and control. Also like the seventeenth-century coffee-house, this unforeseen social space was developed and initiated by private persons following an entrepreneurial spirit, hoping to turn a profit: it was generated from below, challenging the pre-eminence of the spaces prepared by authority for civic participation.

EPILOGUE

Milk and Sugar

It had been a copy shop before it closed. The hoardings went up a couple of months later and after a few weeks – very few – it became a Starbucks, sporting the familiar green logo of a stylised mermaid rising out of the sea, the comfortable furniture, the bar bearing a large, but unremarkable, espresso machine. There had been nothing like it in the area before and now it was full of people, in the morning, at lunchtime and in the evening. Starbucks, as has often been said, is everywhere. In all the more prosperous parts of town, in malls, main streets, high streets, shopping districts, downtowns, shopping villages, there has been an unprecedented explosion in coffee-shops, all of which seem to follow the same tried and tested model. This is a commonplace observation: as true in England as California, or in Bahrain, New Zealand and Japan.

As a brand, Starbucks burst upon the scene in the mid 1990s, although the company's history reaches back thirty years before that to the counter-culture movement of the mid 1960s in California. In 1966 a Dutch immigrant, Alfred Peet, opened a whole-bean coffee bar at the corner of Vine and Walnut in Berkeley. Unusually for the time, he roasted his own coffee, using high-quality beans of named origin, and served it highly roasted and strong. Berkeley was an area at the front line of the hippy movement, of anti-Establishment feeling and anti-war protests. This was an important moment in the history of food, too, for this period saw the first stirrings of the whole-food movement, which championed organic food production methods against the increasingly homogenised, branded, corporate food industry. As the home of the Beat poets and student protest, cafés and coffee-shops played an important part in nurturing San Francisco's cultural revolution in the 1960s. Members of the protest movement established a network of 'GI coffee-houses' in army towns outside the gates of military bases, where they used the conviviality of the coffee-house to disseminate seditious ideas and copies of the underground press to soldiers.[1]

Focused on roasting and selling high-quality coffee beans, however, Alfred Peet's business maintained a discreet distance from the protest movement, keeping his focus on connoisseurship not politics. The retail environment at Peet's was not a coffee-house: he saw serving coffee in the store as a way of marketing coffee beans. But Peet's gourmet coffee, like that of other small-scale roasting enthusiasts across America and Australasia, cultivated a dedicated niche market for high-quality coffee. In 1970 three college graduates who shared an enthusiasm for Peet's coffee banded together to open a coffee shop in Pike Place Market in Seattle, doing their own roasting. Casting around for a name, one of their number, Jerry Baldwin, came up with 'Starbuck', a name with no special meaning to them other than a pleasing sound and look (although they later found out it was the name of the first mate in Melville's *Moby Dick*, a man without much interest in coffee). By 1973 the Starbucks coffee business had three stores, mainly selling their own gourmet roasted beans for home consumption.[2]

Ten years later Starbucks had expanded to six stores and was the biggest gourmet coffee roaster in Washington state. The transformation of Starbucks from this small-time coffee roaster to a global chain of coffee shops was brought about by Howard Schultz, a New York business school graduate who was initially hired to revitalise the marketing of the company. On a business trip to Milan in 1983, Schultz had a vision of how Starbucks could be more than a niche coffee roaster. One morning, he recalls, he went into a little espresso *caffè*:

> Behind the counter, a tall, thin man greeted me cheerfully, "*Buon giorno!*" as he pressed down on a metal bar and a huge hiss of steam escaped. He handed a tiny porcelain demitasse of espresso to one of the three people who were standing elbow-to-elbow at the counter. Next came a handcrafted cappuccino, topped with a head of perfect white foam. The barista moved so gracefully that it looked as though he was grinding coffee beans, pulling shots of espresso, and steaming milk at the same time, all while conversing merrily with his customers. It was great theater.[3]

In his corporate biography, *Pour Your Heart Into It*, Schultz celebrates this moment as a kind of commercial epiphany: 'I discovered the ritual and the romance of coffee bars in Italy.' Schultz not only admired how they turned coffee making into a ceremonial drama, but also their commitment to a local community of regulars. The *caffè* was a central part of the daily schedule of its regulars, the focus of their neighbourhood, and an arena for their social and civic life. Visiting Milan and its *caffès* gave Schultz an object lesson in coffee-house history: here was a live, working model, he thought, of the historical legacy of coffee-house culture.

On his return to Seattle Schultz tried to interest his employers in his idea, but the coffee roasters thought it was too exotic for American consumers. Schultz believed in his vision enough to leave Starbucks and start a business in downtown Seattle that concentrated on selling prepared coffee drinks. At Il Giornale, as he called it, he pioneered the sale of a range of hot milky coffees – not just cappuccino (espresso with about the same amount of hot steamed milk) but also caffè latte (espresso with a lot of milk) – in a multitude of combinations. The Il Giornale experiment changed Schultz's vision of a stand-up espresso bar. American customers, he decided, wanted to sit down, they wanted a warmer and more casual atmosphere (jazz replaced opera on the soundtrack, waiters in bow ties became baristas in T-shirts). Schultz's experiment at Il Giornale allowed him to refine the idea he had stumbled across in Milan. Rather than a stand-up espresso bar, the new model was more like a 'neighbourhood gathering place'. Howard Schultz's lesson, he decided, was not about coffee but about sociability. His coffee bar proposed to 'reinvent a commodity. We would take something old and tired and common – coffee – and weave a sense of romance and community around it. We would discover the mystique and charm that had swirled around coffee through the centuries. We would enchant customers with an atmosphere of sophistication and style and knowledge.'[4] This was to be the second espresso invasion of America, but this time it broke away from its Little Italy commercial ghetto into the mainstream of malls and high streets.

In 1987, with his experience of running and refining Il Giornale, Schultz was able to buy Starbucks itself, whose original owners were selling up. With backing from venture capital, Starbucks began to expand, using a highly refined business model to replicate stores across the country. Expansion immediately began outside its home location in Seattle, to Vancouver, Portland, San Francisco and Los Angeles on the West Coast, and further afield to Chicago, Denver and New York. Within a couple of years Starbucks was a national brand. Schultz hired executives from other branded chain franchises such as McDonald's, Pepsi, Kentucky Fried Chicken and Taco Bell. These people brought with them the commercial knowledge of the chain store, not only how to develop systems to deliver the same product in all its outlets, but also an understanding of the processes by which the chain could automate its replication, such as finding locations, hiring and training staff, and establishing local suppliers. The founders' enthusiasm for the gourmet coffee was supplemented (or replaced, some might say) by the culture of management and corporation. The first international stores outside Canada opened in 1994 in Singapore and Japan, and by 2003 there were stores in thirty nations outside the United States. Some are wholly owned subsidiaries of Starbucks Corporation (such as those in Britain, Australia and Thailand), while in others local licencees represent the company (such as those in Taiwan, New Zealand, China, Qatar, Bahrain, Saudi Arabia). Revenue in 2003 exceeded $4.1 billion,[5] with predictions for continued growth: the company has a vision of a future with as many as 25,000 stores, 15,000 of them outside North America.[6] In 2003 Starbucks was more than twenty times larger than its nearest rival in the American market and was the largest coffee-house chain in several other markets (Japan, Britain, New Zealand and the Middle East).

The phenomenal growth of Starbucks is unprecedented in the history of the coffee-house and not without its consequences. In expanding at this rate, Starbucks has consistently amazed investment analysts with its continuing profits. 'We've become jaded – and oh so bored – with Starbucks' comps [same-store sales] growth,' comments LouAnn Lofton at the Internet investment site Motley Fool, but 'only because it's always so strong'.[7] Globally, other companies have followed the Starbucks route, but none so successfully. In England several companies established espresso coffee-shop chains to rival Starbucks, using broadly similar business plans and offering the 'Seattle' coffee range of lattes and macchiatos. Starting up a 'chain of US-style coffee bars in London', the founders of Coffee Republic reasoned, 'wasn't novel or original or revolutionary', but there was a gap in the market, and profits to be made.[8] Costa Coffee had been established in 1971 as a coffee roaster by two Italian brothers (Sergio and Bruno Costa), who opened their first coffee shop in 1978: by 2003 the chain had more than 300 outlets. Caffè Nero (over 130 outlets in 2003) began in 1990 with a single stand-up espresso bar in Kensington, London: the company floated on the stock market in 1996. Starbucks arrived in Britain in 1998, buying the Seattle Coffee Company, a chain established in 1995 by two Americans from Seattle, which had grown to 98 stores (Starbucks had 360 stores in 2003). Caffè Ritazza, by contrast, was created as a coffee-bar brand by Compass group, the world's largest food service group with annual revenues of more than £10 billion (their outlets are mainly in transport hubs like airports and train stations where the brand operates alongside other company brands like Pizza Hut and Burger King).

The coffee-bar chains are not solely an Anglo-American phenomenon. In Germany, Tchibo has grown from its first coffee shop in 1955 to a chain of over 1,000 across Europe. Italian coffee traders such as Lavazza, Illy and Segafreddo have various different franchise coffee-house chains. Growth has often been achieved by acquisition, cannibalising other chains. In America, Starbucks bought out the Boston-based Coffee Connection (1994), the San Francisco-based Pasqua (1998), Seattle's Best Coffee (2003) and Torrefazione Italia (2003), converting their stores to Starbucks outlets. Diedrich Coffee has acquired its rivals Gloria Jeans and Coffee People. In Britain, Costa Coffee was acquired in 1995 by Whitbread plc, a brewing company that diversified extensively into the hotel and catering trade. Another coffee-bar chain, Aroma, was purchased by McDonald's in 2000, but despite large investment it suffered heavy losses and was sold again to Caffè Nero.

Long-term growth in the branded coffee-bar market can be hard to maintain, however. The British chain Coffee Republic, which was founded in 1995 by Bobbie Hashemi, expanded to over 100 outlets by 2001, at which time the management confidently talked of reaching 200 coffee shops within a short time. Spiralling costs and massive pre-tax losses of over £10 million in 2002 forced a rethink. During 2003 the chain shrank to half its former size and some branches were converted to a different business model called Republic Deli, with more focus on food and higher throughput of customers, more like another key rival, the sandwich chain Pret à Manger. Reinforcing this retreat from the coffee-house model, these branches removed their sofas and armchairs in favour of less comfortable seating appropriate to the 'ten-minute eat, drink and meet market'.[9] Starbucks' success, clearly, is no lucky accident, but it has shown itself to be wary of highly evolved 'mature' markets in this sector, notably those of France and Italy. In 2004, however, the first Starbucks was opened in Paris. Although it gained useful experience in similar markets such as Spain and the Middle East, the company expressed wariness about opening in 'a country where family-run cafés are the standard hangout for everyone from truck drivers to philosophers'. Howard Schultz remarked, 'It is with the utmost respect and admiration for the café society in France that we announce our entry into the market.'[10]

Without doubt, Starbucks is the most successful branded coffee-shop chain: it is the meta-prototype. What the company did was change its customers' relationship to coffee, a commodity which, though a staple beverage, was an unexamined part of quotidian life. Market research has consistently shown that the coffee-bar chains have grown the market for coffee, giving both them and the premium coffee they serve a 'new cachet'. 'When a product becomes hip,' brand analysts argue, 'the whole category can prosper.'[11] For most customers the coffee-bar chains offered a higher-quality product than they were used to, introducing huge numbers of people to speciality gourmet coffee beans through its espresso-based drinks. Better coffee was matched by significantly improved standards of interior decoration and store locations. Starbucks has consistently chosen locations close to its customers: on the main street, in the mall and airport, in lobbies and concourses, on the 'going-to-work side of the street'.[12] Everything about the interior is designed to reinforce the core values of the company. Music, artwork, aromas and surfaces are all designed to enhance sales. Providing sofas and armchairs signal to customers that they may relax and hang around, even if they do not get the chance to sit on them themselves. Newspapers indicate an invitation to read, to write, to linger. Artwork on the walls reinforces the organic and natural aspects of coffee and its production (in a colour range which rests heavily on warm earthy colours enlivened by a green and leafy iconography).

The soundscape of Starbucks coffee-houses is dominated by the throaty roar of the espresso machine, the conversation of customers and baristas, and by carefully selected music: all stores play the same music, provided centrally by in-house music planners; customers are invited to purchase a recording to play at home. Above all, the olfactory landscape of the coffee room is dominated by the smell of coffee: in-store notices announce that smoking is banned so as not to interfere with this aroma. The verbal contours of the coffee room are established by the staff, whose training requires their interactions with customers to be friendly, conversational and coffee-centred. The staff themselves are chosen, and carefully trained, to reflect brand quality (no visible tattoos or piercings, bright personality, no backchat). This is not only a carefully considered environment, but it is also one that can only be maintained by extraordinarily high levels of surveillance and regulation.

Perhaps the most complex part of the Starbucks coffee-house environment is its relationship to coffee. As well as serving coffee, Starbucks does much to reinforce the cultural value of coffee at the expense of other core products it also retails, predominantly milk and sugar, but also tea, chocolate and baked goods. In his outline of the company's core values, Schultz refers repeatedly to 'the romance of coffee'. These deep-seated associations, he argues, can be evoked through aroma, but also through reiteration. Explanatory brochures, placed next to the service points, invoke the erudite and refined knowledge of the gourmet coffee world: explaining the 'story of good coffee' (a guide to roasting), 'the world of coffees' (a guide to coffee bean origins), or the 'experience [of] the perfect cup' (a guide to espresso preparation). Printed in-store materials render this recondite knowledge base into an accessible form: by expecting that its customers are interested in the finer aspects of coffee connoisseurship, Starbucks shows them respect, flattering their curiosity. The cultural history of coffee shapes the Starbucks experience by establishing the equation between coffee-houses and the urbane refinement of higher cultural values. In this way Starbucks (at least in the Anglophone world) has successfully repositioned the coffee-house experience as aspirational, urbane and sophisticated. The determined focus on coffee as a product of high cultural value averts attention from those more discreditable aspects of the Starbucks experience (its location in mass culture, the industrialised scale of its production, the preponderance of milk and sugar in its products).

Repositioned in this high cultural territory, the company proposes that it is not unreasonable to pay more for coffee. Without access to the figures themselves, it is nonetheless self-evident that the gross margins on coffee served in any branded coffee-bar chain are very high.

Some estimates place the total cost (including materials, staff costs and service) at less than 40–50 cents for a cup of coffee charged at up to $3 or $4. With profit margins of 80 per cent plus, the coffee beans themselves are a very minor part of the cost. For this reason the cost of a cappuccino does not come down in times of historically low prices for coffee on the international commodities market, as the coffee is a very small part of its cost. Much more money is spent on staff (wages, training, recruitment), the cost of the coffee shop itself (rent, plant, maintenance) and the cost of replicating the chain (servicing debt, opening new stores and brand advertising). Even including these costs, gross margins on coffee-shop coffee are very high and good profits can be achieved. The key index of this is Starbucks' enviable 'comps' sales figures, like-for-like sales revenues in the stores it has already opened. For the twelve years between 1991 and 2003 the company's comps were 5 per cent or better, while overall sales revenue in 2003 rose by nearly 20 per cent.[13] Starbucks' revenues continue to grow very quickly, but not simply because the chain is opening more stores (and becoming more indebted). Rumours in the finance world, however, suggest that outside America this level of comps growth has been much more difficult to achieve, particularly in the two other countries with large numbers of Starbucks outlets, Japan and Britain.

Starbucks has become famous for its coffee lingo, derived from the particular urban argot of Seattle in the 1980s. Italian coffee bars around the world (whether in San Francisco, Melbourne or London) had always used terms similar to these: for example, Melbourne coffee lingo calls an espresso a 'short black' and a latte a 'flat white'. At the Caffè degli Specchi in Trieste in Italy, a nineteenth-century grand *caffè* on the city's main piazza, customers are offered sixty-seven different kinds of coffee, each with a specific name and all with a long heritage in the locality. But at Starbucks, and other Seattleised coffee-bar chains, ordering a coffee has become a farcically complex operation in which the size, variety of milk, strength, caffeination and flavouring of the beverage are all detailed separately, using specific and artificial terms. These terms have a certain archness: 'wet' means without foam, 'skinny' means to use skimmed milk, 'with wings' means the coffee is to take away. Seattleised coffees are also colossal in volume. Drinks are sold in varying sizes: in the language of Starbucks, these are called tall (12oz or 260ml), grande (16oz or 340ml), venti (20oz or 450ml). Given that a shot of espresso is about one fluid ounce (30ml), these drinks are overwhelmingly dominated by milk: even with its standard two shots, a grande or venti has seven to eight times as much milk as coffee. These drinks are not coffee drinks flavoured with hot milk, but hot milk drinks flavoured with coffee. By contrast, in Italy a cappuccino is strongly coffee-flavoured because it contains only as much milk as coffee. As Howard Schultz recalls in his memoir, when he first opened Il Giornale in Seattle in 1985 the Italian coffee drinks had to be 'translated' for American consumers who were simply not ready for the stronger flavours of Italian espresso and cappuccino.[14]

Nonetheless, milk is a dormant concept at Starbucks, repressed beneath the overwhelming commitment to the romance of coffee. Although the chain's consumption of milk is vast, almost no mention of its origins, suppliers, chemistry, preparation or flavour is made in any of the corporate literature. Yet the semiotics, history and economics of milk are radically different from those of coffee. Unlike the volatile oils and alkaloids of coffee, milk is composed of proteins, fats and lactose (a dissaccharide comprised of glucose and galactrose). As an idea, milk connotes the maternal, mammalian and nourishing, quite unlike the associations of coffee. As an item of mass consumption fresh milk has a very short history, even shorter than that of coffee, for its consumption was rare before the mid nineteenth century. Before that fresh milk was simply too unstable and dangerous to drink regularly. In the 1660s Pepys ate cream with gusto and occasionally drank buttermilk, the sour-tasting liquid that remains after milk has been churned to make butter. But milk was rarely added to coffee before the nineteenth century: coffee with milk was made by boiling milk with the coffee grounds, a preparation mainly intended for invalids.[15] 'Don't put Milk to it', argued one tract in 1722, because it 'spoils the Virtue of all Coffee'.[16] In the late nineteenth century new techniques of preservation, such as pasteurisation and refrigeration, made fresh milk safe to drink, and eliminated its associations with typhoid and other diseases. From around this time, too, historian Melanie Dupuis argues, dairy milk was extensively promoted by nutritionists, food marketers, educationalists and agriculturalists as the perfect food for children and young adults. As a result, in the twentieth century the consumption of fresh milk increased dramatically, especially among young people.[17] In the form of Seattleised coffee, the coffee-bar chains deliver unusually high doses of milk to an adult market usually resistant to milk consumption. The milkiness of the coffee-bar chains powerfully suggests the extent to which they have revised the historical legacy of the seventeenth and eighteenth-century coffee-house. The sociability encouraged by Starbucks is based on consumption, not conversation. The interior arrangements of the coffee shop recalls the communal space of the early coffee-house, but atomises people into distinct individuals, promising customers peace and security from others, not encounter and discussion.

In noticing the rapid growth of coffee-bar chains in the urban environment, it is often observed that monotony comes with ubiquity. Of course, no one would confuse a Caffè Nero outlet with a Starbucks, or an Au Bon Pain with an Illy Caffè. But equally, coffee-bar chains have some features in common, features that are deeply embedded in their chain structure. Each chain establishes prototypical solutions to retail problems across its markets: it seeks to identify single answers, and established patterns of response, to the daily difficulties of running a coffee shop. In the same way that the coffee, food and interiors of the coffee bars have a stylistic consistency, so too do the management solutions. Each chain has its own coffee academy where the staff are taught the key values of the company, how its product management systems work and how to perform its signature customer service. A coffee-bar chain is above all an assemblage of information: a digital phenomenon as much as a set of cups and tables, or a gathering of people. But the overwhelming feeling encountered in these coffee shops is their similarity to each other. In a study of airports, shopping malls and motorways, the French spatial theorist Marc Augé coined the term 'non-places' to describe this experience. Characteristic of non-places, Augé suggests, is their repetitive construction, to which individuals connect in a uniform manner and no organic social life is possible.[18] It does not matter whether you visit a Starbucks in Tokyo, Santiago de Chile, Hawaii, or Vienna: everywhere you go they are the same. Some people no doubt find this comforting and the sales argue strongly that it is a successful formula. Many thousands of people – notably young women – now incorporate the coffee-house sociability in their lives, when there was none before. But as distinct locations become deracinated and homogenised, many more people experience this ubiquity as a sense of loss. Plangent eulogies about the lost paradise of the independent coffee-house abound, commemorating the idiosyncratic, organic, local construction of civic space in the great cafés of Vienna, London's vintage Formica working-man's cafes, or the classic French street café, with its zinc-topped bar and smell of stale Gauloises.[19]

Despite their claims to being local and their commitment to the community, many people find the relationship between the corporate chains and neighbourhood unclear. Starbucks enthusiastically embraces the notion of corporate benevolence: encouraging staff participation in neighbourhood philanthropic projects, allowing coffee-house spaces to be used by community groups and, at a corporate level, developing relationships with several international charities (CARE, Conservation International). Howard Schultz speaks approvingly of the 'third place' theory developed by the sociologist Ray Oldenburg in a folksy book entitled *The Great Good Place*. Oldenburg argues that coffee shops, like pubs in England and cafés in France, offer a 'third place' between home and work where people may meet as equals on neutral ground, where conversation may flourish, individuals may acquire the social polish gained by association with others and society may reap the benefits of such collective reasoning.[20] His nostalgic survey of such places further suggests that society is damaged by the omission of third-place environments from many suburbs and cities in the present day. As Schultz suggests, a Starbucks branch *might* play an important role in the civic function of a community, providing an emotionally warm and receptive space for collective engagement in society. But, equally, it is not clear that they actually do. A plaintive symbol of these ambitions is seen in the encouragement coffee-house chains have given to wireless Internet (wi-fi), by which means individuals using their own laptops can participate in the on-line 'community' of the Internet, all the while remaining oblivious of the living world around them.

Despite its 'third space' ambitions and its claims to be an ethical company ('coffee that cares'), Starbucks has attracted the ire of a good many social justice protestors. Like McDonald's, Starbucks has found that size and ubiquity brings with it a unique level of attention, as is demonstrated by the dedicated Starbucks-bashing website 'ihatestarbucks.com'. At the anti-globalisation demonstration in Seattle in November 1999, focused on the World Trade Organisation (WTO) annual convention, Starbucks branches were singled out for attack, and ransacked by a mob of anarchists, unionists and environmentalists. Since then, Starbucks has been a regular focus for activists' agitation. Within the United States, it has been accused of using its size to influence the market. Starbucks is repeatedly attacked in Naomi Klein's *No Logo* for monopolistic practices, such as swamping a locality with clusters of outlets until independent competition is driven under.[21] It is regularly accused of paying low wages, as it pays most staff only a little more than the minimum wage. However, unusually for an employer in the food service sector in the US, it has a health insurance scheme for its employees and grants long-term staff, even part-timers, shares in a partnership scheme. Practices like these have earned Starbucks praise in some quarters: the company was rated number twenty-one on the '100 Best Corporate Citizens' list compiled by *Business Ethics* magazine in 2003, which rated corporate performance in terms of environment, community relations, employee relations, employee diversity programmes and customer relations.[22]

Sustained protests have been launched also at the ethics of the coffee served in branded coffee-bar chains. The five largest Western coffee roasters (Nestlé, Sara Lee, Kraft, Procter & Gamble, and Tchibo) have been accused of encouraging overproduction of coffee, engineering a catastrophic fall in prices for the coffee growers in Third World countries. Since the year 2000 real prices have fallen to historically low levels on the New York international coffee market. Oxfam reports that over 25 million coffee producers have been forced into dire poverty while, by contrast, Western consumers pay unusually high prices for their prepared coffee drinks, especially in gourmet coffee-bar chains. In 2001 growers received the equivalent of 14 cents for a kilo of green coffee in Kenya, but American consumers paid up to $4 for a beverage containing a small spoonful of roasted coffee. Following the 'value chain' from the grower, Oxfam estimated the price of coffee was inflated by 7,000 per cent before reaching a British consumer.[23]

In response, some activists have urged the coffee-bar chains to make more use of Fair Trade coffee. Since its emergence in the 1970s, the Fair Trade movement has sought to avoid the international commodities market, and pay a fair and stable price for coffee by forging direct links between consumers and producers. In response to consumer pressure, most branded coffee-house chains have introduced certified Fair Trade coffee. Pursuing a related, but independent, course, Starbucks claims to buy 74 per cent of its green coffee at fixed, long-term prices, guaranteeing coffee farmers economic stability. In addition, through its 'Commitment to Origins' scheme, it has promised to source all its coffee from growers and producers who meet stringent environmental and social guidelines – although Oxfam expresses some doubts whether small farmers will reap any benefit from it.[24] As economists have noted, the model of Fair Trade coffee in any case only serves a small and specialised sector of coffee production and consumption, and it is unclear how it might be extended to embrace the general coffee global economy.

In the lactification of the coffee-house, the branded chains have eviscerated the bitter flavours of the coffee-house history. The hogo of sirreverence has been cleansed and decontaminated. The heritage with which Starbucks prefers to identify is the romance of the coffee bean, rather than the less palatable coffee-house history of gossip, scandal and sedition, reliant on the contestatory forms of irony and satire. As this book has explained, the early coffee-house retained an aura of refractory fanaticism cultivated in the English Revolution, when republican plotters had commandeered coffee-house debates. The satiric *A Character of Coffee and Coffee-House* observed that many believed 'that a Coffee-house is dangerous to the Government, that seeds of Sedition are here sown, & Principles of Liberty insinuated'.[25] In the 1670s government spies opined that the uncontrolled and unlimited nature of their conversation, and their encouragement of egalitarian social mixing, made coffee-houses treacherous nests of trouble-making and subversion. The coffee-house remained the location of the mob and the crowd in the eighteenth century: playing a key role in the American Revolution, for example.

The more recent 1950s espresso-bar history, redolent of teenage rebellion, with its concatenation of anti-adult sensationalism, juvenile crime and pop music, its intimate relation to beat poetry, student radicalism and counter-culture, is anathemised by the corporate culture of the branded chains, with their shiny happy people consuming expensive milk products. The sociability of the chain coffee bar has cut its links with the vengeful, transgressive crowd, on the verge of insurrection. It is not simply that the mob has been excluded by the anodyne luxury of the corporate coffee shop, but that these places cultivate a sociability designed to reform the mob into a more tranquil, even docile, crowd of consumers. In the sanitised, lactified form of the branded chain, the coffee-house is no longer oppositional, rebellious and dissident. This is their profit, but our loss.

APPENDIX

The Spread of the Coffee-House

1511	Mecca
1532	Cairo
1554	Constantinople
1652	London
1655	Oxford
1664	Cambridge
1665	Yarmouth
1669	Bremen
1670	Boston
1671	Marseilles
1671	Paris
1673	Edinburgh
1673	Glasgow
1683	Venice
1685	Vienna
1694	Leipzig
1696	New York
1700	Salzburg
1703	Philadelphia
1714	Prague
1718	Stockholm
late C18	Madrid

NOTES

Abbreviations
BL British Library
PRO Public Records Office, National Archives, London
CLRO Corporation of London Record Office, London
GL Guildhall Library, London
CSPD *Calendar of State Papers, Domestic*
HMC Historical Manuscripts Commission

PREFACE

1 Samuel Johnson, *A Dictionary of the English Language* (London: W. Strahan, 1755).
2 The best guide is Richard von Hünersdorff and Holger Hasenkamp, *Coffee: a Bibliography*, 2 vols (London: Hünersdorf, 2002).
3 Thomas Babington Macaulay, *The History of England from the Accession of James the Second*, 2 vols (London: Longman, Browne, Green and Longmans, 1849), I, pp. 366–70.

CHAPTER I

1 George Sandys, *A Relation of a Journey Begun An. Dom: 1610. Foure Bookes. Containing a description of the Turkish Empire, of Ægypt, of the Holy Land, of the Remote Parts of Italy, and Islands adjoyning* (London: W. Barrett, 1615), pp. 29–30.
2 Ibid., p. 31.
3 Ralph Preston to the East India Company, 1 January 1614, in *Letters Received by the East India Company from its servants in the East*, ed. William Foster, 2 vols (London, 1897), II, p. 261.
4 Fynes Morison, *An Itinerary, Containing his Ten Yeeres Travell* (London: John Beale, 1617), p. 262.
5 Ibid., p. 265.
6 Henry Blount, *A Voyage into the Levant* (London: John Legat, 1638).
7 Sandys, *Relation*, pp. v–vi.
8 Jonathan Haynes, *The Humanist as Traveler: George Sandy's Relation of a Journey begun An. Dom. 1610* (Rutherford: Fairleigh Dickinson University Press, 1986), p. 18.
9 Sandys, *Relation*, p. 65.
10 William Biddulph, 'A Letter written from *Aleppo* in *Syria Comagena*', in Theophilus Lavender, *Travels of certaine Englishmen into Africa, Asia, Troy, Bythinia, Thracia, and to the Black Sea* (London: Th. Haveland for W. Aspley, 1609), pp. [vi], 60.
11 Ibid., p. 65.
12 William Lithgow, *The Totall Discourse, Of the Rare Adventures, and painefull*

Peregrinations of long nineteene Yeares Travayles (London: Nicholas Okes, 1632), pp. 151–2.

13 George Manwaring, 'A true discourse of Sir Anthony Sherley's Travel into Persia', in E. Denison Ross, *Sir Anthony Sherly and his Persian Adventure* (London: George Routledge & Sons, 1933), pp. 175–226, pp. 186–7.

14 William Parry, *A new and large discourse of the Trauels of Sir Anthony Sherley Knight, by Sea, ouer Land, to the Persian Empire* (London: Valentine Simmes for Felix Norton, 1601), p. 10.

15 Pedro Teixeira, *The Travels of Pedro Teixeira*, trans. William F. Sinclair, Hakluyt Society, ser. 2, no. 9 (London: Hakluyt Society, 1902), p. 62.

16 Biddulph, *Travels*, p. 66.

17 Sandys, *Relation*, p. 66.

18 Ibrahim-I Pechevi [Ibrahim Peçevi], *Tarih-I Peçevi*, 2 vols (Istanbul, 1864–7), I, p. 363; trans. Bernard Lewis, *Istanbul and the Civilisation of the Ottoman Empire* (Norman, Oklahoma: University of Oklahoma Press, 1963), p. 134.

19 Sandys, *Relation*, p. 33.

20 Kurt Weber, *Lucius Cary, Second Viscount Falkland* (New York: Columbia University Press, 1940), pp. 82–156.

21 Peter Clark, *The English Alehouse: a social history 1200–1830* (London: Longman, 1983), pp. 145–65.

22 Biddulph, *Travels*, p. 66.

23 Teixeira, *Travels*, p. 62.

24 Manwaring, 'Sherley's Travel into Persia', pp. 186–7.

25 Parry, *Trauels of Sir Anthony Sherley*, p. 10.

26 Richard Beale Davis, *George Sandys: Poet-Adventurer: a study in Anglo-American Culture in the Seventeenth Century* (London: Bodley Head, 1955).

CHAPTER 2

1 James Douglas, *A Supplement to the Description of the Coffee-Tree* (London: Thomas Woodward, 1727) pp. 19–20. For a modern translation see Bernard Lewis, *Istanbul and the Civilisation of the Ottoman Empire*, pp. 132–3.

2 Evliyâ Çelebi, quoted in Ralph Hattox, *Coffee and Coffeehouses: the Origins of a Social Beverage in the Medieval Near East* (Seattle: University of Washington Press, 1988), p. 81.

3 William Biddulph, *Travels*, pp. 31–85, p. 66.

4 Pedro Teixeira, *Travels*, pp. 62–3.

5 Ibid., p. 121.

6 C. van Arendonk, 'Kahwa', in E. van Donzel, B. Lewis and Ch. Pellat (eds), *The Encylopaedia of Islam*, 2nd ed. (1st ed. 1909; Leiden, E. J. Brill, 1978).

7 Douglas, *Supplement*, pp. 15–16; Hattox, pp. 32–6.

8 Van Arendonk, 'Kahwa'.

9 Ibid.

10 Al-Shaykh Abd al-Câder Ibn Mohammad al-Ansârî al-Djazîrî al-Hanbali, 'Umdat al-Safwa fi hilli al-qahwa', Bibliotheque Nationale, Mss Arabe, no. 971.

11 Antoine Galland, *De l'Origine et du Progrez du Café* (Caen: Jean Cavelier; Paris:

Florentin & Pierre Delaulne, 1699); Jean de La Roque, *Voyage de L'Arabie Heureuse* (Paris: André Cailleau, 1716); trans: Jean de La Roque, *Voyage to Arabia the Happy* (London: G. Strahan and R. Williamson, 1726) pp. 217–306; Douglas, *Supplement*, pp. 12–21.

12 Karl H. Dannenfeldt, *Leonhard Rauwolf: Sixteenth Century Physician, Botanist and Traveller* (Cambridge, Mass.: Harvard University Press, 1968).

13 There is no specimen in the herbarium, and no illustration in the 1583 edition of the *Raiz*. See ibid., p. 276, no. 312 '*Coffea arabica*'.

14 Rauwolf, *Itinerary* (1582), trans. Ray, (1693), pp. 91–2.

15 Kurt Sprengel, *Historia rei herbariae* (Amsterdam, 1807), I, pp. 378–80.

16 Leonharti Rauwolfen, *Aigentliche beschreibung der Raisz* (Laugingen: Leonhart Reinmichel, 1582).

17 Dannenfeldt, pp. 15–24, 221. Karen Meier Reeds, *Botany in Medieval and Renaissance Universities* (New York: Garland Publishing, 1991), pp. 35–6.

18 The hypothesis is discussed and rejected in Douglas, *Supplement* (1727), pp. 7–11.

19 Antonius Faustus Naironi (Banesius), *De Saluberrima potione Cahue, seu Café nuncupata discursus* (Rome: Michaelis Herculis, 1671); trans. C. B. [Bradley?] *A Discourse on Coffee: its Description and Vertues* (London: Geo. James for Abel Roper, 1710), pp. 4–6.

20 Stewart Lee Allen, *The Devil's Cup* (Edinburgh: Canongate, 2000), pp. 58–9.

21 Carolus Clusius, *Exoticorum Libri Decem: Quibus Animalium, Plantarum, Aromatum aliorum* (Antwerp: Raphelengii, 1605), p. 236.

22 Prosper Alpinus, *Prosperi Alpini De Plantis Aegypti Liber. In Quo non pauci, qui circa haerbarium materium irrepserunt* (Venice: Franciscum de Franciscus Senensem, 1592), 26. *De Bon.* Cap. XVI.

23 John Parkinson, *Theatrum Botanicum, the Theatre of Plants. Or, An Universall and Compleat Herbal* (London: Tho. Cotes, 1640), p. 1622.

24 Arthur Coke Burnell and P. A. Tiele (eds), *Volume I: The First Book containing his description of the East, in The Voyage of Jan Huyghen van Linschoten to the East Indies. From the Old English Translation of 1598*, 2 vols (London: Hakluyt Society, 1895), p. xxxix.

25 Rawley, *Life of Bacon*, Works I: p. 9; quoted in Lisa Jardine and Alan Stewart, *Hostage to Fortune: The Troubled Life of Francis Bacon* (London: Victor Gollancz, 1998), p. 475.

26 Ibid., p. 479.

27 Francis Bacon, *Historia Vitæ & Mortis* (Londini: In Officina Io. Haviland, impensis Matthaei Lownes, 1623), pp. 219–20.

28 Francis Bacon, *Sylva Sylvarum: or A Naturall Historie. In ten centuries* (London: J. H. for William Lee, 1627), Century VIII, no. 738, p. 191.

29 Robert Ralston Cawley, *Unpathed Waters: Studies in the Influence of the Voyagers on Elizabethan Literature* (Princeton: Princeton University Press, 1940), p. 243.

30 Robert Burton, *The Anatomy of Melancholy*, 6 vols (Oxford: Clarendon Press, 1989–), *Volume II, Text*, Nicolass K. Kiessling, Thomas C. Faulkener, Rhonda L. Blair (eds), (Oxford: Clarendon Press, 1990), pp. 249, 247, 250–1.

31 Thomas Johnson, *The Herball or General Historie of Plantes* (London: Adam Islip,

Joice Norton, and Richard Whitakers, 1636), III, chap. 159, 'Of divers sorts of Indian Fruits', p. 1549.

32 John Parkinson, *Theatrum Botanicum*, pp. 1622–3.

33 Louis Chauvois, *William Harvey: His Life and Times: His Discoveries: His Methods* (London: Hutchinson Medical Publications, 1957), p. 173.

34 Geoffrey Keynes, 'Harvey's Use of Coffee', *The Life of William Harvey* (Oxford: Clarendon Press, 1966), pp. 406–9.

35 John Aubrey, *Brief Lives*, ed. John Buchanan-Brown (London: Penguin Books, 2000), p. 145.

36 John Evelyn, 'De Vita Propria' (1697), in *The Diary of John Evelyn*, ed. E. S. de Beer, 6 vols (Oxford: Clarendon Press, 1955), I, pp. 14–15.

37 La Roque, *Voyage to Arabia*, pp. 280–1.

38 Keynes, *Harvey*, Appendix VII, pp. 459–63, p. 460.

CHAPTER 3

1 GL Ms 11588/4, f. 36; W. J. Harvey (ed.), *List of the principal inhabitants of the City of London, 1640* (London: Mitchell and Hughes, 1886), p. 18; Alfred Beaven, *The Aldermen of the City of London, Temp. Henry III–1908*, 2 vols (London: Eden Fisher & Company, 1908), I, p. 87.

2 Philip Jones (ed.), *The Fire Court: Calendar to the Judgements and Decrees of the Court*, 2 vols (London: William Clowes, 1966–70), I, pp. 264–5.

3 Percival Boyd, *Roll of the Drapers Company of London* (London: J. A. Gordon at the Andress Press, 1934); Minute books of the General Court of the Levant Company, 13 January 1653, PRO SP 105/151, p. 186.

4 Lewes Roberts, *The Merchants Mappe of Commerce* (London: Ralph Mabb, 1638), chap. 273, p. 259.

5 Evliyâ Celebi, quoted in Daniel Goffman, 'Izmir: from village to colonial port city', in *The Ottoman City between East and West: Aleppo, Izmir, and Istanbul*, Edhem Eldem, Daniel Goffman and Bruce Masters (eds), (Cambridge: Cambridge University Press, 1999), p. 79.

6 Joseph Pitton de Tournefort, *A Voyage into the Levant*, trans. J. Ozell, 2 vols (London: D. Browne, 1718), II, p. 377; Sonia P. Anderson, *An English Consul in Turkey: Paul Rycaut at Smyrna 1667–1678* (Oxford: Clarendon Press, 1989), p. 123, 6; Laurent d'Arvieux, *Memoirs du Chevalier d'Arvieux*, ed. Jean-Baptiste Labat, 7 vols (Paris: Charles-Jean-Baptiste Delespme, 1735), 1, p. 123.

7 *The Travel Diary of Robert Bargrave, Levant Merchant (1647–1656)*, ed. Michael G. Brennan (London: The Hakluyt Society, 1999), pp. 73–4.

8 Anderson, *English Consul*, p. 11.

9 Ralph Hattox, *Coffee and Coffeehouses*, pp. 72–91.

10 Evliyâ Çelebi quoted in Goffman, 'Izmir', p. 79.

11 Jean de Thevenot, *Relation d'un Voyage fait au Levant* (Paris: Claude Barbin, 1664); trans. Archibald Lovell, *The Travels of Monsieur de Thevenot into the Levant* (London: Henry Clark for John Taylor, 1687), pp. 32–4.

12 Paul Rycaut, *The History of the Turkish Empire, from the Year 1623, to the Year 1677* (London: J. D., 1687), pp. 67–74. See also Alfred C. Wood, *A History of the Levant*

Company (Oxford: Oxford University Press 1935), pp. 90–2; and Gwilym Prichard Ambrose, *The Levant Company mainly from 1640–1753* (B. Litt dissertation, University of Oxford, 1932), pp. 241–57; Bargrave, *Travel Diary*, p. 109.

13 *CSPD 1651*, 22 September 1651, pp. 445–6; *CSPD 1651–52*, 31 May 1652, pp. 269–71.

14 W. Bruce Bannerman, *The Registers of St Stephen's, Wallbrook and of St Benet Sherehog, London*, Harleian Society Register Section, nos 49–50 (London: Harleian Society, 1919–20), p. 63.

15 Houghton, 'Discourse on Coffee', p. 312.

16 'General Sessions of the Publick Peace holden for the City of London' 16 August 1654: CLRO: Alchin Coll. Box H/103.(7) [printed].

17 David Underdown, *Revel, Riot, and Rebellion: popular politics and culture in England 1603–1660* (Oxford: Clarendon Press, 1985), pp. 268–9; Christopher Durston, 'Puritan Rule and the Failure of Cultural Revolution, 1645–1660' in *The Culture of English Puritanism, 1560–1700*, Christopher Durston and Jacqueline Eales (eds), (Houndsmills, Basingstoke: Macmillan Press, 1996), pp. 210–2.

18 William Oldys, 'Notes on Trees', BL Add Mss 20724, 90r.

19 Ambrose, pp. 21–2.

20 'The Diarie of the Life of Anthony à Wood Historiographer and Antiquarie', BL Harley Ms 5409, fol. 43.

21 *Life and Times of Anthony Wood, antiquary, at Oxford 1632–1695*, ed. Andrew Clark, 5 vols (Oxford: Clarendon Press, 1891–1900), I, pp. 168–9.

22 John Stow, *A Survey of London reprinted from the text of 1603*, ed. Charles Lethbridge Kingsford, 2 vols (Oxford, Clarendon Press, 1908, 1971), p. 193.

23 Samuel de Sorbiere, *A Voyage to England, Containing many Things relating to the State of Learning, Religion, and other Curiosities of that Kingdom* (London: J. Woodward, 1709), p. 16.

24 *The Accounts of the Churchwardens of the Parish of St Michael, Cornhill from 1456 to 1608*, ed. William Henry Overall (London: Alfred James Waterlow, 1868), p. 255.

25 GL. Ms 04072, vol. 2, part II, fol. 206v, 2 September 1656 (fol. 207v).

26 Samuel Hartlib, *Ephemerides*, no. 254, 4 August 1654, *The Hartlib Papers*, 2nd ed. (Sheffield: HROnline, Humanities Research Institute, 2002), HP 29/4/29A-B.

27 PRO SP 105/151/216, 7 July 1654.

28 Markman Ellis, 'Pasqua Rosee's Coffee House 1652–1666', *London Journal*, 29: 1 (2004).

29 *A Broad-side against Coffee, Or, the Marriage of the Turk* (London: J. L., 1672).

30 'Condition of a Victuallers Recognizance' (1673), CLRO: Alchin Coll. Box H/103.(14).

31 'General Sessions of the Publick Peace holden for the City of London', 16 August 1654, CLRO Alchin Coll. Box H/103.(7) [printed].

32 Grocers Company Register of Apprentices, 1629–1666, GL: Ms 11593, vol. 1, fol. 139r; Grocer's Company, Wardens Accounts, 1642/3–1651/2: GL Ms 11571 vol. 13, unnumbered.

33 Richard Newcourt, 'A letter expressing some Inconveniencies amongst many of the Old City, And some Reasons for the New Modelling of the Same', 1666, GL Ms 3441, p. [1].

34 Richard Neve, *The City and Countrey Purchaser and Builder's Dictionary* (London: John Nutt, 1703), p. 71.
35 GL Ms 04072, vol. II, part 2, fol. 213r.
36 Ukers (*All about Coffee*, pp. 43, 64) claims without evidence that Rosee opened the first coffee-house in Korten Voorhout in The Hague in 1664.
37 GL: Ms 04083, fol. 41r.
38 Houghton, 'Discourse of Coffee', p. 313.
39 Hartlib, *Ephemerides*, no. 254, 4 August 1654, HP 29/4/29A-B.
40 GL Ms 04071, vol. II, fol. 194r, 197v, 201r, 202v, 206r.
41 GL Ms 04072, vol. II, part II, fol. 217r, 221r.
42 PRO: Lay Subsidies E 179/252/27.
43 Stephen Primatt, *The City & Country Purchaser and Builder* (London: S. Speed, [1667]). See also Dan Cruickshank and Neil Burton, *Life in the Georgian City* (London: Viking, 1990), pp. 209–36, p. 218.
44 John Schofield, *The Building of London from the Conquest to the Great Fire*, 3rd ed. (Stroud, Gloucestershire: Sutton Publishing, 1993), pp. 168–70.
45 Douglas, *Supplement*, pp. 30–1.
46 Wardmote Inquest Book, St Dunstan's in the West, Guildhall Library, Ms 3018/1. Monday, 21 December 1657.
47 John Evelyn, *A Character of England* (London: Jo. Crooke, 1659), pp. 28–9.
48 *The Vertue of the Coffee Drink. First publiquely made and sold in England, by Pasqua Rosee* ([London], n.p., n.d. [1666?]). BL: C.10.f2.(372).
49 GL Ms 04072, vol. 2, part II, fol. 231r; Grocer's Company, Wardens Accounts, 1663–1671: GL Ms 11571 vol. 15, 1665–6, p. 3; Grocers Company Register of Apprentices, 1629–66, GL: Ms 11593, vol. 1, fol. 297v; Grocers Company, Wardens Accounts, 1663–167 GL Ms 11571 vol. 15, 1666–8, p.7.
50 *Parish Registers of St Michael Cornhill*, p. 257. GL Ms 04071, vol. 2, fols 210v, 209v, 215r, 213r, 216v.
51 CLRO: Alchin Coll. Box H/103.(12); Guildhall Ms 04071, vol. 2, fols 219r, 223r, 224v, 228r, 229r.
52 Thomas Vincent, *God's Terrible Voice in the City*, 5th ed. (London: George Calvert, 1667), pp. 51–2.
53 Joseph Lemuel Chester (ed.), *The Parish Registers of St Michael Cornhill, 1546–1754* (London: Harleian Society Register Section, 7, 1882), p. 257; Guildhall Ms 04071, Vol. Il, fol. 238r.
54 Houghton, 'Discourse of Coffee', p. 313.
55 John Shand, 'The First Coffee House', *Manchester Guardian*, Monday, 17 March 1952.

CHAPTER 4

1 *A Commonwealth and Commonwealths-Men Asserted and Vindicated* (London: Henry Fletcher, 1659), p. 1. Thomason E.988 (19) dated 28 June 1659.
2 *Englands Monarchy Asserted and Proved to be the Freest State, and the Best Commonwelth Throughout the World* (London: W. G. for Richard Lowndes, 1660), p. 1.
3 *The Diurnal of Thomas Rugg, 1659–1661*, ed. William L. Sachse, Camden Third Series,

vol. 91 (London: Offices of the Royal Historical Society, 1961), pp. 29, 10.

4 For a general account of these events see Ronald Hutton, *The British Republic, 1649–1660* (Basingstoke: Macmillan, 1990) and Samuel H. Gardiner, *The History of the Commonwealth and Protectorate 1649–1660*, 4 vols (London: Longmans, Green, 1894–1903).

5 *The Character of the Rump* (London: n.p., 1660), p. 1.

6 Aubrey, *Brief Lives*, p. 136.

7 *Englands Monarchy Asserted*, p. 1.

8 John Beale to Hartlib, 14 December 1658, Hartlib Ms 51/43A-B, *The Hartlib Papers Second Edition* (Sheffield: HROnline, Humanities Research Institute, 2002).

9 *Endless Queries: or, An End to Queries* (London: n.p. 1659), pp. 3–4.

10 *No New Parliament: or some Queries or Considerations Humbly offered to the present Parlament Members* (London: n.p., 1660).

11 Mercurius Philalethes, *Select City Queries: Discovering several Cheats, Abuses and Subtilties of the City bawds, Whores and Trapanners*, part I (London, n.p. 1660 [1659]), p. 7.

12 *Select City Queries*, part III, p. 18.

13 *The Wandring Whore*, 6 parts (London: n.p., 1660), II, p. 7.

14 David Smith, 'The Struggle for New Constitutional and Institutional Forms', in John Morrill (ed.), *Revolution and Restoration: England in the 1650s* (London: Collins and Brown, 1992), pp. 15–34; J. G. A. Pocock, 'Introduction', in James Harrington, *The Commonwealth of Oceana and A System of Politics* (Cambridge: Cambridge University Press, 1992), pp. vii–xxv.

15 Aubrey, *Brief Lives*, p. 135.

16 Samuel Johnson, *A Dictionary of the English Language* (London: W. Strahan, 1755).

17 Peter Clark, *British Clubs and Societies, 1580–1800: The Origins of an Associational World* (Oxford: Clarendon Press, 2000).

18 *The Rota, or, A Model of a Free-State Or equall Common-wealth: once proposed and debated in brief, and to be again more at large proposed to, and debated by a free and open Society of ingenious Gentlemen* (London: John Starkey, 1660).

19 *The Censure of the Rota Upon Mr Miltons Book* (London: Paul Giddy, Printer to the Rota, at the sign of the Windmill in Turne-Againe Lane, 1660), p. 3.

20 Henry Stubb, *The Rota, or News from the Common-wealths-mens Club* ([London]: n.p., [1659]).

21 Aubrey, *Brief Lives*, p. 135.

22 *A Proposition in order to the Proposing of A Commonwealth or Democracie* ([London], n.p., n.d.]).

23 Aubrey, *Brief Lives*, p. 136.

24 Ibid., pp. 136–7.

25 Samuel Butler, *Characters*, ed. Charles Daves (Cleveland: Press of Case Western Reserve University, 1970), pp. 256–7.

26 Samuel Pepys, *Diary*, ed. R. Latham, 11 vols, (London: HarperCollins, 1995), I, pp. 13, 14.

27 Ibid., pp. 17, 20.

28 Ibid., p. 24

29 Ibid., pp. 39, 45.

30 *Bumm-Foder or Waste-Paper to wipe the Nation's Rump with, or your Own* ([London], n.p., [1659]).

31 [Roger L'Estrange], *A Plea for a limited Monarchy* (London: T. Mabb for William Shears, 1660). E.765.(3), dated 20 February 1660.

32 Pepys, *Diary*, I, p. 61.

33 Godfrey Davies, *The Restoration of Charles II, 1658–1660* (San Marino, California: Huntingdon Library, 1955), pp. 293–5.

34 Pepys, *Diary*, p. 63.

35 *The New Grove Dictionary of Music and Musicians*, ed. Stanley Sadie, 2nd ed. (London: Macmillan, 2001).

36 Pepys, *Diary*, I, p. 63.

37 *Mercurius Phanaticus. Or Mercury Temporizing*, no. 2 Wednesday, 14 March to Wednesday, 21 March [1660] (London: Praise-God Bare-Bones at the sign of the Anabaptist Rampant in Fleet Street, 1660), p. 11.

38 *A Proclamation Against Vicious, Debauch'd and Prophane Persons* (London: John Bill and Christopher Barker, 1660), dated 13 May 1660.

39 Alazonomastix Philalethes, *Free Parliament Queries: Proposed to Tender Consciences; and Published for the use of the Members now Elected* ([London], n.p., 1660), p. 1.

40 John Toland, 'The Life of James Harrington' in *The Oceana of James Harrington*, ed. John Toland (London: the Booksellers of London and Westminster, 1700), p. xxx–xxxvii.

41 Aubrey, *Brief Lives*, p. 136.

42 *The Character of a Coffee-House. Wherein Is contained a Description of the Persons usually frequenting it, with their Discourse and Humors. By an Eye and Ear Witness* ([London], n.p., 1665). p.6.

43 Aubrey, *Brief Lives*, pp. 136–7.

CHAPTER 5

1 Pepys, *Diary*, IV, pp. 434, 437, 438.

2 Edward Phillips, *The New World of English Words, or, a general dictionary* (London: E. Tyler for Nath Brooke, 1658).

3 William Allen, *A Conference about the next succession to the crown of England* (N. [London]: R. Doleman, 1681), pp. 2, 3.

4 *A Character of Coffee and Coffee-Houses. By M.P.* (London: John Starkey, 1661), p. [1].

5 Pepys, *Diary*, I, p. 315.

6 Ibid., III, p. 40.

7 Karl Westhauser, 'Friendship and Family in Early Modern England: The Sociability of Adam Eyre and Samuel Pepys', *Journal of Social History*, 27: 3 (1994), pp. 524–5.

8 John Phillips, *Speculum Crape-Gownorum: or, an Old Looking Glass for the Young Academicks, new Foyl'd* (London: E. Rydall, 1682), p. 21.

9 Pepys, *Diary*, IV, pp. 22, 162, 412–14.

10 *A Character of Coffee and Coffee-Houses*, pp. [1], 5–6.

11 *The Character of a Coffee-House . . . By an Eye and Ear Witness*, p. 2.

12 *A Brief Description of the Excellent Vertues of that Sober and wholesome Drink, called Coffee* (London: Paul Greenwod, 1674).
13 Ben Jonson, *Leges Convivales. Rules for the Tavern Academy, or, Laws for the Beaux Esprit* (London: Tho. Bassett, 1692).
14 Erving Goffman, *Behaviour in Public Places: notes on the social organisation of gatherings* (New York: Free Press, 1966).
15 *A Character of Coffee and Coffee-Houses*, p. 10.
16 *The Maidens Complaint Against Coffee. Or, the Coffee-House Discovered, Besieged, Stormed, Taken, Untyled and laid Open to publick view* (London: J. Jones, 1663), p. 4.
17 *A Character of Coffee and Coffee-Houses*, p. 5.
18 *Remarques on the Humours and Conversations of the Town Written in a Letter to Sr. T. L* (London: Allen Banks, 1673).
19 *A Character of Coffee and Coffee-Houses*, pp. 6-9.
20 *Women's Petition Against Coffee* (London: n.p., 1674), pp. 4–5.
21 *Character of Coffee and Coffee-Houses*, pp. 4–5.
22 *Women's Petition Against Coffee*, p. 4.
23 *The Character of a Town-Gallant* (London: for W. I., 1675), pp. 2, 7.
24 R. H. [Richard Head], *Roteus Redivivus: Or the Art of Wheedling, or Insinuation* (London: W. D., 1675), pp. 2–3, 197–8.
25 E. P. Thompson, 'Time, Work-Discipline and Industrial Capitalism', in *Customs in Common* (London: Merlin Press, 1991), pp. 352–403.
26 *Character of Coffee and Coffee-Houses*, p. 5.
27 Henry Peachum, *The Worth of a Penny, or, A Caution to keep Money* (London: S. Griffin for William Lee, 1667), p. 21.
28 Ibid., rev. ed. (London: Samuel Keble, 1687), pp. 26–7.
29 Alexander Pope, *The Rape of the Lock* (1714), in *Twickenham Edition of the Poems of Alexander Pope, Volume II, The Rape of the Lock and other poems*, ed. Geoffrey Tillotson (London; Methuen, 1940), III, II. pp. 109–10.
30 See Steven Pincus, '"Coffee Politicians Does Great": Coffee-Houses and Restoration Political Culture', *Journal of Modern History*, 67 (1995), pp. 807–34, 815–17. Pincus gives several instances of women in coffee-houses, but all are unreliable.
31 Francis Grose, *A Classical Dictionary of the Vulgar Tongue* (London: for S. Hooper, 1785), unpaginated.
32 Edward Ward, *The London-Spy Compleat, in Eighteen Parts*, 2nd ed. (London: J. How, 1704), part II, pp. 25–32.
33 Anthony Hewitson (ed.), *Diary of Thomas Bellingham: an officer under William III* (Preston: Geo. Toulmin & Sons, 1908), p. 44.
34 *The Covent Garden Magazine; or, Amorous Repository*, 2 (January 1773), p. 37.
35 *The Free-Thinker*, no. 223 (4 April 1720), p. [1].
36 *The new Bath guide; or useful pocket companion*, new ed. (Bath: R. Cruttwell, 1799), p. 39.
37 Oliver Goldsmith, *The Life of Richard Nash, Esq.* (London: J. Newbery; Bath: W. Frederick, 1762), p. 43.
38 Tobias Smollett, *Humphrey Clinker* (1771), Letter to Miss Willis, 26 April.
39 *A Cup of Coffee: or, Coffee in its Colours* (London: n. p., 1663).

40 *CSPD 1667*, 24 August 1667, p. 455.
41 John Spurr, *England in the 1670s: 'This Masquerading Age'* (Oxford: Blackwell, 2000), pp. 165–78. p. 165.
42 Tim Harris, *London Crowds in the Reign of Charles II: Propaganda and politics from the Restoration until the Exclusion Crisis* (Cambridge: Cambridge University Press, 1987), pp. 27–8. See also C. John Sommerville, *The News Revolution in England: cultural dynamics of daily information* (New York: Oxford University Press, 1996), pp. 75–84.
43 Pepys, *Diary*, III, p. 35.
44 Ibid., V, p. 105.
45 Roger L'Estrange, *The Intelligencer; published for the Satisfaction and Information of the People*, no. 1, Monday, 31 August 1663, p. 1.
46 J. G. Muddiman, *The King's Journalist [Henry Muddiman] 1659–1689: Studies in the Reign of Charles II* (London: John Lane the Bodley Head, 1923), p. 179. Joad Raymond (ed.), 'The Newspaper, Public Opinion, and the Public Sphere in the Seventeenth Century', in *News, Newspapers and Society in Early Modern Britain* (London: Frank Cass, 1999), pp. 109–40, p. 126.
47 14 Car. 2 cap 33 (1662): *An Act for preventing Abuses in Printing Seditious Treasonable and Unlicensed Books and Pamphlets; and for Regulating of Printing and Printing Presses* in *A Collection of the Statutes at Large, Now in Force*, 2 vols (London: Assigns of John Bill and Christopher Barker, 1667), I, pp. 167–9.
48 *CSPD 1667*, 26 July 1667, p. 333.
49 Sorbiere, *A Voyage to England*, p. 54.
50 *CSPD, 1663–1664*, 5 August 1664, p. 660.
51 *Lorenzo Magalotti at the Court of Charles II: His 'Relazione d'Inghilterra' of 1668*, ed. and trans. W. E. Knowles Middleton (Waterloo, Ontario: Wilfred Laurier University Press, 1980), p. 124.
52 Andrew Marvell, *The Rehearsal Transpros'd: Or, Animadaversions Upon a Late Book Intituled, A Preface Shewing What Grounds there are of Fears and Jealousies of Popery* (London: A. B. for the Assigns of John Calvin and Theodore Beza, 1672), ed. D. I. B. Smith (Oxford: Clarendon Press, 1971).
53 Edmund Hickeringall, *Gregory, Father-Greybeard, with his Vizard off: Or, News from the Cabal in Some Reflexions Upon a late pamphlet Entituled The Rehearsal Transpos'd* (London: Robin Hood, sold by Nath Brooke, 1673), p. 5.
54 Richard Leigh, *The Transproser Rehears'd: or the Fifth Act of Mr Baye's Play. [...] Shewing what Grounds there are of Fears and Jealousies of Popery* (Oxford: for the assignes of Hugo Grotius and Jacob Van Harmine, 1673), pp. 48–9.
55 *The Lift of Edward Earl of Clarendon*, 3 vols (Oxford: Clarendon Printing-House, 1759), III, pp. 675–8.

CHAPTER 6

1 'The Diarie of the Life of Anthony à Wood Historiographer and Antiquarie of the most famous University of Oxford', BL Harley Ms 5409, p. 45. See also *The Life and Times of Anthony Wood*, ed. Andrew Clark, 5 vols (Oxford: Oxford Historical Society at the Clarendon Press, 1891–1900), I, p. 201.

2 Norma Aubertin-Potter and Alyx Bennet, *Oxford Coffee Houses 1651–1800* (Kidlington, Oxford: Hampden Press, 1987).

3 Wood, *Life*, II, p. 60.

4 9 November 1664, 'Stat. Acad. 494', quoted in J. E. B. Mayor (ed.), *Cambridge Under Queen Anne* (Cambridge: Cambridge Antiquarian Society by Deighton, Bell & Co., 1911), p. 419.

5 Roger North, *The Life of the Honourable Sir Dudley North, And the Honorable and Reverent Dr. John North*, ed. Montague North (London: for the editor by John Whiston, 1746), p. 249.

6 See Pincus, '"Coffee Politicians Does Great"' pp. 807–34, pp. 813–4.

7 *Domestic Intelligence, Or News from City and Country*, no. 53, 6 January 1680; see also Sarah Richards, *Eighteenth-Century Ceramics: Products for a Civilised Society* (Manchester: Manchester University Press, 1999), pp. 135–6.

8 William Boyne, rev. George Williamson, *Trade Tokens Issued in the Seventeenth Century in England, Wales, and Ireland* (London: Elliot Stock, 1889), II, part 2, p. 1382.

9 Rev. J. Dodds (ed.), *The Diary of William Cunningham of Craigends* (Edinburgh: Scottish History Society, 1887), pp. 37–9. Alexander Fenton, 'Coffee-drinking in Scotland in the 17th–19th Centuries', in Daniela Ball (ed.), *Kaffee im Spiegel europäischer Trinksitten/Coffee in the Context of European Drinking Habits* (Zurich: Johann Jacobs museum, 1991), pp. 93–102; J. D. Marwick (ed.), *Extracts from the Records of the Burgh of Glasgow A.D. 1663–1690* (Glasgow: Scottish Burgh Records Society, 1905), 11 October 1673, p. 172.

10 N. de Roever, 'Koffie- en Chocoladehuizen', *Uit onze oude Amstelstad*, 3 vols (Amsterdam: S. L. van Looy, 1890), I, pp. 116–23.

11 Thera Wijsenbeek, 'Ernst en Luim: Koffiehuizen tijdens de Republiek', in Pim Reinders and Thera Wijsenbeek (eds), *Koffie in Nederland: Vier eeowen cultuurseschiedenis* (Zutphen: Walburg Pers; Delft: Gemeente Musea Delft, 1994), pp. 36–9.

12 Carl Bridenbaugh, *Cities in the Wilderness: the First Century of Urban Life in America 1625–1742* (New York: The Ronald Press Company, 1938), p. 109. See also Sylvia Doughty Fries, *The Urban Idea in Colonial America* (Philadelphia: Temple University Press, 1977), pp. 54–7, 120–2.

13 *A 7th Report of the Record Commissioners of the City of Boston containing the Boston Records from 1660 to 1701* (Boston: Rockwell and Churchill, 1881), pp. 58, 60, 64, 68, 73, 76, 87.

14 Ibid., pp. 104, 110, 118, 128, 139, 156.

15 Daniel Neal, *The History of New-England* (London: J. Clark, R. Ford and R. Cruttenden, 1720) p. 587.

16 *Boston Records 1660–1701*, pp. 204, 207.

17 George Emery Littlefield, *Early Boston Booksellers 1642–1711* (Boston: The Club of Odd Volumes, 1900), pp. 148–64.

18 Edwin G. Burrows and Mike Wallace, *Gotham: a History of New York to 1898* (New York: Oxford University Press, 1999), p. 108.

19 William Harrison Bayles, *Old Taverns of New York* (New York: Frank Allaben Genealogical Company, 1915), pp. 67–77.

20 Bellomont to the Lords of Trade, 2 January 1701, in E. B. O'Callaghan and Berthold Fernow (eds), *Documents Relating to the Colonial History of the State of New York* (Albany, New York, 1853–87), IV, p. 826.

21 Adrian Howe, 'The Bayard Treason Trial', *William and Mary Quarterly*, 3rd ser., 47: 1 (1990), pp. 57–89, p. 60.

22 Bridenbaugh, *Cities*, pp. 267, 269, 432.

23 Jean de La Roque, *Voyage*; trans. *A Voyage to Arabia the Happy*, p. 289.

24 Antonius Fausius Naironi (Banesius), *De Saluberrima fiotione Cahue, seu Çafé nuncupata discursus* (Rome: Michaelis Herculis, 1671); [Jacob Spon], *De L'Usage du Caphé, du Thé et du Chocolate* (Lyon: Jean Girin et Barthelemy Riviere, 1671).

25 La Roque, pp. 282–3.

26 Ibid., pp. 289–92.

27 Jean Moura and Paul Lovet, *Le Café Procope* (Paris: Perrin, 1929).

28 La Roque, pp. 292–3.

29 Quoted in W. Scott Haine, '"Café Friend": Friendship and Fraternity in Parisian Working-Class Cafés, 1850–1914', *Journal of Contemporary History*, 27: 4 (1992), pp. 607–26, p. 608.

30 Thomas Brennan, *Public drinking culture in eighteenth century Paris* (Princeton, NJ: Princeton University Press, 1988), pp. 78–88. See also Jean Leclant, 'Le café et les cafés à Paris', *Annales Economies, Sociétés, Civilisations*, 6: 1 (1951), pp. 1–14.

31 Cemal Kafadar, 'A Death in Venice (1575): Anatolian Muslim Merchants Trading in the Serenissima', *Journal of Turkish Studies*, 10 (1986), pp. 191–218., p. 216.

32 Danilo Reato, *The Coffee-House: Venetian Coffee-Houses from 18th to 20th Century* [sic] (Venice: Arsenale Editrice, 1991), p. 19.

33 *The Maxims of the Government of Venice. In an advice to the Republick* (London: J. Morphew, 1707), p. 15n.

34 3 May 1754, Nota Manus (Medri), *Agenti Segreti Veneziani 1705–1797*, ed. Giovanni Commisso, (Milano: Longanesi, 1984), pp. 41–2.

35 'Commernoriali', Biblioteca di Museo Correr, Venice, XII, c. 25r, quoted in Reato, *Coffee-House*, p. 96.

36 Pompeo Molmenti, *Venice: its individual growth from the earliest beginnings to the fall of the Republic*, 2 vols (London: John Murray, 1908), I, pp. 173–6.

37 Arthur Young, *Travels, during the years 1787, 1788 & 1789. Undertaken more particularly with a View of Ascertaining the Cultivation, Wealth, Resources, and National Prosperity of the Kingdom in France* (Bury St Edmunds: J. Rackham, 1792), p. 225.

38 Ulla Heise, *Coffee and Coffee Houses* (West Chester, Pennsylvannia: Schiffer Publishing, 1987), pp. 205–6. A sketchbook of Richard Wilson, inscribed 'Studies and Designs [. . .] done at Rome ye year 1752, Caffe delle Inglesi' is in the Victoria and Albert Museum, London. See Denys Sutton, *An Italian Sketchbook by Richard Wilson* (1968), pp. 15–16.

39 James Boswell, *Boswell on the Grand Tour: Italy, Corsica and France 1765–1766*, Frank Brady and Frederick Pottle (eds), (New York and London: McGraw-Hill Book Company, 1955), p. 71.

40 'Memoirs of Thomas Jones', ed. A. P. Oppé, *The Walpole Society*, 32 (1946–8), pp. 1–142, pp. 53, 54.

41 Margaret Farrand Thorp, 'Literary Sculptors in the Caffè Greco', *American Quarterly*, 12: 2 (1960), pp. 160–74.

42 Thomas Barker, *Double Eagle and Crescent: Vienna's Second Turkish Siege and its historical setting* (Albany, New York: State University of New York Press, 1967), p. 336.

43 Harold Segel, *The Vienna Coffeehouse Wits 1890–1938* (West Lafayette, Indiana: Purdue University Press, 1994), pp, 8–9. See also Karl Teply, *Die Einführung des Kaffees in Wien* (Vienna: Verein für Geschichte der Stadt Wien, 1980).

CHAPTER 7

1 *'A Proclamation for the Suppression of Coffee-Houses'* (London: John Bill and Christopher Barker, 1675), dated 29 December 1675.

2 *The London Gazette*, No. 1055, Monday, 27 December 1675.

3 Robert Hooke, *The Diary of Robert Hooke, 1672–1800*, Henry W. Robinson and Walter Adams (eds), (London: Taylor & Francis, 1935), p. 205.

4 12 Car. II (1660), *A Grant of Certain Impositions upon Beer, Ale and other Liquors, For the Encrease of His Majesties Revenue during his Life.*

5 22 & 23 Car. II (1670), *An Act for an Additional Excise upon Beer, Ale and other Liquors.*

6 15 Car. II (1663), *An Additional Act for the better Ordering and Collecting the Duty of Excise, and Preventing the Abuses therein.*

7 *A Satyr Against Coffee* ([London], n.p., [1674?]).

8 Williamson Newsletter, 19 January 1672, HMC, *The Manuscripts of S. H. Le Fleming, Esq., of Rydall Hall* (London: HMSO, 1890), p. 88.

9 *'A Proclamation to Restrain the Spreading of False News, and Licentious Talking of Matters of State and Government'* (London: John Bill and Christopher Barker, 1672).

10 *'A Proclamation to Restrain the Spreading of False News, and Licentious Talking of Matters of State and Government'* (London: John Bill and Christopher Barker, 1674).

11 *Letters to Sir Joseph Williamson*, ed. W. D. Christie, 2 vols (Camden Society, new ser. VIII and IX, 1874), II, p. 24.

12 A Lover of his Country, *The Grand Concern of England Explained* (London: n.p., 1673), p. 24.

13 *CSPD 1676–1677*, 13 October 1676, pp. 366–7.

14 *Letters to Sir Joseph Williamson*, I, pp. 38, 73, 138, 112, 194; II, p. 68.

15 See J. R. Jones, 'Parties and Parliament' in J. R. Jones (ed.), *The Restored Monarchy, 1660–1668* (London: Macmillan, 1979), pp. 48–70.

16 Andrew Marvell, *An Account of the Growth of Popery and Arbitrary Government in England* (Amsterdam [London]: n.p., 1677), p. 54.

17 David Wootton (ed.), *John Locke: Political Writing* (London: Penguin, 1993), p. 45.

18 Newsletter to Sir Daniel Fleming, No. 1693, 4 January, *HMC Fleming*, p. 123.

19 *'A Proclamation for the Suppression of Coffee-Houses'* (London: John Bill and Christopher Barker, 1675), dated 29 December 1675.

20 Hatton newsletter, 1 January 1676. BL: Add Ms 29555, fol. 288r.

21 Ibid., 6 January 1676. BL: Add Ms 29555, fol. 292r.

22 Basil Duke Henning, *History of Parliament: The House of Commons 1669–1690: Members* (London: Secker & Warburg for History of Parliament Trust, 1983), II, p. 246.

23 Hatton newsletter, 6 January 1676. BL: Add Ms 29555, fol. 292r.

24 Andrew Marvell, 'A Dialogue between the Two Horses', in George deF. Lord, *Poems on Affairs of State Augustan Satirical Verse 1660–1714* (New Haven and London: Yale University Press, 1963), I, pp. 275–83.

25 15 Car. 2 (1663). 'An Additional Act for the better Ordering and Collecting the Duty of Excise, and Preventing the Abuses therein'.

26 Andrew Browning, *Thomas Osborne, Earl of Danby and Duke of Leeds 1632–1712*, 3 vols (Glasgow: Jackson, Son & Co. 1951), p. 194.

27 Hatton newletter, 8 January 1676. BL: Add Ms 29555, fol. 296r.

28 'Notes by Williamson of a debate in the Privy Council', PRO: State Papers: Domestic, Car. II, 378, no. 40.

29 Roger North, *Examen ... Together with some Memoirs ... tending to vindicate the Honour of the late King Charles the Second* (London: Fletcher Gyles, 1740), p. 141.

30 *History of Parliament: The House of Commons 1669–1690: Members*, II, p. 667.

31 *CSPD 1675–1676*, pp. 496–7.

32 Ibid., p. 496.

33 Hatton newsletter, 8 January 1676. BL: Add Ms 29555, fol. 296r.

34 Those present were Heneage, Lord Finch, the Lord Chancellor; Sir Francis North, Chief Justice of the Court of Common Pleas; Sir Richard Rainsford, Chief Justice of the King's Bench; Sir Edward Turnor, Chief Justice of the Exchequer; and Sir Hugh Wyndham, Hon. Vere Bertie and Sir Timothy Littleton of the Court of the Exchequer. BL Add Ms 32518, fol. 227v; Edward Foss, *A Biographical Dictionary of the Judges of England, 1066–1870* (London: John Murray, 1870); John Sainty, *The Judges of England 1272–1990* (London: Selden Society, 1993); DNB.

35 *CSPD 1675–1676*, p. 500; BL Add Ms 32518, fol. 228r.

36 Ibid., pp. 496–7.

37 'Condition of a Victuallers Recognizance (1673)'; CLRO: Alchin Coll. Box H/103.(14).

38 *CSPD 1675–1676*, p. 497.

39 Hooke, *Diary 1672–1800*, p. 210; Hatton newsletter, 11 January 1676. BL: Add Ms 29555, fol. 298r.

40 *'An Additional Proclamation Concerning Coffee-Houses'* (London: John Bill and Christopher Barker, 1676), dated 8 January 1676.

41 'A Proclamation for the Better Discovery of Seditious Libellers' (London: John Bill and Christopher Barker, 1675), dated 7 January 1676; *The London Gazette*, no. 1059, 10 January 1676.

42 Newsletters to Sir Daniel Fleming, no. 1697. 18 January 1676, in *HMC Fleming*, p. 124.

43 *CSPD 1675–1676*, 16 January 1676, p. 516; 12 January 1676, p. 510; 13 January 1676, p. 511.

44 *CSPD 1676–1677*, 8 August 1676, p. 268. See also *CSPD 1676–1677*, 2 September 1676, p. 309; 4 September 1676, p. 312; 26 September 1676, p. 338; 13 October 1676, pp. 366–7; 18 October 1676, pp. 372–3; 23 October 1676, p. 382; and Perry Gauci, *Politics and Society in Great Yarmouth, 1660–1722* (New York: Oxford University Press, 1996), pp. 136–42.

45 *CSPD 1675–76*, 15 and 16 February, pp. 559–61; 18 February, pp. 562–3.

46 Shaftesbury and Buckingham, *Two Seasonable Discourses concerning this present Parliament* (Oxford: n.p., 1675), John Locke, *A Letter from a Person of Quality* ([London]: 1675), Marvell, *Growth of Popery.*

47 *The Case of Francis Jenkes* (Amsterdam [London]: n.p., 1677); *CSPD 1676–77*, pp. 185, 253–4.

48 Bulstrode Newsletter, 30 June 1676 (Harry Ransome Center, University of Texas Ms, Pforzheimer 103c, vol. IX, file 1).

49 Hooke, *Diary*, p. 249.

50 Bulstrode Newsletters, 15 September 1676 (Pforzheimer 103c, vol. IX, file 2).

51 *CSPD 1676–77*: 17 November 1676, p. 419; *Calendar of Treasury Books, 1676–1679*, comp. William Shaw, V, part 1 (London: HMSO, 1911), 12 January 1677, p. 419; 25 June 1679, p. 813.

52 *CSPD 1676–1677*, 24 February 1677, p. 569.

53 *CSPD 1677–1678*, 5 February 1678, p. 627.

54 *HMC: Report on Manuscripts in Various Collections* (London: HMSO, 1901), I, p. 157.

55 Mark Knights, *Politics and Opinion in Crises 1678–81* (Cambridge: Cambridge University Press, 1994), pp. 153–92

56 *News from Colchester* (London: Richard Janeway, 1681), p. 2.

57 *The True Domestic Intelligence*, no. 48, 19 December 1679. Mark Knights, 'London's "Monster" Petition of 1680', *The Historical Journal*, 36, 1 (1993), pp. 39–67, p. 53.

58 *A Moderate Decision of the Point of Succession* (London: R. Janeway, 1681), p. 1.

59 *Heraclitus Ridens*, no. 1, 1 February 1681; no. 12, 19 April 1681.

60 *The Observator*, no. 394, 29 August 1683; no. 399, 6 September 1683; *CSPD July–September 1683*, 1 September 1683, p. 232.

61 John Oldmixon, *The History of England, During the Reigns of the Royal House of Stuart* (London: John Pemberton, Richard Ford, Richard Hett, John Gray and Thomas Cox, 1730), p. 781.

62 Paul de Rapin Thoyras, *The History of England*, trans. N. Tindal, 15 vols (London: James and John Knapton, 1726–31), XIV, p. 73.

63 David Hume, *The History of Great Britain* (London: A. Millar, 1757), II, p. 245.

64 BL Egerton 226, fol. 479. Thanks to Chris Reid for this reference.

CHAPTER 8

1 'Accompt of Coffee Houses in the severall Wards in May 1663', CLRO: Alchin Coll. Box H/103.(12).

2 *The Character of a Coffee-House. By an Eye and Ear Witness*, p. 2.

3 Charles Daves (ed.), 'Introduction', in Butler, *Characters*, pp. 256–7.

4 R. Campbell, *The London Tradesman* (London: T. Gardner, 1747), pp. 281, 269–70.

5 *A Trip through the Town. Containing Observations on the Humours and Manners of the Age*, 4th ed. (London: J. Roberts, 1735), pp. 6–7.

6 Douglas, *Supplement*, p. 31. George Constantine also told Douglas that 'Nicholas, a Grecian' was an early proprietor of the Rainbow Coffee House in Temple Bar, and that 'a Turk' kept one in Henrietta Street, Covent Garden.

7 CLRO: Alchin Coll. Box H/103.(12).

8 *The Intelligencer*, no. 7, Monday, 23 January 1665, p. 51.
9 *The Character of a Coffee-House.*
10 Douglas, *Supplement*, p. 33. See Jonathan Harris, 'The Grecian Coffee House and Political Debate', *London Journal*, 25, 1 (2000), p. 2.
11 *The Maidens Complaint Against Coffee*, p. 1.
12 *The Coffee-Mans Granado Discharged Upon the Maidens Complaint Against Coffee* (London: J. Johnson, 1663), p. 3.
13 CLRO: Alchin Coll. Box H/103.(12).
14 Lillywhite, no. 147, p. 127; no. 1501, pp. 635–7; no. 624, p. 625; no. 1531, p. 647; no. 331, p. 188.
15 Emma Clery, 'Women, Publicity and the Coffee-House Myth', *Women: a cultural review*, 2, 2 1991, pp. 681–77.
16 Tom Brown, *Amusements Serious and Comical, Calculated for the Meridian of London* (first published London, 1702) in *The Works of Mr. Thomas Brown. Serious and Comical, in Prose and Verse,* 4 vols (first edition 1707; 5th ed., London: Sam Briscoe, 1715), III, pp. 71–2.
17 *The Mens Answer to the Womens Petition Against Coffee* (London: n.p., 1674), p. 3.
18 *The Spectator*, no. 87 (Saturday 9 June 1711), ed. Bond, I, pp. 371–2.
19 Andrew Moreton, *Every-Body's Business is No-Body's Business* (London: T. Warner; A. Dodd and E. Nutt, 1725), pp. 21–2.
20 Markman Ellis, 'The coffee-women, *The Spectator* and the public sphere in the early-eighteenth century', in *Women and the Public Sphere*, Elizabeth Eger and Charlotte Grant (eds), (Cambridge: Cambridge University Press, 2001).
21 *The Velvet Coffee-Woman: or, the Life, Gallantries and Amours of the late Famous Mrs. Anne Rochford* (Westminster: Simon Green, 1728), pp. 33, 10.
22 Macky, *Journey Through England*, Letter IX, (1714), p. 107.
23 *The Velvet Coffee-Woman*, p. 35.
24 Henry Fielding, *The Covent-Garden Tragedy. As it is Acted at the Theatre-Royal in Drury-Lane By his Majesty's Servants* (London: J. Watts, 1732), p. [21.]
25 *The Life and Character of Moll King, Late Mistress of King's Coffee-House in Covent-Garden* (London: W. Price, [1747?]), pp. 5, 8. Helen Berry, 'Rethinking Politeness in Eighteenth-Century England: Moll King's Coffee House and the Significance of "Flash Talk"', *Transactions of the Royal Historical Society* (Cambridge: Cambridge University Press, 2002), 6th ser., IX, pp. 65–81.
26 Campbell, *London Tradesman*, p. 270.
27 *Knavery in all Trades: or, The Coffee-House A Comedy. As it was acted in the Christmas Holidays by several Apprentices With great Applause. With License* (London: J. B. for W. Gilberton and H. Marsh, 1664), pp. 21–2.
28 Museum of London, no. 7143. See Frank Britton, *London Delftware* (London: Jonathan Home, 1987), p. 177.
29 Thomas Sydserf, *Tarugo's Wiles: or, the Coffee-House A Comedy. As it was acted at his Highness's The Duke of York's Theatre* (London: Henry Herringman, 1668), Act III, p. 16.
30 Ibid., pp. 17–18.
31 Steele, *The Spectator*, no. 49, Thursday, 26 April 1711, ed. Bond, p. 211.

32 Steele, *The Tatler*, no. 1, Tuesday, 12 April 1709, ed. Bond, I, p. 21; no. 69, Saturday, 17 September 1709, ed. Bond, I, 481.
33 Steele, *The Spectator*, no. 24, Wednesday, 28 March 1711, ed. Bond, I, p. 104.
34 *The Women's Petition Against Coffee* (London: n.p., 1674), p. 2.
35 M. P., *A Character of Coffee and Coffee-Houses* (London: John Starkey, 1661), p. 2; *Women's Petition*, p. 5; *Maidens Complaint*, pp. 3–4.
36 *Coffee-Mans Granado*, p. 7; *Cup of Coffee; A Satyr Against Coffee*, ([London], n.p., [1674?]).
37 *Knavery in all Trades*, p. 21.
38 *The Character of a Coffee-House, with the Symptomes of a Town-Wit* (London: Jonathan Edwin, 1673), pp. 2, 3.
39 *The Ale Wives Complaint, Against the Coffee-Houses* (London: John Tomson, 1675), p. 4.
40 *Knavery in all Trades*, Act I, Scene 2, p. 8.
41 *Coffee-Mans Granado*, p. 6.
42 Pepys, *Diary*, 4 October 1661 (II, p. 191); 17 January 1663 (IV, p. 16).
43 BL Add 15226, fol. 59r; Douglas, *Supplement*, p. 33.
44 *Ale-Wives Complaint*, p. 3.
45 Ernesto Illy, 'The Complexity of Coffee', *Scientific American*, 286: 6 (June 2002), pp. 86–93.
46 Kenneth Davids, *Home Coffee Roasting* (New York: St Martin's Griffin, 2000).
47 Helene Desmet-Gregoire, *Les Objets du Café dans les sociétés du proche-orient & de la mediterranée* (Paris: Presses du CNRS, 1989), pp. 28–33.
48 Douglas, *Supplement*, p. 33.
49 Pope to Arbuthnot, 4 July 1714, *The Correspondence of Alexander Pope*, ed. George Sherburn, *Volume 1, 1704–1718* (Oxford: Clarendon Press, 1956), p. 234.
50 'Memoranda medica', BL Sloane 645, fol. 19r. See also 'Letters to and from Dr Bellingham concerning chymical medecines, secrets', 1675–1681, BL Sloane 647, f. 8r.
51 Davids, *Home Coffee Roasting*.
52 *Knavery in all Trades*, p. 21; Butler, 'A Coffee-Man', p. 257.
53 *Broad-side against Coffee; Women's Petition Against Coffee*, p. 5.
54 Thevenot, *Travels*, p. 33.
55 J. S. Buckingham, *Travels among the Arab Tribes* (London: Longman, Hurst, Rees, Orme, Brown and Green, 1825), p. 352.
56 'Memoranda medica', BL Sloane 645, fol. 19r.
57 BL Add 15226, f.59r.
58 Historical Manuscripts Commission, *Report on the Manuscripts of the late Allan George Finch, Esq* (London: HMSO, 1922), II, pp. 144–5.
59 Edward Bramah and Joan Bramah, *Coffee Makers: 300 years of art & design* (London: Quiller, 1989), pp. 26–9.
60 Maria Eliza Rundle, *A New System of Domestic Cookey; formed upon principles of economy: and adapted to the use of private families*, 2nd ed. (London: John Murray, 1810), p. 283.
61 Douglas, *Supplement*, p. 33.

62 Pepys, *Diary*, V, p. 105.

63 John Chamberlayn, *The Manner of Making Coffee, Tea and Chocolate* (London: William Crook, 1685), pp. 14–15.

64 James Lightbody, *Every Man his own Gauger. Together with the Compleat Coffee-Man* (London: A. Baldwin, undated [1698]), p. 62.

65 Laurence Sterne, *The Life and Opinions of Tristram Shandy, Gentleman*, ed. Mervyn New (London: Penguin, 1997), p. 429.

66 Comenius to Hartlib, 28 December 1657, trans W. J. Hitchens, in *The Hartlib Papers Second Edition* (Sheffield: HROnline, Humanities Research Institute, 2002), 7/111/6A-7B.

67 *Mercurius Politicus*, no. 435, 23 September 1658, p. 887.

68 Pepys, *Diary*, I, 25 September 1660, BL 12/7(1)..

69 *Anno XII. Caroli.II.Regis. A Grant of Certain Impositions upon Beer, Ale and other Liquors, For the Encrease of His Majesties Revenue during his Life* (London: John Bill, 1660), p. 253.

70 *Mercurius Publicus*, no. 11, 12–19 March 1663, p. 177.

71 George Birdwood, *Report on the Old Records at the India Office* (London: Eyre and Spottiswoode, 1890), p. 26.

72 Richard Ames, *The Bacchanalian Sessions: or the Contention of Liquors: with A Farewell to Wine* (London: E. Hawkins, 1693), p. 16.

73 Nahum Tate, *Panacea: a Poem Upon Tea: In Two Canto's* (London: J. Roberts, 1700), p. [10].

74 Duncan Campbell, *A Poem Upon Tea* (London: Mrs. Dodd, J. Roberts, J. Wilcox and eight others, 1735), p. 13.

75 K. N. Chaudhuri, *The Trading World of Asia and the English East India Company, 1660–1760* (Cambridge: Cambridge University Press, 1978), pp. 385–406. See also William Ukers, *All About Tea*, 2 vols (New York: The Tea and Coffee Trade Journal Company, 1935); and Alan Macfarlane and Iris Macfarlane, *Green Gold: the Empire of Tea* (London: Ebury, 2003).

76 J. B., Writing Master, *In Praise of Tea. A Poem. Dedicated to the Ladies of Great Britain* (Canterbury: for the author, 1736), p. 9.

77 John Wesley, *A Letter to a Friend, concerning Tea* (Bristol: Felix Farley, 1748), pp. 4–5.

78 Jonas Hanway, *A Journal of Eight Days Journey from Portsmouth to Kingston Upon Thames. To which is added, an Essay on Tea* (London: H. Woodfall, 1756).

79 Stephen H. Twining, *The House of Twining 1706–1956* (London: R. Twining, 1956), pp. 4–13.

80 *T. T. Ledger C, 1715–1722*. R. Twining & Co. Archives, Andover, Hampshire. Mss 5/3/1, ff 24, 59, 98, 130, 229, 260, 288, 299, 320, 345.

81 J. A. Johnston, *Probate Inventories of Lincoln Citizens 1661–1714* (Woodbridge, Suffolk: Lincoln Record Society and Boydell & Brewer, 1991), p. 79.

82 Gladys Scott Thomson, *Life in a Noble Household 1641–1700* (London: Jonathan Cape, 1937), pp. 167–70.

83 J. Theodore Bent (ed.), *Early Voyages and Travels in the Levant* (London: Hakluyt Society, 1893), p. 263.

84 John Stevens (trans.), 'The Travels of Peter Teixeira from India to Italy by Land', Volume V of *A View of the Universe: or, New Collection of Voyages and Travels*, 7 vols (London: J. Knapton, A. Bell, D. Midwinter et al, 1708–10), p. 38.

85 Nurhan Atasoy and Julian Raby, *Iznik: The Pottery of Ottoman Turkey*, ed. Tanni Petsopoulos (London: Alexandria Press in association with Thames and Hudson, 1989), plates 7, 8, 19, 20, 21, 22.

86 *Thomas Platter's Travels in England*, ed. C. Williams (London: Jonathan Cape, 1937), p. 73.

87 Arthur Lane, *Later Islamic Pottery: Persia, Syria, Egypt, Turkey* (London: Faber and Faber, 1957), p. 59.

88 T. Volker, *Porcelain and the Dutch East India Company* (Leiden: E. J. Brill, 1965), pp. 34–5, 48–9; David Howard, *The Choice of the Private Trader: the Private Market in Chinese Export Porcelain* (London: Zwemmer, 1994), pp. 13–17.

89 Frank Britton, *London Delftware* (London: Jonathan Horne, 1987), pp. 35–7.

90 Lorna Weatherill and Rhoda Edwards, 'Pottery Manufacture in London and Whitehaven in the 17th century', *Post-Medieval Archaeology*, 5 (1971), pp. 160–81, p. 164.

91 'Trade-card of the Nottingham Potter James Morly, *c.* 1700 (Bodleian Library)', in Bevis Hillier, *Pottery and Porcelain 1700–1914: England, Europe and North America* (London: Weidenfeld and Nicolson, 1968) plate 70.

92 Michael Archer, *Delftware: The Tin-Glazed Earthenware of the British Isles: a catalogue of the Collection in the Victoria and Albert Museum* (London: Stationery Office, 1997), p. 349.

CHAPTER 9

1 Pepys, *Diary*, 3 November 1663, IV, pp. 361–2.

2 Walter Rumsey, *Organon Salutis. An Instrument to Cleanse the Stomach* (London: R. Hodgkinsonne for D. Pakeman, 1657), pp. [vii], 27, 4–5.

3 Aubrey, *Brief Lives*, pp. 277–8.

4 Hooke, *Diary 1672–1680*, 6 May 1676, p. 230.

5 *Mercurius Politicus*, 11–18 June 1657, no. 367, p. 7857; Rumsey, *Organon Salutis*, p. [v].

6 Michael Hunter, Antonio Clericuzio and Lawrence M. Principe (eds), *The Correspondence of Robert Boyle*, 6 vols (London: Pickering and Chatto, 2001), II, pp. 153–66; A. R. and M. B. Hall (eds), *The Correspondence of Henry Oldenburg*, 13 vols (Madison, Milwaukee and London, 1965–86), II, p. 51.

7 Rumsey, *Organon Salutis*, pp. xi, xx–xxii.

8 Thomas Sprat, *The History of the Royal-Society of London, For the Improving of Natural Knowledge* (London: T. R. for J. Martyn, 1667), p. 256.

9 N. D., *The Vertues of Coffee. Set forth in the Works of Lord Bacon his Natural Hist., Mr Parkinson his Herbal, Sir George Sandys his Travails, James Howel Esq; his Epistles* (London: W. F., 1663), p. [3].

10 Leonard Twells, 'Life of Pococke' in Edward Pococke, *The Theological Works*, 2 vols (London, 1740), p. 81.

11 Edwarde Pococke, *The Nature of the Drink Kaubi, or Coffe, and the Berry of which it is made, Described by an Arabian Phisitian* (Oxford: Henry Hall, 1659).

12 *Correspondence of Robert Boyle*, I, pp. 325, 327; *The Hartlib Papers*, 2nd ed. (Sheffield: HROnline, Humanities Research Institute, 2002), Ms 42/4/42A-4B; *The Diary and Correspondence of Dr. John Worthington*, ed. J. Crossley, vol. 1 (Chetham Society, vol. XIII, Manchester 1847), pp. 120–8.

13 *The Vertue of the Coffee Drinke* ([London: n.p., 1670]). BL: 778.k.15 (9).

14 *The Women's Petition Against Coffee*, pp. 1–2.

15 Simon Paulli, *Commentarius de abusu tabaci et herba thee* ([Strasbourg]: Argentorati, 1665); trans. Robert James, *A treatise on tobacco, tea, coffee and chocolate*, (London: T. Osbourne, 1746), pp. 118–19, 163.

16 Adam Olearius, *The Voyages & Travels of the Ambassadors sent to the King of Persia*, trans. John Davies (London: Thomas Dring and John Starkey, 1662), p. 322.

17 Paulli, p. 165.

18 J. D. T. Bienville, *Nymphomania, or, a Dissertation on the Furor Uterinus*, trans. Edward Sloane Wilmot, (London: J. Bew, 1775), pp. 57–9. Thanks to Adriana Craciun for this reference.

19 Samuel Hahnemann, 'On the Effects of Coffee. From Original Observations', in *The Lesser Writings of Samuel Hahnemann*, trans. and ed. R. E. Dudgeon (London: W. Headland, 1851), p. 464.

20 Jack E. James, *Understanding Caffeine: A Biobehavioral Analysis* (London: Sage Publications, 1997), pp. 125–6.

21 *Women's Petition Against Coffee*, pp. 3–5.

22 'Substance-related disorders', *Diagnostic and Statistical Manual of Mental Disorders*, 4th ed. (Washington, DC: American Psychiatric Association, 1994), pp. 173–272.

23 *The Mens Answer to the Womens Petition Against Coffee, Vindicating Their own Performances, and the Vertues of that Liquour* (London: n.p., 1674), pp. 1, 4.

24 *A Brief Description of the Excellent Vertues of that Sober and Wholesome Drink, called Coffee* (London: Paul Greenwood, 1674).

25 Antonius Faustus Naironi (Banesius), *De Saluberrima potione Cahue, seu Café nuncupata discursus* (Rome: Michaelis Herculis, 1671).

26 Naironi, *A Discourse on Coffee: its Description and Vertues*, trans. C. B. (London: Geo. James for Abel Roper, 1710), p. [vi].

27 N. D., *The Vertues of Coffee*.

28 Naironi, *Discourse on Coffee*, pp. 25–6.

29 Naironi, *Discorso della Salutifera Bevanda Kahve, ò vero Café*, trans. Frederic Vegilin (Roma: Michele Hercole, 1671).

30 Naironi, *Discourse on Coffee*, p. iii.

31 [Jacob Spon], *De L'Usage du Caphé, du Thé et du Chocolate* (Lyon: Jean Girin et Barthelemy Riviere, 1671); trans. John Chamberlayne, *The Manner of Making Coffee, Tea and Chocolate* (London: William Crook, 1685).

32 Philippe Sylvestre Dufour, *Traitez Nouveaux & curieux du Café, du Thé & du Chocolate* (La Haye: Adrian Moetjens, 1685).

33 Iacobus Sponius, *Tractatus Novi De Potu Caphé; de Chinensium Thé; et de Chocolate* (Paris: Petrum Muguet, 1685).

34 Article IV, *Nouvelles de la Republique des Lettres*, III: 5 (Mai 1685), pp. 497–509.

35 [Jacobus Sponius], *Drey Neue Curieuse Tractatgen, von dem Trancke Café, sinesischen*

The, und der Chocolata (Budissen [Bautzen?]: Verlegung Friedrich Arnsts, Druckt Andreas Richter, 1686); Angelo Rambaldi, *Ambroisio Arabica, Overo della Salutare Bevanda Café* (Bologna: Longhi Stampatore Arcivescouale, 1691): Iacobus Sponius, *Tractatus Novi* (Genevæ: Cramer & Perachon, 1699).

36 Nicolas de Blegny, *Le Bon Usage du Thé, du Caffé et du Chocolat* (Lyon: Thomas Amaulry, 1687).

37 Thomas Willis, *De Anima Brutorum, Quae Hominis Vitalis ac Sensitiva est, Exercitationes Dua* (London: E. F. for Ric. Davis, 1672), p. 232. Thomas Willis, *Two Discourses concerning the Soul of Brutes, Which is that of the Vital and Sensitive of Man, Englished by S. Pordage* (London: Thomas Ding, Ch. Harper and John Leigh, 1683), pp. 133, 134–5.

38 Thomas Willis, *Pharmaceutice Rationalis sive Diatriba de Medicamentorum Operationibus in humano Corpore*, 2 vols ([Oxford]: Theatro Sheldoniano, 1674) 'Potus Coffee', Sect VII, Cap. III, pp. 327–9; Thomas Willis, *Pharmaceutice Rationalis: Or, The Operations of Medicines in Humane Bodies*, 2 vols in one (London: Thomas Dring, Charles Harper, and John Leigh, 1679), pp. 136, 154–5.

39 Thomas Willis, *The London Practice of Physick* (London: Thomas Bassett and William Crooke, 1685), pp. 68–9.

40 Charles Raven, *John Ray, Naturalist: his Life and Works* (Cambridge: Cambridge University Press, 1942).

41 J. Theodore Bent (ed.), *Early Voyages and Travels in the Levant* (London: Hakluyt Society, 1893). See John Ray, *Further Correspondence*, ed. Robert Gunther (London: for the Ray Society, 1928).

42 John Ray, *Correspondence*, ed. Edwin Lankester (London: for the Ray Society, 1848), p. 190.

43 John Ray, 'Coffee frutex ex cujus Fructu sit Potus', *Historia Plantarum*, 3 vols (London: Henry Faithorne, 1686, 1688 and 1704), II, Lib. XXX., Cap. III, pp. 1691–3.

44 Labelled 'from Moca in Arabia felix by Mr Clyve', it is in the Sloane Herbarium in the Natural History Museum, London, preserved among specimens collected by a ship's surgeon called Handisyd in 1690–2. J. E. Dandy (ed.), *The Sloane Herbarium* (London: British Museum, 1958), H.S.8., fol. 93.

45 Richard Bradley, *A Short Historical Account of Coffee* (London: Em. Matthews at the Bible in Pater-Noster-Row, [1715]) [Royal Society Library: Biology-Small, RCN 29716]; Richard Bradley, *The Virtue and Use of Coffee, with Regard to the Plague, and other Infectious Distempers* (London: Eman. Matthews and W. Mears, 1721); James Douglas, *Arbor Yemensis fructum Cofé ferens: or, a Description and History of the Coffee Tree* (London: Thomas Woodward, 1727); John Ellis, *An Historical Account of Coffee, With An Engraving and Botanical Description of the Tree* (London: Edward and Charles Dilly, 1774).

46 J. K. J. De Jonge, *De Opkomst van het Nederladsch Gezag in Oost-Indie* (Amsterdam: Frederick Muller, 1875), pp. cxxxxiv–cxxxv; C. G. Brouwer, *Dutch-Yemeni Encounters: Activities of the United East India Company (VOC) in South Arabian Waters since 1614* (Amsterdam: D'Fluyte Rarob, 1999), pp. 267–8.

47 James Petiver to Patrick Blair, 12 February 1712, BL Sloane 338: 27v–31r, fol. 28v. For the best account of this matter see Richard Coulton, *Writing and Gardening in*

Eighteenth Century London (unpublished Ph.D. dissertation, University of London).

48 William Oldys, 'Notes on Trees', *c.* 1761, Add Mss 20724, fol. 9r.

49 André Charrier and Julien Berthaud, 'Botanical Classification of Coffee', in *Coffee: Botany, Biochemistry and Production of Beans and Beverage*, Michael Clifford and Ken Willson (eds), (London: Croom Helm, 1985), pp. 14, 55.

50 Anton van Leeuwenhoek, 'Epistola de 9 Mey, 1687, ad Regiam Societatem: Quo ordine farinacea substantia sive material seminbus infundatur, de fabis vulgo dictis Coffi', *Continuatio Epistolarum, datarum Ad longe Celeberriman Regiam societatem Londiensem* (Lugduni Baravorum: Cornelium Boutestin, 1689), pp. 13–19.

51 Thomas Birch, *The History of the Royal Society of London for Improving Natural Knowledge*, 4 vols (London: A. Millar, 1756), IV, p. 540.

52 Ernesto Illy, 'The Complexity of Coffee', *Scientific American*, 286: 6 (2002), p. 90. See also H. B. Heath, 'The Physiology of Flavour: Taste and Aroma Perception', in *Coffee*, R. J. Clarke and R. Macrae (eds), 6 vols (London: Elsevier Applied Science, 1988), III, pp. 141–70, p. 143.

53 John Houghton, 'A Discourse of Coffee', *Philosophical Transactions*, 21: 256 (September 1699), pp. 315–16.

54 Samuel Taylor Coleridge, *Collected Letters*, ed. Earl Leslie Griggs, 6 vols (Oxford: Clarendon, 1956), II, pp. 446, 468, 481.

55 Hahnemann, *Lesser Writings*, pp. 450–69, p. 454.

56 Bennett Weinberg and Bonnie Bealer, *The World of Caffeine: the science and culture of the world's most popular drug* (London: Routledge, 2001), pp. xvii–xxi.

57 Ferdinand Friedrich Runge, *Neueste Phytochemische Entdeckungen zur Begründung einer wissenscaftlichen Phytochemie* (Berlin: G. Reimer, 1820), pp. 144–59. Coleridge's copy (with marginalia) is BL: C.126.g.5.

58 Stephen Braun, *Buzz: the science and lore of alcohol and caffeine* (New York and Oxford: Oxford University Press, 1996). See also James, *Understanding Caffeine*; B. B. Fredholm, 'Adenosine, adenosine receptors, and the actions of caffeine', *Pharmacology and Toxicology*, 76 (1995), pp. 93–101; and Marshall Brain, 'How Caffeine Works', *Howstuffworks*, <http://home.howstuffworks.com/caffeine.htm> accessed 14 October 2003.

59 Barry D. Smith and Kenneth Tola, 'Caffeine: Effects on Psychological Functioning and Performance', in *Caffeine*, ed. Gene Spiller (Boca Raton, New York: CRC Press, 1998), pp. 251–99.

60 Hahnemann, *Lesser Writings*, p. 458.

61 Institute of Medicine, *Caffeine for the Sustainment of Mental Task Performance: Formulations for Military Operations* (Washington, DC: National Academy Press, 2001), pp. 2–3.

62 James, *Understanding Caffeine*, pp. 40–55.

63 Braun, *Buzz*, p. 133.

CHAPTER 10

1 César de Saussure, *A Foreign View of England in the Reigns of George I & George II: the letters of Monsieur César de Saussure to his Family, translated and edited by Madame Van Muyden* (written 1729, first ed: London: John Murray, 1902), pp. 164–5.

2 Pepys, *Diary*, V, p. 37; IX, p. 175.

3 James Boswell, *The Life of Samuel Johnson*, ed. R. W. Chapman (London: Oxford University Press, 1970), p. 770.

4 Brice Harris, 'Captain Robert Julian, Secretary to the Muses', *ELH*, 10: 4 (1943), pp. 294–309.

5 William Empson, *The Structure of Complex Words* (London: Chatto & Windus, 1951), pp. 84–100.

6 John Dennis, *Letters Upon several Occasions* (London: Sam. Briscoe, 1696), unpaginated insertion between pp. 128–9.

7 *Letters of Wit, Politicks, and Morality* (London: J. Hartley, W. Turner, and Tho. Hodgson, 1701), p. 216.

8 *The Humours and Conversations of the Town* (London: R. Bentley and J. Tonson, 1693), pp. 107–8.

9 Aphra Behn, *The Luckey Chance, or an Alderman's Bargain. A Comedy* (R. H. for W. Canning, 1687), pp. [iii], [v].

10 A. B. [Aphra Behn?], *Rebellions Antidote: or a Dialogue Between Coffee and Tea* (London: George Croom, 1685).

11 Thomas Brown, *The Reasons of Mr. Bays Changing his Religion* (London: S. T., 1688), p. [9].

12 J. Harold Wilson, 'Rochester, Dryden and the Rose-Street Affair', *Review of English Studies*, 15: 59 (1939), pp. 294–301.

13 Simon Alderson, 'The Augustan Attack on the Pun', *Eighteenth-Century Life*, 20: 3 (1996), pp. 1–19, p. 9.

14 John Macky, *A Journey Through England* (London: J. Roberts for T. Caldecott, 1714), p. 111.

15 Joseph Spence, *Observations, Anecdotes, and Characters of Books and Men*, 2 vols (Oxford: Clarendon Press, 1966), I, p. 77.

16 Alexander Pope, *The Correspondence of Alexander Pope*, ed. George Sherburn, 5 vols (Oxford: Clarendon Press, 1956), I, pp. 305–6.

17 *Twickenham Edition of the Poems of Alexander Pope*, ed. John Butt, 10 vols (London: Routledge, 1939–67), IV; George Sherburn, *The Early Career of Alexander Pope* (Oxford: Clarendon Press, 1934), pp. 63–6, 115–48; Peter Smithers, *The Life of Joseph Addison* (Oxford: Clarendon Press, 1954), pp. 306–8, 323–7.

18 *The Connoisseur*, no. 1, Thursday, 31 January 1754, I, p. 4.

19 *Memoirs of the Bedford Coffee House. By a Genius* (London: J. Single, 1763).

20 *The London Packet*, 8 November 1770, newspaper cutting in BL 12314.ee.11.

21 Pope to Wycherly, 20 May 1709, in *The Correspondence of Alexander Pope*, I, p. 60.

22 *The Correspondence of Robert Boyle*, II, pp. 347–8.

23 Hobbes, 'Dialogus physicus', quoted in Shapin and Shaffer, pp. 112–13.

24 *Coffee-houses Vindicated in answer to the late published Character of a Coffee-House* (London: J. Lock for J. Clarke, 1675), p. 5.

25 Lisa Jardine, *The curious life of Robert Hooke: the man who measured London* (London: HarperCollins, 2003).

26 Robert Hooke, *The Diary of Robert Hooke, 1672–1680*, Henry W. Robinson and Walter Adams (eds) (London: Taylor and Francis, 1935), pp. 463–70.

27 Hooke, *Diary*, p. 103.

28 Ibid., p. 107. Hooke purchased 'coffee powder' from Garraway's too (p. 107).

29 Rob Iliffe, 'Material doubts: Hooke, artisan culture and the exchange of information in 1670s London', *British Journal for the History of Science*, 28: 3: 98 (September 1995), pp. 285–318, p. 317.

30 For example, Hooke, *Diary*, pp. 383, 385, 416. See Stephen Inwood, *The Man Who Knew Too Much: the strange and inventive life of Robert Hooke*, 1635–1703 (London: Macmillan, 2002), p. 246.

31 Hooke, *Diary*, pp. 430–1.

32 Thomas Birch, *The History of the Royal Society of London for Improving Natural Knowledge*, 4 vols (London: A . Millar, 1756), IV, pp. 2, 38.

33 Edward Tyson, *Phocæna, or The Anatomy of a Porpesse, dissected at Gresham College: with a Preliminary Discourse concerning Anatomy, and a Natural History of Animals* (London: Benjamin Tooke, 1680), p. 10.

34 Cambridge University Library, Royal Greenwich Observatory, Ms. 1.50. (K). in Iliffe, pp. 316–17,

35 Michael Cooper, 'Hooke's Career', in Jim Bennet, Michael Cooper, Michael Hunter and Lisa Jardine, *London's Leonardo – The Life and Work of Robert Hooke* (Oxford: Oxford University Press, 2003), p. 7. The fullest account of the experiments is in Steven Shapin and Simon Schaffer, *Leviathan and the Air-Pump: Hobbes, Boyle, and the Experimental Life* (Princeton: Princeton University Press, 1985), pp. 45–9.

36 *Difficiles Nugæ, or, Observations Touching the Torricellian Experiment* (London: W. Godbid for William Shrowsbury, 1674).

37 *An Excerpt out of a Book, Shewing That Fluids Rise not in the Pump, in the Syphon, and in the Barometer, by the Pressure of the Air, but Propter Fugam vacui. At the occasion of a Dispute, in a Coffee-House, with a Doctor of Physic* ([London] n.p., n.d. [1675]), pp. 1, 8.

38 Colin Ronan, *Edmond Halley: Genius in Eclipse* (London: Macdonald, 1970), p. 125.

39 *The Correspondence of John Flamsteed, the First Astronomer Royal*, Eric Forbes, Leslie Murdin and Frances Willmoth (eds), 2 vols (Bristol: Institute of Physics Publishing, 1995–7); vol. II, *1682–1703*, 1 February 1687, p. 332; 12 February 1687, p. 335.

40 Hooke, *Diary*, pp. 199–200, 205–6.

41 Robert Hooke, 'Diary 1688 to 1693', in R. T. Gunther (ed.) *The Life and Work of Robert Hooke (Part IV)* in *Early Science in Oxford*, X (Oxford: for the author, 1935), pp. 69–265; T. E. Allibone, *The Royal Society and its Dining Clubs* (Oxford: Pergamon Press, 1976), p. 15.

42 R. P. Stearns, 'James Petiver, Promoter of Natural Science, c. 1663–1718', *Proceedings of the American Antiquarian Society*, 1952, n.s. 62, pp. 243–365, pp. 252–3.

43 Pettiver to Breynius, December 1692, BL: Sloane 4067, fol. 81.

44 Stearns, 'Petiver', pp. 252–3.

45 Larry Stewart, *The Rise of Public Science: Rhetoric, Technology and Natural Philosophy in Newtonian Britain, 1660–1750* (Cambridge: Cambridge University Press, 1992), pp. 101–41.

46 T. H. Levere and G. Turner, *Discussing Chemistry and Steam: The Minutes of a Coffee House Philosophical Society 1780–1787* (Oxford: Oxford University Press, 2002). See especially Jan Golinski, 'Conversations on Chemistry: Talk about Phlogiston in the Coffee House Society, 1780–1787', pp. 191–205.

47 See Helen Berry, *Gender, Society and Print Culture in Late-Stuart England: the cultural world of the 'Athenian Mercury'* (Aldershot: Ashgate, 2003), pp. 11–34; Emma Clery, 'The *Athenian Mercury* and the Pindarick Lady', *The Feminization Debate in the Eighteenth Century: Literature, Commerce and Luxury* (Basingstoke: Palgrave, 2004), chapter 2.

48 Houghton, *Philosophical Transactions*, 21: 256 (1699), p. 317; *The Athenian Mercury,* II: 4 (6 June 1691), p. [1].

49 John Evelyn to John Beale, 17 July 1670, in *John Evelyn Letter Book*, quoted in Douglas Chambers, '"Elysium Britannicum not printed neere ready, &c.": *The Elysium Britannicum* in the Correspondence of John Evelyn', in Therese O'Malley and Joachim Wolschker Bulmahn (eds), *John Evelyn's "Elysium Britannicum" and European Gardening* (Washington, DC: Dumbarton Oaks, 1998).

50 'The Life of John North', in Roger North, *The Life of the Honourable Sir Dudley North*, ed. Montague North (London: for the editor by John Whiston, 1746), p. 249.

51 John Houghton, *A Collection for Improvement of Husbandry and Trade*, 15: 461, Friday, 23 May 1701.

CHAPTER II

1 L. Grenade, 'Les Singularitéz de Londres, 1576', in Ann Saunders, *The Royal Exchange* (London: London Topographical Society, 1997), p. 48.

2 Lewes Roberts, *The Merchants Map of Commerce*, 2nd ed. (London, 1671), p. 12.

3 Ned Ward, *The London-Spy Compleat, in Eighteen Parts*, 2nd ed. (London: J. How, 1704), p. 66.

4 John Strype, *Survey of the Cities of London and Westminster,* 2 vols (London: A Churchill, J. Knapton, R. Knaplock et al, 1720), I, ii, p. 149.

5 'A new & correct plan of all the Houses destroyd and damaged by the fire which began in Exchange Alley, Cornhill, on Friday, March 25, 1748', in *London Magazine*, March 1748, opp. p. 138.

6 'A Perticular of Writeings [on] the two houses in Exchange Alley', *c.* 1700, Appendix F. in John Martin, *'The Grasshopper' in Lombard Street* (London: Leadenhall Press, 1892), p. 299.

7 *Kingdom's Intelligencer,* no. 51, 15–22 December 1662, p. 815.

8 *Mercurius Publicus*, no. 49, 4–11 December 1662, p. 802.

9 BL Add Mss 5100 (55*, fol. 166r–v); PRO, E 179/252/32 (3), p. 2 (R).

10 *Mercurius Politicus*, no. 435, 23 September 1658, p. 887.

11 Lorna Weatherill, *Consumer Behaviour and Material Culture in Britain, 1660–1760* (London: Routledge, 1988), p. 157.

12 'A Coffee-House Scene', *British Museum Quarterly,* 6: 2 (1931–2), pp. 43–4.

13 *The London Gazette*, no. 865, 2–5 March, 1675.

14 *Mercurius Publicus*, no. 49, 4 December 1662, p. 802.

15 *The Intelligencer*, no. 19, 7 March 1664, p. 157.
16 E. E. Rich (ed.), *The Minutes of the Hudson's Bay Company, 1671–1674* (Toronto: Champlain Society, 1942), p. 8.
17 *Particulars and Conditions of Sale, of all that Plantation, or Freehold Estate, called Studley-Park, situate In the Parish of Saint George, in the Island of Tobago; [. . .] together with the Negroes, Stock, and Utensils, hereafter mentioned; Which will be Sold by Auction, By Messrs, Young and Brooks, On Thursday the 30th of September, inst. 1773; At Garraway's Coffee-House, Exchange Alley, at One o'Clock in the Afternoon* ([London]: n.p., n.d. [1773]).
18 *The Tatler*, no. 232, 30 September 1710.
19 BL: Sloane 647, fol. 122r–v.
20 Pepys, *Diary*, I, p. 284; III, pp. 185–6.
21 See also Brian Cowan, 'What was masculine about the public sphere? Gender and the Coffee-House Milieu in Post-Restoration England', *History Workshop Journal*, 51 (2001), pp. 127–57.
22 P. G. M. Dickson, *The Financial Revolution in England: a study in the development of public credit 1688–1756* (London: Macmillan, 1967).
23 Ranald Michie, *The London Stock Exchange: a History* (Oxford: Oxford University Press, 1999), pp. 15–20.
24 Anthony Hilliar, *A Brief and Merry History of Great Britain* (London: J. Roberts, J. Shuckburgh, J. Penn and J. Jackson, [1730]), p. 21.
25 Macky, *A Journey Through England*, p. 208.
26 Ephraim Chambers, *Cyclopædia or an Universal Dictionary of Arts and Sciences*, 2 vols (London: James and John Knapton, 1727), I, p. 246; Edward Hatton, *A New View of London, or, an Ample Account of that City* (London: John Nicholson, 1708), I, p. 30.
27 The figure of 3,000 is stated by Walter Besant, *London in the Eighteenth Century* (London: Adam & Charles Black, 1902), p. 308; Leslie Stephen, *English Literature and Society in the Eighteenth Century* (1903; London: Methuen & Co., 1966), p. 22; Jürgen Habermas, *The Structural Transformation of the Public Sphere: An Inquiry into a Category of Bourgeois Society*, trans. Thomas Burger (Cambridge: Polity, 1992), p. 32; Pat Rogers (ed.), *The Eighteenth Century: the context of English literature* (London: Methuen, 1978), p. 46; and E. J. Clery, 'Women, Publicity and the Coffee-House Myth', p. 169. The figure of 2,000 is stated by Aytoun Ellis, *The Penny Universities: a history of the coffee-houses* (London: Secker & Warburg, 1956), p. xiv; and Peter Stallybrass and Allon White, *The Politics and Poetics of Transgression* (London: Methuen, 1986), p. 95. Bryant Lillywhite's *London Coffee-Houses* identifies 2,033 different coffee-houses that operated between the mid seventeenth and mid nineteenth centuries, but many of these were short-lived businesses of which only a subset were ever open at the same time.
28 John Ashton collected a list of about 500 coffee-houses mentioned in newspapers during the reign of Queen Anne (John Ashton, *Social Life in the Reign of Queen Anne* (London, 1882), Appendix B); George Rudé, *Hanoverian London 1714–1808* (London: Secker & Warburg, 1971), p. 77.
29 A. L. Beier and Roger Finlay, 'Introduction: The significance of the metropolis',

in A. L. Beier and Roger Finlay (eds), *London 1500–1700: The Making of the Metropolis* (London: Longman, 1986), pp. 1–34.

30 William Maitland, *The History of London, from its Foundation by the Romans, to the Present Time* (London: Samuel Richardson, 1739), Book II, pp. 519–20. There were about 300 cafés in Paris at this time, Thomas Brennan, *Public Drinking and Popular Culture in Eighteenth-Century Paris* (Princeton, New Jersey: Princeton University Press, 1988), pp. 86–7.

31 John Houghton, *A Collection for Improvement of Husbandry and Trade*, 2 (6 April 1692), p. [1].

32 *The Impartial Protestant Mercury*, 25 November 1681, p. [2].

33 John McCusker, 'European Bills of Entry and Marine Lists', *Harvard Library Bulletin*, 31: 3 (1983), pp. 209–55; 31: 4 (1983), pp. 316–39, pp. 316–26.

34 Alex Preda, 'In the enchanted grove: Financial Conversations and the Marketplace in England and France in the 18th Century', *Journal of Historical Sociology*, 14: 3 (September 2001), pp. 276–307.

35 Michie, *Stock Exchange*, pp. 19–20.

36 Narcissus Luttrell, 21 January 1692, *Parliamentary Diary*, ed. Henry Horwitz (Oxford: Clarendon, 1972), p. 147.

37 Ward, *London-Spy*, part XVI, pp. 390–1.

38 *The Craftsman*, no. 77, 23 December 1728, II, p. 345.

39 [Daniel Defoe], *The Anatomy of Exchange-Alley: or, A System of Stock-Jobbing* (London: for E. Smith near Exchange-Alley, 1719), p. 35.

40 Edward Matthew Ward, *The South Sea Bubble*, exhibited in Royal Academy in 1847. See James Dafforne, *The Life and Works of Edward Matthew Ward, R.A.* (London: Virtue and Company, 1879?), unpaginated. Engraved 1853.

41 Susanna Centlivre, *A Bold Stroke for a Wife, a Comedy* (London: W. Mears, J. Browne, and F. Clay, 1718), IV, 1, pp. 35–42.

42 Mortimer, *Every Man his Own Broker*, pp. 81–2.

43 Mitchel Abolafia, *Making Markets: opportunism and restraint on Wall Street* (Cambridge, Mass.: Harvard University Press, 1996), p. 49.

44 *The Spectator*, no. 46, 23 April, 1711, ed. Bond, I, p. 196.

45 Raymond Flower and Michael Wynn Jones, *Lloyd's of London: an Illustrated History* (Newton Abbott: David and Charles, 1974), pp. 20–32. See also Frederick Martin, *The History of Lloyd's and Marine Insurance in Great Britain* (London: Macmillan, 1876); Charles Wright and Ernest Fayle, *A History of Lloyd's from the founding of Lloyd's Coffee House to the Present Day* (London: Macmillan, 1907), pp. 64–125; D. E. W. Gibb, *Lloyd's of London: a study in individualism* (London: Corporation of Lloyd's, 1957), pp. 1–57.

46 Mortimer, *Every Man his Own Broker*, p. 72n.

47 S. R. Cope, 'The Stock-Brokers find a home: how the Stock Exchange came to be established in Sweetings Alley in 1773', *Guildhall Studies in London History*, II: 4 (April 1977), pp. 213–19. See also Dickson, *Financial Revolution*, pp. 490–505.

48 *The London Chronicle*, 11: 852 (8 June 1762), p. [1]

49 Cope, 'Stock-Brokers', p. 217.

50 *The Morning Chronicle*, no. 1291, 13 July 1773, p. [3].

51 *The Conduct and Scandalous Behaviour of the Porters in Exchange Ally* (London: Mrs Dodd, Mrs Nutts and Mrs Cooks, n.d., [1750?]).

52 Bayles, p. 128.

53 John F. Watson, *Annals of Philadelphia and Pennsylvania*, 3 vols (Philadelphia: John Pennington and Uriah Hunt, 1844–79), I, pp. 393–5, III, pp. 203–4.

54 Carl Bridenbaugh, *Cities in Revolt: Urban Life in America 1743–1776* (New York: Alfred A. Knopf, 1955), pp. 161–2. See also Edwin B. Bronner, 'Village into Town' in *Philadelphia: a 300-year history* (London: W. W. Norton, 1982), p. 56; Robert Earle Graham, 'The Taverns of Colonial Philadelphia' in Luther Eisenhart, *Historic Philadelphia: From the founding until the early nineteenth century* (Philadelphia: American Philosophical Society, 1953), pp. 318–25.

55 Bayles, quoted p. 278.

56 Henry W. Domett, *A History of the Bank of New York*, 2nd ed. (G. P. Putnam's Sons, 1884), pp. 7–15.

57 Madison to Jefferson, 10 July 1791, *The Republic of Letters: The Correspondence between Thomas Jefferson and James Madison 1776–1826*, ed. James Morton Smith, 3 vols (New York: W. W. Norton, 1995), p. 696.

58 Edmund Stedman and Alexander Easton, 'The History of the New York Stock Exchange' in *The New York Stock Exchange*, ed. Edmund Stedman (New York: Stock Exchange Historical Co., 1905), pp. 17–43; Peter Eisenstadt, 'How the Buttonwood Tree Grew: the Making of a New York Stock Exchange Legend', *Prospects: An Annual of American Cultural Studies*, 19 (1994), pp. 75–98.

59 Kenneth Jackson (ed.), *The Enyclopedia of New York* (New Haven, Conn.: Yale University Press, 1995).

CHAPTER 12

1 'Joseph Addison, *The Spectator*, no. 10, Monday, 12 March 1711, ed. Bond, I, p. 44.

2 Peter Borsay, 'The Culture of Improvement', in Paul Langford (ed.), *The Eighteenth Century* (Oxford: Oxford University Press, 2002), p. 189.

3 Lawrence E. Klein, *Shaftesbury and the Culture of Politeness: Moral discourse and cultural politics in early eighteenth century England* (Cambridge: Cambridge University Press, 1994), pp. 3–14.

4 Samuel Johnson, 'Addison', *Lives of the English Poets*, 3 vols (Oxford: Clarendon Press, 1905), II, p. 93.

5 Addison, *The Spectator*, no. 409, ed. Bond, III, pp. 528–9.

6 Johnson, 'Addison', II, p. 93.

7 Calhoun Winton, *Captain Steele: the early career of Richard Steele* (Baltimore, Maryland: Johns Hopkins University Press, 1964), p. 77.

8 De Souligné, *Old Rome and London Compared*, 2nd edition (London: J. Harding, 1710), p. 155.

9 Guy Miège, *The New State of England*, 3rd ed. (London: R. Clavel, H. Mortlock, and J. Robinson, 1699), II, pp. 17, 19–20.

10 Richard Steele, *Correspondence*, ed. Rae Blanchard (Oxford: Clarendon Press, 1968), p. 198.

11 Steele, *The Tatler*, no. 1, Tuesday 12 April 1709, ed. Bond, I, p. 15.

12 Steele, 'Dedication', *The Tatler, Volume 1, Nos 1–50* (London, 1710), ed. Bond, I, p. 8.

13 See J. G. A. Pocock, 'Virtue, rights and manners', *Virtue Commerce and History: Essays on Political Thought and History, Chiefly in the Eighteenth Century* (Cambridge: Cambridge University Press, 1985), pp. 48–9; Michael G. Ketcham, *Transparent Designs: Reading Performance and Form in the 'Spectator' Papers* (Athens: University of Georgia Press, 1985), pp. 167–71.

14 Steele, *The Spectator*, no. 346, ed. Bond, III, p. 289.

15 Steele, *The Tatler*, ed. Bond, I, pp. 16–17.

16 Bruyere, in *The London Journal*, 1727, quoted in Lillywhite, p. 641.

17 Karl Ludwig, Baron de Pollnitz, *The Memoirs of Charles-Lewis, Baron de Pollnitz*, 2 vols (London: Daniel Browne, 1737), II, pp. 462–3.

18 Lewis Theobald, 'Coffee-House Humours Exposed', *The Censor*, II, no. 61, 12 March 1717, pp. 210–12.

19 *The Spectator*, no. 1, ed. Bond, I, pp. 3–4.

20 John Calhoun Stephens (ed.), *The Guardian* (Lexington, Kentucky: University Press of Kentucky, 1982), p. 19.

21 Addison, *The Spectator*, no. 317, ed. Bond, III, pp. 152–6.

22 Addison, *The Spectator*, no. 31, ed. Bond, I, pp. 127–32.

23 Johnson, 'Addison', II, p. 92.

24 Steele, *The Spectator*, no. 49, ed. Bond, I, pp. 208–9.

25 Ibid., pp. 209–11.

26 Ibid., p.211.

27 Norbert Elias, *The History of Manners* in *The Civilising Process*, trans. Edmund Jephcott, (1st ed. 1938; Oxford: Blackwell, 1994), p. 66.

28 Steele, *The Spectator*, no. 49, ed. Bond, I, p. 210.

29 Ibid., no. 206, ed. Bond, II, p. 309.

30 Ibid., no. 236, ed. Bond, II, p. 417; no. 114, I, p. 469.

31 Lawrence Klein, 'Coffeehouse Civility, 1660–1714: an aspect of post-courtly culture in England', *Huntingdon Library Quarterly*, 59, 1, (1997), pp. 30–51, p. 49.

32 Theobald, *Censor*, II, no. 61, 12 March 1717, pp. 213–16.

33 Erasmus Jones, *The Man of Manners: or, Plebeian Polish'd* (London: J. Roberts, undated [1737?]), pp. 56–7.

34 'Rules of Behaviour, of general use, Though Much Disregarded in this Populous City', *The London Magazine*, 49, May 1780. p. 197.

35 John Hill, *The Inspector*, no. 4, 2 vols (London: R. Griffiths et al, 1753), I, pp. 15–18.

36 Samuel Johnson, 'The Rambler, No. 195', ed. W. J. Bate and Albrecht B. Strauss, vols III–V, *The Yale Edition of the Works of Samuel Johnson*, 10 vols (New Haven and London: Yale University Press, 1969), V, pp. 252–7.

37 Ian Gilmour, *Riots, Risings and Revolution: Governance and Violence in Eighteenth-Centuy England* (London: Hutchinson, 1992), p. 52.

38 Steele, *The Tatler*, no. 141, ed. Bond. II, p. 306.

39 Edward Ward, *Vulgus Britannicus: or, the British Hudibras* (London: James Woodward and John Morphew, 1710); canto XI, pp. 119–21.

40 Ibid., canto IV, p. 50; canto XII, pp. 138–9.

41 Daniel Defoe, *The Lay-Man's Sermon Upon the Late Storm* (London: n.p., 1704).

42 G. D. Scull, *The Montresor Journals*, Collections of the New-York Historical Society for the year 1881 (New York: for the Society, 1882), pp. 336, 344, 346, 363, 369.
43 Edwin G. Burrows and Mike Wallace, *Gotham: a History of New York to 1898* (New York: Oxford University Press, 1999), pp. 191–244.
44 William Harrison Bayles, *Old Taverns of New York* (New York: Frank Allaben Genealogical Company, 1915), pp. 277–80.
45 Michael G. Ketcham, *Transparent Designs: Reading Performance and Form in the 'Spectator' Papers* (Athens: University of Georgia Press, 1985), p. 170.
46 *A View of Paris* (London: John Nutt, 1701), pp. 24–5.
47 Thomas Brennan, *Public drinking and popular culture in eighteenth century Paris* (Princeton, NJ: Princeton University Press, 1988), p. 132; Robert Isherwood, *Farce and Fantasy: Popular Entertainment in Eighteenth-Century Paris* (New York: Oxford University Press, 1986), pp. 25–6, 240–5.
48 La Roque, *Voyage*, pp. 293–4.
49 Brennan, *Public drinking*, pp. 128–34. See also W. Scott Haine, *The World of the Paris café: Sociability among the French Working Class, 1789–1914* (Baltimore: Johns Hopkins University Press, 1996), pp. 2–12.
50 Dena Goodman, *The Republic of Letters: a cultural history of the French Enlightenment* (Ithaca, New York, 1994); Roger Chartier, *The Cultural Origins of the French Revolution*, trans. Lydia G. Cochrane (Durham, North Carolina, 1991).
51 Daniel Gordon, '"Public Opinion" and the Civilising Process in France: The Example of Morellet', *Eighteenth-Century Studies*, 22: 3 (1989), pp. 302–28, p. 309.
52 Thomas Nugent, *Travels through Germany*, 2 vols (London, Edward and Charles Dilly, 1768), I, p. 162.
53 Young, *Travels in France*, pp. 146, 156.
54 *Il Caffè, o sia Brevi e Vari Discorsi*, 2nd ed., 2 vols (Venezia: Pietro Pizzolato, 1766), I, pp. 1–9; James Wheelock, 'The Anonymity of the Milanese "Caffè" 1764–1766', *Eighteenth-Century Studies*, 5: 4 (Summer 1972), pp. 527–44.
55 Ulla Heise, *Coffee and Coffee Houses* (West Chester, Pennsylvannia: Schiffer Publishing, 1987), pp. 130–7.

CHAPTER 13

1 Henry James, 'London at Midsummer' (1877), *English Hours*, ed. Leon Edel (Oxford: Oxford University Press, 1981), pp. 90–1.
2 Isaac d'Israeli, 'Introduction of Tea, Coffee and Chocolate', *Curiosities of Literature*, 3 vols (London: John Murray, 1817), III, p. 378.
3 'Coffee-Houses and Smoking', *New Monthly Magazine and Literary Journal*, 16 (1826), pp. 50–2, p. 51.
4 Simon Smith, 'Accounting for Taste: British Coffee Consumption in Historical Perspective', *Journal of Interdisciplinary History*, 27: 2 (1996), pp. 183–214.
5 Elizabeth Boody Schumpeter, *English Overseas Trade Statistics, 1697–1808* (Oxford: Oxford University Press, 1960), table XVIII.
6 Smith, 'Accounting for Taste', pp. 183–214.
7 Peter Earle, *The Making of the British Middle Class: Business Society and Family Life in London, 1660–1730* (London, 1989), pp. 295, 387.

8 Jonas Hanway, *Letters on the Importance of the Rising Generation of the Laboring Part of our Fellow-Subjects*, 2 vols (London: A. Millar and T. Cadell, and C. Marsh and G. Woodfall, 1767), pp. 180–1.

9 Arthur Young, *The Farmer's Letters to the People of England*, 2nd ed. (London: W. Nicoll, 1768), pp. 268–70.

10 Hanway, *Letters*, p. 181.

11 J. R. Ward, 'The Industrial Revolution and British Imperialism, 1750–1850', *Economic History Review*, 47: 1 (1994), pp. 44–65, p. 53.

12 Ukers, *All about Tea*, II, pp. 389–96.

13 Jane Pettigrew, *A Social History of Tea* (London: The National Trust, 2001).

14 Virginia Woolf, 'Sketch of the Past', (1940). BL Add Mss 61973.

15 Peter Bird, *The First Food Empire: a History of Lyons & Co.* (Chichester: Phillmore & Co., 2000); Erica Rappaport, *Shopping for Pleasure: Women in the Making of London's West End* (Princeton: Princeton University Press, 2001), p. 103.

16 James Boswell, *Boswell's London Journal 1762–1763*, ed. Frederick A. Pottle (New York: McGraw Hill Book Company, 1950), pp. 74–6.

17 Horace Walpole, *Correspondence*, ed. W. S. Lewis (New Haven: Yale University Press, 1937–83), IX, p. 7; XXXIX, p. 108.

18 Charles P. Moritz, *Travels, Chiefly on Foot, through Several parts of England, in 1782* (London: G. G. and J. Robinson, 1795), pp. 92–3.

19 Iain McCalman, 'Ultra-radicalism and convivial debating-clubs in London, 1795–1838', *English Historical Review*, 102 (1987), pp. 309–33; *Radical Underworld: prophets, revolutionaries and pornographers in London, 1795–1840* (Oxford: Clarendon Press, 1993), pp. 195–8.

20 John Thelwall, 'The Natural and Constitutional Rights of Britons' in *The Politics of English Jacobinism: Writings of John Thelwall*, ed. Gregory Claeys (Philadelphia: University of Pennsylvania Press, 1995), p. 53.

21 Henry Mayhew, *The Morning Chronicle Survey of Labour and the Poor: The Metropolitan Districts* (London: Caliban Books, 1981), pp. 2–7.

22 E. Hepple Hall, *Coffee Taverns, Cocoa Houses and Coffee Palaces: their rise, progress, and prospects* (London: S. W. Partridge, 1878); T. Joff [Thomas Jowghin], *Coffee House Babble: The History of some Temperance Coffee Houses* ([London: [n.p., 1915]); Antony Clayton, *London's Coffee Houses, a stimulating story* (London: Historical Publications, 2003), pp. 125–32.

23 Hugh Barty-King, *The Baltic Story: Baltick Coffee House to Baltic Exchange, 1744–1994* (London: Quiller Press, 1994), p. 3.

24 Percy Colson, *White's 1693–1950* (London: William Heinemann, 1951).

25 *Flora Tristan's London Journal: a survey of London in the 1830s*, trans. Dennis Palmer and Giselle Pincetl (London: George Prior, 1980), pp. 244–5.

26 Henry James, 'Letter to Alice James, 2 March 1877, *Selected Letters*, ed. Leon Edel (Cambridge, Mass.: Belknap Press, 1987), p. 146. See also Leon Edel, *Henry James*, 5 vols (New York: Lippincott, 1962), II, p. 284.

27 *The City; or, The Physiology of London Business; with sketches on 'Change and at the coffee houses* (London: Baily Brothers, 1845).

28 *The Times*, 28 January 1873, p. 10.

29 R. S., 'A City Coffee-House', *The Cambridge Review*, IV: 95 (2 May 1888), p. 336.

30 Hippolyte Taine, *Italy: Florence and Venice*, trans J. Durand (New York: Leypoldt & Holt, 1869), p. 230.

31 T. J. Clark, *The Painting of Modern Life: Paris in the art of Manet and his followers*, rev. ed. (Princeton: Princeton University Press, 1999), pp. 205–57.

32 Charles Baudelaire, 'The Eyes of the Poor', in *Paris Spleen*, trans. Louis Varese (New York, 1947), p. 52.

33 Haine, *The World of the Paris Café*.

34 Ruth Iskin, 'Selling, Seduction and Soliciting the Eye: Manet's *Bar at the Folies-Bergère*', *Art Bulletin*, 77: 1 (1995), pp. 25–44.

35 Haine, *Paris Café*, pp. 207–32.

36 Harold Segel, *The Vienna Coffeehouse Wits 1890–1938* (West Lafayette, Indiana: Purdue University Press, 1994), p. 4. See also Michael Rössner, *Literarische Kaffeehäuser Kaffeehausliteraten* (Wien: Böhlau, 1999).

37 Alfred Polgar, 'Theory of the Café Central' (1926), trans. Harold Segel, in Segel, *Vienna Coffeehouse Wits*, pp. 267–70.

38 Friedrich Torberg, *Die Tante Jolesch oder der Untergang des Abendlandes* (1975), trans. Harold Segel, quoted in Segel, *Vienna Coffeehouse Wits*, pp. 16–18.

39 Leslie Frewin, *The Café Royal Story: a living legend* (London: Hutchinson Benham, 1963).

40 Osbert Sitwell, *Laughter in the Next Room* (Boston: Little, Brown & Co., 1948).

41 Oscar Wilde, *Letters*, ed. Rupert Hart-Davis (London: Rupert Hart-Davis, 1962), pp. 426, 435.

42 Arthur Symons, *The Café Royal and other essays* (London: The Beaumont Press, 1928).

43 Painting untraced. It was sold at Christie's to Charles Forté in 1968, to be hung in the Café Royal (*The Times*, 9 November 1968, p. 8).

44 Guy Deghy and Keith Waterhouse, *Café Royal: Ninety Years of Bohemia* (London: Hutchinson, 1955).

45 John Betjeman, *Collected Poems* (London: John Murray, 1997).

46 Thomas Babington Macaulay, *The History of England from the Accession of James the Second*, I, pp. 366–70.

47 W. H. Davenport Adams, *Good Queen Anne; or Men and Manners, Life and Letters in England's Augustan Age*, 2 vols (London: Remington & Co., 1886), I, pp. xi-xxiii, 357–73.

48 Leslie Stephen, *English Literature and Society in the Eighteenth Century* (London: Duckworth and Co., 1904), p. 39. See Noel Annan, *Leslie Stephen: The Godless Victorian* (London: Weidenfeld and Nicolson, 1984); Mark Girouard, *Sweetness and Light: The 'Queen Anne' Movement 1860–1900* (New Haven and London: Yale University Press, 1977).

49 John Timbs, *Club Life of London with Anecdotes of the Clubs, Coffee-Houses and Taverns of the Metropolis During the 17th, 18th, and 19th Centuries*, 2 vols (London: Richard Bentley, 1866); Edward Forbes Robinson, *The Early History of the Coffee-Houses in England* (London: Kegan Paul, Trench, Trübner & Co., 1893).

50 George Macaulay Trevelyan, *England Under Queen Anne: Blenheim* (London: Longmans, Green and Co., 1930), pp. 82–3.

51 George Macaulay Trevelyan, *English Social History: a survey of six centuries Chaucer to Queen Victoria* (1942; London: Penguin Books, 2000), pp. 338–40.

52 Hermann Westerfrölke, *Englische Kaffeehäuser als Sammelpunkte der literarischen Welt hit Zeitalter von Dryden und Addison* (Jena: Frommannschen Buchhandlung, 1924).

53 Hans Speier, 'Historical Development of Public Opinion', *American Journal of Sociology*, 55: 4 (January 1950), pp. 376–88, 376, 381.

54 Jürgen Habermas, *The Structural Transformation of the Public Sphere: An Inquiry into a Category of Bourgeois Society*, trans. Thomas Burger (Cambridge: Polity, 1992); Richard Sennett, *The Fall of Public Man* (1977; London: Faber and Faber, 1986); Terry Eagleton, *The Function of Criticism: from the 'Spectator' to Post-Structuralism* (London: Verso, 1984), p. 9; Stallybrass and White, *The Politics and Poetics of Transgression*, pp. 80–118.

55 Jürgen Habermas, *Strukturwandel der Öffentlichkeit* (Darmstadt and Neuwied: Hermann Luchterhand Verlag, 1962). See also Markman Ellis, 'The coffee-women', pp. 27–52; Brian Cowan, 'What was masculine about the public sphere?', *History Workshop Journal*, 51 (2001), pp. 127–57; and Craig Calhoun, *Habermas and the Public Sphere* (Cambridge, Mass. and London: MIT Press, 1992).

CHAPTER 14

1 Susan Cooper, 'Snoek Piquante', in *Age of Austerity*, Michael Sissons and Philip French (eds), (London: Hodder and Stoughton, 1963), p. 35.

2 John Wain, *Living in the Present* (London: Secker & Warburg, 1955), p. 11.

3 G. S. Fraser, 'Sensibility and Sense', *Times Literary Supplement*, 1 February 1957, p. 65.

4 Mark Pendergrast, *Uncommon Grounds: The History of Coffee and How it Transformed the World* (New York: Basic Books, 1999), pp. 147–8, 240–1.

5 *Picture Post*, 61: 10 (5 December 1953), p. 57.

6 'The Englishman's Coffee', *The Times*, 10 January 1953, p. 7.

7 'High Prices for Beverages', *The Times* (Annual Financial and Commercial Review), 13 September 1954, p. xvii.

8 'Coffee Crisis in America', *The Times*, 3 February 1954, p. 7.

9 Louie Salvoni, 'Espresso and its origins', in Rolf Cornell and Steven Sullivan, *Esprit d'Espresso: a guide to making and enjoying espresso and cappuccino at home* (London: Dastro Publishing, 1991), pp. 16–17, p. 16.

10 Edward and Joan Bramah, *Coffee makers: 300 years of art and design*, pp. 140–5.

11 'Gaggia Lux Espresso machine' [Advertisement], *Caterer and Hotelkeeper*, 26 September 1953, pp. 2–3.

12 '9d a cup: a report on coffee bars illustrating the greatest social revolution since the laundrette', *Architectural Design*, 24: 6 (June 1954), pp. 175–7, p. 177.

13 'Coffee Time', *The Times*, 3 October 1955, p. 11.

14 Martha Gellhorn, 'So Awful to be Young', *Encounter*, 6: 5 (May 1956), pp. 42–8; Edward Bramah, *Tea & Coffee: a modern view of Three Hundred Years of Tradition* (London: Hutchinson, 1972), p. 70.

15 J. W. Ashton, 'U.K. Coffee Trade is Making Steady Progress', *Tea and Coffee Trade Journal*, 111: 6 (December 1956), p. 22.
16 B. A. Young, 'Coffee-Bar Theory and Practice', *Punch*, 231 (5 December 1956), pp. 670–2, p. 670.
17 *Coffee Bar and Coffee Lounge*, 2 vols, December 1959–December 1961. BL: PP.7612.ag.
18 Ibid., 1: 6 (June 1960), p. 11; 'I am the Queen of Soho', *Picture Post*, 72: 3 (21 July 1956), pp. 12–13; Neville Barker, 'Soho Fair', *Listener*, 53 (17 March 1955), p. 466.
19 'Australia's "Good Life"', *The Times*, 12 March 1956 p. 11.
20 Gábor Tóth, 'The Impact of Design and Technology', *The Daily Grind: Wellington Café Culture 1920–2000*, (Online: <http://www.nzhistory.net.nz/mph/cafe/gabor.html>, accessed 15. 11. 03).
21 Mark Pendergrast, *Uncommon Grounds*, p. 266.
22 Lillian Schaaf, 'Café ¡Ole!: the brave bean: 25 ways to serve it', *Esquire: The Magazine for Men*, 3: 3 (March 1956), pp. 52–3, 98–100.
23 'High Prices for Beverages', *The Times*, 13 September 1954, p. xvii.
24 '9d a cup', p. 175.
25 John Pearson, 'Revolution Espresso', *The Listener*, 55: 1401 (5 January 1956), p. 10; 'Coffee Bars Pop Up All Over London', *Tea and Coffee Trade Journal*, 108: 3 (March 1955), p. 28.
26 '9d a cup', p. 176.
27 Marghanita Laski, 'Espresso', *Architectural Review*, no. 1118, (March 1955), pp. 166–7, p. 166.
28 Sidney Perkowitz, *Universal Foam: the story of bubbles from cappuccino to the cosmos* (London: Vintage, 2000), pp. 45–9.
29 'Coffee Bars Pop Up All Over London', p. 28.
30 Laski, 'Espresso', p. 167.
31 B. Young, 'Coffee-House Rock', *Punch*, 232 (8 May 1957), p. 589.
32 Stephen Gardiner, 'Coffee Bars', *Architectural Review*, no. 1118, (March 1955), pp. 167–73, p. 168. See also Alan Hess, *Googie: fifties coffee shop architecture* (San Francisco: Chronicle Books, 1996).
33 Gardiner, 'Coffee Bars', p. 168.
34 Bramah, *Tea & Coffee*, p. 71.
35 Laski, 'Espresso', p. 165.
36 Gardiner, 'Coffee Bars', p. 168.
37 Ibid.
38 Quoted in Young, 'Coffee-House Rock', p. 589.
39 Gardiner, 'Coffee Bars', p. 168.
40 Pearson, 'Revolution Espresso', p. 10.
41 Laski, 'Espresso', pp. 167, 168.
42 Pearson, 'Revolution Espresso', p. 10.
43 Gellhorn, 'So Awful', p. 43.
44 Ibid., pp. 42–8.
45 '9d a cup', pp. 175–7.
46 *Two Broad-Sides against Tobacco* (London, J. H., 1672), p. i.
47 Laski, 'Espresso', p. 167.

48 Young, 'Coffee-Bar Theory', p. 670.
49 Laski, 'Espresso', p. 167.
50 Richard Hoggart, *The Uses of Literacy: Aspects of working-class life with special reference to publications and entertainments* (London: Chatto and Windus, 1957), pp. 37, 203–4.
51 George Sutherland Fraser, 'The Writer's London', *Times Literary Supplement* (2 March 1956), p. 133.
52 Eric Hobsbawm, *Age of Extremes: the short Twentieth Century, 1914–1991* (London: Michael Joseph, 1994), pp. 329–30.
53 Mark Abrams, 'The Facts of Young Life', *Encounter*, 6: 5 (May 1956), pp. 35–42; Abrams, *The Teenage Consumer*, LPE papers, no. 5 (July 1959), pp. 3–11.
54 Christopher Booker, *The Neophiliacs: a study of the revolution in English life in the Fifties and Sixties* (London: Collins, 1969), p. 39.
55 Robert Fabian, *London After Dark* (London: Naldrett Press, 1954), p. 10.
56 Arthur Tietjen, *Soho: London's Vicious Circle* (London: Allan Wingate, 1956), p. 145.
57 Derek Amos Kirby (pseud. Marty Ladwick), *Soho Street Girl* (London: Kaye Publications, [1954]), p. 9.
58 *Daily Express*, 29 May 1958; 17 June 1958; 22 July 1958.
59 '"Aimless Café Society" of Juveniles', *The Times*, 9 December 1958, p. 3.
60 Daniel Farson (dir.), *Living for Kicks*, Associated Rediffusion for ITA, Wednesday, 2 March 1960.
61 Daniel Farson, *Never a Normal Man* (London: HarperCollins, 1997), pp. 220–4.
62 G. S. Fraser, 'Sensibility and Sense', *Times Literary Supplement*, 1 February 1957, p. 65.
63 Kenneth Allsop, *The Angry Decade: a survey of the cultural revolt of the nineteen fifties* (London: Peter Owen, 1958), p. 40. See also Humphrey Carpenter, *The Angry Young Men: a literary comet of the 1950s* (London: Allen Lane, 2002).
64 Colin Wilson, 'The Outsider, Twenty Years On', *The Outsider* (London: Phoenix, 1997, 2001), p. 1.
65 Gardiner, p. 172,
66 'Colin Wilson recalls the Soho years', *Abraxas* 13 (online: http://www.stormkoader.com/abrax7/Bradley.html), accessed 20 November 03.
67 Quoted in Tom Maschler (ed.), *Declaration* (London: MacGibbon & Kee, 1957), p. 5.
68 Angus Wilson, 'A Bit Off the Map', in *A Bit Off the Map and Other Stories* (London: Secker & Warburg, 1957), pp. 7, 11–12.
69 Lindsay Anderson, 'Get Out and Push!', in Maschler (ed.), *Declaration*, pp. 153–78, p. 176.
70 Michael Kenny, *The First New Left: British Intellectuals after Stalin* (London: Lawrence & Wishart, 1995), p. 111.
71 Stuart Hall, 'The "First" New Left: Life and Times', in Robin Archer et al (eds), *Out of Apathy: Voices of the New Left Thirty Years On: Papers based on a Conference organized by the Oxford University Socialist Discussion Group* (London: Verso, 1989), pp. 11–38, p. 18.
72 Kenny, *The First New Left*, pp. 15–19.

73 'Editorial', *Universities and Left Review*, 1: 1 (Spring 1957), pp. i–ii.

74 Stuart Hall, 'The "First" New Left', p. 28.

75 Kenny, *The First New Left*, p. 21.

76 *Universities and Left Review*, 1: 2 (Summer 1957), p. 3.

77 Ibid., 1: 3 (Winter 1958), p. [ii]; Pendennis, 'Pea Soup and Irish Stew', *Observer*, 2 November 1958. The fullest account of the foundation of the Partisan and its subsequent trading history is Caroline Bamford, 'The Politics of Commitment: The Early New Left in Britain 1956–1962', (unpublished doctoral thesis, University of Edinburgh, 1983), pp. 295–302.

78 *Picture Post*, 69: 7 (12 November 1955), p. 27.

79 'The Partisan', *Universities and Left Review* (Autumn 1958), p. 66. On women and the New Left see Sheila Benson, 'Experiences in the London New Left', and Lynne Segal, 'The Silence of Women in the New Left', in Robin Archer et al (eds), *Out of Apathy*, pp. 107–16.

80 Christopher Hill, 'Republicanism after the Revolution', *New Left Review*, I: 3 (May–June 1960), p. 51.

81 Stuart Hall, 'Politics of Adolescence', *ULR*, 6 (Spring 1959), p. 2.

82 Raphael Samuels, 'Born-again socialism' in *Out of Apathy*, p. 44.

83 Michael Kullman, 'The Anti-Culture Born of Despair', *Universities and Left Review* (Summer 1958), p. 52.

84 Derek Allcorn, 'The Unnoticed Generation', *Universities and Left Review* (Summer 1958), pp. 54–8.

85 The Labour Party, *The Younger Generation* (London: The Labour Party, 1959), p. 23. See also Catherine Ellis, 'The Younger Generation: The Labour Party and the 1959 Youth Commission', *Journal of British Studies*, 41 (April 2002), pp. 199–231.

86 Diana Cicely Keppel, Countess of Albemarle, *The Youth Service in England and Wales: Report of the Committee Appointed by the Minister of Education in November, 1958 Presented to Parliament . . . February 1960* (London: HMSO, 1960), pp. 18, 54–5.

87 'Coffee Bars for "Teenagers"', *The Times*, 22 March 1958, p. 4; 'Youth of Brighton "Bored": Official Coffee-Bar Proposed', *The Times*, 3 July 1959, p. 4.

88 *New Left Review*, 1: 1, (January 1960), p. 51.

89 Leone Gold, interview quoted in Bamford, p. 301.

90 Eric Hobsbawm, *Interesting Times: a twentieth-century life* (London: Allen Lane, 2002), pp. 212–14.

91 Gardiner, 'Coffee Bars', p. 167.

EPILOGUE

1 Abbie Hoffman, *Steal this Book* (New York: Pirate Press, 1971), Fred Gardner, 'Hollywood Confidential: Part 1', *Vietnam Generation Journal*, 3: 3 (November 1991), [<http: //lists.villlage.Virginia.edu/sicties/HTML_docs/Texts/Narratives/Gardner_Hollywood_1.html> accessed 8.12.03].

2 Mark Pendergrast, *Uncommon Grounds: the history of coffee and how it transformed our world* (London and New York: Texere, 2003), pp. 292–316.

3 Howard Schultz, *Pour Your Heart Into It: how Starbucks built a company one cup at a time* (New York: Hyperion, 1997), p. 50.

4 Ibid., p. 77.

5 'Starbucks Fiscal 2003 Results', Starbucks Press Release, 13 November 2003 <http://www.Starbucks.com/aboutus/pressdesc.asp?id=349> accessed 20 November 2003.

6 'Starbucks Confident it will become a global brand', *Austin American Statesman*, 16 April 2003, p. C3.

7 LouAnn Lofton, 'Starbucks' Sales Yawner', Motley Fool, 30 October 2003 <http://www.fool.com/News/>, accessed 7 December 2003.

8 Sahar and Bobby Hashemi, *Anyone Can Do It: Building Coffee Republic from our Kitchen Table* (London: Capstone, 2002), pp. 33–6.

9 Celia Brayfield, 'Coffee to Go – the End of Café Society', *The Times*, 2 October 2003, T2, p. 6.

10 Jamey Keaten, 'Starbucks to break into France's café culture with first Paris store', *Marketing News*, 37: 22 (27 October 2003).

11 Vijay Vishwanath and David Harding, 'The Starbucks Effect', *Harvard Business Review*, March–April 2000, pp. 17–18.

12 Schultz, *Heart*, p. 246.

13 LouAnn Lofton, 'Starbucks' Growth Strategy', Motley Fool, 14 November 2003 <http://www.fool.com/News/>, accessed 7 December 2003.

14 Schultz, *Heart*, p. 87.

15 Maria Eliza Rundle, *A New System of Domestic Cookery; formed upon principles of economy: and adapted to the use of private families*, 2nd ed. (London: John Murray, 1810), pp. 283–4.

16 *Of the Use of Tobacco, Tea, Coffee, Chocolate and Drams* (London: H. Parker, 1722), p. 12.

17 Melanie Dupuis, *Nature's Perfect Food* (New York: New York University Press, 2001). See also Ken Albala, 'Milk: Nutritious and Dangerous', in *Milk: Beyond the Dairy. Proceedings of the Oxford Symposium on Food and Cookery 1999*, ed. Harlan Walker (Totnes, Devon: Prospect Books, 2000), pp. 19–30.

18 Marc Augé, *Non-Places: Introduction to an Anthropology of Supermodernity*, trans. John Howe (London: Verso 1995).

19 George Mikes, *Coffee Houses of Europe* (London: Thames and Hudson, 1980); Marie-France Boyer, *The French Café* (London: Thames and Hudson, 1994); Adrian Maddox, *Classic Cafés* (London: Black Dog Publications, 2003).

20 Ray Oldenburg, *The Great Good Place* (New York: Marlowe & Go, 1989).

21 Naomi Klein, *No Logo* (London: Flamingo, 2000), pp. 134–9.

22 '100 Best Corporate Citizens', *Business Ethics*, 31 March 2003 (online: <http://www.business-ethics.com/100best.htm>, accessed 2 April 2003).

23 Charis Gresser and Sophia Tickell, *Mugged: Poverty in Your Coffee Cup* (London: Oxfam International, 2002), p. 26.

24 Ibid., p. 40.

25 M. P., *Character of Coffee-Houses*, p. 8.

INDEX